NEARER THE MOON

WORKS BY ANAÏS NIN

NEARER THE MOON

From *A JOURNAL OF LOVE*

*The Unexpurgated Diary
of Anaïs Nin*

1937–1939

*With a Preface by Rupert Pole
and Biographical Notes and Annotations
by Gunther Stuhlmann*

HARCOURT BRACE & COMPANY

New York   San Diego   London

N O T E

The text of *Nearer the Moon* is taken from diary books fifty-three through sixty as numbered by Anaïs Nin. Titles are respectively: "Journal de Fata Morgana and Un Dieu Qui Rit," "Bateau Vendu," "Maya," "Parenthesis," "Les Mots Flottants," "Nearer the Moon," "Book of Metamorphosis" (also called "Book of Maya," "The Only Way to Conquer the World Is to Make It Transparent," and "Ne Touchant à la Terre que par le Sexe"), and "Le Tubéreuse aux Muqueuse Pleureuse."

All translations of passages in French and Spanish were made by Jean L. Sherman. Invaluable help in the preparation of the typescript was given by Lisa Guest.

Readers should note that the spelling and styling of foreign-language words and phrases have been allowed to stand as they appear in Anaïs Nin's original diary.

—R. P.

C O N T E N T S

An eight-page section of photographs follows page 176

PREFACE

Nearer the Moon continues the "Journal of Love" series, following *Henry and June*, *Incest*, and *Fire*. It includes the years 1937 to 1939, ending, like the second volume of the *Diary of Anaïs Nin*, with Anaïs's departure (temporary, she thought at the time) from her beloved France.

After fifty-two years of diary writing, in 1966 Anaïs Nin finally felt able to publish her diary without hurting others. This she did by editing out her personal life, including her husband and her lovers. Seven volumes were published under the title *The Diary of Anaïs Nin*, covering her life from 1914 to 1977, when she died of cancer at the age of 74. Toward the end of her life Anaïs and I discussed the original diaries, and she asked me to publish all her diaries just as she wrote them.

Nearer the Moon continues Anaïs's relation with Henry Miller and with Gonzalo Moré and his wife, Helba. Its theme is maturity, for Anaïs has finally acquired the wisdom to see through and understand both Henry and Gonzalo: "Henry has changed. In all his men now he seeks analysis, philosophy. He plays the god-role. He has become serious, spiritual, a little tired physically, moving away even from his angers and hatreds, from chaos."

With Gonzalo, Anaïs is finally forced to confront politics and communism. She states, variously: "Communism—what a farce. I stand alone. I stand only for life and for truth against *all* laws." And: "If I enter communism I have to adopt prejudices I never had. I never had a sense of class or possession. I lived the essence of communism." Further: "So . . . in the Arabian restaurant, I became a communist *for the others*. . . . I believe in it for the others. For myself I only believe in liberation by illusion and poetry. . . . I return to the dream and the drug."

In this volume Anaïs also settles with her father, Joaquin Nin. He tells her: "Until I met you I knew pleasure, women, but it was love I wanted and it was love I found with you. After that marvelous, violent climax everything else would seem tasteless and disgusting. My career ended there. And you?" She responds: "With an honesty I have rarely shown I said gently, 'I have Henry and Gonzalo.' "

Maruca, her father's second wife, tells Anaïs: "I am divorcing your father." He threatens suicide, but Anaïs does not believe him. She feels he deserves all this pain for his egotism: "My poor father 'died' at . . . his thousandth concert in Paris. . . . People rushed to the stage. It was not the heart. It was anguish, sadness, solitude, death. . . . He died alone, on the stage. Today, he weeps over himself. I weep over him. I think even then my weeping is more profound."

This diary clarifies Anaïs' relation with her husband, Hugo, as well. She cannot love him physically, but she needs him as "anchor" to keep her from going crazy. "My very young father, I need you. I feel very small. I don't understand. . . . I am in your arms. Protect me."

Like all Anaïs's diaries, this one is an exploration of the self, of the inner journey. She discovers playful humor, telling her father she is working for the Fascists and Gonzalo that she is working for the Communists. She enjoys provoking her father with the title of her book, *House of Incest*. She tells Gonzalo, "I'm Henry's wife and Hugh's mistress." Anaïs struggles to deal with the burdens of the world, but she continues to live only for love. "Someday I'd be locked up for love—insanity." "What a great struggle to keep the balance between: so Henry would no longer destroy himself or me, so Gonzalo would stop destroying himself or me. There are days when I feel the fullness of my inferno on earth. My Karma was not to become an angel. I was born one, but on the contrary, to live my life fully on earth, as woman, incarnated in love, by love. . . . I hold this secret drug which does not destroy me and which permits me to hold on to the ecstasies."

"*Ne touchant à la terre que par le sexe* (We touch the earth only through sex)."

"I wanted passion—I got it, and its punishment too. I asked to be loved for my skin, feet, mouth, body, sex. And I got all the violence that accompanies desire."

As she reaches maturity as a woman, Anaïs matures as an artist as well. "I can write well about anything. I see clearly the difference between analysis and direct presentation of the drama. I am inside now—I hate comments."

Anaïs wrote her diary at "white heat," as soon as possible after the event. And this is the way she would have liked to live. "Left to myself I would like to burn up until I die, live my whole life in a few years of intensity, like Rimbaud, like so many of the mystics. I don't feel attached to life as a continuous thing. I don't want it to last. I want to burn quickly and die early. Hugh fights to keep me alive. And what keeps me alive is my protective instinct toward others. So many people depend on me. When I got ill this winter I realized how many people I failed to sustain. And it was for them I struggled for strength again. *Au fond I have never done exactly what I wanted.*"

Anaïs's intuition of peace proved wrong. In 1938 the threat of war hung over Europe. "Everything became ugly, tense, destructive. Individual life was annihilated. . . . [Henry] got sick at the disruption of his life. . . . Gonzalo [is jubilant] over what the war might mean to the revolution."

She observes her father, clinically: "Father is selling his furniture and his marvelous collection of books on music to go back to Cuba, back to the womb, . . . swallowed by the birthplace again after seeking to escape for thirty years."

And with chaos all around her, Anaïs reconstructs the world for herself. "I was never in it . . . so I am not to be destroyed with it. I always lived beyond it. . . . We were never of the world in the present. . . . I am attached to the cosmic rhythm. I am related only to the few human beings I love. I do not belong to my epoch. . . . Anyone who remembers as much as I do, and who can live in the future, and beyond class, race, time, touches the world at certain points but does not belong to it."

At the conclusion of this volume, Anaïs resigns herself to return to America. "I leave for America without joy, torn and divided between tenderness and passion. Hating the passion at times. I must remember it is not final, only temporary. Going to New York I can help them all. . . . But I, I am sacrificed. It is not what I want."

Everyone thinks it will be a short war. Anaïs has no idea she will never live in France again, that this is the last diary to be written there: "And today, because all my life has been nothing but love, and not art, and not the idea, and not immortality, I carry all my diaries with me so that if I sink into the sea they sink with me and no one I loved will ever suffer."

NEARER
THE MOON

MARCH 4, 1937

*P*ARIS. GONZALO [MORÉ] SAID: "WAY UP IN THE mountains in Peru—mountains twice as high as Mont Blanc—there is a small lake set inside a bower of black rocks, an immensely deep lake among black rocks, polished like black marble in the middle of eternal snows. The Indians go there to see the mirages. What I saw in that lake was a tropical scene—richly tropical. We call these mirages *fatamorganas*. You should take that as a pen name for your diary."

COMES THE MOMENT WHEN I CHOKE—WHEN ALL I have lived, seen, heard, felt, overwhelms me, comes up into my throat, drowns me. When the abundance bursts open, when I have to shout.

Comes the moment of white hysteria, of red menstrual blood, the moment of overflow.

Comes life to a climax, an orgasm.

Everything pointing to an orgasm:

"*Poème de l'extase*"—Scriabin.

Dream of René's murder.

Dream of Gonzalo and flame of his life being Helba's dancing.

The dancing of Uday Shankar.

Lawrence Durrell's *Black Book*.

Talk with Henry [Miller] and [David] Edgar.

Talk in the dark in bed with Henry saying: "You are the only one I ever yielded to, Anaïs."

Tenderness with Gonzalo.

Elena [Hurtado] back on surface, does not remain deep.

Swimming.

Talk on pretense between [Jean] Carteret, Evreinoff, and I.

Letters—floods of letters.

[My brother] Joaquin's playing applauded by the king of Spain.

Mother climbing the sixty-five holy steps in Rome on her knees.

Helba's jealousy.

Elena's jealousy.

Spring: *esquivant un geste pâle*.

Suicides. People throwing themselves into the Seine under my window.

Swimming really, in water, to match the inner swimming.

Pushing Betty to use her fins!

Humor.

Writing Durrell about his book.

Fears—of losing Gonzalo—fear of discovery.

Not jealousy of the past but of this past's survival. The nondeath of it! It never dies in the artist.

Nanankepichu [the houseboat] darkened by René. When René worked for us I was too liberal with money. When there was less to do (light the fire, chop wood, get water) he did less and less and claimed more and more money, demanded it, waited for me in the morning, telephoned, visited Gonzalo, endangered our secret, grew nasty, ugly, mean, dark. Gonzalo, as with the old man, grows turbulent, erratic, dark, tumultuous. The air gets tense, heavy, loaded with hatred. *Nanankepichu* begins to look like the site of a crime. In this isolation, in this darkness among this wood groaning, the rain falling in the room, the steps sounding louder, the water lapping, hatred and rapaciousness, injury, anger looms immense and monstrous. Against the smoke of our caresses, this brusque money wrangle, this glare of the world's battle, René's laziness and bad will loom dark and twisted. If my comb disappears it is René who has taken it, and the vision of the filth in which he lives looms immensely, revolting. Gonzalo's anger turns to poison. The noise of the chain tying and untying the little boat, the fury of the Seine's current, the suicides, the old man who still sings when he sees us and bangs his milk cans together, René unable to rouse our pity with his attacking manner, letting the dirt accumulate, the water enter the boat, the dampness gather. All this, with the holes in the floor, the door cracking, the darkness and heaviness of the *péniche* gave me a dream in which Gonzalo cut the neck of René, cut his head off with the same difficulty one has cutting meat . . . and all over the floor of our room were fragments of flesh, entrails, blood, in a pile with rags and broken chairs and coal.

Knocks on the door. It is René saying if we don't leave with him now, we will have to wait until eleven o'clock. We can't wait. We get up resentfully.

We left in the sunshine, angry at René. Gonzalo would be

returning in the afternoon to pump the water out. At five-thirty I passed by, intending merely to smile on him from the quay, and to go on to Henry.

Gonzalo was not there. René came out sulkingly.

I went to Henry. He was writing about my diary. I cooked him a good dinner and we went to the movies. I telephoned Gonzalo several times. At 8:30 he was not home and Helba [his wife] and Elsa [his niece] were anxious. My mind reeled. Something had happened to him. Worse than all this, Gonzalo had dreamed the night before that he was dying gently. Something had happened to Gonzalo. He had quarreled with René or he had tired himself with the pump (his heart is not very strong because of the ether he took).

After nine o'clock I can't call up. The *concierge* will not answer. My imagination tortured me, but my instinct said no. If something had happened I would feel it. I would not be alive. I could not be alive.

Walking at Henry's side I felt a desperation. I felt that if I lost Gonzalo and his warmth, his caresses, nothing could hold me on earth. More than anything, more than this marriage with Henry was this moment of caresses, of abandon, of all things said by the touch, this touching, the miracle of human flesh touching . . . bread and wine. Life. The flesh of Gonzalo.

Henry and I walking. The Western world. The movies. The compromises with life. Exploitation. Commerce. Paris. All the poetry in Henry in his WORDS. Henry and Edgar: WORDS. The snow of analysis. For Henry has changed. In all his men now he seeks analysis, philosophy. He plays the god-role. He has become serious, spiritual, a little tired physically, moving away even from his angers and hatreds, from chaos.

We are lying in bed, spoon fashion. I am hoping he will not desire me. He is tired, quiet, spiritualized. We lie gently together, falling asleep softly, quietly. Nothing has happened to Gonzalo, I feel, or I could not sleep.

Dreamed that Gonzalo was saying: "Helba's dancing was the flame of my life." And I wept with jealousy and said: "You will lose me, you will lose me." Woke up serene. Breakfast with Henry.

Walked to Gonzalo's place. Knocked. No answer. Knocked. And Elsa, half asleep, opened. Gonzalo, half asleep, came. We went out together, drank burned, stale coffee, kissed.

Later in the café, alone, kissed each other into delirium. This was the flame. Kisses ripped the flesh open, yielding, drunk. Gonzalo on fire, wild. He murmured: "I'm so degenerate, I almost prefer thinking about being inside of you to really taking you." Enjoying this frenzy without possession. And I had just come from seeing Helba. Helba struggling to dissolve her jealousy with love as I used to do. Helba acting as I acted toward [Henry's now ex-wife] June. Helba saying: "How could I *not* love you, Anaïs, we are sisters. You have saved my life. When you came I wanted to die. You saved my life. I don't love Gonzalo as a man. He is a child. He has done me so much harm. He is really an Indian, he just wants to drink and be with his friends. I have to sew for him continually. He tears everything. He sticks wine bottles in his pockets and they are always torn. He does nothing for me. He is full of crazy ideas, full of *candeur;* of naïveté. He can't think of tomorrow. He is just a child. If you love him I am glad, because of the kind of woman you are, because you are full of quality and you are an artist." We kissed fervently. Kisses annihilating jealousy, closing the wounds of hatred. From her I go to Gonzalo waiting for me at the café.

[Conrad] Moricand, telling us about the auction sale of all his belongings, how much he suffered, how the rapaciousness, lust, and greediness of the people fighting over his drawings, paintings, books, intimate belongings, souvenirs, trophies, symbols, magic gifts, tokens of love, bartering with cupidity, calcinated him like those trees one sees in the South still standing but with their entrails burnt out.

"Perhaps it is true that those who unveil the mysteries always have tragic lives."

"It is the same with the analysts, all the unveilers," I said, and I thought of Durrell's *Black Book*, where Pandora's box was opened too wide. And I was grateful to Gonzalo for closing my eyes with caresses, with kisses.

Moricand looked at Carteret and said: "You are Rimbaud *gai*."

And Carteret said: "There is something nonhuman about you."

"Don't be afraid to say it. There is something fatal."

The Medusa came in, Elena, with her hair done by Antoine, like a Greek goddess in a white toga and said: "Last night I dreamed about a temple with columns made of people, and I could not get to it because there was an abyss under my feet."

"People were almost afraid to clap at the dancing of Uday Shankar. The feeling of magic was so strong they felt as if they were in a temple," said someone. At this everyone looked at my Persian dress and at my gestures and knew I was a part of that world in which everything was said with the body. That I could forget all the thought of the Western world, all the analysis of the West, and take all meaning into my body and give it out in the gesture. I want to dance.

Hugh held the tiny Siamese cat baptized "Pepe-le-Moko" and Bravig Imbs said: "The Siamese is an exaggerated cat."

Hugh answered: "I have an exaggerated wife."

In the middle of his talk Moricand stopped: "Blank—a blank. That happens when I suddenly begin to *watch myself* talking . . ."

"I call that the absences," said the Medusa. He was telling her about Therese Neuman.

The nearest I could come to magic: Moricand, [René] Allendy, Carteret, Otto Rank. Western magic?

Evreinoff points to his toe, leans over his toe explaining: "In this Petrograd school one was taught to conceal the outward marks of timidity. For example a singer, instead of twisting her hand was taught to twist her toe."

"There are things one can pretend to be," I said, "all that is lying inside of one, latent, unconscious. As soon as you act a role, if this role corresponds to a dormant self—this self awakens, becomes reality. But if you act a false role, something outside of yourself, you get sick, uneasy, as in the Gilbert and Sullivan play—the poet who was not a poet, who was pretending, got a terrible cramp."

Pepe-le-Moko made a sound like a dove, then a curly sound like a monkey and fell asleep inside of Hugh's coat, with his head hung on the lapel.

In the morning I copied out diary forty-six, which is a kind of desert—not even mirages. During lunch I asked myself: was it a pure hazard that in Spanish, English, and French the words

PASSION
COMPASSION

are almost the same plus the *com* which means *with* in Spanish. . . .
How near the words.

Night. Henry and I talking, sitting on his bed. I am saying things
which Henry used to laugh at, and now takes seriously. How he
represented what in me loved war, violence, and chaos—which I
could not express—my masculine soul; and I, by my gentleness, represented the tender in him. "It is true," said Henry, "it was only with
you I could express tenderness."

"You could be your real self."

With me and with his close men friends, who were always gentle
and feminine. The rest of the world arouses him to combat. "It is
thus one arrives at one's own balance because through you I expressed
my martial self. That is what C. G. Jung calls the anima and animus."

In the dark I said: "A strange paradox—I who never fought,
fought violently *for* you."

"And I who never yielded, I yielded to you. You are the only one
I yielded to."

When Henry said this I felt peace, peace and faith. I ceased to be
afraid of separation—of loss. I ceased to fear Elena.

With Gonzalo there is no talk. Everything is said with the mouth,
the tongue, the moisture, the hands, the locked bodies, the touch, the
murmured chaotic words, a sigh, a deep breath, a bite. When he walks
before me and I see his body, his large haunches, his way of swaying,
his joyous head carried high—I desire him, his husky voice in my
ear, his laughter, his terrific angers—he blazes with anger and violence.

I had to learn to be helpless, to stand by the wall waiting so he
can carry me, to be afraid so he can go first, to be passive, dependent.
I do this laughingly. The shifting rhythm from my role in Henry's
life (Henry's complete helplessness in life) is a difficult one to accomplish in one day! Gonzalo likes to wait on me.

What I adore in him is the feeling, the humanness, the personal
feminine way of living. He cannot be objective. He is always in the
moment. When I awoke this morning, eyes swollen from the sunlamp,

I thought first I would leave secretly so he would not see my eyes. I would walk in six inches of water to the ladder. But then I thought of his desire to serve, his sympathy, how angry he would be. I abandoned myself to his great caring. I covered my face with my gypsy handkerchief and awakened him. Instantly he was awake, responsive, fervent, tender.

I have to be three or four days in a dark room—sunburn on eyelids. I hide my face behind a black mantilla.

Henry and I talking about our friends. Why it is outside we feel discord—I am against him. Henry said together we are like hydrogen and oxygen. We produce water. But outside, the elements don't mix, mine with your friends—yours with mine. His men are flabby and my women almost wear mustaches!

I asserted before Edgar that I would continue the diary because it was a feminine activity, it was the personified creation, the opposite of the masculine alchemy. I want to remain on the untransmuted, untransformed, untransposed plane. This alchemy called creation has become, for me, as dangerous as the machine—feeling, emotion are diverted at the source, used as the sacred fluid of sex, to other purposes. What comes out of the factory: pottery, sculpture, painting, books, rugs, architecture, I now regard with fear, just as when I reached a moment with Rank where I *saw* too much, *unveiled too much*—the psychological terminus, where Henry and I stood for a few blinding moments of too much awareness.

It was only lately that I was able to sum up the three errors of analysis: First—Idealism, to expect the perfect relationship, that is, balance, another perfection of the absolute. Second—To consider all escapes as bad, as evasions. (This flight creates another world, a creative world in creative individuals. Repudiation of actual world is right, fecund.) Third—Desire to get back into the womb can become, in a creative way, a making of a womb out of the whole world, including everything in the womb—the city, the enlarged universe of *Black Spring*, of Durrell's *Black Book*—the all-englobing, all-encompassing womb, holding everything. Not being able to reenter the womb, the artist becomes the womb. Analysis does not count the creative product of the neurotic desire.

Crime: Not to tell Elena about Gonzalo as she then would feel free to court Henry; to seduce and enchant her so that she feels no man who has me can ever be won away from me.

At the same time I exalt her to herself and help her to create herself and her life, to paint, write, and believe in herself.

Stuart Gilbert says: "In the last volumes [forty-three, forty-four, forty-five] you have developed a real style of your own—a technique. They are wonderfully done."

Helba said: "How could I not love you, and that little neck of yours and the catlike nose"—almost exactly Gonzalo's own words and feelings.

MARCH 30, 1937

*D*EPRIVED OF THE OPIUM OF INTENSITY I FELL into an abyss. For the world a picturesque effect: Mélisande veils, Tibetan woman, Arab woman, eyes veiled, mystery—a week in darkness. The tenderness of Hugh, the passion of Gonzalo, the egotism of Henry: "That's good. You will have time to meditate"—so I meditated on his egotism, his absolute lack of humanness. I have hated him fully for a week, and adored Gonzalo, and spoiled Hugh with tenderness. Henry has hot blood and a cold soul—there's no doubt about it. It is never love which moves him but his appetite, his desire, his pleasure.

No meditation. Melancholy and darkness. I need my work, my intensity to sustain the illusion of happiness.

APRIL 1, 1937

*H*EALED. DESPERATELY SAD, I WENT TO HENRY AND found, as usual, a man *innocent*, a primitive who cannot love in my way—joyous, philosophical, unmoved. I stormed, wept, felt the primitive appetite, desire, sensual love, no compassion and no giving. Henry could not understand my feeling. He and Edgar in icy objective worlds, *ideas*, new words, books, Durrell's letters, technique of watercolor, analysis, a conference given by Henry on *"la vie intégral,"* review of his book in *Le Mois*, letters. Read me thirty pages he wrote on my diary—magnificent. Edgar all mind, all idea, as [Walter] Lowenfels and [Michael] Fraenkel are discovering with Henry all that I already know.

Henry's answer was to take me. I did not respond. I kept weeping, my whole core shattered by this eternal discovery that you cannot put all your life in the hands of One. Henry is still the Son, and a completely egotistical son.

I left him.

Violent contrast with Gonzalo. In Gonzalo's very gesture—first kiss—an immediacy, a warmth, a strength of love, an awareness. All my pain melts away in the fervor. The life flows through my veins. Instead of *ideas* Gonzalo's talk is all You—Me. I want to help him. He laughs at this. Between his work he kisses me. For ten days I was deprived of a night with him, and it was like death. Oh the sweetness, the warmth, the life in him. Body to body. At dawn I murmur: "Were you really born this way, Gonzalo, so tender? Is it natural? It won't wear off? You won't fade or shrink?" We laugh together. He laughs, laughs. Life again. He can even be concerned over Pepe-le-Moko, who got very sick. He will even show tenderness to a cat.

Too late, much later, Henry is stirred, awakened, and when I came last night he acts like a child who tries very hard to be tender. Too late and unreal. He won't let me peel the onions. He closes the curtains. We talk. The nightmare is over because now and then I see Henry as a monster—I suddenly fall into darkness and he gets deformed. I get angry that he took all my ideas to write about [Hans] Reichel. I get angry that even to write about my diary he used all I had told him and Edgar about the mirrors as if it were his own, handing it back to me, the very theme of a story I was writing. Inconscient? Innocent. He is telling me he bought himself a penknife he had wanted for a long time: "Only eleven francs, Anaïs, but I felt guilty." He looks naïf like a child. I melt. I absolve him because he cannot see, cannot feel. I ask myself: Is this monster I see now and then in Henry what others see in his writing, and which no one can feel in his *presence*—is it all the twist in me which pictures cruelty enlarged just as he saw June's cruelty enlarged? Is it in me, the deformity, the sudden ugly visage (the phrases he utters: "I don't really care about Edgar—I'm just curious about his ideas, that's all"), or is there in Henry this cannibal devouring and never loving?

Doubt tortures me. There is a twist in me, my fear of interpretation. When Henry goes to buy bread in the morning and locks me in absentmindedly, I say: "He has forgotten that I am here." But he returns and says: "See, I want to lock you in so you'll stay."

How to construe?

He says I misconstrue—and I am so willing to believe, to trust. So yesterday he wraps me in care. We fall asleep holding each other. His small head, pale hands, small body, his gray hair, the stoop of his shoulders arouses something in me which is no longer desire but a terrible kind of maternal yearning.

"With you," I said, "it must be always a holiday, always Sunday."

"Why not," says Henry, "why not?"

APRIL 6, 1937

To CONSTRUE—TO MISCONSTRUE. WHAT? THE whole universe? All life suddenly looks monstrous again, and yet is it a monster? How many days and nights have I expected catastrophe which did not happen, how many hours during six years have I imagined the loss of Henry, Henry loving another, and Henry is still there. What is this pall of anxiety, the expectation of the nerves, the fears in full sunshine *compared with my life as others see it?* The envy of other women, my life, my lovers! All women jealous of me. The days when I am outside of the monster, the days of peace, of normal vision, when Hugh does not look to me like a martyr, when Henry does not look like a rogue without scruples, when Gonzalo does not seem about to murder someone out of jealousy, the days when I can laugh at everything—those are the days which make me doubt the monster—its presence, its reality. That is why I cannot rest, I cannot be idle, I cannot sleep as much as others, that is why I seek my joys so desperately, my activity, my creations, my loves, my friends. I say to myself: Now it begins, it begins to gnaw at me again, the disease. I was dreaming of Henry betraying me, of Gonzalo betraying me. I say it begins again, the sickness—see—the world changes as I look at it. When I am told *The House of Incest* is sold at the bookstalls for one franc—someone tore out the dedicated first page and sold it—the whole malignity of people grimaces at me. Who did it? Who among those I know sold my book as junk? I blush with humiliation. [Richard] Osborn is here, penniless. He will sponge on Henry because he knows behind Henry there is the banker's wife. He may even go to sleep at the studio—there is an extra bed. More money, expense. Henry sentimental. I say: "Can I trust you with one hundred francs?" "No," said Henry, "give me fifty francs." "The boat has to be pumped for days," said the proprietor of *Nanankepichu*. "The carpenter must lift the floor to see if there is a leak, there is so much water in the bottom it may sink." No more wine in the barrel. Gonzalo's eyes hurt and I read in a book that alcoholism and drugs affect the glands and ultimately the eyesight and diminish the sexual power. It is true, when Gonzalo first met me he was worried about his diminishing potency but since then he drinks so much less and has gained vitality miraculously and potency. Anxiety. If Gonzalo lost his eyesight and his beautiful sensuality.

Elena wants to buy a car and take short trips, to Rouen, for instance. Henry, who has not seen Elena, says: "I would rather not go on big voyages—just stay around Paris and take short trips. See Rouen, for instance." The day Henry discovers Elena has a car and a friend who is a printer, his whorish nature will be set on fire, his taking, using, prostitute nature. How good if I could leave behind the tragedy and break with Henry—break ahead of life, of fatality, of my fear, of the inevitable—free myself—to give myself wholly to Gonzalo who is my *life*. Because of the disease in me, the poison, the cancer of doubt and fear, Henry has become my death, and even though he can make love to me, prove his passion, take me with frenzy, even though sensuality solders, resolders, even though he has ordered a blank book for my diary from [Jack] Kahane, and written thirty pages about my diary, and looks at me with unchanged, innocent, expressionless blue eyes. Even then . . .

APRIL 7, 1937

EVEN THEN—I LEAVE HENRY ASLEEP, I GO TO [OUR apartment at] quai de Passy, take a long, voluptuous bath, have dinner with Hugh, rest, leave him in bed at 10:30, take the bus to *Nanankepichu*. Gonzalo's caresses touching all my body, all the places Henry never touched, Gonzalo's warm hand and sensitive fingertips touching all my body, electrifying the skin, awakening the nerves, rousing the blood and Gonzalo taking me from behind which has never stirred me, and now I have a long, powerful

13

orgasm, and this makes me so happy, to yield to him wholly, to abandon myself wholly, that I almost weep with pleasure, and he has the same emotional overflow after the orgasm as I have, he says: *"abrázame, abrázame, chiquita."* He wants nearness, the love again, he is grateful. *Abrázame, abrázame.*

I awake joyous. The world is clear and soft, at peace. The trees, the sky, the boat are peaceful. Henry lies asleep in me, silent, and my flesh has opened and yielded to Gonzalo, to Henry, in one day and night and so divided, shared, the anguish ceases, I feel the axis again, the normalcy, the joy.

Leaping out of the taxi in the sunny morning I meet Joaquin who has come back from Italy and he says: "Where do you come from?" I laugh behind my hands as I did when I was a child. We have breakfast together.

Joaquin. Mother. Diary 46 unfinished. Thurema [Sokol] longing for me. Fifteen- and twenty-page letters of confessions from patients to answer.* Call up to store away the fur coat. Buy music paper to type on music lines the pages of orchestra writing. Take Helba to the doctor. Take sun baths. Bring Mother flowers. Have Gonzalo's drawings framed. Fatigue. Refusing invitations. Harassed by the [George] Turners, no time to meet [Eugene] Jolas, who asked to meet me. Stuart Gilbert asking: "Are you writing?" Pepe-le-Moko eating holes in the towels. Carrying candles and towels and soap to *Nanankepichu.* Taking notes in the bus. Henry saying joyously: "I will die of tranquility." Enjoying his life, living with a deep enjoyment of peace. Writing steadily. Content. The moment in the bath is the only moment for meditation. I love the richness.

---

*After following psychoanalyst Dr. Otto Rank to New York during the winter 1934–1935, and again early in 1936, Anaïs Nin had briefly worked as a lay psychotherapist under his guidance and subsequently on her own.

*H*ELBA IS SO SICK I WILL TAKE HER TO MY DOCTOR. This after a tender afternoon together when we kissed and exchanged confidences. I took her to the doctor. I translated what she said. The man she was married to at fourteen gave her syphilis. She had been pronounced cured years ago. (My god, my god, Gonzalo has syphilis. Gonzalo has syphilis!)

"When was the last blood test made?" asked the doctor. "What kind of cure were you given?"

"Two months ago my blood was tested. I was given mercury injections."

He turned to me because she could not hear him: "That explains the deafness."

"Did your husband—"

"No, my husband did not catch it. He has been tested several times. I was already cured when I met him. And we have had no relations for six years." (Gonzalo, Gonzalo, how ugly all this is! How terrible. Poor Helba!)

Poor Helba. I kissed her with sudden, deep pity. She was frightened to have spoken. She lay on the couch, half undressed. I saw her legs, her sex, her black hair. I felt a pang of jealousy when I thought Gonzalo had caressed and kissed these legs, this black hair.

In the taxi Helba was terrified: "I beg you tell no one, Anaïs. Gonzalo will be furious if he knows I have told you this. He has begged me not to tell you. He hates disease, he says it is so ugly, he puts you always as someone in a dream, he does not want you to know about these things. Today I said the Turkish woman might come to see me at the same time as you. He was furious. He said he didn't want you to meet her, she was vulgar and she talks about operations. He thinks you are a dream."

"Helba, don't be afraid. It will be our secret—between women."

"Oh, Anaïs, why do you do all this? Nobody has ever done this for me. Gonzalo does nothing for me, he is a child, he dreams his time away."

I wanted Gonzalo desperately, to see the life in his eyes, to feel his mouth, after all this death and rotting of flesh, these ulcers. *Nanankepichu.* Candlelight. Water lapping. The dream.

I could not see Gonzalo because Henry was waiting for me, a very tender Henry, following the design of my mouth with his fingertips. We indulged in sleep, an orgy of sleep. I wanted to sleep to forget, I wanted tomorrow—the sun, the breakfast, and the morrow came sensual and warm, burst of foliage, lulling air, sun. Gonzalo came in the morning. Quai de Passy full of *"alegría phýsica,"* [sic] rejoicing to find me looking luminous and gay. Reassured by his mouth, kisses *pour chasser les mauvais esprit.* Gone the shock.

"Before I met Gonzalo I was a demon as you are now with men," said Helba.

I realized fully what I meant to Gonzalo. I felt no more jealousy. Strange this jealousy which I do not feel about Helba as a woman but of Helba the dancer—her creation—exactly as Gonzalo is jealous of Henry's genius. Helba the dancer represents what I value highly: the dance as a living expression. I always feel Gonzalo can't love my writing as much as he loves her dancing. So mad is jealousy and so far does it reach! Just as I can't love his work as I love Henry's.

I feel a *malaise* until I write certain things down. This scene irritated me today like something I could not rid myself of. Deliverance!

A P R I L   1 2 ,   1 9 3 7

Gonzalo's bronze glow—his mouth—vital flesh burning. All this effaced the monstrous apparitions. A night together. A Sunday afternoon stolen by tricks— a long afternoon. The nights sensual. The days sensual. The softening days prolonging the caresses of the night. The wheel turning, the days turning, cracking with fullness, the leaves bursting out of dead branches, the sun lancinations, new dust in the air, then Henry and the purely naked sensual fusion, then Gonzalo and voluptuousness, intricacies, dreams, three hours of caresses like music through the veins. He is like a woman, he quivers under my hands, with my fingertips I touch his eyelids, his temple, his ears, with my whole hand I grasp his neck, touch the pulsing throat, softly, lightly I touch the back, down the spinal column, and around the hip, the hand slips down the curves of the hips, in the valley that leads to the hair, touches the hair. He feels even a caress on the arm, on the shoulder! I buried my head suddenly into the darkness of the bed, my mouth found the black hair, the legs—he was quivering all over with pleasure. He falls into a trance.

Then Helba, and disease, and tears, and melancholy, and all my jealousy dissolving because she says: "Gonzalo loved me as I loved him—not as a woman really, as a friend. He was not jealous. I never felt man really—all through my life. My first experience was too much. . . . Married at fourteen to a sadist—who beat me and forced himself on me."

Only reality heals the torments of the imagination. Reality. Reality. I laugh at my jealousy. When there was the sensual connection between Henry and June I thought I was jealous because it was sensual. And now I transfer jealousy to the plane of creation, knowing it is not a sensual connection. I center my jealousy on Helba's work. I laugh today. I see myself clearly as the one who captivated Gonzalo's senses, how I am June now, how I mean color and health and joy to Gonzalo—*life*. And I laugh at myself. . . .

So Helba and I are walking and while we talk I am thinking that Helba and Henry can be poets in writing or on the stage but they cannot *live* poetry—in life they are prosaic. Is this an accident, this parallel, or is this art in life the magic element which communism will destroy and which is fated to disappear from human life? Poetry in life. It is amusing that Gonzalo and I—after traversing all the realisms, all the realities of poverty, of caricature, Henry's prosaic life, Helba's naturalism—have been drawn to each other after a long detour and stand at the beginning of our life again, I mean, at the poetic peak, at the moment when the sense of wonder blinded us, when dreams obscured all life for us.

No matter how human my life with Henry, and no matter how human Gonzalo's life with Helba, a secret world survived which neither Henry's writing nor Helba's dancing completely fulfilled: the poetry and the fire in life, in the body, in caresses, flowering in the veins, in tenebrous moments, below daylight, a secret. Gonzalo touches things in me which are *beyond* me, which were dormant in my blood, secret affinities of race, beyond us, ancestral, mysterious, something which the present self, free today, has never lost.

Race. And yet not race. No other Spaniard touched this. But Gonzalo does. And I do in him. Memories. Odors. Images. Images of race. Madonna faces of the sixteenth century. Catholicism and sensuality. Religion only as a sensual experience. Incense and pride.

I know now, from my caresses with Henry, that the mystery of flesh is a deep one—always, if a mouth touches flesh profoundly, if the blood quivers, if the rhythm is one, there must be a marriage somewhere—somewhere that is not apparent, sometimes never comes to the surface, never materializes, embodies itself, formulates itself. It may remain a mystery. In the cells. Consciously, what happens with words, we don't know. There errors can happen, dissonances. One has to believe in a marriage without white veils and orange blossoms, this marriage in darkness which sometimes cannot be prolonged in daylight. One has to believe in this marriage under water, voiceless and wordless.

In this way I am falling in love with Gonzalo. The day does not exist. I know nothing of the day. The day I speak Henry's language or rather he has come to speak mine. I can say things I could not say before. He understands more. Caricature, I read, is a sign of madness. Deformation in art is a puzzle, yet. A puzzle Rank could not solve.

At night I speak Gonzalo's language. Sometimes I feel the orgasm, sometimes not. It does not matter. He opens my flesh tenderly and ardently like so many petals. Each day he touches a new nerve, each day his caresses remain longer inside of me. The pleasure runs from the roots of the hair to the toes. Each day Henry and I say less to each other with our bodies.

A year ago it was possession every day or every other day, then twice a week, then once a week. Fewer caresses in between possession. Then today I could not respond wholly because I felt Gonzalo in me, Gonzalo's eyes, Gonzalo's jealousy.

First this marriage, and perhaps we shall marry in daylight, too, perhaps from the dark roots flowers will suddenly pierce the ground and flowers of the same nature. I don't know. Perhaps when this happens I shall regret the chaos, the darkness.

Henry and I have reached the mystical stardust marriage, with gemlike words and when he says: "I am more interested in Neptune (Anaïs) than in Uranus (Henry)," that is what he means.

APRIL 13, 1937

*I*CANNOT REMEMBER WHAT I SAW IN THE MIRROR as a child. Perhaps a child never looks at the mirror. Perhaps a child, like a cat, is so much inside of himself that he does not see himself in the mirror. He sees a child. The child does not remember what he looks like. Later I remember what I looked like. But when I look at photographs of myself at one, two, three, four, five years old, I do not recognize myself. The child is One. At one with himself. Never outside of himself. I can remember what I did but not the reflections of what I did. No reflections. Six years old. Seven years old. Eight years old. Nine. Ten. Eleven. No image. No reflection. Feeling. I can feel what I felt about my Father's white mice, the horror they inspired in me, the revolting odor, the taste of a burnt omelet my Father made for us while my Mother was sick with child. The feel of the beach, of the air in Barcelona, the feel of the balcony there, the fear of death and the writing of a testament, the feelings in church, in the street. Sounds in the Spanish courtyard. Voices. The appearance of others. Not the image of the self. No picture in my mind's eye of what I wore. The long black cotton stockings of Spanish children I saw in a photograph. Yet at six years old the perfection of the blue ribbon on my hair, shaped like a butterfly, preoccupied me since I quarreled to have my godmother make it because she made it better than anyone. I must have seen this bow in the mirror then. I do not remember whether I saw this bow, the little girl in a short white dress, again in a photograph taken in Havana where all my cousins and I stood in a row according to our height, all wearing enormous ribbons and short white dresses.

In the mirror there never was a child.

The first mirror has a frame of white wood. In it there is no Anaïs Nin but Marie Antoinette with a white lace cap, a long black dress, standing on a pile of chairs, the chariot, riding to her beheading. No Anaïs Nin. An actress. A girl of fourteen grimacing, portraying despair, fury, terror. Other personages. Charlotte Corday pushing a dagger into the back of Marat. A beggar woman. A princess. An orphan. But the first mirror in which the self appears is very large, inlaid inside of a brown wood wall. Next to it the window pours down so strong a light that the rest of the room is not reflected in the mirror, but the image of the girl who approaches is brought in luminous relief—against a foggy darkness the girl of fifteen stands with frightened eyes. She is looking at her dress, a dress of shiny worn blue serge which was fixed up for her out of one belonging to a cousin. It does not fit her. It is meager, it looks poor. The girl looks at the blue serge dress with shame. It is the day she has been told in school that she is gifted for writing. They had come purposely into the class to tell her. She who was always quiet and who did not wish to be noticed, was told to come and speak to the composition teacher before everyone, to hear the compliment. And the joy, the dazzling joy which had first struck her, was instantly killed by the awareness of the dress. I did not want to get up, to be noticed. I was ashamed of this meager dress with a shine on it, its worn air, its orphan air, its drooping rainfall aspect. Ashamed. The girl looks at the dress.

There is another mirror inlaid in dark brown wood. The girl is looking at the new dress which transfigures her. What an extraordinary change. She leans over very close to look at the humid eyes, the humid mouth, the moisture and luminousness brought about by the change of dress. She walks up very slowly to the mirror—very slowly as if she did not want to frighten the reflection away. Several times, at fifteen, she walks very slowly toward the mirror. The face is mask-like. It does not smile. The girl is in a trance. All day in a kind of trance. She does not want to frighten the reflection—herself. Someone has said she is very pale. She approaches the mirror and stands still like a statue. Immobile. Waxy. She never makes a gesture. Immobile. Confronting herself. Surprised. Somnambulistic. She only moves to become someone else. She moves in the mirror now, not as Anaïs Nin who goes to school, writes in her diary, and grows vegetables and flowers in the backyard. She moves to be a tragedienne. She acts. In the mirror there is Sarah Bernhardt, Melisende, Faust's Marguerite, queens, monsters, woman limping, a woman dying of poison, *la dame aux camélias*, Thaïs with her veils, a woman praying.

Anaïs Nin is immobile, haunting, like a picture caught in a painting, moving in a dream. She is decomposed before the mirror into a hundred personages, recomposed into paleness and immobility and silence. At sixteen, it is Anaïs looking at the mirror with her hair up for the first time, a question in her glance. In the eyes a question—in the mouth, in the eyebrows, a question.

APRIL 14, 1937

WHAT I FIND HUMOROUS IS TO MOCK THE ORDER of the world, to tell my Father I'm working for the fascists when I need his [mimeograph] machine and to pretend to Gonzalo to care about the communists, not a double-faced character but fundamentally not caring for either, no more than Henry cares for ideas seriously. I don't take these things seriously. I find it humorous to irritate my Father with the title of my book *The House of Incest* (he, telling Elena, imagine what people will think!), precisely because I know his hypocrisy. Humor in shattering hypocrisies—or mocking men's system of thought, telling Gonzalo I'm Henry's wife and Hugh's mistress because I am amused by the idea of *not* being Hugh's wife (Mrs. Guiler, wife of submanager of National City Bank) in Passy, the bourgeois world. Humor in carrying the diary about, and thinking of juxtapositions *as the world would see them*, not as I *feel them.*

The old Abbé Lancelin coming every day to convert me—whose door-ringing I finally did not answer. One morning, while he was ringing persistently, I was sorting out the pages in the diary relating the incident of flagellation! He rings the bell, the gray-bearded abbé whose eyes lingered with pleasure on my face, and I am numbering pages on incest, flagellation. And it makes me laugh. Laugh. That the world should have brought itself to such foolishness, incongruous impasses! Through sheer idiocy. I laugh. The same with faithfulness, loyalty, and other ideals!

Pierre Bresson says that symbolical, stylized language impedes the human participation.

People admire *House of Incest*, but they warm up, explode over the childbirth story.* The human. The direct.

Letter from Lawrence Durrell: Dear Anaïs Nin: I feel a pig if I don't write and tell you what a splendid writer you are—though of course you know. It was that last thing you sent, the Dionysiac little birth scene. That rang the bell *and* returned the penny: as you know, only a real heavy's strength will do that. . . . I have always dreamed of a sort of hypothetical goal which the woman writer would reach. . . .

Writing as a woman. I am becoming more and more aware of this. All that happens in the real womb, not in the womb fabricated by man as substitute. Strange that I should explore this womb of real flesh when of all women I seem the most idealized, the most moonlike, a Persian miniature, a dream, a myth. And it is I descending into the real womb, luring men into it, struggling to keep man there, and struggling to free him of me! To help him create another womb. The

---

*The story "Birth," adapted from reflective diary entries, appeared for the first time in the inaugural issue of Dorothy Norman's New York literary magazine, *Twice a Year* (fall–winter 1938), but Anaïs Nin had passed around copies of her manuscript.

diary ends in Fez, in a city, in the street, in the labyrinth for me because that is the city which looks most deeply like the womb, with its Arabian night gentleness, tranquility, and mystery. My self—woman—womb—with grilled windows, veiled eyes, tortuous, secret cells.

When I leave Henry at ten in the evening, saying I have posing to do, with only a half hour between his kiss and Gonzalo's, I cannot cross the bridge as lightly, and half of me remains imprisoned in the fine wrinkles on the edge of Henry's eyes, his laughing wrinkles, in the corner fold of his humorous, soft mouth, and the wave of desire for Gonzalo envelops me again with languid eyes and palpitating eyelashes, and a mouth that seems to await pain tremblingly.

APRIL 20, 1937

THE QUAI D'ORSAY CLOCK POINTS TO ALMOST noon! With eyes half asleep I look at it, unbelieving, as I stand on the little rotted wood stairway leading from our room to the deck of *Nanankepichu*. "Gonzalo, it is nearly twelve!" He springs up. We had talked late into the night, about madness. I said no one became mad except from loneliness, I said while there is someone near you who sees what you see, you don't go mad. "See, Gonzalo, the lamp hanging there, it has the color of the moon."
"Yes, it has the color of the moon."
"Then if you see it like that we are both sane, or both crazy and we have a world of our own."

The rain is falling. Home at quai de Passy. Every first and every fifteenth of the month, Hugh makes very seriously and earnestly a budget: He hands me 3,200 francs, or 6,400 a month. My allowance, 500; Lantelme, 200; Mother and Joaquin, 1,500; house, 500. With this I have to pay: Henry's rent, 650; Henry's food, 1,500; Helba and Gonzalo (more than I confessed giving), 1,500; rent of *Nanankepichu* (unconfessed), 300; Lantelme (more than I confessed giving), 700; my expenses, 500; Mother and Joaquin, 3,000. I pay 8,150. I have 6,400. 1,750?????

Money in hand I pay right and left. After a week I have nothing. I have to borrow or take it from Hugh's pocket, or we have a windfall! We have debts. Henry got 3,000 francs royalties [on *Tropic of Cancer*] and my own share [advanced for] the printing. We paid 400 francs taxes; 500 francs Henry gave to Osborn; 100 francs to Reichel, in payment for a painting I have been buying slowly; 50 francs debt to Edgar; 300 francs debt to Durrell. He gave me 1,000 with which I paid bills I had long ago said I had paid. Bought myself a pair of shoes, and Henry bought a shirt and tie. And when I arrived two days later Henry had only red beans for lunch, heavy red beans I could not digest and when I met Betty [the copyist] at the Dôme, I told her about the red beans and ordered Vichy! How we laughed.

I never worry about money. But I often have to play desperate tricks. [Cousin] Eduardo [Sanchez] and Hugh do the worrying. Every month I juggle through. And at the blackest moment something happens! A check comes, a patient pays me, Hugh's mother relents.

So today it is raining. George Turner on the telephone: "Can't I see you?" He is back from a cruise around the world: "I thought I was cured, had forgotten you, Anaïs, but I'm still crazy about you. . . ."

Elena: "Come over. It's a sad day. I want to see you."

I elude them all. I want to be alone. Walk the streets. *Pursue my game*, my secret life, my fantasy. I want to buy enormous candles for *Nanankepichu*, sweep the room, change the sheets. I walk in the rain. On the way I try on hats I cannot buy, but for a few minutes I pretend. I take the copied diaries to the vault. At six I am marketing for Henry, with Betty who laughs at my life. I peel potatoes and string beans. Henry is out meeting Léon-Paul Fargue. It is raining. He will be glad to walk in and find a good dinner waiting. While I peel the vegetables I rage a little because people prefer the childbirth to the coral and the dream and the Atlantide. They like the naked female world. Human life. This black narcissus growing on top of the diary's back like a mushroom on a wet roof, they don't like.

At the Dôme Feri stops me: "Why doesn't Eduardo write me? I'm getting mad."

"You must know why he doesn't write you. It's all over."

"When can I see you?"

"There is no more bond between us. We have nothing to say to each other."

He walks away angrily.

APRIL 21, 1937

I DON'T KNOW WHY I CAN'T GET AS HUMANLY close to Elena as I did to Thurema. At moments we do. When she is at home, quiet and deep, we talk deeply about life, but soon I feel, as I did with Louise [de Vilmorin], that we are playing. I see the colored balls of our imagination, I see the nonhuman eyes, and I don't trust her. People feel that in her, the nonhuman. People are afraid of her. Something in her inspires a nonhuman attachment. *Sur elle*, human feelings seem to slip, they *glisser*—yet she talks about her life in tragic terms, and Louise's life was tragic, but it does not move me. She seems unreal. A brilliant, multicolored Medusa, capable of great evil unconsciously. One feels the vampire in her, the taker, the one who destroys, in contradiction to the facts, the conscious life of Elena as a generous woman, as a healer, as a creator. She has truly two faces and she only believes in one of them. She has two aspects: Elena at home, sewing, serious, tragic almost, maternal, the Catholic girl who is afraid of sinning, and Elena outside, with mocking eyes, a sardonic mouth, an adventurous air. This aspect frightens people, freezes them, or amuses them. "Which is my real self?" she asks me.

Absolute duality. As there is in me. Betty copying the New York diary of a year ago can't believe all this passion, tumult, pain, and fever could be taking place under my calm, peaceful, sphinxlike exterior.

Elena exteriorizes her fever, as June did. I live it deep down, and secretly. As an actress I present a facade to the world, of innocence and tranquility.

The night I spent with Gonzalo, Henry went to a movie on the Champs-Elysées and walked home, passing by the Pont de la Concorde at midnight, so near to *Nanankepichu*. The same night, Hugh went to the café where Allendy's group meets*—Carteret etc.—and walked back home passing by the Pont Royal at about midnight. Another time, Gonzalo and I were walking from *Nanankepichu* to the café because he was thirsty and Emil [Savitry], the photographer, was leaning over the quays, studying the *péniches* for a possible composition. It was dark and he did not recognize us.

Living out my relationship with Henry in Elena's presence, and keeping my relationship with Gonzalo a secret, makes the first seem very real and the second a life of the imagination. No mention to anyone except Eduardo, the existence of the *péniche* makes it seem a dream. A warm dream.

Gonzalo says we were made of the same paste but in baking us he was kept in the oven too long and got darker! I can watch our two skins for hours with delight. They are made of the same tones. I have not the whiteness of the Anglo-Saxon but a creamishness, a banana color, a moon glow and baked longer this would produce Gonzalo's color.

I like secrets.

Everything that is natural and right with Henry, crowded streets, cafés, movies, is wrong with Gonzalo, and we run away from it. We created a dream which unfolds in *Nanankepichu*. No one in the Dôme knows where he goes when he leaves precipitately about ten at night.

Henry's love for the ordinary, natural human aspect of Paris, and his exaggerated expectations, demands, and disillusions with traveling because nothing is as extraordinary as he imagined it to be is a par-

---

*Dr. René Allendy, the psychoanalyst who befriended Antonin Artaud and other surrealist artists, apparently was involved with left-wing political activities, as were many of the surrealists under André Breton's influence.

adox. His acceptance of ordinary, natural human beings stands in the way of his finding the extraordinary, I tell him. This he does not understand. I find the extraordinary in proportion to my rebellion against the natural. It would seem as if he dodges the extraordinary in order to be forced to create it, while I seek and find the extraordinary and don't have to invent it: Rank, Louise, June, Elena, Gonzalo, Fez. Henry enjoys the familiar and the known, fears the unknown: Corfu, Lawrence Durrell. The extraordinary *in life, realized*, makes him uncomfortable. He does not recognize it. He does not like it until it has become familiar, human, natural.

I am at home in the marvelous. Absolutely at home. And uncomfortable and paralyzed in the common. What Henry enjoys around him are the unpicturesque, the not-striking, the common street, the face of a clock, a homely house, a prosaic café, just like the people around him. Faced with the created marvel, he does not see that it matches his dream, or his writing. The transformed, created, illumined material he looks at as upon a scarecrow.

MAY 1, 1937

WE SAW A *CLOCHARD* WHO WORE A SCOTCH CAP. I said to Gonzalo: "Ask him if he is Scotch and if he is we will give him a bottle of wine, in honor of Scotch ancestors." Gonzalo's father. Hugh's mother.

When Gonzalo talks about ritual, the first theater on the altars of the Catholic Church, the extraordinary fantastic ceremonies full of mystery and grandeur, I feel that I recover a lost world which is beyond my everyday self, the world of my race. When he raves against the vulgarity of the Western world, the scientific epoch, the lack of ritual and significance, I understand. When he fears we are tainted, I understand, tainted with consciousness. But we know deep down we have kept a chalice and an altar, a mystery. I know what passionate affinity attracted me to Fez, what deep roots are stirred in me by the

Orient. I had all this sense of form and ritual in the life of dress and symbolism, of continuous significance, and the power of falling into a trance, of moving out of myself by exaltation, away from violence.

A gorgeous world of grandeur and hierarchy, of faith and worship. A lost world. Religion as poetry.

[Antonin] Artaud attempted to recapture the illusion and symbolism, to break with the realism in the theater.

Henry always says: "Why don't you get a beret"—like the servant girls, coquettes, students, like everybody?

Even in hats I like hierarchic coiffures: hats like Russian tiaras, hats like aureoles, hats like crowns, like Venetian headdresses, like Egyptian, Greek, or Indian headgears.

The softening, relaxing influence not of woman but of the men I choose! The sleepy, lazy, soft, weak men! Sexual enjoyment all a matter of relaxation or tension. Frigidity is brought about by tension. Tension due to resistance of some sort—psychic, psychological. I resisted responding to Gonzalo out of love for Henry. But now I have completely divided myself. At times I have a fear of this *dédoublement*. Perhaps I shall divide beyond unity. But I do not feel broken. I feel balanced over a great net. No abyss, scission, split, madness, but sanity and harmony. I feel a great joy and no remorse.

Helba took a black cat under her protection. The black cat vomited a worm. Helba went into convulsions. Her face twisted, her eyes protruding. "The worms are inside of me. That is why I'm sick. They have eaten into my intestine and the food does not stay. Take the cat away. You have caught worms too, Gonzalo."

Worms. Death. Fear of death. Of burial. Of worms. Insane over the worms. Her eyes show no recognition.

At the same moment Osborn haunts Henry's studio. He lies on the couch and sticks his tongue out, and tries to chew the tip of it. Or he stands before the mirror cutting his hair with his left hand and contemplating his unshaven face. Or he comes showing his penis in his hand to Edgar and Henry saying: "It looks quite healthy, doesn't it, it doesn't look like syphilis." He asks Henry, "How would you go from Litchfield, Connecticut, to Boston?"

He has built up an imaginary legal case against an imaginary man who has stolen one of his manuscripts, sold it for a fabulous price to a Hollywood producer. He thinks Hugh dismissed him from the bank because he drank Pernod, frequented Montparnasse, and had a mistress. He wants Henry to hold his money and deal it out to him in small sums.

Rank had visited him in the asylum in Connecticut. Had said: "I am Otto Rank." "So you say!" answered Osborn.

Rank had said: "Guilt. He is loaded with guilt, envy, jealousy. He is jealous of Henry as a writer and of what you gave Henry."

Henry is haunted, obsessed, uneasy. He wants to leave Villa Seurat. He hides, is afraid to typewrite—yet will not go and visit Durrell in Corfu.

I hold the money for all of them. Henry hands it over to me. I have to send envelopes with one hundred francs to Osborn by way of other people. I sent Gonzalo once, who does not know Osborn is a friend of Henry's.

Yesterday afternoon I took Gonzalo to the doctor for his eyes. He found him run-down, but not sick. A wonderful physique. Unusual vitality. No syphilis traces. Gonzalo and I walked back through the Bois, passed le boulevard Suchet, where I first visited Rank, passed boulevard Suchet studio. At seven we parted at the Passy subway station. At seven Hugh and Horace [Guicciardi] were bicycling through the Bois while I walked back along the rue de Passy to the little restaurant on the rue Boulainvillier, where Henry and I used to eat when we stayed in the rue des Marronniers. I was meeting Henry there because he wanted to elude Osborn. Great softness. I observe the great changes in Henry, his spiritualization, his interest in clairvoyance, astrology, the mysterious, the far-from-the-earth. He has become wise, as I was, and I have become emotional. He looked tired and very serious. When we laugh at the movies he takes my hand. We sit in a café. We talk about clairvoyance. I leave him at midnight, saying I have to go home because the next morning Hugh and I are leaving very early for a bicycle ride. I leave him to meet Gonzalo.

Gonzalo is disgusted, nauseated by politics, the petty self-interest, the petty jealousies, the petty quarrels. He is hurt, disillusioned. Our night is not happy. The mad violinist, who is a Freudian, has told him that his fear of spiders reveals his fear of woman and homosexuality. Gonzalo is affected. He has begun to be anxious over the fact that he prefers to take me always from behind. "Am I abnormal?" he asks. I laugh his fear away. I tell him I think the real reason is a kind of punishment for what I wrote in my novel about legs parted, a phrase which aroused his jealousy and carved an irradicable image in him. So much so that he remembered it one night when he was lying over me and suddenly the phrase flashed through his mind and he closed my legs and his desire died. "You see, Gonzalo, I mistrust all explanations now because you can always give two of them, one physical, one metaphysical. So let us leave all that alone." I was sad to see Gonzalo conscious.

Hugh, however, does not let me live in a *brume* of feeling. He is reading Rank, discussing him, he is analyzing his friends. I have to hear all this that I know too well and which I have left behind. But I listen through a veil. I am far away, far away.

I get tired of Edgar's mental acrobatics. Henry urges me again to talk. I stop as soon as I feel misunderstood. Edgar, like Fraenkel, talks geometrically. I can't answer that. I was very simple and sincere and told Henry why I withdrew. Not as he thought, through hostility, but through shyness, inadequacy, lack of faith in myself as a talker. I am not ashamed of my weakness.

MAY 9, 1937

WHAT I FAILED TO SAY TO EDGAR WAS: SELF-analysis is destructive, it generates only introspection, the labyrinth, division. It is always false, based on false premises. It is paralyzing.

Analysis should be only endured at the hands of another as a healing process. There is no self-analysis—there is neurosis. It is anti-creative. It is a form of pause, not motion.

When at times I lean over a Gonzalo half asleep, half drunk on caresses and I am awake, alert, my imagination on fire, he often closes his eyes and says: "*Tengo pereza. I am lazy. Pereza espiritual. Pereza cerebral.*"

A blessing.

"Strange," he says, "the unexpected effect you had on me. Although we do nothing but dream together, although you drug me, although *Nanankepichu* is a dream, you have a dynamic effect on me. I want action."

He has been made secretary of the Peruvian Communist Party.

Waiting in the café I write these words: "On *being* the womb." And it unleashes a tremendous new feminine world. I am completely divorced from man's idea world. I swim in nature. On being the womb. Englobing.

All the artists, the intellectuals, rushing to find the blood rhythm in war and revolution. I go wherever there is pulsing blood. Nothing can shatter my individual world. No storm on sea or earth. Communism they call it. It is the drama, the poem, and the rhythm of hatred, desire, lust, war, passion. The rhythm of illusion. I will call it the madness of perpetual analogy.

Identification.

Because I love I identify myself. Everything is identified. People are mingled inside of me. There is flow between all of them, an absence of separateness.

I give Gonzalo medicines for Helba and I get into the subway, not for Passy but for Alesia, where I stop in the rain to buy food for Henry who is signing contracts with Stock for the translation of his books.* When he comes I am peeling strawberries. He talks excitedly but says he is not excited because it has all come too late. It is raining. We eat slowly. Afterward I work on volume thirty-eight, changing

---

*Editions Stock in Paris apparently never issued any translations. A French edition of *Tropic of Cancer*, published by Denoel, appeared in 1945, and a translation of *Black Spring* several years later.

the names of Artaud, Allendy, et al. Strange how many years I missed Gonzalo. Henry had met him. Artaud knew him. Roger [Klein] knew him. Natasha [Troubetskoia] knew him. There was my happiness and it did not come until I was ready for it. Before Henry I was not ready for Gonzalo, spiritually. Henry brought him to me when I needed him not to go mad with jealousy and the inhumanness of my life with Henry. How grateful I am for all this which makes me believe in God. How each friend and each lover represents the world in us, the unborn potential world and makes it be born. I traversed a sensual pleasure world to arrive at my spiritual devotion world of Gonzalo, clothed in ardent flesh, but a kind of communion flesh. Ironically, Henry is becoming a saint and is saying his life was an error. "Write this in your journal, Anaïs, I like to be with myself now." *Il se receuille. Et moi je me donne.* He communes with himself. I give of myself. I live in the dark yet sun-warmed flesh of Gonzalo which I *hear* burning—a sound of fire.

When Helba and I walk together she makes me happy telling me: "Gonzalo is a changed man, and I am so happy, Anaïs. He was very unhappy before. A man cannot live without love, and Gonzalo was not easy to satisfy. All the women wanted him, all of them wanted him. But he would see them once perhaps and come back unhappy and refuse to see them again. He did not care about women. They sought him out while he always found something wrong with them. With you, he is ecstatic. And I'm happy, because I knew this had to happen sometime but I am happy it's you and I know you would not take him away from me because I need him. I used to fear some woman coming and taking him where I would never see him again. And you, you're a part of me. I'm not unhappy."

Hugh is with Carteret, Henry with Edgar, when I am with Gonzalo. Each one reflects Hugh's and Henry's mood of the present. Hugh always mystical, occult, analytical. Henry spiritualized, mentalized. Henry shares analysis with Edgar, while I have passed on into another plane. *La nuit.*

MAY 25, 1937

*E*VER SINCE OSBORN CAME, HAUNTED HENRY'S STUdio, borrowed money and food, Henry, while acting with compassion and wisdom, became more and more depressed. His passivity, acceptance, inertia tied him in a knot. I tried to help him. I suffered from his fatigue, bad moods, despondency. I understood. He was far away, cold, impersonal, abstracted, jellied.

My own madness came back. I began to imagine he was tired of me, indifferent. My understanding wore out. I was hurt. Gonzalo's caresses and fervor could not dispel my greatest sources of pain: any feeling of distance between Henry and me, of separateness, of lack of vital exchange. For the last three days, after a dark evening with Henry I fell into darkness myself. Henry's remoteness, Henry's deadness. I tried to find a cause for my misery. I grasped on his last act of selfishness (spending all his royalties on an illustration of the *Scenario* which represents all my own images out of *House of Incest*).* But that was not the cause. Yesterday morning I went to him feeling rebellious, hating his passivity—full of poison. He was sick, he wanted to be left to sleep. I left him. I spent the afternoon with Gonzalo. We fixed up our rooms, worked together. His kisses, humanness, warmth, nearness warmed me. But I was still sad inside. I went back to Henry at six. He had slept all day. He was soft, gentle, caressing. I told him what I felt. He said he felt shattered inside, tired, needed *recueillement*, meditation. We had dinner and sat in a café, talking quietly. He said: "I feel I have never lived on the same level as the

---

*Henry Miller's *Scenario* (A Film with Sound), "directly inspired by a phantasy called 'The House of Incest' written by Anaïs Nin," as the dedication read, was published by Miller himself under the Obelisk Press imprint, in July 1937, in an edition of two hundred signed and numbered copies, with a frontispiece illustration by Abraham Rattner, an American artist living in Paris.

one I write on." Continually, he says the things I felt and did not attack because they were his nature. Now he knows.

"Except with you, and now Edgar."

"I suppose you did that not to be alone—not to go mad. You closed your eyes in life. If one's eyes are too open one can't live, like Rank, for instance."

He was very near again. Apropos of Elena he said: "Doesn't she dress frumpishly?" He does not seem attracted. He was human and near, and I felt great joy again, and all the ideas, angers, rebellions, resentments, and criticisms which had separated me from him vanished again. All the poison vanished.

I had to leave him to meet a train, Henry Mann and his wife, and then Gonzalo. But I was happy again.

To separate makes me mad. And when my sickness comes back, doubt of him, of Gonzalo, I am very near to madness. I imagine my isolation, and I go mad inside, a delirium of doubts and fears.

JUNE 5, 1937

DREAM: A LONG PATH OF ICE. A WOMAN WALKING on it with a great terror of the ice breaking. Runs away in a panic. Hugh decides he will try. I tell him not to because he is heavier. He begins to walk over it and I hold him. The ice breaks. I am holding Hugh so he does not fall into the pit but I feel the heat that comes from it and I pull Hugh out of this hell. We all have to pass through a narrow aperture to reach a certain place. I feel the usual anxiety before a hole and decide to take another route. I leap like a deer over lakes, bushes, hills. I get to an isolated castle—old, ravaged, with many rooms locked with huge keys. The rain is pouring in through the windows and the floor is rotting. I open all the rooms. I come upon a room and through a glass door I see a man sitting with his back turned, sitting in an absolutely empty room. He is blond. I get panicky and I run away, carrying one of the keys.

When I join the others, Lyon, the manager of Helba and Joaquin, has decided I am to dance an Indian dance with my body painted in gold and feathers. I say to Gonzalo: "I think it is Helba who would do this better." He agrees. A man says: "If you got into that castle, can you prove it?" I say: "I have one of the keys." "Then you are a hysterical woman," he answered.

The son of Henri Matisse, Pierre, was on the same train with some friends. They met Henry and said to him: "We saw Anaïs meeting some people. She looked very radiant and was with a very romantic-looking dark man."

I had told Henry about my having to wait two hours for the train the night I left him, but I had not told him I was with Gonzalo. When I came to Villa Seurat Henry first of all kissed me with unusual fervor and then began to tease me about my lie. The jealousy made him desirous and extraordinarily tender. I was exalted with happiness. When he fears to lose me he clutches at me. We become aware of our love.

Yet last night, a whole evening in *Nanankepichu* could make me happy, too. I could respond fully to Gonzalo, almost sob with joy when the orgasm came in both of us so miraculously in rhythm.

Durrell writes: "I have no doubt, not a shadow of doubt about you as an artist. The sense of dislocation proves that to me more fully! Loneliness is the password...."

> *From a letter to Lawrence Durrell:* ... I could say to you what Henry said about me in the diary: "Eyes too open." And I see yours are closing a bit—the metamorphoses. You are already somewhere else. You reached life by divination first, I take it, as I reached it. How much I like Gregory [in *The Black Book*] and his sincerity and his cosmic reachings. I wonder where you are now, metamorphically speaking. I'm in the night looking for silence. The head quiet and everything else, and all the other cells and tentacles, breathing. Wonder why you called me the submarine superwoman. That made me laugh, yet it is accurate. Only it took me many years to recover

my fins and my swimming stride. I was trying to walk (like the penguins?) and to think like a man. I was very impressed by man's thinking.

JUNE 13, 1937

*J*OLAS COMES, AS IF ABOUT TO CHARGE, HEAVY with German mysticism, disillusion with the poet's *temporal* concessions, praising *House of Incest* as a marvel of language, beauty *"qui m'a donne de grande frayeurs*, sickened as I am with the actual." So we talk in harmony, a kind of opaque Wagnerian language. I hear the "mantic" horse hooves, I feel the bath of mists, and the "Language of the Night," with its red cover and very black letters,* takes the form of a man tormented with an anxious smile and a mystical fatigue.

Desperate with fragmentation, suffering because it is Henry and Durrell who understand my work and whose work I love; because it is Jolas and not Gonzalo who damns politics; because Gonzalo is writing anti-fascist trash, such as the fascists write about communists; because it is Gonzalo who keeps the blood flame alive; because some of my prayers still rise toward a God, and I want Oneness.

"You have the hands of a sculptor," Gonzalo says, because he has seen Hugh's metamorphoses. Hugh is in life now, touching everything with his own hands, feeling, enjoying, drawing, talking until dawn with his friends, walking through Paris, reading Rank's *Le Double*. I asked Ponisowsky, a Russian friend, to buy one of Gonzalo's drawings, saying I would pay him back. Wanted Gonzalo to have faith. I knew someone would buy Elena's work, but I was afraid for his. Gonzalo

Transition, one of the most influential avant-garde English-language magazines published in Paris in the late 1920s and early 1930s, used emphatic black and red typography and its editor, Eugene Jolas, advocated a "new magic, new words, new abstractions, new hieroglyphics, new symbols, new myths," as his purpose.

is happy, working feverishly at his political campaign. I took some suits my mother had collected for the Franco Red Cross and gave them to Gonzalo. Gonzalo put one on at his *vernissage* and then the giver, David Nixon, appeared and Gonzalo had to hide. He wanted to hide anyway. He is savage, and wild with timidity. He looks right and left, out of somber eyes, with a bowed head, for a door.

Henry is aging, his beautiful health weakening, he goes to the dentist, to the doctor. He takes medicine but even over his hands, reddened by fever rash, I can yearn with the desire to englobe him, caress him, protect him.

Helba still expresses her love for me and each time I see her she adds strangely to my faith in Gonzalo's love—telling me how women pursued him but how he ran away because he wanted the ideal. Only when I say: "Hugh is changing. He may fall in love someday," a shadow falls over her face and she says: "You will suffer then."

Obsessed with deformation, with what I am with Gonzalo for instance. Angry when I have said something not true. He acts on me as a confuser, I leave my cosmic realms.

When Henry talks about his impersonal friendships I tried to explain to him my impersonal pity, which he does not understand. I am pushed by a force greater than myself to create, to give hope and pity *even* when I personally don't care for the other. To be benefic. With Elena, whom I would like to see dead, I have acted creatively, as a life-giving force. It is I who give Elena her faith in herself. And it is I who cure Helba, whom I also wish to see dead. It is I who restore her to her dancing, to life; something greater than myself which I obey. I have to act out my white magical power. Yet perverse and diabolical actions haunt me, attract me. And it is diabolical of me to have kept Henry and Elena apart. I should have said to Elena: "You are not, as you think, monstrously large. There are men like Henry who like that." But in place of this I have done a more subtle act of creation, continuous and effective.

"Before," I said to Hugh, "you were drinking life through a straw."

Bill's book has been accepted in New York, so all my patients have given birth and know realization of their desires. Henry Mann here with his new wife. Betty facing New York to conquer it.

For Moricand I found a fabulously rich man who appointed him court astrologer—or rather, *Bourse* astrologer. The man's mistress appointed him lover. And so he shines with secret, malefic glee. I sewed colored stones on my black velvet curtains unevenly placed as the stars. Marvelous. Carteret falls into a trance when he sees them. This is the fairy tale.

Inside of my illusion, as inside a cellophane balloon, I sit raging because when people come, more than two or three, I begin to suffer. I thought Moricand, who knows me by the route of Neptune, must be disillusioned. I can't talk. I can't manifest myself. I'm paralyzed. But my dress, my colors, my stones, my decor, my gestures—perhaps they talk. It becomes an anxiety, because I cannot be passive either, listen, efface myself. Was introduced to [André] Breton and almost turned my back on him, in a panic.

Henry tests himself, in a mood of self-assertion, by giving a talk to a group of people. Failed. Went blank.

There is still work to be done on this picture. Many things are missing. Communication haunts me, imperative, vital. I hate the failures. It is like stuttering.

JUNE 16, 1937

THE DIABOLICAL TANGLE OF THE PRINTING MA-chine: We discovered a printing machine for two thousand francs. A perfect, small, neat, easily run invention. A marvel. The dream of Henry's life, of mine, of Gonzalo. Gonzalo was set on fire. He wants to publish all my things. He wants to run a magazine. He is exultant, active, awake. He gets up early. He doesn't drink. He works feverishly at his propaganda, he draws, he tries to collect the money for the machine. He combs his hair, he dresses with the clothes I took away from my Mother. He is radiant, dynamic. The printing machine here is half literary, half political. The group is mixed.

Meanwhile I am thinking of Henry. Henry's joy if I could get the machine, Henry's work, which is of greater value than Helba's poems, or my work, or the propaganda. How can I get two thousand francs for Henry? Henry dreams. We'll put the machine in his studio. Work there. And so again my desire splits in two directions. And as I walk the streets thinking about it I'm a little anxious because I think: this takes away from my strength, this duality weakens me.

Yet I laugh, too. Spiritually I am with Henry, not Gonzalo.

Monday. After a long peaceful talk with Henry in bed, and after Gonzalo's enthusiasm to print me, I began to work seriously on the mirrors, on this book of mirages and metamorphosis.

Now, how can I get two thousand francs to get the machine for Henry without Hugh knowing it, or Gonzalo?

Sunday. I reread my "Father" MS. It *creaks* with artifice and unnaturalness. All but the feverish passages. Flat brevity due to timidity. I talked to Henry about it. I told him I was grateful to him for his naturalness, which I value highly. He was glad I could see my defects. I helped him with his sincerity in writing. In my diary, with Henry, I am natural. With Hugh and Gonzalo. But not in the world and not in my novels.

I collect clothes from the comfortable ones, saying it is for refugees, and I give them to *my* poor, saying now it is for communists, now for the fascists. I say to Hugh, laughing: "Had a good haul today— or a good holdup." I even give Hugh one of Turner's new silk shirts!

To go and see the machine with Gonzalo I walk quietly from Villa Seurat to the metro of Denfert-Rochereau. In the sun, in Nixon's suit, shaved, he looks bronzed and magnetic. I feel gently amorous, his deep voice stirs me, his smell, his eyes.

My life of lies every day more difficult because all the people we know know each other: Stuart Gilbert knows the [James] Joyces; the Joyces the Turners; the Turners the Jolases; Jolas knows Ponisowsky, who knows Elena, who knows Moricand, who knows Carteret; Carteret knows Allendy; Allendy, Artaud; Artaud knows Gonzalo;

Gonzalo knows Bill Hayter and Arnaud de Maigret and Mayo, who know Henry as well as Brassai and Emil Savitry; Fred [Perlès] knows Emil, Emil knows Buckland Wright, a friend of Hugh's and Horace, who knows Hayter, and Hayter knows Anita de Caro, who knows Henry and [Jack] Kahane. Gonzalo knows the same painters and writers. In his house lives André Dhote, who knows Elena etc., etc. Most of them go to the same *Club du Cinéma* for choice artistic movies, most of them to the same *vernissages*, the same concerts, the same cafés and restaurants. Fred and Artaud saw me meeting Gonzalo. Maigret sees me with Henry. Mayo knocked at Henry's studio last night while I was there. [Abraham] Rattner made a drawing for the *Scenario*, and he stays in the same hotel with the Joneses, where Henry goes to see him, while Henry calls on Jones. [Denise] Clairouin knows Colonel Cheremetieff, Betty's lover, and most of the people I know. At the Villa Seurat lives Lucette Leque, Rank's ex-secretary, a friend of Chana Orloff, who receives Mrs. Rank, who is a friend of Mrs. [Alfred] Knopf, who sent Henry one hundred dollars. Bravig Imbs met Hugh through Horace, and Buckland Wright met Henry. He is a friend of Mrs. Hensley, astrologer, who met Eduardo and came to the house, and who now knows Moricand, who knows Evreinoff, who knows the colonel, who knows Clairouin, who knows all of them! Colette [Roberts] knows Roger [Klein,] who knows Gonzalo loves me, but he's in Spain! Mrs. Jolas knows Gonzalo, Gonzalo knows Edgar, who knows Mrs. Hensley, etc.

A spiderweb closing around me.

JUNE 20, 1937

FATHER AND I ALONE IN MY ORANGE ROOM, Father saying: "Until I met you I knew pleasure, women, but it was love I wanted and it was love I found with you. After that marvelous, violent climax everything else would seem tasteless and disgusting. My career ended there. And you?"

With an honesty I have rarely shown I said gently, "I have Henry and Gonzalo."

"You are younger and you have to follow your own evolutions. It was less profound for you."

"Not less profound—remember, I was in love with you for twenty years when you were not in love with me!"

Every time we kiss each other something hard and pointed breaks inside of us—our will—some strange carapace, the shell around him and my defense against him. There is no nearness possible, only that violent conjunction, an impossible love. Defense, fear, predominate, doubt of each other. A relationship that tortures, baffles me, unhinges me.

With a desire to cling to my wholeness I turn toward Gonzalo at such a moment—turn my love toward him—call him.

Sickness the same day. The devil planted his *"fourche"* into my back—paralyzed me with rheumatism.

Gonzalo comes for only a little while. Sanity.

What is there between my Father, my brothers Thorvald and Joaquin, and me which causes only misery and misunderstandings, undercurrents of cruelty, of twisted, jealous, destructive love?

In all my other loves there is softness and faith.

Hugh so soft, drawing with great sensitiveness. Beginning to live for himself. When Jolas came he took him right over to see his drawings instead of effacing himself as before and exalting me.

I make them all live for themselves, I nurture their egoism! Hugh thinks of his pleasure now, Gonzalo lives to realize his own desires. Hugh becomes aware of his charms, that he possesses El Greco hands, the power to heal; they make him play the role of ideal father, too. He comes home at three in the morning. And every day he exonerates me more. He says: *"Now* I understand why you gave so much. I see the needs around me." Or: "Now I understand why you couldn't be home at fixed hours, one has to leave when the talk ends naturally." He discovers the joy of seeing the sun rise, while drunk on talk. He has his group of friends, their activity, their cycle of interests, conferences, talks, expositions, creations. He is happy.

———

A letter from New York threatening a change came like a thunderbolt. Hugh said: "I won't let them change me, just when life is opening up for me here."

Gonzalo begins his propaganda work tomorrow morning with an office, telephone and stenographers, files and a big desk.

Meanwhile, Andrés Nin, anarchist, is about to be shot. Father says playfully: "Thank God for one less Nin in the world."

Gonzalo says: "Treason, treason."

Gonzalo and I have in common a malady unknown to Henry, *les tristesses ideales*. If something goes wrong, if because I'm sick he comes to see me in my house, feels nervous about Hugh coming, the cat's intrusion, the loud noises of the Exposition, begins to caress me and cannot fulfill his desire, he gets sad. If our time is rushed, and there is brusqueness—if I am moody, one phrase misplaced—he goes away sad. Hugh feels this, Rank, my Father, all the idealists. Henry never. Henry is attuned to dissonances, is not shocked by interruptions, or by grotesque accidents.

This makes me seek with Gonzalo again more and more dreamlike atmosphere, exclusion of the world, of all accidents—and we get more and more sensitive to reality.

When *Nanankepichu* was threatened by the occupancy of the proprietor, quarrels began about the pumping, roof leaking, etc. I cut through all the petty discourses with a dictator-like firmness. I wrote a note: "I will pay more—the three hundred francs for only the room on condition that the pumping is done from outside, that René never penetrates into our room, that you fix the leaking roof and all the things which go wrong and leave us alone—Finish."

Everything was done as if by magic. Gonzalo and I were left alone. *Nanankepichu* became again the dream, the opium den.

But misery is the great reality. That is why artists seek it. It is their only reality. It was my only reality as a child. It gave me the only human reality I ever understood. I sought it out afterward, with Henry, Helba, Gonzalo. All my friends are poor. It also has a religious significance. It represents sacrifice, it is usually the outcome of a choice between artistic and spiritual values and the material. It has a spiritual significance.

I have used all that Hugh gave me to protect, foster, and realize other's dreams—to reinstate poetry. For that I have given all. For that we are moving to a cheaper place. For that I have denied myself voyages, luxuries, clothes. I have kept only what was necessary to my creation in my life. I have nothing around me that is not necessary. Just enough to create an image, an illusion of beauty, an illusion of oriental softness (in reality what there is in my apartment is worth no more than two or three thousand francs!). I have stripped myself joyously. I feel great joy thinking of Henry working in his studio, with his watercolors, his phonograph, his *femme de ménage;* Helba with her medicines, food, and a new box full of stuffs to make new costumes; Gonzalo with paper to draw, pencils, suits to wear; Elsa with one of my dresses, paints. All these are the real gifts, but they would mean nothing: *It was the love.*

Perhaps it is true I do all this to atone for all the marvelous gifts life made me, for what I took, received, absorbed, for the love given me. To atone for the miracle of a fulfilled life! Then if it is atonement I must give more and more. I shall never give enough then. Never enough for all I have received. Gratitude makes me generous, gratitude makes me flow out, yield, abandon, give. I feel so rich. The less possessions I have the richer I feel. Perhaps I'm seeking poverty always. Only Hugh kept me from it.

But when I see what it did to Henry, Gonzalo, and Helba I wonder. Their hope, life, health, everything destroyed. The dream destroyed. No food. No material to work with. No paper, no paints, no costumes, no medicines.

Yet I seek this—every day I come near to it. If Hugh had not fought me I would already be poor.

I am grateful to him. I am grateful to everyone tonight. I feel my weakness fully, as never before. My love of others, my dependency, my . . .

Sh, sh, sh . . .

Sentimentality.

JUNE 21, 1937

COMICAL, ALL THIS. WRITING IT LAST NIGHT AND stopping myself. Felt I was repeating myself and sentimentalizing. Feeling religious. But now it seems it was prophetic. I get the astrology magazine and the predictions for the month are all about *giving*. I have to give even more. And it is true. I have to give up staying in Caux with my Father, staying in Cagnes with Eduardo, or in Corfu with the Durrells, Montecatine with Elena, or Venice with Mother and Joaquin because all Hugh gives me will go to pay Henry's rent, Gonzalo's rent, and to feed them all. No sea. No rest. No vacation. Violá. No Heim beach costumes. No mountain air. No sun on the body. Sacrifice.

Hugh is taking a trip with Carteret. I incited him to take it, he wanted to, he needs it. He has been deprived of vacations, which he needed more than I.

I'm working on the "Metamorphosis" book—passing from the mirrors to water. A second *House of Incest*.

Today passed from a tender morning with Father (now I treat him as I treat Henry—great mellow forgiveness) to a passionate noon with Henry. Then a little writing, resting, and at 9:30 I meet Gonzalo.

I am tired. Resigned. Grateful for all I have.

Gonzalo is good for life because he lives in the present, but that is why he is of less value in the *eternal*, in art. He is immediate, and that is why he is in politics. He lives so much in the present that he has a beautiful gift of direct emotion, as woman has—a beautiful gift in a lover. But now I see the *eternal* values of Henry, in duration, which is so painful in life.

As soon as creation begins there is a need of far-seeing—of thinking of tomorrow. I have so much the sense of creation, of tomorrow, that I could not get drunk, knowing I would be less alive, less well, less creative the next day.

————

When I see my Father now, so gentle, so loving, I marvel at the novel I wrote and begin to think I am insane, that the way I crucified him is undeserved, that the monster I created was an invention, that the deformation was in me. I doubt all I saw, felt. The truth is in the diary. Outside it is insanity. Father is talking about the marvels of the microscope, about the scorpion he saw, the minerals, the gold dust, and I ask myself: Was it a nightmare? In the novel there is ferocity. In the diary, the truth. I clutch at this truth told from day to day. Or I would get lost, lost, lost. Every deformity is a crime committed against the other. Henry deformed June. This crime terrifies me, this magnifying, this microscope of art. Here alone is the human vision restored. The novel is an act of injustice.

I don't want to be an artist.

I want to keep this Father I saw in Valescure and not the monster which my hurt, injured self created later. I want to keep him as he was today, kneeling swiftly, gracefully before me, as I sometimes do before Henry, and telling me about his dreams which are like mine, of the ship passing through the city, of the train leaving and his valises not ready, of flying. I looked at him with sad eyes. I am out of the asylum. Tell me some more, Father, about the microscope. He is ashamed of all he has to get for himself, of his thirsts, his appetites, his whims, his games which he must pursue inexorably while people die and starve around him, of his games in the infinite with microscopes, cameras, a piano. He is ashamed and so he says lamely: "It was to amuse Maruca during her illness."

One's games with colored crystals. Others' needs. Others' needs. Real needs. Dark needs. Vital needs. One's games with poetry, costumes, music, guitars, charcoal, water, colors, words. Vital games of poetry.

Bread—Poetry.

It may seem ridiculous to talk about the sacrifice of luxury, but for me that is a real sacrifice because I was physically created for luxury, and it is a need, a passion, not a superfluity. If I smoke cigarettes at 1 franc 75, as I do, I pay with irritated throat. If I take bad cheap wine I get sick. If I use cheap toilet necessities, bad soaps, my skin spoils. I need beauty as I need food. In homely surroundings I get sad. So my sacrifices are real and made with love. But that is why they are magical. Other people help materially but when the money ends, no miracle. It is ended.

I write about this because it is my *joy*. All the pleasure I take in luxury, I willingly surrender to that awesome religious pleasure I get from creating life, hope, sanity, desire, hunger around me. I feel a deep pleasure when others enjoy. It is deeper than any other.

I was excusing my Father to Hugh, saying how all the money came from Maruca. He was like a child. She ordained. She only liked to give to him for his whims. She did not permit him to give except at her order. It is she who tells him when to give me a present.

Hugh said: "Well, why doesn't your father pretend to ask for himself and then give it to others—as you do."

"Yes, of course, that's how I do it."

We laughed. I made a sound like that of a mouse caught in a trap, in the trap of Hugh's prank to get me to confess something he knows very well.

FATIGUE FATIGUE FATIGUE FATIGUE

Coup de theatre. Hugh prepares to leave with Jean Carteret for Finland and gets a cable from New York: He must sail July 7th to appear in court for the bank—*force majeure*.

More and more I see implied in the diary my struggle against the scientific, intellectual inventions of man. With my feelings and instincts I belied all the theories and psychological explanations of man. What I did with analysis was to use, transform, and finally reject all but poetry. At this point I was fortunate enough to meet Gonzalo, who picks up [James] Fraser's book *Myths of the Origin of Fire* and says: "Why seek the origin of fire? Why not *be* the fire?"

Growing obsession with order, that is, domination. Obsessively I arrange my closet, my papers. Create a light atmosphere. Not one useless, superfluous object. No dress without its hat and coat to match. No unnecessary papers. All papers classified. Medicines in order. Reduction, stylization. Not one object out of place. Tools together. Winter clothes together. I organize, order, arrange. It is a mania. I want to find tools, sewing box, paper, stamps immediately, automatically. Order gives me serenity, order quiets me. I need sedatives. I tremble like a racehorse. I seek quiet. Want all the diaries in one place. Have given away everything I don't use constantly. *Pas de déchets.* Nothing around me torn or broken.

Lying in bed, I invent a new activity. I remake my seashell necklace. I cannot be idle. It is a disease.

Obsessed with fear that because Gonzalo and I are not devoted to each other's work our love will die.

Returning to simple truths. Differentiations between kinds of love. Before the moonstorm* I reached a hysteria of love. I sat in a café and wrote a letter full of love to my mother.

July 3, 1937

HUGH GOING TO NEW YORK MADE IT POSSIBLE TO get the press for Gonzalo. Gonzalo was in ecstasy. To him it means financial independence, prestige, domination in his propaganda work. His pride is now aroused. I have awakened his energy, his love of leadership, dispelled his sense of guilt which made him afraid to live for himself, ashamed to do anything for himself.

We went to buy the machine together. We danced around it. I could not have got the money from Hugh to give Henry the machine, naturally. Even if I could I think I would have given it to Gonzalo because all Henry's writing is now accepted and published. He does not *need* the press. He wanted to use it for me, he said, to do the diary.

---

*Anaïs Nin often referred to her menstrual period as the "moonstorm" or the "moon cycle."

Gonzalo needed it and can earn his living with it. His joy was wonderful to see.

Afterward I thought a little wistfully, how I could have had the press for myself to do with as I liked, but I cannot ever do this while those I love have a need. I was happier to give it to Gonzalo. Enjoying his joy.

Durrell writes me [about two manuscripts which were later incorporated in *Winter of Artifice*]: "... I wept a bit, because this is the first book in Europe which belongs to a female artist: and it is bitter. I was not concerned so much with interplay of characters but thought all the time how female it was, how the gift was total, always, unreserved, not withheld...."

JULY 6, 1937

*T*ENSION. WORK. RUSH. I CAN WATCH HUGH LEAVE for New York without desire to go, because I have Henry here, and Gonzalo. The New York experience was really burnt out. I only wish I could see Thurema. Too full a life! Who ever thought I could exclaim this, too full, of loves, emotions, creations. It is breaking me down physically.

Bowing over Hugh's needs, giving him all the care, devotion.

JULY 8, 1937

*T*ERRIBLE WRENCH PARTING FROM HUGH. WE sobbed together, clung. All day I sobbed, felt weak, lost, small. Overcome with feeling, hysteria of love. Could not enjoy Henry's or Gonzalo's presence. I think it was his feelings I felt, his sobbing which broke me down, his clinging which hurt me. I don't know. There is in us a love beyond my passion for Henry, my feeling for Gonzalo. In me, at times, the maternal, the nonpassionate, wins over everything.

Yet at night I knew if I were with Hugh on the ship sailing away from Henry and Gonzalo I could not bear it. Someday I'd be locked up for love—insanity. "She loved too much."

What I feel terribly deeply always is the aloneness of the other. I don't want Hugh to feel alone, or Henry, or Gonzalo. The lonely one draws me, the sick one, the suffering one, Hugh facing the ordeal of New York alone, that moves me. For *him* I would go. For myself I need this rest, this solitude.

I am Hugh's refuge and he is mine. Is that the love that makes one less alone, the loyal secure one, or the passion that fuses bodies, or the tender love, devotion, desire, intellectual harmony? Which one am I closest to? Henry, yet not close in the trusting way. Closeness to the Father, to the lover, to the brother. So many kinds of closeness! What is it that annihilates loneliness? Understanding of Rank, the devotion of Hugh, the ardor of Gonzalo, the creative harmony with Henry, the yielding to Henry, my devotion to Hugh? To break and shatter loneliness forever I sit here, cursing loneliness. I sit here, alone in bed, with Hugh in New York, Gonzalo having his dinner with Helba and Elsa, Henry working in Villa Seurat. I am never close enough. I want some impossible communion. I am always lonely, and I can't bear it even for five minutes.

Letter from Faber & Faber to Clairouin: We have been having an exceptionally difficult time deciding about the diary of Anaïs Nin. As you already know from my request for the further material, we were very much interested, yet in the end, and after very great regret, we cannot see how to shape the material into book form which could be published in England. Much of what we should wish to use for the integrity of the book, we should be prevented from using by the restrictions on books in England. In the end the difficulties of the problem have defeated us, and I am sending the volumes back with a great deal of reluctance.

On loneliness, continued:

Nearness to Hugh is more reassuring because he lives for me, breathes through me, is loyal, obsessed and gives me so much. His presence is paternal, eternal, faithful, continuous.

Nearness to Henry profound but less manifest. Henry expresses less. Our connection is cosmic, creative, on high levels, enlarged, at times impersonal, certainly not continuous because Henry shares himself with his work and the world, leads a collective life, does not live for me but for himself.

Nearness to Gonzalo is manifest, emotional, direct, personal, human. Gonzalo's genius is for relationship. He is ardent, he is spontaneous. Connection is more eternal, based on loyalty, wholeness, the total gift of the self.

We laughed last night, at our comedy of errors. Gonzalo and I are so alike in the giving, the self-effacement, we want so much to give the other that we forget ourselves, our own desires, and so when Hugh left and Gonzalo saw me weep he thought I wanted to be alone and he left me at midnight, but I wanted and needed his love and was hurt that he left me. He thought he was being delicate, he respected my sadness, but I grew sadder because I felt that Gonzalo was failing me, was leaving me alone. And slowly the injury in me grew, clouded my days, estranged us.

I went to Henry, and spent the evening arranging his clippings in a book which pleased him, made him want to write.

I met Gonzalo in *Nanankepichu*, where we escape from all the world, all the bonds, homes, devotions, limitations, enclosures. I confided in him. He was amazed. He was hurt because I seemed to be far away, withdrawn. He is sensitive to all my moods. We laughed. I said it is ridiculous how we want to live for the other, and how entangled we get, how through excess of love and delicacy we create immense edifices of misunderstanding. The least word I say makes Gonzalo think I do not want to see him. I think he came only to please me, when he was tired and desirous of staying home. Once, when he met me in the café in the evening and found me writing, he said exactly what I say to Henry at such times: "Go on writing.

Do you want me to go away?" And I was only writing to pass the time, while waiting.

Gonzalo says: "I feel so sure of your love." He is no longer jealous, does not imagine that I see Henry, feels enveloped, and in the warmth, blooms into *le dieu du feu* as I called him, *le dieu du feu* whom he used to drown in wine.

Divided between Shangri-la—the Tibetan heaven—and *Nananke-pichu*—the Indian drug. Running between them, excluding the world, producing poetry. I write about metamorphosis.

July 12, 1937

A NEW DIARY BOOK [NUMBER FIFTY-FOUR]. NOT the small notebook I could hide. A large, honest, expansive book given to me by Henry, on which I can spread out beyond the diary, englobing more, transcending myself. The small notebook I could put in my pocket was mine; this I cannot clutch, hide, restrain, or retain. It spreads. It asserts itself. It lies on my desk like a real manuscript. It is a larger canvas. No marginal writing done delicately, unobtrusively, but work, assertion.

It so happens I am alone. I can leave it on my desk. The house is wholly mine. Perhaps I shall include the world. I neglect the world. Henry was right, what I write is less communicable than what he writes because he has a human love of writing, of words, he takes a sensuous pleasure in writing, it is flesh and food, whereas I, I have a sort of contempt for the sensuous joy of expression. I am like the woman and the mirror, intent on my pursuits, my ideas, on satisfying myself. A lonely quest, a selfish quest which isolates me. He is nearer to all because of the language, because he likes to talk, to say, to formulate, to share. His concern is with communication, mine with myself, my discoveries. We shall look around a bit, my diary, at the enjoyments. We shall dwell on the sensuous pleasures of language. The word made flesh.

Sometimes, in the street, or in a café, I am hypnotized by the "pimp" face of a man, by a big workman with knee-high boots, by a brutal criminal head. I feel a sensual tremor of fear, an obscure attraction. The female in me trembles and is fascinated. For one second I am a whore who expects a stab in the back. I feel anxiety. Trapped. I forget that I am free. A dark fungus layer is awakened, a subterranean primitivism, a desire to feel the brutality of man, the force which can break me open, violate, sack. To be violated is a need of woman, a secret erotic desire. I have to shake myself from the invasion of these violent images, awaken. Henry's writing had that effect on me, Henry's brutality of speech, his barbaric language, his primitive behavior. Food and sex the primal needs.

In Gonzalo, too, I chose the man of nature. Yasurt [Pablo Neruda] said to him: "Where is your horse? You always look as if you had left your horse at the door."

I don't see a lie in idealization. If I have a swollen cheek because the dentist took out a wisdom tooth, I cover my head with a peasant handkerchief, I look like an Aragonesa, the swollen cheek is under a flowered cotton. I show only my brows, eyes, nose, chin. Artifice. Artifice is art, the paradise, the only paradise. Paradise was a place with white-feather pine trees, with fur and mirrors, with glass fishes, veiled lamps, Arabian divans, silk-lined walls, invisible music, dishes shaped like stars, costumes of cellophane. Paradise was artifice. In artifice there is peace, joy, forgetting, enchantment, opium.

July 21, 1937

Anyway such is the moral of the mirror and metamorphosis story I finished today.

Solitude. Hugh in New York. The maid on vacation. Mother and Joaquin in Venice. Father in Caux. Having told everybody I'm traveling, sending my mail via Caux, I have only Henry and Gonzalo to see. It is a strange experience, to wake up when I want to, to be in an empty apartment, free to eat when I please and what I please, free to go out, free to stay out. I lost the sense of time. I sat alone in an empty café, drinking coffee, in a reverie. I walked. I strolled. Nobody expecting me for lunch, or at any hour. Only the nights filled. But there were nights when I could not be with either Gonzalo or Henry, and then I felt loneliness, I felt weak, I crumbled inside. I cannot live alone, yet I love independence, I need it. I have been writing better, in spite of a week of pain and swollen face and great physical fatigue.

The truth is I feel a maternal anxiety over Hugh, his loneliness, but I do not miss him except as a refuge, a protection.

Tonight, alone in bed, Gonzalo at a political meeting, Henry engaged, I am contented. I have worked well. Henry is satisfied with what I have done. Last night we talked so deeply. Another night Gonzalo read *The House of Incest*, lying at my side. I enjoyed his enjoyment. *"Qué sensual, qué sensual,"* he repeated. He responds to the sensation directly. For Henry it is esoteric. He responds to the language, he is fascinated as by something very far from him. He likes the images as an artist. But he does not experience this. Gonzalo feels how deeply I am swimming, with gestures he tries to explain from what region I write. He knows. He knows sensation as June knew it.

Henry suffers from none of the things I suffer from, or Proust suffered from, because he has a stronger contact with reality. Between the times we see each other nothing is destroyed because he does not analyze it, and so it is not questioned or dispersed. He lives in a physical world. Henry will believe something dies or that I cease loving him if he can see it, if I can present a real proof of a dead love. He doubts when he has a fact to doubt, not out of the *"désarroi,"* the anguish of his own being. Henry is furthest from Proust because he lives a physical life with his body, eyes, tongue, appetite. Proust made love more evanescent, tortuous, unstable, unreal, changeable, he experienced greater jealousies because he had less faith, he deformed when he was left alone, he created the separations, the distances, the misunderstandings. If I could write as well as Proust how marvelously I could explain this. Life, passion, become tenuous in our hands in proportion to our mental experiencing of it. Proust did not make a universal study of love and jealousy but an individually Proustian twist.

That is why I touch my life less. I handle it less. I have less doubt, less need to capture, hold, eternalize. I describe just long enough to keep the image, and not long enough to reach dissolution. Whenever I am alone I feel the danger of madness and dissolution, because my life with others, their warm presence, their voices reassure me. I cannot live alone. I have discovered this. I cannot live alone because then I become diseased. My life becomes unreal. I must confess I need Hugh's presence humanly. I need my lovers, but lovers are less there. Henry because he is an artist, Gonzalo because he has a home. This period was a marvelous test of my desire for independence. I like to awaken when I want to, to lie in bed as long as I want to, not to have to give orders for the day and therefore define it, adhere to the plan, I like taking my breakfast when I want to, feeling the whole day loose and slack, write as long as my mood dictates, eat when I am hungry, and eat what I like, follow only my own impulses. I like not being interrupted, feeling no pressure, no responsibilities, no set hours. I like coming into the empty apartment, where I can live in a continuous reverie. But every night, faced with solitude, I cannot bear it. And now I know my diary was created not to be alone. What a weakness. I need this that I rebel against, I need the home which I say suffocates me, this husband I chafe against, I need all this web, ties, responsibilities, care, I curse as an artist.

I felt this in New York, alone with Henry. I ask myself what my life will be when Hugh lives in London, as he will next winter, London and not New York as we feared. Perhaps I can overcome this—learn. When I was thirteen I wrote my diary in the one room we lived in, all of us, Mother, Joaquin, and Thorvald, talking and quarreling.

Insoluble conflict.

A few times I have a kind of remorse toward Henry, cheating him. Yet I know so well now that this is sentimentalizing, imagining a wronged, injured Henry. The truth is that if I were with Henry all the time, his independence would be endangered and our happiness. I know this. I know that it is by spreading out in love that I have not choked him with my jealousy. It is not love I take away from him to give Gonzalo. What Gonzalo possesses is all that Henry does not want, an idealistic me, a romantic me, a love constantly expressed, a personal, human, almost feminine relationship.

Humanly I don't get pleasure, comfort, as Henry and Gonzalo do, from ordinary exchange. It makes me more conscious of separation and that saddens me. I have no disdain. I have regrets. I would like to be near everyone. Less lonely. Woman is more alone than man. The problem of separation, of loneliness, is deeper for her. I don't believe she can find the eternal in art, as Proust did, even when she is an artist.

JULY 24, 1937

*M*Y FIRST QUARREL WITH GONZALO WAS ABOUT time. He says over the telephone: "I'll have dinner and I'll come right over." This is eight o'clock. He arrived at midnight. Another time he said at noon: "I'll have lunch and I'll come right over." He arrived at six o'clock. This is not counting the times I waited in cafés one hour, two hours. I knew it was racial, that all

South Americans are the same. I knew Hugh and I would no longer invite them to dinner because they arrived three hours late. At first I took it well, was indulgent, tried to adapt myself. But if there is anything that gives me a fever and rage it is to wait. I cannot wait. I had to wait all my life for a late Hugh. I never let anyone wait and I expect the same courtesy.

I got angry one night when Gonzalo arrived at midnight. I told him I did not want to be with him, that all my pleasure was spoiled. He himself hates to wait. He gets into a rage. Once I arrived half an hour late and he had gone home in a temper.

One afternoon I wrote the following for him, calling it "Poem to a Timeless One":

Time is not for one's self, it belongs to the other. For one's self there is no time. The universe evolves around one's needs, one's desires, one's moods. Time is for the other to whom a promise was made, as for a miracle, and at the moment of expectation, if one is late, the miracle does not take place. Time is for the one who comes to meet you with his expectations, it is not for yourself who likes to wander, to dream, to get lost in the infinite. A universe without time is the universe inside of one. Time means the hour to meet the other, and it is necessary to the miracle of touch, to the miracle of meeting, touching, and loving. In the great empty space in which we are lost, the hour is the one set even by the planets when they wish to grow nearer each other, or even eclipse each other! Or there would be no conjunctions.

On the envelope I drew a clock, but instead of pointing to the hours, the arrows pointed to a bed, to two glasses of aperitifs, one large, one small (his big glass of Pernod and my little glass of wine), to a mouth. I thought this Chinese delicacy would touch him. The same evening he said: "I will come early after supper." And he came at midnight. I decided I would not open the door. When he rang I said: "Go back home. I'm not going to open the door."

"Why not?" said Gonzalo innocently.

This shook me. My heart began to beat very fast with anger. I did not open. He stood there. At the same time I hoped he would not go away. I regretted deeply our night being spoiled. But I waited. He rang the bell again so gently. If he had rung it angrily I might have remained unmoved, but he rang so gently and softly and I opened. I was still angry and I told him so. Angrier to think that the letter I had written him had no effect on him.

Afternoon: Parc Montsouris. Helba and I talking. Together we have emotional feasts of generosity, universal love, and sacrifice. Helba tells me how much she loves me. She takes a wise, old, maternal tone to say: "For a woman to love Gonzalo is not happiness. He is one who sacrifices woman to himself without knowing it, unconsciously. He is a child. I feel badly at the sacrifices you are making for him."

"We want the same thing, Helba, we want to keep Gonzalo from going to Spain to fight. That is why I gave him the printing machine."

The image of war, of Gonzalo in danger, was so vivid as we sat there drinking coffee near the lake, that the whole beauty of the afternoon was blackened. I felt an intolerable pain.

I walked with Helba. I went to meet Henry. I bought him ice cream, I cooked the food he likes. We spent a quiet evening, he working, I reading. I took a slow bath. Henry played Bach. Every day he seems to become more delicate and wiser and tender. We fell asleep.

I left him after breakfast to meet Gonzalo in *Nanankepichu*—for the last time. The *péniche* was sold. One day we came and found the lock broken, the windows open. The new owner had been inspecting it. *Nanankepichu* was lost. The tear in me was deep. All the marvelous nights I spent there with Gonzalo.

This morning poor *Nanankepichu* so old, the water filtering in. It had to be sold, and it will be taken to dry dock for repairs. *Nanankepichu* the dream. A sadness as I packed, folded the sheets, took down the mirror, the lanterns, placed the candles in a box, our glasses, towels, dishes. *Nanankepichu* lost. Our isolation. Our dream cut off from the earth, suspended over space, floating on a river. Our chalice. Our ciborium. I carried the tiny blue lamp. The little blue lamp fell into the gutter and broke. Strange, Gonzalo, suddenly he swept away all the delicacies and became destructive. Perhaps he conceals his regrets, and his regrets make him angry, and so roughly he pulls down what he loves, his hands get brutal, he tears, breaks, burns. It was he who had lit the tiny blue lamp one night so that I would find it when I arrived, like a mystic church light, and know he was there. And now *Nanankepichu* was destroyed, lost, and the little blue lamp rolled into the gutter.

JULY 25, 1937

I SPENT THE AFTERNOON CLEANING THE HOUSE, marketing, cooking, preparing my room with many pillows on the floor (we both like the Moorish life on the floor). I lit the lamps, the candles, I set the dinner on a very low glass table. I turned on the radio, and was inundated in emotion. The loss of *Nanankepichu*, the jealousy of Gonzalo, the sensual pleasure, the weight of his body, the pleasure of the evenings to come, the voluptuous appearance of my room. Oriental splendor, and the lover of Oriental tales.

"This is a harem," he said, and he yielded to the languor and the warmth. Our dinner was joyous.

In the dim velour night we caressed again, and we discovered a new embrace. Gonzalo lay over me, his whole body covering me, but I lay on my stomach. A new joy. Gonzalo covering my back, holding my hips with burning hands, and I raising only my backside to better feel him inside of me.

I was amazed how a different love has a different expression. Our caresses are altogether different from Henry's caresses, Henry's way of taking me. Sometimes Henry has taken me from behind, but he makes me stand on the edge of the bed and lean over, or he makes me kneel on the bed like an animal. The thrust is always more direct, more animal.

In gestures there is a faithfulness to a different love.

Sitting alone on the pillows this morning, after Gonzalo left, I mused on the eternal quality of love in certain beings. In me love is eternal. A new one is born without destroying the old. The old ones change, alter, but their essence is indestructible. I still feel Hugh alone in New York, his struggles, and I vibrate with maternal tenderness. I feel Thorvald's solitude now without a wife and children. I feel my Father, Joaquin, my mother's growing old. I feel Henry's need of shoes, his aching throat, his difficulties in starting each time, to write *Tropic of Capricorn.* I feel.

Reading *Les Modernes* by Denis Seurat, I take note of all he has to say about sensation. I know where I am modern and where I am not. All he says about sensations applies to me, except the *ennui* which follows upon their exhaustion. I do not know *ennui.* Perhaps because of the more eternal quality of my sensations, they do not die in me. I do not suffer from hangovers. My sensibility, response, vibration, exultancy, enthusiasm, and passion are the same, or deeper than when I began to live. *Ennui*, which haunts the modern man, is unknown to me. I only pray at times to feel less, to find peace and repose.

I want to describe some time what happened to me in Cadiz, very minutely. I have never yet expressed it.*

I awake this morning with a song in my head which I heard at Henry's, a poem by Paul Eluard, sung like a bird's song. One love increases the other. It is a symphony. I am holding Gonzalo in my arms and I hear the mechanical bird of paradise in a café singing from the Villa Seurat, the bird of Eluard and surrealism, which was wound up with the handle of a phonograph.

The sun shines on the duality of day and night, and on eternal love. That which dies in modern man because he is like a potted plant on a balcony, never dies in me because my soul reaches to the other side of the earth, and my roots are infinite.

---

*On their return from a trip to Morocco, Anaïs Nin and her husband had stopped over at various places in Spain. "Cádiz," Anaïs Nin had written to Henry Miller on a postcard dated April 23, 1936, "is the city I describe in a childhood diary. I didn't want to live there, I said, because women could not leave the house, or go out except on holidays." This time, Anaïs Nin had traveled without her diary.

J U L Y   2 6 ,   1 9 3 7

*T*HOSE WHO, LIKE GONZALO AND I, LIVE INTENSELY
for the other and are abnormally aware of oth-
ers' feelings, fall into the habit of lying about their pleasures. I never
say, for instance: I am seeing Elena tonight because I enjoy seeing her,
because we have such a mad way of talking together. But: Elena wants
to see me tonight, she is so much alone and she gets so depressed. As
if I were merely submitting to Elena's need. This is meant, at times,
not to hurt Gonzalo by seeming to enjoy anything outside of him, it
is meant to convey: All my pleasure in life is with you. The rest is
sacrifice or duty. Gonzalo has exactly the same habit. But there is a
deeper reason for all this. We live so much to give pleasure that after
a while I am confused myself as to whether I see Elena for Elena's
sake (because she is alone, because her life is empty of relationships)
or for my own pleasure. The truth is there is such a vast sum of things
I do not do for myself that it has become the dominant impulse. Not
to sacrifice what I love best of all (an evening with Henry or Gonzalo)
and yet to make other people around me happy is my constant
struggle. At times neither Gonzalo nor I are exactly truthful because
we have enjoyments outside of our love, but they are certainly lesser
ones. We are true in saying we yield to others' needs because I have
often sacrificed my pleasure to alleviate Henry's sickness, or Hugh's
depressions. Gonzalo, too, makes me wait two hours while he helps
a friend who does not know French to send a cable to his family.

The true identification with others and the desire to give (old
religious sacrifice) is erroneously confused with masochism in psychology because it says we give out of guilt, out of atonement, we give
to suffer, but no account is taken of the divine *pleasure* which attends
the giving and makes it a natural function of the religious, or the
passionate, pleasure-loving soul! I am far from the Catholic hypocrisies, but I am returning to religion. Gonzalo, last night, lying on my

bed, talking about sensual life and Catholicism, kissing, and saying: "You're a true Catholic. *Tu aimes le péché*. You love the sin and absolution and regrets and sinning again."

JULY 26, 1937

GONZALO GIVES ME THE FEELING OF A DREAM ALready dreamed, of a being I have already seen, or one who reproduces in life the gestures, the atmosphere, the images imprinted in my blood, in the blood of my race. What awakens in me is a world so far away that it is like watching the sun rise from a mountain and seeing valleys, rivers, mountains not seen the night before. The world is so enlarged I reach the deserts of Arabia, the skin color of the Hindus, the mysterious lives of the Incas. It is not in this life I saw him because I was torn away from Spain too young, before seeing or tasting it. It is not in this life that I have seen Gonzalo on horseback, wearing white boots, furs, and corduroy, with his burning eyes, somber face, and wild black hair. But I have seen him. It is not in this life that I have seen Gonzalo's face in passion, worshipful like a man receiving Communion. But I have seen him lying at my side and I have heard him say hoarsely: *"Mójame, mójame, mójame, chiquita."* It is like the obscure memories which assail one while traveling through lands to which we did not know we were bound in any way. Some roots in me were buried in the sixteenth-century Spain of the troubadours, with its severity, its rigid forms, the domination of the Church, the claustration of women, the sensuality of Catholicism. Gonzalo re-creating his childhood, the stylized life of the Jesuits, the culture, the wild life in the mountains, the hunting and fishing, recreated for me a natural, blood-and-flesh paradise so different from the artificial art paradise I created with Henry, where Henry and I found not only our childhood again but a paradise created out of our inventions, with a language of our own, outside and beyond life: a creation. And this other life, which makes this life more marvelous but less often attained, fused, is the life which Gonzalo's artless paradise of mythical life in the forest (with the lake, the mirages, the mountains, the air) sometimes surpasses, sometimes seems insufficient to me.

I see the deep significance of Gonzalo's indifference to art except as a voluptuous form of enjoyment. It is not, for him, a necessity. He lives inside of life, and he touches the infinite when we lie in bed and after he has possessed me.

Henry can be *in* this life and then removed from it in the other, in the created one. A secret dissatisfaction with mere being, a need to fuse the two keeps him in motion. We created Shangri-la.

And I ran between both, knowing that it was not in art I found *"le moment éternel,"* as Proust did. It is in life. It is not to reach it, attain it, possess it that I write. It is not because I have missed it. It is out of the joy I feel upon experiencing it. Proust went so far in transmutation that he finally can only enjoy Albertine by metamorphosing her into music. Henry never enjoyed June when she was there. Henry is the one who misses the actual moment, a half of him always arrives late at the banquet. There is nothing perverse about his appetite, but there is with his timing. Passion made me arrive on time. But once, long ago, I was equally fragmented.

The paradise of my childhood was already an invented one, because my childhood was unhappy. It was by acting, pretending, inventing, that I enjoyed myself. Reality gave me no joy.

Gonzalo had no need to invent. There was the mountain of legendary magnificence, the lake of fantastic proportions, the extraordinary animals, the tales of witchcraft of the Indians. He took his ecstasy from the air he breathed, his drug from religion, his sensual pleasure from battle, physical power, domination, his poetry from solitude and the Indians. He rode horseback all night to visit the first girl he loved, he leaped walls to meet her, she risked her mother's fury, it was all written in the *Romancero*.

The paradise of my childhood was under the library table, covered to its feet by a red cloth with fringes, which was my house, and the little piece of oilcloth I was given of which I made the doormat of my house and on which I wiped my feet ostentatiously. The paradise of my childhood was music which filled the house, books which filled my father's shelves, in games drawn from books and music, enacting history, the chariot of Marie Antoinette made of chairs, and later, during the catastrophe, the world seen through a piece of colored glass in one of the windows of the *Château les Ruines.**

JULY 29, 1937

SO MUCH MORE DIFFICULT FOR ME TO ENTER Gonzalo's world of politics. I could easily abandon the personal world with Henry because it was to enter creation, but to abandon my personal world with Gonzalo for politics, to console Gonzalo for the pain of learning that his own brother in Peru ran a "fascist" newspaper and was considered the *valet de plume* of capitalism, is a feat for me of self-abnegation. Yet he needs to talk to me, he is alone spiritually, and just as I endured all Henry's constant confessions of his past, descriptions of his whole life no matter how they affected me because I wanted his to be natural, so I have to endure Gonzalo's anger, passion, despair over events I cannot value highly. Last night I felt a moment of sadness after a whole evening of puerile worldly preoccupations. Our dream was spoiled. I withdrew—to come out of myself again because Gonzalo needs me, to talk until he had emptied himself, liberated himself, to counsel him, guide him, lull him, and finally make him sleep with his head on my breast. How strange that the political anxiety, the hatreds, struggles of this world, can poison a man's happiness. All our personal happiness poisoned by the existence of a world I despise.

When Henry comes to Passy, which is not very often, he falls under the charm of the very objects, habits, surroundings which he does not allow me to manifest in his studio—but for their strangeness.

---

*It was at the château *Les Ruines* in Arcachon, in the South of France, in 1914, where Anaïs Nin experienced the traumatic separation from her father which broke up the family.

Whereas with Gonzalo it is familiar to him—the Moor in him (in school he was called the Moor) is awakened. He knows how to sit on pillows, how to eat from low tables, he likes dimmed lights.

Letter to Hugh: Sometimes I worry about our separation, sometimes I think I will be more with you when we are together again than when I am trying to live out a split life with the *"désordres astral,"* as Cheremetief calls them. The necessity of split is strange. I have been thinking about it. When you go I stay home because then the split is made by your being away, I am cut in two as it were. And at the same time, through it all, it is not the wholeness that is lacking at all, it is but the double life which you yourself have felt the need of. To keep us from that unchanging life which we admit as spiritually unfecund. Strange, strange, and hard to bear humanly. I imagine that the time you and I will be together we will be more closely together than we are when I am flitting in and out, minus all the conflict of feelings which arise when I am flitting right near you and you so near me.... The diary thing worked out as I predicted, that is, I foresaw the obstacle, and I prepared myself spiritually for this: to make out of it now with care and time a sort of Proustian work, with more art and fullness. I regard the nonpublishing as a destiny, meant to push me into art and away from the document. I will take each piece of the diary and transform it.

To Henry, fragment from an old letter: I came away yesterday with a million children from you, all about the fairytale, and the lurid walk, and I am making notes on the fairytale and wishing I could write it with you. I could not help thinking all the while of how many things are born when we were together. I was in such a high mood that I wanted to...

I will write someday a long *"Promenade en Taxi"* which will describe all that happens in a taxi, the reveries, the preparations to act, the introspective analysis of what just happened, the feeling of escape and detachment, the preparation between the two levels of life.

It was in Cadiz that I lay down in the hotel room while Hugh was out and fell into a dolorous obsessional reverie, a continuous secret music of fears, jealousy and doubt. And it was in Cadiz that I stood up and broke the evil curse, as if by a magical act, that is, I broke the evil curse of obsession. From that day on suffering became intermittent, subject to incidents, not a perpetual condition. *J'ai pu me distraire.* I was able to amuse myself. I could live hours without thinking of Henry or imagining what he was doing. I could leave him Friday and forget about him until Monday. There were silences in my head, periods of peace and enjoyment. I could abandon myself wholly to the pleasure of other relationships, to the beauty of the day, to the sensuous lulling trance of a warm bath. It was as if the cancer in me had ceased gnawing, the poisonous travail of introspection. It seemed to have happened swiftly, like a miracle, but it was the result of years of struggle, of analysis, of passionate living, of the crucifixion in New York. From that moment on, what I experienced were emotional dramas which passed like storms and left peace behind them. I experienced crises of jealousy, but not continuous chronic condition relieved only by Henry's presence.

Then I met Gonzalo and being with him when I was not with Henry completed the separation from Henry in my thoughts. I arrived at a deep and complete happiness without Henry. Also, the spectacle of Gonzalo's jealousy, although it reminded me often of my own, mysteriously freed me of mine. My feelings passed into his, I forgot my own jealousy in my desire to calm his, to invent ways of freeing him of it. Some of my jealousy also transferred itself to Helba.

One night I sat in Henry's studio pasting up the press notices on *Tropic of Cancer* and *Black Spring.* Henry was jubilating over them. I was very happy for a moment, doing this for Henry, which made so visible and tangible his progress as a writer, his communication with the world, his recognition.

Then I remembered that it was Gonzalo who had pasted Helba's press notices, and I imagined he had done it with the same love and pride and I began to suffer. I made a parallel between our loves. Yet it takes Helba's revelations to me of the absence of passion in their relationship ("Gonzalo was never jealous of me as a woman—he loved me like a brother. Very soon we had no desire for each other") to console me. Jealousy is such a strange malady that it is the devotion of Gonzalo to Helba that I am jealous of, whereas it was Henry's passion, sensual enjoyment of all women that I was jealous of before. I always imagine a greater love to have existed between Henry and June or Helba and Gonzalo, and that is the true source of my suffering. Yet Henry himself told me: "I never was as close to June as I am to you." And Gonzalo has amply proved that I am his passion as Helba never was. I insist on not seeing the analogy Gonzalo makes between his relationship to Helba as being like mine with Hugh.

I don't know if it is not the very immensity of my own love, its very ramifications, its almost cosmic expansion and its division, which makes me so unsure of others' fidelity and in such great need of it. I lose myself in such conjectures.

Yesterday Henry came for lunch here at Passy. After lunch he had a headache and he lay down on my bed. About an hour afterward Gonzalo telephoned that he wanted to see me about six. I knew Henry could only catch a few words like *"bueno, hasta luego."* I said to him: "It is Gonzalo calling me because Helba wants to see me," and I began to talk about Helba's deafness, to put all the emphasis on Helba. But Henry's instinct was not misled. He got up and said: "How strange it is to hear you rattling off in Spanish. One lives with a woman, one thinks one knows her well, and all of a sudden because she begins to talk in a foreign language one does not know where one stands anymore."

"But you know me very well," I said. "I do not express myself in Spanish but in English. In English I can say everything. In Spanish only the most elemental things."

"Not too elemental, I hope," said Henry.

When Gonzalo came in the evening he was happy because of the affection growing between Helba and me. It is strange, what completely annihilated my jealousy and finally aroused my affection was Helba's dolorous confession of the isolation in which her deafness left her. I had spent an afternoon with her and then sent her a letter: "I want you to hear me saying clearly: Never feel alone again because I am near you with a deep affection."

Gonzalo's pleasure at this harmony irritated me. I could not help saying: "It gives you great pleasure to see Helba and me close but you would never do the same for Henry or even tolerate my friendship for him."

Gonzalo jumped as if I had whipped him, trembling with rage. He hurled at me all the gossip he heard in Montparnasse about Henry's unscrupulousness, monstrosities, infidelities, thieveries. He said he knew I was seeing Henry, that I had been with him the night before, that this was an unbreakable bond, that this was intolerable to him. He didn't want me ever to see him again, or correspond with him, that he loathed Henry because Henry was a repulsive monster whereas he loved Hugh, who was a marvelous human being who really loved me. "Henry used you, made you suffer, that is why I hate him." He was like an insane man.

I saw I could never expect from Gonzalo the very detached impersonal generosity which he wanted Helba and me to have for each other. I cannot deceive his instinct, and his jealousy is well founded. But last night I denied, pleaded, and talked really as if there were nothing between Henry and me but friendship. I lose myself in my own lies because I would like to be able to see Henry without this feeling that I am risking my happiness with Gonzalo each time. What abysses! I cannot come out of a movie with Henry without incurring the danger of my very life being shattered. I live like a spy and I am so tired, so tired.

One of the principal sources of pain in my life with Henry is that he is not in harmony with himself. He is full of confusion and contrariness and the conflict inside of him is so continuous that he projects it on all those around him. Each day he destroys what he has said the day before. He attacks in me the very qualities he praised; I am a victim of his contrariness. He acts crazily about food, as about deeper subjects. If I am tranquil he wants me aggressive. If I am active, restless, he wants me passive. Then if I defend myself against personal comments he says: "You should not take it personally." He is a sea of discord and contradictions.

I was naive enough to believe all he said and to try and mold myself. Now I always bristle up and say: "I have accepted myself as

I am. Leave me alone, even my defects. I can see the good of them."
He attacks my lack of interest in slang. Well, it isn't my language. I
have no need of it. By elimination and selection I have found my tone,
color, individual style. He is the woman and I am the man. I am more
consistent, more to be depended on. Hell, forget Henry the irrational,
erratic Henry.

My error was to care too much about all Henry said. I took him
seriously. I must be more indifferent. I have really believed so earnestly
that he was wise, I suffered from his aimless statements. I thought he
was a man in his thinking and it is really the opposite. That is why
Fraenkel used to say I was a better thinker.

Gonzalo's language reveals him. His favorite word is: *"atmósfera."*
He liked the atmosphere. It was "a marvelous atmosphere." Or a bad
one. *"No tiene qualidad. Un cuerpo sin qualidad. Qualidad espiritual."*

"Prodigioso." Extremes of enthusiasm: *"Maravilloso. ¡Qué prodigio!
Irreal* of *realidad.* Irreal. Vital. *Mística. Línea."*

Gonzalo, too, is full of contradictions and confusions. He worships
the old, he hates science, the machine, yet he embraces communism.
He is religious, and he loves beauty, and yet he goes to political meetings, he can listen to blind, stupid speeches, he can go to mass meetings, walk the streets with the workmen, or attend an airplane exhibit.
He hates realism, but he makes drawings of bums, drunks, hobos,
prostitutes in the most naturalistic style. He loves deformity. He likes
magic but he does not believe the psychic being can be affected physically by sorrow, a loss, a defeat. He is aware of time, he can say it is
five o'clock without looking at a watch but he cannot arrive on time.
He knows scientific statistics and he lives in chaos. He worships delicacy yet he destroys everything around him, he burns rugs and furniture, he stains everything, his papers are dirty, his clothes are always
torn or stained. The most extraordinary absence of equilibrium: He
cannot draw a straight line (I can draw a perfect circle without a
compass), he cannot frame a picture straight, cut a page without man-
gling it. He cannot organize: He can make several futile trips through
the city caused by lack of foresight. He can come to Passy and then
discover the place we had decided to go to was near where he started
from. All my suffering comes from caring too much, from faith and

naïveté, from an implicit abandon of myself which is not consistent with my strong inner conviction.

Henry never suffered from unreal anxieties, only from realities (his greatest neurosis is the fear of being left without food so that I have to keep his closet stocked with provisions in an effort to calm this anxiety).

The malady consists in the selection of a trend of thoughts which is destructive, a wallowing in all the negative, frustrating aspects of one's life. For example, dwelling on what one cannot obtain, on one's defeats, on a desire for unlimited power, on selfish tyrannical obsessions. If I begin thinking that Gonzalo should abandon Helba for me instead of remembering that I have abandoned neither Hugh nor Henry for Gonzalo, thinking of destroying in Gonzalo's life that very thing I preserve in mine, that is a malady. If I dwell on Henry's defects and let rebellion accumulate for all the times I have been generous and forgiving. If I think for long hours on the people who have disregarded *The House of Incest* rather than on Lawrence Durrell's glowing letters. If I meditate on my failures rather than on my joys, possessions, pleasures. Destruction, which I do not carry out in life (I never demolish, strike down, punish, kill, in life), seems to install itself at the source of my energy and devour it. Because I never destroy in life, destruction gnaws at me like some animal I keep inside of my breast. Would it not be better to free it, to let it cause its ravages, to rebel against Henry at the moment, as June did, in front of him rather than in solitude, to destroy all my past, my old loves, my ideal fidelities, and demand the same of Gonzalo, to plunder, to kill Helba for my own selfish power satisfaction? How to liberate the snake I carry in my breast which eats into me when I cease being active, or living at a wild fevered rhythm? For two days I have been sick. Is solitude forever forbidden me? I read, I write, I take a rest I need, yet I am haunted again. Why? Would creation feed the monster? Must I write?

A truth overlooked by psychoanalysis is that after analysts have classified a relationship as "masochistic," as Rank classified mine with Henry, they have not considered that what may seem to be the seeking of suffering is sometimes one's spiritual salvation. They completely forget the fact of the soul's salvation, that perhaps this suffering inflicted by Henry's total absence of understanding is the very one which deepened me and humanized me, which forced me into self-expression (I always have to explain to Henry, he divines nothing). Who is to say what is destructive and what creative? One can observe the signs of deterioration, or death, in a human being but who is to say what caused it? Hugh seemed dead, inert for many years. I treated him in a way many people would consider inhumanly, yet I was the cause of his resurrection—and he knows it. He sobbed when he left for America: "You made me, you made me." Henry, perhaps, helped me to find my strength, by his constant challenges.

If it is true that I have the defect of being hypersensitive, of being easily wounded, it is also true that I have an uncanny divination of others' feelings. Gonzalo is amazed how I guess all he feels, expose it, explain it, heal him . . . an opening of the soul, a penetration.

Henry is always admiring what is outside, not what is there. There is no convergence. It is when he is with others that he appears to others to be obsessed with me. To others he talks about me. To me he always talks about others.

Helba complains that Gonzalo cannot live except with a group around him. He too, like Henry, lives in shoals. Hugh is an exception to this masculine shoal habit.

Gonzalo or Henry arrive from the street with a glow on their faces. They come from the most innocuous places, a café, a talk with an anonymous, nondescript, colorless person, an opening, an exhibit of paintings. They denigrate what they have seen or heard. But the glow is there. It is the glow of exercise, of motion, of circulation. It comes from the flux and reflux, the waves. It is impersonal and woman is wrong to be jealous of it. It is the shoal pleasure, the health of exercise in collective swimming. Woman looks for depth, and for intimacy.

Dream in Louveciennes: I arrived at a village on my way to getting somewhere, but it was dark already and I wondered if it would be safe to cross the forest in the evening. I passed by a bistro and three workmen offered to escort me, one small man, and two others. I thought this would be no safer than to go alone for the three might be in accord to attack me, but in spite of this I decided to trust them because there was nothing else to do, and because I was fascinated by the danger, and I wondered how it would be to be attacked by three men. They said the easiest and safest route to where I wanted to go was through a house, that this would be a shortcut. So we climbed over a fence and forced the door. The house was high up on a hill. A long series of rooms. I stayed in it a long time because there was so much to see and do in it. It seems to me I stayed so long I almost forgot my original intent. When I found myself out of it I marveled at myself, and how many years spent in a house could pass like a few hours. I knew then that many years had passed, and I could not understand what could have detained me so long. But I was now at the end of my journey, which was simply the other end of the house, or outside of the house. I believe it was while I was in the house that the following strange incident took place: I was looking at a man who was at a window, very near to me, and he looked twice the natural size of a man. I was hypnotized and interested by his face and his size. Then I saw that the size was due to a magnifying glass which someone had erected on the windowsill. I could see where the glass ended, that around it things looked normal. The glass was only half-way on the window, just enough to change the bust of the man. I wondered whether, if this man was looking at me through this glass, he must also see me abnormally large. I went to investigate. The man was not there, only the glass. I looked down at the windowsill, which was a large aperture through which I could look down into a cellar, where a man had a lot of costumes for disguises, beards, and tricks of all kinds. It seems that when he said something fantastic or tricky, just to deceive people, it actually became true or happened many miles away. He had talked about a train accident, and when I got on the train I discovered the accident had already happened before the man had said it. The room was full of ugly, deformed, sick, servantlike women, a procession of them. The man I had seen so big, still very big, was making love to me, and I was attracted. Hugh was there and this man said he would break down with the pain of knowing me married to Hugh. To console him I said, "But be happy because I have decided to be yours, today." Then I thought I should not have told him this, but let it happen as a surprise. I should have let him suffer. I was sorry to have given him happiness so quickly. He said he did not want, above everything else, that I should love George.

AUGUST 3, 1937

My JEALOUSY (MY DISEASE) OF HENRY HAD reached such a development years ago that I could not go out with Hugh without experiencing the whole evening through Henry. It was my identification with Henry which caused me to look at the show through his eyes, to feel the presence of a woman as he would feel it, to look at this women as he would look at her (often a woman I myself would not like). A sensuous hour of soft air, lights, a beautiful woman, they only aroused in me the sensation that Henry was living somewhere in the city and feeling the air, the lights, the woman at the same moment.

Holidays, days when I knew he would be invited to dance, or drink—Christmas, New Year's, the fourteenth of July—were dates I dreaded. The presence of Fraenkel in the Villa Seurat, Fraenkel who often picked up whores and invited Henry to share them, or Maigret's parties, which ended in orgies, all this caused me intolerable torture. I never wrote very much about them because they were like a dark poison I did not want to expose to the light. Now that I no longer feel this, now that perhaps Henry, by his independence, helped me to separate from him, and I am able to live my life, my pleasures, without mixing them with him—I can write of them. I have done the same to Hugh, who has now a life of his own. The only difference is that my work was done with delicacy and my separation from Henry was achieved through my own solitary experience, without help from Henry.

The other day, after writing again about the poison, I sprang up and freed myself again. I bathed and dressed for Gonzalo. I enjoyed my night with Gonzalo to the fullest, plunging into enjoyment of his body. He is afraid to hurt woman with sex. He imagines it is a torture, a cruel act. I left in the morning for the Villa Seurat, still feeling the physical weight of Gonzalo's body, still aware of his fingers, body, legs, of the shape of his body, still smelling his odor. I was very happy, very happy.

I walked to Henry's studio to meet Nancy and Lawrence Durrell. I saw Durrell's eyes, eyes that know everything, eyes like those of a sea animal, both of earth, sky, and water, of seer and prophet, of child and old man. What keenness in them. He sees everything. His soul sees, his body, his creative self, through those clear, clairvoyant eyes. He was as I expected him to be, soft and feminine, healthy and humorous, fawn and swimmer. Immediate vision. Then I saw Nancy, a long-waisted boy with beautiful long leopard eyes, a Greek boy. And then we talked, but it was not very necessary.

With a few people I have had that eye connection, instantaneous transmissions, the eyes' current, a sort of *accrochage*, an encounter of the eyes which skips all reality. At one bound, with Moricand, with Carteret, with June, with Gonzalo, with Thurema. One is instantly inside of them, and they inside of you, by knowing.

When they left, Henry took me with passion and I responded: animal, animal, animal, animal. A kind of appetite, impersonal, food, like Henry's.

We spent a quiet evening. We saw a movie *[Massacre]*. I saw workmen revolting, a fight with the police, injustice, suffering, hunger. At that moment, because of the actor Richard Barthelmess's suffering, because the police shot into the workmen, because the machine left them without bread, I embraced communism if only for the reason Gonzalo embraced it, as a possible relief of injustice, not a cure, because injustice is inherent in man, incurable, but it can be combated. All my talks with Gonzalo led to this, but the real act of conversion happened like a miracle in a cheap movie house, seeing a cheap movie.

It struck me again, as several times before, that my individual suffering should be merged into the other, that just as when I was a girl and laid aside my personal introspective suffering at the loss of my Father to take care of my mother and my brothers, and lost myself in serving others. Or that, just as I identified once with the war, and with war-torn France, I should again adopt the world's trouble in replacement of my own. Of course, the personal life deeply lived expands to truths beyond itself. My struggles with myself are not valueless. They represent the struggle of thousands. But they lead to the greater one. I don't know.

Meanwhile this month I have rested and enjoyed solitude, paying no heed to the desperate and childish letters of my former patients because I am tired of being used.

This morning overwhelmed with love letters from Hugh and Thurema, still so very happy and so grateful, so grateful. When I am happy I always want to turn to Christ again. Maybe it is just that I am *comblée* [fulfilled], and so I want to give by way of communism.

It seems to me now that when I write, I only write consciously, or at least I follow the most accessible thread. Three or four threads may be agitated like telegraph wires at the same instant, and I disregard them. If I were to capture them all I would be really cornering and capturing the nimblest of minds, revealing innocence and duplicity, generosity and calculation, fear and courage. The whole truth. I cannot tell the whole truth simply because I would have to write four pages to the present one, I would have to write always backward, retrace my step constantly to catch the echoes and the overtones because of the slipperiness of the vice of embellishment, the alchemy of idealism which distorts the truth at every moment. The danger in careful backwalking to pick up what fell out of the net, the danger of falling into introspection, that monster who will chew too long on one morsel, achieve absolute mastication and deterioration, who will wither all it touches rather than illumine it.

Peru:* One doesn't walk on level ground. One is forever climbing stairs that rise in enormous square steps toward a black sky. Weary, eternal stairs, stones set one on top of the other, going up toward the clouds. Exhausting stairs, each stone higher than a man's step. Stairs made by others, those whose faces are carved in granite, those who drink the blood of sacrifices, those who laugh at man's efforts, their laughter frozen in granite toward the belly of the mountain. A man grows weary reaching its high passes, grows weary coming down, his shoulders bent under the weight of invisible curses. He finds foot-

---

*In Spanish in the original.

prints, traces of huge footprints; can they be the white boots spotted with burnt earth?

The world ends here. Behind these walls there are no roads at all. Here the drowned land weeps, here weep men who have not seen daylight. There is no sea, but one hears the rhythm of blood; the wind decapitates and clouds fall perorated by sand. Lava of volcanoes freezes in the form of dead stars, fever dwells with ashen eyes, laughter burns as it falls and clouds emerge from the openmouthed earth. Here the world ends and here the world begins.

Letter to Hugh: Pleased that you like Thurema. It is not a foil I seek, it is always the woman who lives entirely by her instincts, in chaos, and like nature. I love that in other women because it represents my own instinctive nature which I hold in check as much as possible, which I seek to transcend by some creative and superior force which makes me not want to destroy others, and all instincts freed are destructive. Having more or less (you know about the less) dominated my instincts of possession, power, egotism, enslaving, appetite, I like to see it—the whole jungle—in other women. I don't like superior women, I like the jungle.

Evening: Helba and I met. Helba, whose abdication, whose rise above jealousy finally helped me to rise above it, and who acts as I acted toward June, turning it all into love. Helba and I sit talking with an honesty no man would imagine us capable of, with a direct-ness incredible in women. At one moment Helba even asked me: "Were you jealous of me?" I said: "Yes, I was." And we kissed.

Walking through the Bois I tell her the legend of the mandragora and she jumped and said: "I had been thinking of a dance inside the trunk of a tree, waving my arms as branches with tortuous twisted gestures, the feet like roots." I said: "And I have just finished a story where the woman turns into a tree." (Metamorphosis). We talked excitedly with an exaltation which accompanies creation, this sudden miracle. And I walked home with a joyous feeling, Helba and I were now flying away from destruction into creation, we had climbed gen-erous stairs up into creation, and we had talked about the diabolical in us, how she felt like a saint in life, melted with goodness, and how the diabolical came out in the dance, how sudden it was, the storm in her and how it became a dance. And I told her how I wrote during the moon cycle, discharged all the turgid, dark, brooding elements into writing.

My first afternoons with Helba had been lifeless and like a visit to the hospital. I saw her only out of compassion. But each time she was less inert, less sick, less depressed, and today we really could reach the creative sources of our being, walk through enchanting stories, we were transported into fantasy. And I was joyous to have brought her to life and perhaps back into creation. Just as happy as I am now to see that Gonzalo does not drink anymore, that he is full of energy and joy, that his work is effective, that he is manifesting the power in him. Miracles. Miracles. I feel a little drunk, that all this happens to others and to me, that I am like an inexhaustible well, that life flowed out of me in great continuous miraculous sources and I am again religiously, primitively grateful.

Gonzalo lies on my bed and he talks like a king or a dictator. He shows his gift for domination and leadership. He has made, in two months, large and wide unifications. There is power in him. His weakness is like mine: He can rule himself, drive himself, create, he has the vision, but he cannot use others, he does not know how to use others, make others work for him. That is why he serves communism yet he is not bound to it by any contract. He will not, cannot, submit to anyone, he wants to bring his own group to it, and be allowed independent work. He works for the collective but he can't bear to give up his liberty.

He lies on my bed after a day's full work, and he says: "Is it possible that two years ago I was just a Montparnassian, a Bohemian?"

"Never deep down," I said, and I remember when I first put my finger on the springs of his real nature, what it was I touched one day which exploded like dynamite: His pride, his aristocracy, his rulership, his devotion and compassion. I remembered how he awakened at my side like a man suddenly whipped—whose manhood suddenly and violently asserted itself. With his sexual conquest, his conquest of his type of woman, his first image, his first ideal, the one he did not attain the first time, his life began again where it had started, as a

76

lord of vast lands, owner of slaves, soldier and mayor of his village. I like this domination in Gonzalo. I awakened it because I sensed the pride in the slave, I could not let him be a slave.

"I believe, *chiquita*, that you and I were not only attracted to each other for human reasons but that destiny was planned and we are the instruments for a greater purpose. Somehow, we were thrown together to serve humanity."

Strange, ever since I have considered communism not as an absolute, which my wisdom denies, but as a palliative, as a fatality, as a purifier because it is new, as inevitable, as a punishment for the disintegration of the individual, as a possible redemption of the individual, I am at peace.

Desire. Gonzalo came for dinner, but after dinner we had work to do. I had to proofread the English version of a communist pamphlet. Gonzalo prowled around me, kissing me. I pushed him off, laughing, because I could not work with the softness inside. Even my eyes would blur when he kissed me. At eleven he was to deliver the work and see [José] Bergamin at the café. I said: "You'd better not come back." (He was absolutely exhausted, after a day of work and tension.) But Gonzalo was determined to return. I felt it. And I felt he had to return, that desire obsessed us. He came back very late, everything had conspired to detain him, even meeting a friend at the café who said: "Helba and Elsa are at my studio with a few Spanish friends. You'd better come." And then Helba expected to be taken home, but Gonzalo left the café, left the party, left Helba, and rushed back to me with a body so warm it made me shiver. "I had to come, I had to come back, *chiquita*." "I wanted you to come back. I wanted you." He touched me. I was wet, so wet. Sliding in and out of me, he said: "I like to see how I hurt you, how I stab you in there, in the little wound."

I am writing this very slowly, so it will last, so it will last eternally. I am sitting in a café, inside of the softness of a summer day like an ermine paw. I am writing because I want it to last, Gonzalo pounding into me, so heavy his body and so rich with flesh, the flesh so firm, so strong, so thick, so hot. Everything seems miraculous again, the temperature, how was such a thing created, the softness in the air, the trees, the fountains of the Champs-Elysées, the men and women walking. How was Gonzalo's voice created, out of what marvelous sounds no music ever caught, no instrument ever emitted? How was this flesh shaped so, animated with a soul, with desire, with tenderness? How was it drawn to me, fixed, to what depths can our love go, what marvelous new worlds every day? A city never entirely known, a forest never possessed, a sky which changes every instant, an earth which turns and brings new feelings every day? Can life continue unrolling this way with a freshness never withered, a new face, new marvels? Can one arrive so many times at fullness without touching bottom? Every year new leaves, new skin, new loves, new words. One day I weep at change, but then there is no death, there is this everlasting continuity, nothing is lost, it is transformed. A man can come and arouse your desire, make you drunk, sleep in your arms, possess you without pain. This absence of pain with Gonzalo, that is what I am grateful for. Henry was a torment. Gonzalo not. A fire which does not burn, a fire like the magician's whip which does not hurt, or have I learned to walk magically over hot coals without burning?

AUGUST 5, 1937

I HAVE KNOWN LAWRENCE DURRELL FOR A THOUsand years. He is irremediably, familiarly, intimately a friend. One can talk about everything, and at the same time there is no need of it. How well he knows Henry. Talking about the "Max" story he said: "You are frightening, Henry, the way you have cut the cord—the umbilical cord from what you describe. No pity, no love, just the all-seeing monster, the savage vision, exposure. Something really outside the human. If I were a Jew this story would kill me."*

*Published in James Cooney's magazine *Phoenix*, Volume 1, Number 3 (fall 1938), "Max" also became part of the title of *Max and the White Phagocytes*, a collection of miscellaneous items, dedicated to Betty Ryan, published by the Obelisk Press, Paris, as part of the Villa Seurat series, in October 1938.

Always for me this has made me shiver and admire. I could do it in the "Birth" story, in the diary, but not as Henry does it. Then he wonders why people are terrified, why Fraenkel got sick when he read the story, just as I wonder why the "Birth" story has such terrific effect on people.

Letter to Patrick Evans: . . . You know what happens when one writes. It is an arithmetic that happens in the dark. It only becomes valuable, illumined with a sort of life glow, vital, when it creates a current, when there is someone at the receiving end, when there is an echo, an answer. Everything else is a sad affair, sitting alone, writing. . . .

Transposition of emotion by either the unconscious or conscious. My mother profoundly upset by Joaquin's interest in Thurema, not conscious of it, talked to me for a whole afternoon about homosexuality and Eduardo, ending by asking me if I thought my brother might be a homosexual, without realizing that at that moment she wanted to hear me say: yes he is, which would have reassured her that she would not lose him to Thurema.

The conscious transposition I have often noted. When I went to Henry the morning Hugh left for New York and felt emotional, on the verge of tears, quite broken inside. I had to see Henry, at the same time I could not conceal my turmoil. I consciously erected a situation which would explain my condition, which would let me talk emotionally about something else, which relieved me of the pent-up feeling. I shifted the cause of my unbalance, dramatized the danger of our being sent to New York. I said Hugh had just received a telephone call from New York, that I was afraid that the bank was inhuman. At times Henry's instincts tell him I am unnerved by something else but I lead him into blind alleys. He cannot quite find the real cause. He has not discovered Hugh's absence yet. So the emotion, disguised, flows out. Most women are unaware of this. I become aware as I lie. With me the unconscious is tremendous, vast, an ocean which is constantly manifesting its presence, but it always becomes conscious as I live. It is very rare when I don't know what is happening to me—when I am blind. The chaos, the storm, the furies, the anguish, they come as fiercely as in all women but very quickly I swim on the surface, my head comes out, the mermaid. I see, I hear with human eyes and ears.

AUGUST 6, 1937

TIME. WHEN I EXPERIENCE A GREAT DEAL BE-tween the night I spend with Gonzalo, and our next night together, I have the feeling we have been separated a long time, as if I had taken a long voyage. If nothing happens and I keep my reverie centered on him then it seems as if we had hardly been separated at all. The evening I spent with Henry and the Durrells, because it was spent in an art world, because we talked about so many things, stirred up so many feelings, awakened so many new ideas, seemed like a full week. I had been in Greece, in their house on the rocks fiercely licked by the waves. I had been in the Himalayas, in England. I had been in the world of madmen I saw with Carteret, whose speeches I read out to Larry.* I had been in a new Paris with Larry, visiting the Exposition as upon a playground of whimsical possibilities. His humor had reminded me of [John] Erskine even though it is much more delicate and poetic. When I saw Gonzalo again the next evening, I felt great distances had spread between us. I had dust on my feet, the song of Ravel's "Birds of Paradise" in my head, the joy at Durrell's understanding of my writing and of me. I had been very far away.

*On a visit to the Palais de Justice Anaïs Nin and Jean Carteret had witnessed the interrogation of a "madman" by a police psychiatrist that became the basis for the story *"Le merle blanc,"* written in French, which appeared in the September 1937 issue of *The Booster.* An English version, "The White Blackbird," is included in the recently published collection *The Mystic of Sex and Other Writings*, edited by Gunther Stuhlmann (Santa Barbara, CA: Capra Press, 1995). The same material eventually became the final section of the story, *"Je suis le plus malade des Surrealists,"* in *Under a Glass Bell* (rev. ed., Athens, OH: Swallow Press/Ohio University Press, 1995).

At other times Gonzalo takes me so deeply into his warmth, shuts the door of our little flesh tabernacle so intimately, pours such a circle of passion around me, snorts his jealousy like a cage around me, envelops me in his gift for nearness, for human contact, that I return to Henry's art world as if to a glacier. Impersonal, impersonal. So personal about himself, Henry, ruled indeed by the moon in him, but so impersonal about others, yes, he never enters others, that is the great difference. He is observer, eye, ear, mouth. He eats. He does not penetrate. He sacks human beings, cuts them open, exposes their vitals, like the butcher. He can do it because he does not care. I am the opposite. I am personal with others, and relentless about myself. It is myself I expose in the diary and the others I idealize, love, or lose myself into! It is about my own experience I can write monstrously.

Letter to Dr. Esther Harding: I cannot keep myself from writing you. I already wrote you once what I felt while reading your books. I have just been rereading *Woman's Mysteries.* I am deeply struck again by it, the chapters on the Inner Meaning of the Moon Cycle, and on the Virgin Goddesses.... I cannot tell you how much they mean to me. I tried to when we met in New York, but I felt that we did not communicate then at all. I know what happened. I had met you in the world of your creation, in an unreal atmosphere. I was overawed by what you had written. I wanted so much to communicate with you that it intimidated me. You are a psychologist and you will understand what happened. I dressed up, because I was timid. I wore everything I had that was not usual, not familiar, and not simple. I hid myself behind my foreignness. I did everything to make myself remote, the opposite of what I wanted. I don't know what my visit meant to you. I was terribly sad afterward. I knew I had not been able to talk to the woman who wrote those two books in which I find enclosed an unusually complete, total feminine psychology and philosophy. I was always saying the psychologists had not seized woman, but you did. I am sad that all my unnatural fear and doubts of myself created that false impression and separated us. I had so much to tell you that in a naive, unrealistic way, I had brought you my diary all the way from France, a diary I have never wanted to show, with a desire not only to be understood by you, but greater still, of proving to you the deep truth of all you had written. . . .

It is really extraordinary, dear Dr. Harding, but I have had two analyses, one by a French Freudian, the other by Dr. Otto Rank himself, for whose philosophy I have a great respect, yet neither of these illuminated woman for me or woman's nature as you do. It was truly a man-made psychology. I was able to make use of it to heal myself by efforts of my own, by my own individual creative instinct, but you expressed the true understanding.

I sent you my book *House of Incest*, because afterward I saw in it expressed symbolically so much that you had touched upon. I instinctively sought the sea, and life under the sea. I used the ship as a symbol and then I read that you consider the water the unconscious waters of instinct, and you write about the crescent boat of the goddess. I have used all my instincts in creation. During the moon cycle I usually shut myself in, and I write. Feeling overwhelmed by the dark blood you describe so well, I canalized this into poetry. I usually do then my best and most poetic writing. I turn away from those I love so as not to hurt them. The maternal and the egotistical passions are both strong in me. How well you explain where they meet, interact. I can tell you how deeply you write because I have lived through all the phases beginning with an absolute sacrifice of my feminine instincts to play the mother, the muse, passing through rebellion and assertion of the instincts, through destruction, acting many roles in relation to different men, loving and not loving, and finally coming to that one in-herself through art. If ever my diary of fifty volumes gets published I hope you will be the one to write the preface for it.

Dear Dr. Harding: It was good of you to write me when I know how busy you are. You analyzed my letter perfectly. I was an analyst myself for two years and so I understand what you meant about trying to bring into a casual visit a contact which can be achieved either in friendship or in the patient and doctor relation. Of course, having been analyzed, and having analyzed so many people, I did not imagine I came to you with a need, or for purely a personal confession. I thought rather that I admired your work and that it was Esther Harding the writer I wanted to talk to, being myself a writer, and I laid aside all thought of analysis. I know how often people have turned to me personally who ought to have submitted to the analyst in me. I understand perfectly how the only way for you to deal with those who are not your friends is to take care of them. Perhaps unconsciously, I was seeking understanding, it is true, of what I call communication. But more than this, stronger than all this, was my admiration of your work and my desire to tell you this because I know it is good, I know it helps one to know our books are understood. There is no hope of my going to New York for a long time. My whole life is settled here. So for the moment please consider my letters as mere tokens of admiration.

Everything that is not jealousy is life. Beautiful flow between Larry, Henry, and me. It is while talking together that I discover that I possess Henry; it is while talking together that I discover my own strength as an artist; that I get nourished, stimulated; that I stimulate Larry and he Henry. Henry's love is nourished by Larry's tremendous admiration of me. My feeling for women's inarticulateness is reawakened by Nancy's stuttering, stumbling loyalty to me as the one who does not betray woman but expresses her.

When they discuss the problem of my diary, all the art theories are involved. When they talked about the geological changes undergone by an accident with time and that it was the product of this change we called art, and I asserted this process in me took place instantaneously, Henry said: "But this would upset all the art theories." I asserted I could feel the potentialities of our talk last night while it happened as well as six months later. I cited the birth experience which varies so little, the version written as soon as it happened and the version three years later. "But then why did you feel the need of rewriting it?"

"For a greater technical perfection, but not to re-create it."

They said: "We have a real woman artist before us, the first one, and we ought to bow down instead of trying to make a monster out of her."

As soon as I won out I was doubtful, deep down. I know Henry is the artist because he does exactly what I do not do. He waits. He gets outside of himself.

This last month I have been rewriting the whole diary in my head. What a prodigious thing I might do, both the document and the art product, both the human and the created, side by side, monster and woman, inside and outside. What a feat that would be! All I know is that I am right, all I do is right for me.

The woman artist has to fuse creation and life in her own way— or in her own womb, if you prefer. She has to create something different from man—something not monstrous, in man's sense, not de Chirico, not the art paradise. She has to create the mystery, the storm, nature, the moon itself, the madness of nature, the terrors, the natural paradise of sex, the inferno of sex, the battle with art and against art.

The art of woman must be this that is born out of a flesh womb and not from the cells of the mind. She must be, in her art, the very myth in motion. She must marry the elements and the synthetic products of man, she must be the link, the cord, the perfume which man destroys. The instant she fails in this the world will be plunged in darkness. And man's city hanging in the sky will perish with it.

She must create that which man originally destroyed, the very world of unity first issued from God, which man shattered and split with his proud consciousness. It is this dividing of the paradise made by God into fragments, so as to piece it together in a man order, rule it, that Henry and Larry tried to reenact the other night. They tried to lure me out of the womb. Why? I have to create for man or woman this very tragic seeking of a lost bond, of a shattered wholeness. I have to create that which will deliver us from aloneness, the mirages of art, the suffering of our separateness . . . that which recalls Rimbaud from his death.

Note by Durrell: "I fold up and give in. What she says is biologically true from the very navel strings."

The birth of the magazine *The Booster*, inherited by Fred [from the American Country Club in Paris], and dominated by Henry, reawakened my rebellion against Henry's atmosphere of begging, stealing, cajoling, schoolboy pranks, slapstick humor, vulgar exuberance.

AUGUST 10, 1937

As to personalization being a possessive instinct I said to Henry, "I don't believe it. Certainly I am not possessive. I leave plenty of air around you, don't I?

"Of course—but that is the strongest possession. Why, in a way, you're much more possessive than other women. When you leave me, when you efface yourself, vanish, when you most forgive, tolerate, understand, when you are most silent, when you leave most air around me, you possess me more than the woman who takes one by the throat and whom one can shake off! Why, at times I feel as if I were living with an Egyptian sorceress."

Letter to Thurema: . . . I got a letter from Hugh all about you at the same time as yours. I was delighted. He liked you, of course he liked you. He writes warmly. He says: "Everything about her breezy, tremendous gusto, outrushing generously into life and suffering from it. Conflict between the outrushing and ingoing tide. She talked to me about Joaquin and I told her what I thought. Our evening went so well. She took off nearly all her bracelets and rings and gave them to me for you. Marvelously generous. I say I like her very much.

I can see why you loved her." So, will you ever believe, why should you ever have been afraid? How could you not believe in yourself? All my love does not give you faith in yourself. Reread my letters. I prescribe that every day. Reread what I write and you will see what you are. I am not blind. As a matter of fact all I wrote in the diary I finally poured back in the letters. There is nothing you do not know. I have written you how I see you, how you seem to me, and what you are to me.

If you want to know: Seeing and hearing you in New York saved my life, inspired me and stimulated me more than you can ever imagine. I was drunk on you, you forget that always. You always get love and compassion mixed up. I love you, and other people I feel pity for. They are entirely different. Separate. Your weakness, since you insist on having one, takes nothing away. You know my weakness, you know I have more of that than you, yet it changed nothing in you. Your weakness is only your lack of faith in yourself, and that certainly does not disillusion me, how could it? It is human. . . .

Oh, Thurema, I should not have started this because now I recall your mouth so vividly and the nights in the Barbizon Plaza, our talks in the dark. Really I miss you. I envy Hugh seeing you. Hugh hearing your voice.

Gonzalo is working hard with his press, will begin to earn a living soon. Hugh and I got him the printing machine, he has plenty of orders. He is very human, delicate in relationship, loyal, and faithful. You would like him. He is the opposite of Henry. He sacrifices himself for others, is full of *nobleza*, and a soft, tolerant, easy rebelliousness. The name I have given him describes him well: Leóncito. He has a lot of the lion, the goodness and the nobility. He devours nothing but meat, never eats human beings as Henry did; I had quite a time to keep him from going to fight in Spain. He has the nature to go and get killed for what he believes in. Helba is getting her health back slowly, and even her deafness has improved.

Little Brown has refused the diary, too. Don't be sad. I am going to get to work and change it, make novels of it, and it will be less dangerous for those it might hurt. I will use it as a notebook and write novels slowly. Instead of a human document I may make something artistic out of it. We will see. None of them dared risk the money involved, and there was the problem of cutting out. But it has helped to make me a name, so whatever I send them now they read carefully. I have gained their respect.

I am wearing your ring as I write. I wish you would read a book called *The Way of All Women*, by Esther Harding. It is immensely illuminating about woman, really marvelous. Don't deprive yourself anymore to send me money, *querida*. I was very touched, really, and grateful, but you must not go on. *Te quiero tanto, y te abrazo con toda mi fuerza.*

Fred Perlès again. Horseplay. Wasted energy, common destructiveness. Feebleness, hypocrisy, callousness, extortion. Again the air gets vitiated, stupid. It is not my humor. I turn to the Durrells. I like their climate, their humor. People mock and despise this side of Henry. Everybody knows it is his vulgar side, his infantile side. Nobody sends subscriptions, except those who have just met Henry and Fred and don't know they are throwing money and interest down the drain.

This atmosphere of truly American humor, burlesque, I turn violently away from.

The waste, the waste, is what I can't bear. Playing the fools, the buffoons, the jesters. This bores me. Now I discover I have loved Henry and hated sides of Henry at the same time, and those sides revolted me, sent me away from him.

And Henry, when he gets power of any kind, uses it to satisfy his vanity, to be able to kick people around, to express his resentments, his envies, his jealousies. Everything he does is right, he says. He has a puerile vanity—wants everything published. Has a sort of negative resentment against selection, elimination. A love of insulting, a sort of belated Dadaism, the worst aspect of surrealism.

AUGUST 11, 1937

I WENT BACK TO HENRY AND THE DURRELLS, not to be alone. I was surprised at myself. Shocked. I cannot be alone. I did not need to see Henry or the Durrells. I had been with them the night before. I did not want to be alone. The soft evening, the illuminated city drew me out. I was happy to be walking with Henry and the Durrells, with anyone, a strange, impersonal animal pleasure at nearness. I understood for the first time why people are together without good reason, not for each other's charm, creative sparks, or love sparks—just to be together, not to be alone. I understood Henry—never alone. What a change in me. We walked. We had little to say. We were just together, that is all, the four of us, walking, eating. I was happy. I was watching Durrell.

He is a little amazed at himself, as someone who discovered a disease in himself. Under the golden-tanned skin, the blond hair, the sea-bottom eyes, behind the poetic gestures, mellow and human, he has found a cataract of words, a universe of nuances, shadows, quarter tones. Not by way of neurosis did he uncover the imagination he has. He is like a sailor, a mountaineer who has been visited by revelations. There is a miracle about his creation. He is a bit amazed. He walks the familiar streets with a vague uneasiness. The wine bottle has become symbolical. This expresses all he is fighting against. He does not want to lose the warmth, the flesh, the odor, the reality.

At times Gonzalo's jealousy (he had another attack of it after reading only the June episode in "Chaotica")* angers me because it

---

*At various times, Anaïs Nin used "Chaotica" as the title of her story, drawn from diary material, which eventually became the first part of the original edition of *The Winter of Artifice,* under the title "Djuna." It presents her infatuation with June Miller, who has become "Johanna," and, simultaneously, with "Hans," the writer.

reawakens my own jealousy, not only my old jealousy of Henry but also of Helba. The things he says arouse my own resentments, revolts. For a night I feel as poisoned as he is—by the past. I cannot say I like his jealousy. True, when it first flares up I may feel a pleasure, a perverse pleasure in his blind, jealous, instinctive love, at seeing the storm, at his suffering. But after a moment I am drawn into the dark abyss and I feel my own dark furies. And it hurts me, lacerates me, as much for his suffering as mine. I begin to see how growing away from the loved one does not diminish the love but increases it. I would be tired of the current between Henry and me if we lived all alone, but this current is vivified, enriched by the currents around us. I discover new aspects of Henry in his relationships with others, and life takes the place of the exchange between us which is naturally attenuated now. What is love? If Henry and I cease to feel each other directly it does not mean that what I am to Durrell leaves him un-stirred. It does stir in him a new feeling for me. What Henry is to others keeps alive in me an illusion which at times I almost lose, that of his aliveness, because I see the ebb flowing back, I witness his deadness while he works.

The more I go out the stronger I become aware of Gonzalo's seduction, of the beauty of his nature. It is the life flowing around me that keeps me so sensitized to his presence, so alert to his charms, so physically, electrically responsive. There is no doubt that we flow in an individual way through a non-individual world to which we are connected. Every disconnection is death. I breathe an air, not Gon-zalo's, but it is an air which vivifies our love. To breathe. To admire. To respond. I am rediscovering that to possess is to kill. I have lived by the law of not possessing by force, of my creative love for others —but deep down it was a demon clamoring to possess. Thus did Rank kill his own happiness, and Gonzalo would if he could have me all to himself.

August 12, 1937

I FELT THAT NANCY AND LARRY WERE A LITTLE uneasy, a little lost, a little ready for flight, after ten days of the Villa Seurat and the Dôme circus. I felt their loneliness. I asked them to come and see me last night while Henry and Gonzalo were engaged. We sat on the floor by the enormous window, had coffee sitting on pillows in the dark. All the light comes from the *Exposition* below the window. And we talked intimately. They recoil from what I recoil from. They wanted Greece again, after walking through the slippery, greasy, putrid world of Fred, Mechanze, Brassai, et al. It is not moral repulsion, we said, it is heraldic.

I enjoyed hearing Larry and Nancy's contempt, sadness. Larry saying: "I get impatient. I can't stand idiots very long. One should not have contempt, but..." I felt less alone. I was happy. In the dark we seemed to be able to say everything. Larry was exposing his fear of "going mad" if he continued writing.

He is afraid of what I will write about him, but I said: "So am I of what you will write, yet I can't stop talking because I know you know me anyway."

The Dôme at nine in the morning. Antonin Artaud waving his magic Mexican stick and shouting: "I don't want this rotting away while I am alive."

Today Henry is so changed I can hardly believe it. His hundred-dollar check from Knopf he spent with wisdom and generosity. He gave me the Tibetan sandals I wanted, he helped Reichel instead of throwing it away on Fred's magazine. I was amazed.

AUGUST 15, 1937

HENRY IS MORE AFRAID TO BE ALONE THAN EITHER Larry or I. He is so afraid he will accept any company, anybody, any circumstance. He seems independent because he likes to insult his equals, he likes to separate himself from the intelligent, the valuable men. But he is so afraid to be alone that he prefers a mediocre movie, any street, any café, or anybody to solitude. To estrange, insult Herbert Read or Otto Rank, satisfies his vanity. To surround himself with inferiors flatters his vanity.

AUGUST 16, 1937

FOUND MY HAPPINESS AGAIN WORKING WITH Gonzalo. A small low-ceilinged room with two windows on an old French garden on the rue de Lille. Two enormous tables, one with the press on it. I printed two thousand strips for pamphlets. Cut them. Gonzalo writes letters. What neither Helba nor June could do is to find the deep reason for the apparently stupid, perverse behavior of Henry and Gonzalo. The true reason why he does not take a workman to help him is pride, independence, a possessive feeling toward the machine, a hatred of big enterprises, wants to do it all himself. Likes the personal, the universe ruled by one's self and one's self as workman. I understand this. So I told him this, I entered into the spirit of it. I am doing the work.

AUGUST 18, 1937

*I*T IS TRUE THAT WHEN THINGS DO NOT WORK OUT ideally—are broken, spoiled, failed—I experience a sadness completely out of proportion to the event, like Rank's sadness when I spilled my bag as the train was leaving Philadelphia, after a perfect weekend. Whatever mars the marvelous, the dream, gives me a great shock. Last night Gonzalo said he would come right after supper. He came at midnight because "Elsa had not fixed supper and they had quarreled all evening and spent hours looking for biscuits for Helba who can't eat bread." The excuse seems feeble. The disorder and stupidity of their lives, the waste and ugliness of it revolts me. I close against Gonzalo. I don't want his caresses. He fell asleep in my arms, feeling innocent.

I got out of bed and went to Hugh's bed, thinking of Hugh. I was weeping, lying there among his drawings. "Take me into your arms, Hugo, you alone keep me from going crazy. I am no better now than when I was thirteen years old weeping all night over sorrows which seemed enormous. Somehow, at times I feel all confused and lost by the craziness of Henry and Gonzalo. At times I feel like a child, without courage and without laughter. Take me into your arms, my young sweet father. I have given you strength and you keep me from going crazy. No one can understand, because they look for visible causes. Visibly it is not hard to live with Henry or Gonzalo, but deep down it is maddening. They are worse than women, with their disorder, contrariness, their bohemianism, their lack of awareness, they are like weights on my life, and they create a sort of darkness in which I fall. Because I love them I dissolve in them, and I hate the way they live. I can't understand the way they live with their childish quarrels, their incapacity to discipline themselves, their slack, loose, wasted lives. My young father, my very young father, I need you. I feel very small. I don't understand. I have so much courage, fire, energy, for many things, yet I get so hurt, so wounded by small things. No better than those attacks of melancholy I had as a child. No nearness to anyone but you, because Henry is all sand and yielding and dispersion, without strength or wisdom, and Gonzalo has no will, no strength, he is not a man, he gets tangled in life as a child does and I feel haunted by a terrifying melancholy which I struggle wildly to kill—and I can't. I feel waylaid by madness, when I see Gonzalo's confusion, Henry's confusion, and Thurema's, it seems to me that everybody is floundering, blindly, in an infernal sort of darkness, and only you, my young father, you and I can find ourselves at times in a haven—so tranquil and wise you are, and so much older, and there is a core to you. I lie in your bed. Protect me. I am in your arms. Protect me."

One day Edgar came to see Henry with Heinz Henghes, a German sculptor. He had supercilious, irritating manners, but his face was soft, feminine, appealing. I was aware of his presence physically—as you feel a storm coming, in your bones. I could not define the feeling—a vague attraction. Great antipathy between him and Henry. I did not see him again for many months. A few days ago I walked into Fred's studio and there he was—soft, alluring, yet somehow dissonant, never knowing when to be hard, when soft, when he should be hurt or not hurt. He reminded me of a softer, more animal Eduardo. I liked the melting eyes, the sharp nose, oriental, oval. Henry insulted him, and I gave him my address. Why, I don't know. I followed an impulse. He came today. He said he had been aware of me the first day, wanted to find me. But with all this psychic undercurrent flowing it was hard to talk. We were both uneasy. When he said: "I would like something lovelier and warmer," I got frightened. Frightened of my old habit of permitting people to get closer to me than I meant them to. I became explicit, about my life, too clear, on account of the fear. We parted very uneasily. I wonder, is it spoiled. Or is it that I don't altogether trust him. I'm afraid of a vulgar trait in him, and we began on too high an altitude. The truth is he attracts me superficially, as so many people do—and I know the rigid core in me which makes it impossible for me to yield to these incomplete relationships, to the pleasant ones, such as my liking for Artaud, for example. *Tant pis.* I am still awkward, awkward before these disquieting, obscure attractions which I don't feel I can yield to *au fond.* I have no fear of depths, and a great fear of shallow waters. I must be a real mermaid.

Other women get in "rut" for sexual nearness. I get such a rut for "nearness"—not necessarily sexual, but nearness. And it eludes me. I feel at moments separate from Henry and Gonzalo . . . from everybody. No one seems to have the key. Or is it I who push myself outside? For example, the day Henry received the proofs of his essay on the diary* (a piece which everybody considers marvelous and in which Henry reveals how far he is from seizing my meaning—me), I saw he had left in two paragraphs of direct, inaccurate crudities about my Father. He said he would make the change. He saw what I meant. In relation to the whole essay they were petty and personal touches. But Henry had been for many days in a world mood—his world self—brutal, mocking, ruthless, jesting, diabolical, and so at night I thought he would send the essay to T. S. Eliot without the changes, and I could hear him say: "You are too soft about people—this will teach you to let anything be said—not to care." All this quite probable, if one knows Henry, but actually not one of the things he has ever done to me. It is when I get the outer Henry and my Henry confused that I fear. And the next day he had made the changes, very subtly, that is, I can bring out wisdom and lucidity in him and do not arouse his combativeness (to Benno, who gave him one of his paintings and was naturally tender with it, Henry says: "It's my painting now, isn't it? You gave it to me, so if I want to I can put my foot through it," which naturally put Benno beside himself with rage).

Letter from Heinz Henghes: I left you—walking within a cloak of glass, having been just born, washed clean—walking—seeing like a detached lens, without commentary—not seeing at all—but BEING, seeing, seen. . . . some things are

---

"Un être étoilique," which for the first time publicized the existence of Anaïs Nin's diary, appeared in T. S. Eliot's London magazine, the *Criterion,* Volume XVII, No. 66, pp. 33–52, in October 1937.

like an alive river or like green things that come up every year and that ask no questions. . . . I should perhaps not write too much, because this is too silent to me, the sculptor, to take form except in stone—but I cannot really believe in this ungenerosity before you. I must tell you, Anaïs, that I came to you afraid, that now my fear has left me. I am not yet clear enough to say what has taken place. . . . We have very much to say to each other. There are many reasons for this. Some are not yet clear to me and for others I do not find the words; one, which is one of the senses your book has given me, is that our suffering has been alike.

Newborn, washed Henghes telephoned insistently. Feminine laughter. I let him come today. I teased Gonzalo about him. I let them meet. A demon pushed me. I had no control over myself. I sat down for an hour talking with Heinz, letting myself be moved, stirred, then I let Gonzalo come (consciously I thought Gonzalo is never on time, if he says six o'clock he will come at seven or eight. Heinz will have time to go). But Gonzalo arrived exactly at six. I had just asked Heinz to leave me. They bowed to each other. When Heinz left, Gonzalo was like a wild animal, dark, leaping, beside himself. For an hour I pleaded, spoke of our completeness together, how nothing could take us away from each other, no one, how all this was an accident, Heinz had come with other people, they had left, he had stayed. Pleaded with words of love. I took his head and laid it on my breast, lulled him. Out of the exhaustion and perhaps to escape he fell asleep—I could not sleep. I moved about restlessly. I stood by the window. The charm of Heinz had faded. I knew all the time it was charm, like the momentary charm of Moricand, of Turner, of Mary Gill. Everything faded beside the depths of Gonzalo's jealousy. I stood by the window for one moment quite crazed. Remembering that the night before I had been with Henry, that Henry had taken me with passion, that I had gone from Henry's place to Gonzalo's office and worked for Gonzalo, that I had rushed home at four to bathe and dress for Heinz, I saw Heinz's face with the soft glowing eyes saying: "I love you." I was afraid.

Heinz laughing with an adolescent laughter, trusting, sensitive, and with the charm of Thurema, the voice of Henry, the voice of Gonzalo.

I was afraid because it was not I, Anaïs Nin, tied to Henry and Gonzalo, but an unknown woman lying down, yielding, opening, spreading—and as if I were forced on a ship and I felt this ship sailing and I felt terrible regret for that which I was leaving, no awareness of where I was going. I don't care where it is I am going, but wherever I go I know now will take me away from Gonzalo, will create a distance between us, for I know what Gonzalo has taken away from Henry. I know all the orgasms I have withheld from Henry and they are only symbols of the feelings I have withheld and gave another. It is not true that there is no betrayal. I am less wholly Henry's— and even if I have enough for both, it is not the same, and now I don't want to fall apart again. I don't want to move away from Gonzalo even for a few hours for the sake of wholeness. I feel dismembered—spreading, expanding, in a joy, but I feel dismembered because I don't play, I really tear myself apart, I give, I am all tired out now from the work for Gonzalo. I want peace. I am not afraid of Heinz. I am afraid of splitting, splitting, fragmenting. If I yield I can yield to an infinite. I can yield to so many. I can become a temple prostitute. And it is all a devouring. When Henry turned to his work I sought lovers, when Gonzalo gives himself to his work, I seek this new game of sensation, to hear men court me, to be desired anew.

I don't know. Don't explain. I had to do all this, so that I could stand by the window resolved not to yield, seeing life like a precious liqueur in a cup, and this liqueur spilling over, I don't want to spill over, as Henry does, one drinks the dregs, one loses the depths, I don't want to taste Gonzalo less by adding a new savor, I fight this dissolution, I fight it, I don't want Gonzalo to feel me escaping him.

He awakes; he says: "It is over now."

I begin to weep hysterically, deeply. I feel injured. It seems to me that Gonzalo's jealousy is unjust. I feel that all I'm saying to him about our love being so complete is true, that he should not be jealous, I feel a fatality, as if the small Anaïs who loves Gonzalo is a small figure carried on a giant wind-gust of dispersion. I feel hurt, afraid, confused. I am weeping, saying: "You are unjust."

What confusion in me, the moon cycle coming, I am drowned in wild instincts, hatreds and coquetries, desires and rebellions. I sway, everyone near me seems to lure me, move me, the sea is inside of me, swaying, heaving, my blood is feverishly mounting, into my head, my thinking is drowned, there is a sea, and dispersion in me, Gonzalo, hold me with your possessiveness, I am like one lost in a giant forest, I walk blindly, forces greater than I push me, the demon is in me, to tease. Heinz will be jealous, he saw Gonzalo. Gonzalo said: "Here on this same couch we kissed, why not you and this man?"

I am weeping because I feel the demon, the woman playing havoc, destroying, so strong, destroying my own peace and happiness— pushed—great outgoing impulses. So soon. Gonzalo, can't you help me, keep me, lock me up, possess me? I don't want this any more than you. We are kissing passionately. Perhaps I did all this—during this moonstorm which awakens all my hungers, my appetites, because I feel separate, and jealousy and pain bring collision, and when madness divorces me from my love, real and warm, nothing but such scenes can answer this tumultuous need for havoc, collision, and so now we lie kissing to resolder, and it is near. Henry was near last night, I have his sperm in me, I laugh. Gonzalo dipping his fingers in Henry's sperm, and being jealous of Heinz, and while Gonzalo slept I went to read Heinz's letter, a love letter.

Letter to Djuna Barnes: I have to tell you of the great, deep beauty of your book *Nightwood.* The last half, above all, moved me so much that I am almost afraid to write you.... I have been truly haunted, murmuring all kinds of lines from *Nightwood.* Haunted really by the emotional power, the passionate expression.... To write to another about a book she has written is like addressing someone in another language. I would like to speak to you in the language of creation. Perhaps the book I am sending you, my *House of Incest,* may tell you even more why I love *Nightwood* so deeply. I mean it may tell you more of how well I could touch its meaning.... Outside of what I write I do not exist or, rather, do not manifest myself. If I speak to you in a letter I reveal nothing.

I can say I understand *Nightwood,* but cannot make you feel the current which it set off. When one writes, one only wants to know if this phrase rushed through someone else's being with the same warmth, meaning, power it had in flowing out of you. . . .

I am not the only one. The person who gave me your book is young Lawrence Durrell, who has just written a magnificent book. We talked about you, praised you warmly, extravagantly, and for a whole week Djuna Barnes ensorcelled us until we said we must write her. It was an obsession. . . .

AUGUST 23, 1937

*M*Y TRAGEDY IS THAT I LOVE DEEPLY BUT I CANNOT live with anyone. I don't yield. Part of me always remains Anaïs Nin, rigid, like myself. The desire to be *with* Henry, to amalgamate, the concessions I made, the compromises, the abdications, they kill me. I want to be with Gonzalo, be ONE, but I cannot altogether. The work at the press, done so stupidly, foolishly. He cannot organize, foresee, therefore confusion, four times as much work, wasted effort. The immediate thing he cannot do. He has to circumvent. Very well. Gonzalo is Gonzalo. But I can't work that way. So I come home, run away, as I ran away from Villa Seurat. I am the man here, with a certain logic, a certain pattern of intelligence, an urge to create and realize and fulfill, which is a joy and which is constantly blocked by my harem. I have to have a press of my own, run it alone.

I have doubts about people who say: I talked, lived, like Montparnasse. As Heinz says: "When I was poor and worked in restaurants I thought and felt like those I worked with." Not me. I was never anyone but myself when I posed or modeled. I could not be. I play roles but they resemble me, no one else.

Funny, today, after days of chaos, I awake strong and firm. Full of austerity and plans, determination and rigidities. I repudiate Henry's magazine, *The Booster*. Reichel, who was being praised by Henry, did not sleep for several nights wondering how he would tell Henry that what he had written about Reichel was crude and Reichel was ashamed to be so crudely "boosted."* Crudities.

As to politics—I'm through. Too immediate for me, too ugly, too homely, petty, and false. I shall try to open the path to the literature which should be born of the revolution, I must live ahead, walk ahead, live in the future—with a vision. I have plans to start the new literature—one beyond all laws, as all great artists were. This should be the moment for great creative amorality.

Gonzalo's character affects, subtly and destructively, our sexual life. He arouses me often, and then dies inside of me with inhibitions, fears, anxieties. A sudden jealousy, a fear of making love after meals (because people die of that, he says), postponements, denials, these make me uneasy so that I cannot abandon myself to the utmost and at times I cannot feel the orgasm. I get anxious—will he stop, will he withdraw, will he suddenly pause, arrest himself, and then this death of an unfulfilled desire I can't bear. I hate it, as I hate death in life, any act of death in life. When he comes begging, later, I am cold— the moment has passed. What destruction in his every breath, desire, love, life. As June was. When I said: "I wrote all my letters this morning because I want to feel light and free," he says: "And I postpone making those packages I have to make for days knowing it will weigh on my mind, preoccupy me for days, *as if I sought not to feel free.*"

At times, by contagion, he does the immediate thing, is happy, but I know in an hour he will find another way to tangle himself up, make himself bound, slave, castrated.

———

*In his "Boost for Hans Reichel," in the September 1937 issue, Henry Miller presented the German-born painter, who was admired by Paul Klee, among other effusive statements as "a sort of tiger-flower, now yellow, now pitch black, and if you squeeze him gently he exudes a sort of cactus milk which is most excellent for nursing horned toads, vipers, tarantulas and Gila monsters. . . . The man himself is but a messenger from the heraldic universe. It may take five thousand years or twenty thousand years to establish the truth of this, but you take it from me, it's a fact."

Part of my seduction is that in life I betray none of these feelings; I laugh, I excuse, I forgive, I understand, I tolerate, I justify, I defend, I accept, I kiss, I laugh. Rebellion and criticism only explode in the diary. I am soft outside, and sincerely so, because while I am in Gonzalo's presence his voice, eyes, charm, body, skin, melt and disarm me, make me yielding, adoring, as Henry's laugh, blue eyes, or softness can persuade, lull, and dissuade me. I melt in their arms. I yield. It is only when I am alone that I rebel. Here is both my force and my weakness. I have the strength to BE irrevocably myself, but not to impose this self or live it out. The impossible me is here. The vituperous, stormy me. The virago, the monster, the never satisfied one. Only here. In life, life melts me.

Why do I always ally myself to destructive forces? And combat them, alter them? When I met Henry and June it was the same. I walked into an inferno of dark destruction. Gonzalo too. But I changed them.

There must be some strong *décalage* in me or the moon cycle would not be so violent—so opposite to what I am. The instinct, held down, enslaved, dominated, erupts too violently.

Heinz's letters coming with rock crystals, rose quartz, an Egyptian torso from a tomb. "It is the first time I live something pure, Anaïs. I feel I can see something new in my work. I was nauseated by the world, and weak, and lost. You confuse me."

He is timid, lost, dazed by me. To evade danger of hurting Gonzalo I left Heinz's letters unanswered. I determined not to see him. I knew I did not care because it did not concern me to elude him. I knew I was playing. I am not in it. I like him, his excitement, his tremblings. I enjoy them. I feel my power. I feel I can act as I please, capriciously, mysteriously, unaccountably.

He goes from me to the Princess de San Faustino, with my *House of Incest* under his arm. She sees the book, buys it, writes me a letter: "I want to know you." She is coming tomorrow.

Meanwhile my time is given to the press, to the birth of Gonzalo's new life.

Hugh writes me: Today I got a letter from you which was magical. It was your letter of the 4th in which you start by saying you want me to have you at my side in the moment of my need. It was magical not only for the marvelous phrase but also because I got it as I was walking out of the club on my way down to my first appearance on the witness stand (for the bank). It was a big ordeal—and here I was walking out to testify and praying for one word from you to help me and give me confidence at the last moment, and there it came with just the words I needed so much. The night before I had taken out of my wallet your lock of hair and held it in my hand and felt the magic of that.

I can give strength. How is that? Perhaps my weakness is not so great as it appears here, where I only record the breaks, fissures, tears, and anxieties.

I came back from a walk with Heinz through the wild, isolated place where he lives, almost with the ragpickers. Then the press, then Henry, and always an undercurrent of anxiety. Gonzalo may see me with Henry, or with Heinz, whom I have sworn never to see again. Or Henry will see me walking the streets with Gonzalo's arm around my shoulder.

Princess de San Faustino looks like a simple midwestern American, a woman of forty, uneasy in her role of princess. She came to see me because *The House of Incest* meant so much to her. She must know anxiety and *dépaysement*.

Angoisse. Queer, no one writes enough about it. The anxiety is the drama today. Not the events. The suffering about the incident which never takes place, the suffering of the imagination.

AUGUST 27, 1937

WELL, WHAT A VAMPIRE I AM, WHAT A VAMPIRE. I can't even seduce, enchant, charm, without getting seduced myself. This Heinz, trembling, sick with excitement, unable to sleep. Come now, I ought to be ashamed to turn my full force and magic on him. What a strange night we had. I was free, Gonzalo was engaged, Henry was busy, Eduardo was busy. I told Heinz I would meet him for dinner. My feelings were mixed. I was interested as by something new, unknown. I was nervous because I felt stirred in his presence, but I know it is not love, and he is in love, so I feel I should leave him alone. I wanted to be protected by outer forces from my own weakness. I am angry that he should stir me.

I appear all in white and he is all in white. Why does he stir me? His face is full of softness, of soul, of feeling, they enmesh one. One falls into the softness. He has the laughter of a child. He is feminine. He is full of candor. He brings me two poems, and a green beetle with a gold-rust stomach. I feel very old, very old. I feel Gonzalo in me, and I am clutching at him. A new fear. A fear of losing Gonzalo. How is it? I never had a fear of adventure before. I never held back. When I wanted Donald Friede, Turner, I took them. Then why am I eluding Heinz? I don't let him touch me. His eyes are wine. I close mine. We talk to elude feeling. I am unnatural. If I follow all my impulses, invite Heinz, why don't I yield? Very humorous, having no fear of love, rushing out to Gonzalo, but having a fear of nonlove, because of the nausea afterward, because of the emptiness it leaves, because in New York I lived by these intoxications. I have left the key under the doormat of my apartment because Gonzalo, who was obliged to go to a political meeting, said: "I will be anxious later." "If you get anxious, Gonzalo, all you need to do is to come after midnight, you will find me in bed, asleep." A gift to love. But also a way to escape from Heinz. And there was a moment during our dinner when I regretted this and might have gone to Heinz's studio. Perhaps I am so sensitive to love desire that the nearness of the other's feelings is contagious. I think I suffer from contagion. And so I give the illusion of loving and I am ashamed of the deceit, of the falsity. I come home early, at eleven, because I felt the falsity, the acting. I can give the illusion of supreme understanding, and men think they have found the ONE. I am pushed by another force in me to thus enter men's lives, get near to them, torment them, leave them. I don't say no, because I want to get as near as possible. I like the moment when, without love, I have entered their soul, I see their body trembling, feverish, the pulse of love, desire. My lack of indifference is taken for love. Vampire. I put my finger on the heart that beats faster because I am there and I feel my own heart beating, but do not love. I am a thief. I come in like the moon to hypnotize as the moon hypnotized Heinz one night in the ugliest section of New York. For an hour he was unconscious. His soul was taken out of him, what did the moon do with it, returned it intact?

AUGUST 29, 1937

*I*ACTED LIKE THE MOON, BUT I WANT TO GIVE Heinz back to himself. My own caprice has passed. And I am happy. When Gonzalo lay in my arms yesterday, his heavy head on my breast, and I looked down on him I felt there are things to be surrendered for the sake of wholeness, in giving up a journey away from him. I want to be bound, enclosed, imprisoned. It is Gonzalo who can do it, not Henry. Gonzalo and his fixity.

When I set the little low table by the balcony, when Gonzalo and I sit on pillows, he lays his head not on the pillows but on the rock crystal lying on the edge. He seeks the pleasure of pain. Or he lays his head against the wooden bars of my bedstead.

Eduardo has returned transformed, swimming in a pleasure world, slender, electric, elegant, decadent, sensual, joyous.

Letter to Heinz: I feel a little like that moon who took possession of you for a moment, who took you out of yourself, and then, as you say, returned your soul to you. I feel I should give you back to yourself, should repeat again that you should not love me, one ought not to love the moon. I don't know how to say it but I have to create this distance between us. That is why I said the other night: "We use words to elude something. We used words—I want to—to get outside of the trance, to awaken ourselves." True, I visited you, but if you say you feel me too much then I shall have to vanish altogether. Too near—if you come too near I will hurt you, because I don't belong to myself, I have nothing of myself to give except my understanding of you, my seeing you. Will you take yourself back, away from me?

PLAN: WRITE *MILLE ET UNE NUITS,* of all the moods of desire, love, all the moods of physical fusions, complete, total descriptions physical and emotional, maternal feelings, "rut" feelings, animal, bestial, erotic fantasies, obscure desires, emotions, moods, unions and disunions, effects, results, contrasts, failures, defeats, yielding, abandon, withholding, fear, mystic trances, furies, jealousies, pains, frustrations, fulfillments, etc.

Talk with Henry. I feel he is created now, as a writer. He is published, accepted, known. I can now work for myself. I will publish the diary slowly.

AUGUST 31, 1937

GONZALO LOST ONE OF HIS FRONT TEETH CHEWING a bone. It made his smile timid, ashamed, even more indrawn than it is at times. For his laugh, like his sensuality, is inside of his body, not open, obvious. But once he laughed openly at something I said, and I saw this hole in the front of his mouth and something strange stirred in me, a kind of desire, a physical stirring as before a sexual opening. I wanted to enter Gonzalo through this aperture in his mouth. The absence of the tooth was like a gateway, breach, vulnerable opening. It made him less entire, less man, exposed, defenseless, weaker. I felt my strength aroused, and this defect in the completeness of his body, this hole, became a drawing, pulling abyss. I wanted to enter it with some knifelike, phalluslike strength.

I have felt this thrust of myself into Henry's weakness at times, his passivity. I have felt myself incisive, active, entering this mass of chaos, of moving sand, this eluding, elusive, frightened flesh, as a man violating the flesh of woman—on strong days. And then, I fall back, and become myself sea, sand, and moisture, and no embrace then seems violent enough, brutal enough, bestial enough. I want to feel the weight, the pressure in me of man the beast, and I sought this violence in Henry's writing, and did not find it, I sought it in Gonzalo's primitivism, and did not find it, for the beast in Gonzalo is frightened, hidden, obscure. It leaps out in erotic drawings of torture, of a woman being hung, or eaten by dogs. Gonzalo is not very potent. The nights of fullness, of extreme sensuality are rare. *"Estoy débil, he bebido mucho."* He feels it and gives vague excuses. He has little sperm, little force. In my Father the sap rising was tremendous. In Henry less but still magnificent. Gonzalo is less rich than any, but his sensuality spreads out more into caresses, the warmth of his hands, voice, kissing, enveloping voluptuous embraces. He feels caresses all through the body and gives them, as women do.

How to render this, magnifying without losing the dynamic, dramatic swiftness. I am aware at times, like Proust, of the most intricate nuances. One phrase for which I wait, which I immediately translate, analyze, expand on in myself. How I detected in Heinz the falsities and weaknesses which enabled me to break the moment of attraction. The magnifying glass is in my hands too.

Diary as notebook: Eduardo's sexual life. Being treated as a woman by his cousins in school. Enjoying it deeply. Later treating younger boys as a girl, taking them from behind, but now ashamed of being taken as a woman himself. Never finding his rhythm because he could not bear to be dominated sexually, felt humiliated, ashamed, and afraid of the pleasure it gave him to be taken as a woman. Fighting to retain his active role, seeking younger boys who reminded him of his sister Anaïs, or of me. Feri gave him the keenest sensations of all. Only the sight of a penis really arouses his. Keeping this secret desire to be taken as a woman, eluding the advances of older men. Rhythm impossible. If an equal, no pleasure. Conflict. Ambivalence. If he is inert and is courted, his pride suffers. If he courts and is rebuffed, the defeat paralyzes him. Seeks boys with feminine backsides, prominent. Without hair on their body. Feri and his life as a prostitute. Eduardo as a boy sucking other boys' and girls' toes under a table, under beds.

SEPTEMBER 2, 1937

WITH WRITING IT IS THIS WAY. ONE SAYS: "I FEEL good, too good. I don't need to write. I want to live." One is inside, enjoying. Life is lived without formulation, without echo, without double. Then one day, without reason, life is split into being and formulation. A filmlike activity runs inside of the head, inside of my head I am writing. It is not analyzing or meditating, it is writing. It is a phraseology accompanied by a sense of the importance of what is phrased (like a discovery) and an anxiety to capture, retain. It comes unexpectedly like a fever, and goes away like a fever. It is distinct from all other activities.

All this month I have been writing in my head, I am coming nearer to the realization of what I must do. I know my role. I know that as a differentiation from man I feel and I know what I feel. I know I have as great an ear for nuances as Proust, but also a dramatic, dynamic motion he did not have. I feel I can detect the weight of a phrase as delicately while running, leaping. I know what it is I must do.

But I don't want to begin, because life is sweet, laziness is sweet, because I prefer to sit and remember my last night with Gonzalo, remembering in the womb his sudden force, the directness of his desire, the hardness of himself inside of me, just as I was writing about a certain feebleness in him. I can arouse his strength.

I have no desire for Henry, but I can't bear yet to lose him.

Writing in my head about everything: Rank, New York, the *impudeur* of Rank's ugliness, the analysis, Thurema, Henry's writing, dead dresses, I do not laugh enough yet, I am not detached.

Humorous, ironic things are happening with the publication of Henry's *Scenario,* which he printed using his royalties. First the Princess de San Faustino said: "A scenario on *House of Incest?* How can that be? Why, *House of Incest* is a sort of perfection in itself, nothing more can be written around or about it."

Lawrence Durrell, praising *Scenario,* said: "One of the parts I like best is about the man oiling the mechanism in his chest, the astrologer scene." These were literally taken from pages I left out of *House of Incest.*

Jessica Hensley, who read *House of Incest* and writes me enthusiastically, however reads *Scenario* and says it changed her life, especially page twenty-six. Henry and I were having breakfast together when we read her letter. He looked up the page and his face fell. It was, as he said himself, almost a literal transcription of my water pages. I hate *Scenario* and I never had the courage to tell Henry. It is the worst and basest product of our association and collaboration. In his hands all my material was changed, the very texture of *House of Incest* was changed. He wrote *Scenario* but the ideas were mine, all of them. He only added Henry-like touches: doves coming out of asses, skeletons, noise, and things I don't like, loud and filmlike, the opposite of *House of Incest.* He concretized it, it smells of *L'Age d'or,* Dali paintings, it is absolutely lacking in originality. A monstrous deformed bastard child born of our two styles and a caricature of mine. And worst of all, to me (and I never forgot the day I received it in New York), it revealed how Henry had not penetrated the meaning of *House of*

Incest, could not.* When he told me about writing *Scenario,* I had a fear: He will take *House of Incest* and take possession of it, devour it. But no—it was a sort of vulgarization of all I had done, even a destruction of it. But it is more comprehensible to people like Jessica, more accessible. It will be read and liked by thousands who will never read *House of Incest* or understand it. It will be filmed, popular. And so I will see this ironic thing, my ideas, my atmosphere, my fantasies denatured and made popular by Henry, signed by Henry, the greatest piece of spiritual robbery I have ever seen. And I say nothing. From the beginning I said nothing. He stole my idea of the mirrors to use in the article on my diary. I am angry at my own sentimental weakness. I feel at certain moments a bottomless giving, an indifference to how much is taken away, but at times I have rebellions and my possessive instinct is aroused and then I am angry at myself, furious (the scorpion eats its own tail).

S E P T E M B E R   4 ,   1 9 3 7

WHILE HUGH IS SAILING FROM NEW YORK AND Henry traversing a fit of solitude, I am learning from Gonzalo the perverse pleasure of scenes of jealousy. I must confess I have learned nothing. It is a poison, a destructive thing and adds no piquancy to sensuality. It begins this way: When we are most happy together, lying in the dark, instead of caressing me, Gonzalo is silent and withdrawn. I say: "What is it, Leóncito?" He knocks his

*Before joining Anaïs Nin in New York in January 1935, Henry Miller had sent her the manuscript. In a letter from Paris, dated December 18, 1934, he wrote: "I too am doing something for you. Before Christmas or Christmas day, I shall probably cable you again, saying that 'Alraune' is on its way, and that it's my Christmas present for you. And I am signing your name to it, and I want you to leave it there—providing you agree with the worthiness of the MS. It is *your* book, your *Scenario.* That I wrote it is nothing. I only rewrote what you had done. I only lived out the inspiration you received and which you bequeathed to me."

head with closed fists. "That image of you and the sculptor—I have that nailed right in my head."

"But Gonzalo, he means absolutely nothing to me."

"All I can say is I am glad Hugh is coming back. I will feel more secure." This phrase arouses my fury. So Gonzalo is willing to sacrifice all the joys we had together because Hugh is away to his security— to ease his jealousy. For this I say things to hurt him, perfidiously, unconsciously arriving always at what hurts him most deeply: "Why don't you permit my seeing Henry as a friend?" I know his jealousy of Henry unhinges him completely. I say this because his jealousy, his fears, his reproaches ("when I met you you had two or three lovers at the same time") arouse my jealousy and my fears. All that I control and transmute rises again to the surface, naked, ugly, my jealousy of Helba, together with contempt for her diseased, degenerate body, her ugliness, and my feeling: Why did Gonzalo love Helba? How could Gonzalo love Helba? My rebellion against Gonzalo's Spanish tyranny, against his emphasis on sexual jealousy ("the idea that any man could caress you, have you, drives me crazy"). Now that I have someone primitively jealous I ask myself: Isn't he jealous of my thought, my soul, my spiritual life?

We fall into a sea of inchoate phrases. I want to reassure him so I deny half of what I told him about my life (at the beginning to make myself interesting, like his friends in Montparnasse). Since I am fully aware that I am lying I am also desperately angry at Gonzalo's doubts.

Then he assures me he saw Turner kiss me at the housewarming party—which was not true (kissing was not necessary, we were occupied by other stronger sensations and he was holding me as tightly as he possibly could). And so I begin again to try and efface his first impression of my accessibility. All the time I feel ashamed at the petty quarrel we have fallen into.

The air is dense, our feelings tumultuous. We say false things, mean things, we don't mean what we say, we dig knives into each other, there is a hostility and a pain, a confusion, a blindness. I hate it all. I hate it. It is a poison. It is a black tunnel of doubts which arouses all my doubts of love, my fears, which drowns our uniqueness, separateness, twoness into the diminishing depreciation of other people's experiences.

Poison. Clouding all the beauty, all selflessness, all sacrifice. The instinct clamoring bestially: You are mine, I keep you—here—in the prison of my fear. Everything I want to forget reawakened. Because I love men of forty, they have always loved before me. Henry being a writer has never let me forget June. Gonzalo being Helba's brother does not permit me to forget her. I even have to love her, which I don't really. I feel only pity.

After all this storm, the appeasement is sweet. We awake broken, and our caress is like life after death. I don't know whether love has grown a root, or a poison that will hasten its death. I don't know whether this exposure of the animal awakens the senses, excites desire. In me it arouses pain, a pain of the whole of life, of all jealousies, all doubts and all loneliness. I feel heavy and without desire. Love appears too different, too full of pain. I choke in the nightmare of the past forever poisoning the present.

Is there an obscure joy in this that I miss, as I miss so many morbid masochistic tastes which Helba and Gonzalo have for defeat, misery, poverty, humiliation, pain, entanglement, failure, little deaths of all kinds....

I look at his face and seek the expression of candor and purity he has at times—and I see cavernous eyes, a wrinkle of dark anxiety, animal obscurities I do not penetrate or share.

SEPTEMBER 10, 1937

WAITING FOR HUGH—ALL BROKEN BY MY LAST scene of jealousy with Gonzalo. His last obsession is that there is a corner of my being into which he has not yet penetrated, that he does not possess. It is where I keep alive my adoration of Henry's work. Now that he feels sure of me physically (it is true, almost all these two months I have not felt Henry but Gonzalo, I have desired only Gonzalo), he is jealous of my admiration of the writer. We were sitting in the Arabian restaurant when he said with fearful vehemence: "I know I possess your body, but I want your soul, your spirit, all of you. I feel you are away from me at times." I got deeply angry, desperate and I left him saying I would wait for him outside while he paid. I walked in the rain, sobbing, because I fear his jealousy, it separates us, it makes me aware of all I want to forget. It shows me jealousy is not blind for Gonzalo's jealousy is justified and yet I feel he is winning, winning, and I sob because he said: "There are those who are born to lose, I am born to lose." Rank's words, but what a different situation. Each day I love Gonzalo more, I feel further from Henry's Taoism, sensual jolliness, and nearer by temperament to Gonzalo's darkness. I sobbed for him, at his pain, at his frustration.

He came out. He pulled me into a doorway so I would not get wet, and kissed my tears, my wet hair, my mouth. I will never forget these kisses. We went home. We fought. I held my ground. I would not repudiate the value of Henry's work even to assuage Gonzalo. He shouted: "You can't admire something I loathe. I loathe him and his work." Then he collapsed. "Oh, *chiquita,* I love you, I love you too much. I'm going crazy with jealousy. I fear losing you. I love you more and more." When finally this storm ceased and we could kiss, he drank my tears, he kissed me desperately. He came in my hand, the little white foam between the fingers. Kisses in which I poured my whole being.

What a poison, what a poison. What a violent, dark way of mingling body breath and tears, a way of penetrating into each other with knives.

SEPTEMBER 11, 1937

A KIND OF AMOROUS MADNESS. LEANING AGAINST the mirror and kissing my own face to remind myself of how it feels when Gonzalo kisses it. Holding my own shoulder and imagining Gonzalo holding me. Opening my mouth in the dark to his kiss. Missing him wildly. While the new radio drowns us in pure music, while Hugh's passion flares and he kisses me with ec- stasy—I hate his mouth decomposed by desire—I am beside myself with desire for Gonzalo—with tenderness only for Hugh, with re- bellion at an evening with the Hoffmans, rebellion at the return of friends, limitations, duties, family. Gonzalo glad I will be surrounded, watched, by Eduardo, Hugh, Joaquin, not knowing I can escape all prisons, but that I do not wish to escape.

Desperate before new problems. Hugh in London but planning: "We will go for a month to the Riviera, you will travel with me." Gonzalo. I lived every moment with him these two months, aware of time passing, aware of the privilege. He only realized yesterday he was losing me, and yesterday he suffered. I miss him wildly and my nerves are knotted. No peace, no serenity, no continuity. The joy of seeing Hugh blurred by Hugh-the-husband demanding. Hugh's ten- derness blurred by the fact that he bores me, his talk bores me. I'm shattered again by too many feelings.
What I write in my head . . .

Proustian minutiae. Why is it I like to use strong martian language with Hugh ("it makes me puke," that "bitch," that "bastard"), which Hugh dislikes and associates with Henry. Is it because Hugh is over- delicate, hesitant, foggy, wavering, and I feel rough, incisive, viril in his presence?
With Gonzalo I am delicate and feminine in my language.
With Henry the same.
I like to shock Joaquin and Eduardo.
What is it to be one's self? I took over the word "fuck" from Henry, used it in the diary against my own feeling. It isn't my word, yet it is the word that applies to what Henry does to me, not Gonzalo. It describes Henry's sensuality. For Gonzalo I found other words. Henry is writing about the "Land of Fuck," and the key word was impersonal.

S E P T E M B E R   1 2 ,   1 9 3 7

YESTERDAY SO DEPRESSED BY MY SEPARATION FROM
Gonzalo, by Hugh's plans for the future. I saw
Gonzalo fifteen minutes. Then I met Hugh and Bill Hoffman at a
good restaurant. While they prepared a cocktail I sat alone, smoking,
thinking: Now forget yourself, drink and eat and forget yourself. And
when Hugh and Bill came back I drank and ate, and the Beaune wine
went to my head, and I laughed, laughed, everything faded, my sadness. I asked myself what was I sad about. I laughed, drank, floated,
swayed, laughing to the last drop of laughter, told ribald stories, heard
ribald stories. The cook sat down with us, we talked like idiots. Bill
sneezed interminably and everybody around was forced to smile at
our gaiety, and I could not walk firmly, and everything was soft and
dissolved and comical. At the Boule Blanche, Matahi, the Tahitian
girl, sat with us but Bill only wanted to dance with me, and we danced
so tightly, the place so packed all the backsides rubbed against each
other, Negresses, Mulattoes, Whites in fucking poses, sometimes three
of them glued together, a man and woman dancing together and a
Negress dancing against the backside of the man like a monkey on
top of a dog's back, fucking gestures, everybody sweating, mouths
open with excitement, eyes swimming, Bill's desire against my leg,
fucking gestures, everybody dancing the orgasm and the sliding in
and out of woman, all the penises erect and the women moist, a
Negress taking out one breast to show Bill, a breast with a huge black
button tip like an old artichoke. He slapping their backsides, and his
desire erect and hard against my leg, and I dancing lasciviously with
this anonymous pleasure at feeling a man's desire, an impersonal pleasure, the room reeling, the music like a fucking rhythm, everyone in
the center rubbing sexes, legs, breasts, and laughing and perspiring.
Bill drunk and red-faced: "You're a wonder, you're a wonder, Anaïs,
what a humor you've got." I see a Negro, his hair is long and softly

waved like Gonzalo's, and I feel Gonzalo, but he is far away with my sadness as I am reeling and dancing. I can't catch up with him standing there as he is not moving and I can't stop moving, turning like the earth, the earth is turning on this pivot of erect sex, and the womb is flowering and opening around it like a roof. I am turning and giddy, so giddy I can dance but I can't stand still and my sadness with Gonzalo is standing fixed somewhere and I pass like someone on a merry-go-round who cannot slip his finger accurately in the ring of my sadness and Gonzalo but the long black hair touches me, the desire of Bill does not touch me, it gives me a female pride like anything alive between the legs, it is always good to have something alive between the hand, or legs, a bird, a mouth, a penis, a cat, a hand—anything alive with blood in it, blood in it, I am turning but around the long black hair and the Negro thinks I desire him but I'm dancing around Gonzalo raised in the center of my feelings, his hand on my breast, and while all the backsides rub against each other, I dance and am giddy with wine and love, with my love fixed in space which I cannot touch but which I have drunk—and I can dance but I can't walk, I can laugh but I can't weep, I cannot regret, I cannot feel, the world is turning held on its gongs by long black hair holding me from falling off, my gravity, my wheel, my pulse, like a net of long black hair around my body through which I look at the orgy....

Came out dancing and laughing in the cool dawn.

Gonzalo's jealousy of the art climate around and within Henry so well founded. Gonzalo's effect on my work only like that of a woman inspiring a man with her love, but his politics and my love for him draw me away from my writing. As soon as I saw Larry today, for a few minutes, I was elated and exalted—felt like writing because of his enthusiasm and the interest of T. S. Eliot, who is the first to subscribe to the diary to be published by Henry and who asked to see more excerpts from the diary.*

T. S. Eliot in London had learned about Anaïs Nin's diary through Henry Miller's essay, which would appear in the October issue of the *Criterion* and also, apparently, about Henry Miller's plan to raise funds, by subscription, to begin the publication of Anaïs Nin's diary. In an advertisement in the November 1937 issue of *The Booster,* and via a one-

The other day I saw a little Spanish girl, victim of the war. I wanted to postpone all writing and work with Gonzalo.

I still feel I work for Gonzalo and not for communism. I am not one to work for revolution, no matter whether they are right or not. I am not a warrior. I can't spill blood. I have to work in another way. I am profoundly disturbed by the condition of the world, the suffering. I can't shut my eyes as Henry does. That is my conflict.

SEPTEMBER 14, 1937

Gonzalo and I homeless, wandering in the streets, hungry for caresses, I drawn by his mouth, his odor. On the little café table I place two boxes of cigarettes in the shape of a canopied bed like the one in *Nanankepichu,* with two pieces of sugar. Gonzalo fixes a table with a cigarette and a piece of money. And we sit there longing for *Nanankepichu,* while the rain falls outside, the whores pass by under their umbrellas, and we are sad.

This morning I walk with Eduardo into the surrealist exposition and we talk with André Breton, who is coming to see us Friday evening. Eduardo has not been able to live in a pleasure world without deteriorating and losing part of himself. He is obsessed with clothes, perfume, vanities, his appearance, with the places where one can get beautiful boys, with smart restaurants, smart people. I can enjoy these things without being affected by them. He says: "How does my hair look? I think it was cut too short. Do you think it was cut too short?

---

page flyer, in English and French, Henry Miller announced he would publish the first volume, *Mon journal,* in the original French, in an edition of 250 signed and numbered copies, at one hundred francs, one British pound, or five U.S. dollars, respectively. Checks should be sent to him at 18 Villa Seurat and "in the event of a world war or a universal collapse of world currencies all monies received will be refunded at par."

Does it look mousy? Since I am elegant everybody loves me. Do you think Breton will really come? I think he will come because we are well dressed." At this I nearly murdered him. He talks like the people he lives with, shallow.

SEPTEMBER 16, 1937

*M*Y LOVE FOR GONZALO NOW A PASSION. FINALLY the body enters the other's body, the flesh is married. Separation from him, agony. Yet everything separates us: Hugh more clutching, Helba's sickness, having no place to meet. Finally last night we took refuge in the little Peruvian hotel where we met before—and then I did not respond fully, though I was terribly desirous, ravenous for him.

With the Durrells I live, as with Elena, my love for Henry. Henry is at the center. Durrell, so human, old, understanding, how I protect Henry's playing, and let him use his royalties to get more things published when he should use them to live and relieve me of the strain.

No one knows of my love for Gonzalo, yet he is the warm, the alive, the frenzied flame in me.

Of course, I cannot work. Eduardo comes. Nancy and I hunt for apartments on Montmartre for her and Larry. I run over to see Gonzalo for a few minutes. My days are overfull. Henghes returns, weeping with love and suffering: "I need you so much. I feel so alone. You don't know what I went through when I didn't hear from you." But I don't really care. He moved me for a moment as all helpless, soft people move me. I was only disturbed because he was. I harden against his abandon.

Now I want to lie in bed with Gonzalo all day and all night, meet Henry in space for creation, in an Arctic region.

The moon cycle poisoned me for days with a fear of losing my *home.* Hugh, the me, the fixed center, core. He will live in London. He, my home, my refuge.

SEPTEMBER 20, 1937

YESTERDAY MORNING I AWOKE AT HUGH'S SIDE, IN my quiet home, with Janine bringing breakfast on a tray. I awoke anxious, jealous? Of what? Why? I didn't know. At ten o'clock Elena telephoned, back after a month of traveling, radiant with health, beautiful and interesting. I felt: Now is the time for me to surrender Henry as June surrendered him when she left him in my care when she was going to New York to join the man she had been living with for two years. Just as before I had the superstition that passion ends the sixth year, because it ended six years between June and Henry, between Helba and Gonzalo, between Hugh and me. Now I have the superstition that if I live with Gonzalo two years as June lived with the other man two years then I will lose Henry as she lost him. Instead of understanding that my fear grows in proportion to my *own* separation from Henry, because of my love for Gonzalo growing, or the fact that since passion does not help me I can no longer leap over the differences between Henry and me, I imagine other things. That Elena is the woman for Henry, because she is tougher, she is like a horse full of energy, and full of unused feelings, having an empty life, whereas mine is too full. I also think I am afraid to be left alone with Gonzalo because then suffering begins. I give my whole body and soul to him. I will be creatively lonely in my art world. But if I keep Henry as we are I risk losing Gonzalo—my *life.* Gonzalo's jealousy is absolutely inaccurate. My life with Henry is another kind of life, of creation, in creation. If Gonzalo's jealousy is so inaccurate, is mine of Elena equally so? Is she the one who will step into the separateness and space growing between Henry and me? Is this only imagination, guilt for deceiving Henry, neurosis which prevents me from surrendering the old? I don't know. I spent a tortured Sunday, Sunday which belongs to Hugh, trying to make Hugh's Sunday gay, separated from both Henry and Gonzalo, with the vision of Elena entering my life and taking Henry.

I awoke this morning tired and sad. Feeling physically inadequate before the day, feeling like closing my eyes again. In one day I had to look for a room for Gonzalo and myself; see the doctor for my anemia; see Elena, who said yesterday: "I must see you right away— I only came back to Paris for you"; see Henghes, who has waited a week for today; see Henry, whom I evaded last week because it was Hugh's first week here and because I was ill; see Gonzalo at night. We have only been together for one night in ten days. I had to have the Durrells one night for Hugh and Eduardo, Breton one night for Eduardo. Nothing to say about Breton, there is no music, no spark in him. He is all HEAD.

I telephoned Elena. She is ill, so I forget my anxieties, myself, and I think: let fate take care of it. I will stop playing tricks to keep them apart. I say to Elena: "I'm going to live in London." She says: "If you don't live in Paris I will go to Italy. Nothing keeps me here but you." Today she says: "Can you come with me for an X ray as the doctor is worried. I have a lump in my stomach. I am afraid it is a tumor." She has a horror of cancer.

Ever since Hugh arrived, for ten days it has been cold and rainy. Helba is sick again. Gonzalo did not sleep all night. How the world darkens inexplicably, suffocates one. Eduardo hunting boys, paying a hundred francs for caresses. Eduardo very slim, elegant, perfumed, seeking pleasure. I open the astrology magazine: "Peculiar happenings dealing with occult forces or with death may bring about the subjection to very depressive and oppressive unseen forces. The situation is probably only temporary and does not seem to affect you very deeply. Be firm and do not let yourself be influenced too much by the moods projected upon you by your surroundings."

SEPTEMBER 23, 1937

I AM THE ONE WHO LIVES ENTIRELY BY THE MYS-
terious unconscious but who can best under-
stand what it pushes me to do. What I live with Elena is thoroughly
instinctive and I am pushed into it—to become her friend. Why? And
to fear her. To save her (she says: "Your understanding of me is all I
have"), reassure her: "Elena, I know you have not got cancer, all you
need is a lover." To perfidiously advise her to travel and yet traveling
is the only thing which keeps her healthy, it is true what I say, it
prevents her from realizing her life is empty. I tell her I am not going
to live in Paris so she will not either. All the time I am asking myself:
Is it my intuition that tells me Elena is the woman for Henry now—
or my fear of losing Henry now that our passion is over and I love
Gonzalo passionately?

A drama in the imagination. If the stars had intended them to
meet they would meet—as I met Gonzalo. She would only need to
know I love Gonzalo for her aggressive nature to be aroused. And
this is my secret? Do I seek danger, love danger? Gonzalo could not
bear it last night, being in my apartment while Hugh and Eduardo
were at the theater. He was paralyzed with fear of accidents and
amazed at my audacity. It is a gamble—a war. One must be courageous, I said, take risks. Not think of possible catastrophes. I never
think of this. I feel protected, untouchable. I don't desire destruction,
and so it cannot happen.

A day: Joaquin asleep in my bed because he arrived the night
before, breakfast with talk of Venice, his plans. Eduardo arrives.
Lantelme. Hugh. Lunch. Valises being packed for Joaquin's trip to
Spain, Eduardo's to Italy. Elena telephones: "X ray will not be made
today. When can you come to see me?" At three o'clock I have promised to be at the Deux Maggots to see Henghes. I rush over, talk,

leave, see Elena, reassure her, Henry expects me at five, he is resting. I slide into bed, we talk with tenderness, softness. I slip out of bed at six, to meet Gonzalo. All I feel with him is tumultuous, jealous, emotional. I get easily angry, tyrannical, moody with him. Feelings run wild. No control. No holding back.

SEPTEMBER 24, 1937

I GO TO HENRY AND WE TALK ABOUT SAINTHOOD, wholeness, nature, disease, vigorously, marvelously. The universe is expanded, enlarged, rich. The artist is not WHOLE. Only his work is whole. He says about himself all I have written about him. He says whoever reaches an absolute and dies for it, sainthood or Rimbaud's madness, is right. The artist does not die. Henry touched the bottom of suffering with June but he did not kill himself (as other lovers of hers did). I touched the heights of mystical religious exaltation at fourteen but I did not become a saint. I plead for nature now, against disease, I love the full tree and not the tree with one branch. I shun Helba and seek Elena who is expansive, rich. I argue for Henry's life, wide, expanded, against Joaquin's cloister. I say that my year of sainthood was enough. I must go further. For us there is something beyond abandoning ourselves to one wholeness. I said perhaps wholeness for us is a different thing, not like the wholeness of the peasant, a core, but an equilibrium in space, a synthesis we have to reach further, a coordinate, a sky, an earth, memories beyond ourselves. It is not my sainthood I talk about. Mine only helped me to touch, perceive a million sainthoods. I missed nothing—I gave myself to the experience. But not to the point of death. I gave myself to Henry but not to the point of death. THE ARTIST REFUSES TO DIE. Perhaps our wholeness is different, vaster, beyond the personal wholeness. Perhaps that is why I cannot break with Henry while yet loving Gonzalo personally, wholly. I have no personal will in this matter. Henry is creation. I can't break with creation. We talk, blazing—as before—stirring immense perception in ourselves—then lie in bed, and Henry is passionate and tender, and he arouses the little animal slumbering inside of me, rouses it again, and I yield, and am baffled, and say it is wholeness, or duality? I know the human wholeness of my love for Gonzalo. I know this inhuman love bigger than myself for Henry, too. At certain moments they disturb each other. At other moments they exist simultaneously, beautiful, in a breathtaking equilibrium. I feel whole then, by the fact that each one is deep, rooted in the infinite. Reality may come and break the equilibrium, because it lies in unreality, in some other world, some cosmic current, and life is against the widening, this inhuman expansion of the artist.

First talk alone with Larry. He takes my arm as we walk. He says he feels I don't treat him as if he were twenty-six. It pleases him. I say: "At times I feel you are older than Henry. Henry is never aware of the OTHER. Only of himself. I can see that you know others." He has noticed Henry's impersonality, as if detached from all. I am not a part of Henry as Nancy is a part of Larry. No one is a part of him. His relationships are all on a false basis. Larry understands this, sees this, is aware of my feelings. I knew Larry was more human. He could be Henry's son, and mine. He has a sensitivity to the Other which Henry has not. The separateness I feel so much, the one he creates by his deformations, his collectivism. "I believe in friendship, not in the friend." Detachment. He creates distance. Looking at Larry's young face, but old eyes. Awareness, insight, understanding. I know he is near, in understanding. I knew the day I saw him. Young in his playing, his sense of wonder, old in knowing me as I am. I cannot say what we said. It was elusive. But Larry had put his finger right on the drama—his own drama, because he wants nearness. He feels for the woman, he feels my difficulties.

I talk with him and wonder. Are we in the present or in the past? Henry is in the past? Larry understands my acceptance of the artist and my human rebellions and pains. Then I am not altogether abnormal or weak. Are we in the present? I say now, because Henry, as a wound, has ceased to hurt. I am seeking to love him still but I can only do so negatively, through jealousy. I try to relive my love through an imaginary loss, so as not to really lose him. Through Elena. Elena, windmilling, changing her plans every day.

"I have given notice to leave the apartment. I know you're right because while I traveled I felt right. I was well. The day I came home I got sick."

I know I am right. But the pleasure, the relief I felt when she said: "I will leave my apartment," is as keen as what I felt when she went away on her last trip. And that is because I often imagined her receiving Henry in her apartment in which the colors, blue and green, would please him better than my Spanish colors, black and orange. I never say to Elena something that harms her, but I feel guilty because of my inner desire to keep her and Henry from meeting. At the same time her defects: violence, tyranny, selfishness, make me feel at times I am saving Henry.

Watching Gonzalo cross the street, feeling a yearning tenderness for his body, I think: for his sake, I should surrender Henry, because Gonzalo is too sensitive, too whole to be tortured or betrayed. I never imagine Henry suffering because he detaches himself so easily. Just as Elena does. This "Just as Elena does" brings me back to the resemblance between them which I weigh as a source of attraction, which causes me to fear their intimacy. Elena and Henry have the same degree of coldness, hardness, egoism, animality, and appetite.

Elena is like me in some ways—imagination, psychic power, clairvoyance, the power to play, change herself, be elusive, colorful, acts, facilitates the identification. But she has the physical brutality and masculinity of June, she is heavy, awkward, aggressive, destructive as June was. This augments my fears. What drew me to Elena when I should have been repulsed by her because of my jealousy? When I am with her I enjoy the fine interplay between us, color, suppleness, in spite of jealousy. Her brilliancy, her expansiveness, extraversion, mimetism. She identifies herself with me too.

"Are you writing, Anaïs?"

I always say no. I call this breathing. I forget I write every day.

Larry said: "I don't want to disappoint you, destroy your idea of me."

"You can't, what I know is always true."

"Don't get run over, Anaïs, you're unique."

————

Sensuality made our love real, Henry's and mine. With the end of sensual appetite, the creative plane was real. But the difference became more marked, of character, habits, friends, tastes, humors, way of living, philosophy, attitudes in life.

I slide so quickly between contrasting atmospheres, I find myself in one day in such different places. One moment I am in a cheap movie house with Henry, with smelly workmen, monsters of all kinds, apaches, a movie near Alesia in which the water closets all have holes in the doors for voyeurs. One moment I am with Hugh, who likes to have tea in refined places. In the café Deux Maggots with Eduardo, Henghes, Breton. In Mother's bourgeois apartment with the walls covered with photographs and bad paintings, the place stuffed with bric-a-brac, lace over the table, doilies, unmatched pillows. Next I am in the rue de Lille, where communists are studying a plan to expose the capitalists.

Incidentally, here I could have played a diabolical role—I didn't because it could ruin Hugh. Gonzalo needed a piece of information to complete a statistical "case" which I knew to be among the bank files (information concerning investments, which families in France owned what industries, etc.). Hugh's secretary is communistic, and more loyal to me than to Hugh. I could have had the folder from her.

The next moment I am walking with Larry. I never give my dress time to lie still, to get tired, the wind is always blowing through it. A dress like a tide, always in movement. I lie in a strange hotel room with Gonzalo. With a hunger for his warmth, his body.

I will never be able to describe the states of *eblouissement,* the trances, the ecstasies produced in me by lovemaking. More than any communion, more than any creative joy, the infinite for me lies in the unity achieved in passion. The only moment when I am at rest, when I really feel I am breathing, that I can sleep, is when I lie entangled with the one I love. That is the summit, the grace, the miracle.

In all the creative ones, Henry, Larry, me, there is an order. In all the uncreative ones, Elena, Gonzalo, June, there is chaos. Henry's order is now a mania. I cannot displace a spoon in his studio. Being all in the present, instantaneous awareness does not mean wholeness. I have it. Rank did not believe in my wholeness. Larry says my idea of wholeness attained by an equilibrium between duality is not a true one. All I do is not break the final cord. But I am near insanity always when this equilibrium is menaced by a loss, a cold mood of Henry's, or the sickness of Gonzalo, or Hugh's departure for America.

As I won't stop living to write, I can only fill the diary. Joaquin arrives this morning. Mother at two. Henghes telephones. Nancy comes in a moment. Hugh is home. It is a windmill. Larry accuses me of being more chameleon than he—after seeing me one evening at home with Hugh and Eduardo. No longer, he says, the woman who can take care of herself and others, but a girlish person one feels like serving, helping, protecting. The sacred youthful idol, helpless and out of a dream. He could not recover from the contrast. He started to talk about putting me in a play, a labyrinthian idea he had. I said if you put me there I will stop acting in life.

The truth is when I laugh at my transformations, I am at the same time a little tired of them. It seems to me I traverse a hundred quarters a day, breathe so many airs, am so sensitive to the changes, suffer from dualities and triplicities, ask myself what is it I can talk to Larry about that belongs neither to Gonzalo nor Henry, and who is the Anaïs who talks to Henghes and whom he believes he knows, the capricious inaccessible one who refuses to be touched? Tired. Yes, this is not wholeness except when the feelings speak strongest. If I have two hours of freedom there is no hesitancy. I rush to see Gonzalo, but when I leave him to meet Hugh for dinner I am torn asunder with regrets while I think about the Villa Seurat and weep because I don't understand the natural cause of the end of a love. I do not say it is natural, the natural death, I ask myself who has caused this, Henry or I. I am saying good-bye to Gonzalo and I say it is not that I am indifferent to the greater dramas, but that drama is everywhere the same, and it is not my destiny to live the drama of Spain, the simple one, death, war, agony, hunger. It is my destiny to live the drama of feeling and imagination, reality and unreality, a drama without dynamite, without explosions.

When I was fifteen I identified myself with war and sainthood, masochism and humility, heroics and tragedies. Now it all happens in another world, in myself, and myself is an artist who remembers each day more what each day of my life touches in the past. I leaped beyond war—the drama that hastens death, accelerates the end. Perhaps it is a greater agony to live this life in which my awareness makes a thousand circles while others' makes only one, my span seems smaller and it is really greater because it covers all the obscure routes of the soul and a body confessing themselves. It is my thousand-year-old womanhood I am recording. It would be simpler, shorter, swifter not to give this deepening perspective to my life, and lose myself in the simple world drama of detective-story intrigues and crimes.

I am not a pathological liar. I do not lie out of compulsion or disease but with lucidity and intelligence to be able to live the life of my feelings, instincts, nature, without destroying. It is the only solution I have found. Naturally there comes a time when my lies cause new lies and I get enmeshed. The change of life, Hugh leaving for London must cause a denouement. Elena appearing also causes me to live the drama spiritually, ahead of its dramatic timing. Forces me to admit my relationship with Henry has died, or become unreal. Love of Gonzalo also forces me into liquidation of the past. When Hugh leaves Gonzalo will discover my nights with Henry (how often he nearly discovered them while Hugh was in New York) and Henry will discover he cannot enter freely into my house, he will discover Gonzalo. Elena entering into my life is also a denouement, because she can discover my lies if she is intimate with Helba, or with Henry. I do trapeze work to keep them all separate. But it cannot last. All I know is that I have no joy in being with Henry. But if I imagine myself alone with Gonzalo I feel artistic loneliness. Maybe that is what I need, to be alone in creation. Near in feeling to someone. The joy Gonzalo's body and feelings give me are my only reality. When I pass my hand all over his body, and finally he takes me with frenzy, I feel joy. Human joy. His emotions are like mine. His nervousness, restlessness, sensitivity, quick awareness, insomnia, doubts.

I have gone beyond enjoying arousing desire in man. There was a time when I liked that. There is always a man I can fire sexually. I do not care. Henghes's desire I destroyed. I transported him on a plane of intelligence. With humor too. I said I would not permit him to enjoy his suffering, despair at realizing he was not the successor of Henry. I destroyed his mirage. His feelings were real. He had not been exalted over anyone. For seven years after he lost the wife he loved. Then I opened his eyes. I let him feel my strength, which is not obvious, I made him drop his softness, and he showed his analytical power, his psychological games, dramas. I forced him into a mental world where feelings were excluded. "I love someone, it is not Henry." He charms me, but I do not trust him. I feel an absence of core. The mimetism and adaptability. In the taxi he laughed his feminine harp laugh, as Larry calls it. I lost interest in him because his falseness is different. It made me think of mine and its trueness.

I left him standing in the rain and ran to meet Gonzalo, whose warm kiss made me whole. Another night in a hotel room. But the reality of warmth, nearness. In the dark he feels the same. His eyes are alight with feeling. Everything else I can do without, but not this feeling. He falls asleep, and then I am gnawed by loneliness again. Why? Gonzalo is in my arms, asleep. This must be my madness, this solitude must be self-made. I am lying alone, puzzling the meaning of things which do not perplex Gonzalo, gnawed by feelings unknown to Henry, troubled by questions neither Rank nor any philosopher can answer, writing only a diary which Henry says should be nailed with a big nail against the wall of his studio muted forever, and I ask myself is it fear in Henry, is Henry personally afraid of the diary as my sole mystery?

Is there possibly another reason why everybody is against it, one that is not purely ideological?

Larry was here today. Larry divided between Henry and me, sharing Henry's hardness, laughter, masculine objective world, and all the time better able than Henry to put himself in woman's place, feeling with a sensitiveness which Henry has not got. After the big talk about, or against, the diary, he feels: Perhaps Anaïs is right and we are wrong. Henry does not doubt. Larry says: "Henry achieves the happy-rock feeling for himself but he likes to hack away at other's foundations. As I go home and hack away at Nancy with a little hatchet—after respecting you and accepting you for several hours."

"That is why," I said, "relationship in general is a difficult and tragic thing. I feel that Henry undermines and sows doubts in me. He only strengthens me by my defenses against his attacks. He does not ever give me the feeling that I can be right for myself as much as he is for himself. He cannot accept my differences as I accept his. If I hack away it is in the diary, never in life."

I confide in Larry because I feel he understands both Henry and me. I feel right about the diary. I won't stop. It is a necessity. But why does Henry attack it? He says I give good justifications for it each time, but that he does not believe them.

OCTOBER 1, 1937

MEANWHILE I COMBED PARIS FOR A PLACE IN which Gonzalo and I could live. I went all through Montparnasse. I walked through the Île Saint-Louis, all along the quais, rue de Seine, rue du Bac. I answered an advertisement for a boat. No response. Nancy said yesterday: "I saw a place you would like." The night before I had dreamed of a little place on top of a hill, in a garden. The little house I wanted. But it had no bath. Only a hallway full of showers. I walked under the showers and was annoyed because they wet my hair (I have always been against showers because of the wet hair). I saw my house very clearly. So yesterday afternoon, although Gonzalo had coaxed me to stay at the press, although I could have helped with the work, I tore myself away and went to Montsouris. Then Nancy said: "I have seen another little place you would like." And I went to see it.

It was a little house, a little studio, kitchen, and shower in a garden—built by an architect behind his own home. Or being built. It was a dream. With a separate entrance through a garden wall. A little peak-roofed studio with a front and top light. A piece of garden. Tranquility. I was crazy with joy. And only three hundred francs a month. I went to see it with Gonzalo. He loved it. He loves the shower (he has no bathroom in his apartment now). We move into it the fifteenth of October. I said to Nancy: "I am not taking the place. It was too small. It is already rented because I did not go at twelve as I had promised." And thus the secret was established. I forgot that in the morning I had determined I should live in Montmartre to avoid encounters with Henry. This place was too unique. I thought ironically: Well, it was fated to make my life more difficult. I am so near Henry and the Durrells, I skirt tragedy. We are so near to each other. I will have to go out with a black widow's veil and an old woman's dress. I will have to buy a mask. What a game!

I love difficulties. But really, was it not ordained. I console myself, smiling. Good. We all live in the same quarter now. It will be easier. Fewer taxis. When Gonzalo leaves me in the morning, I can walk around the corner and see Henry. Less traveling back and forth. All I need is to bring Hugh near and soon we shall all live in the same house and I will have to slip in and out of keyholes. How delightful! Truly. I will get myself a costume. But Gonzalo knows my walk from blocks away. Such a lovely little house. In such a dangerous place. Difficult to keep my secret as I had to keep the secret of *Nanankepichu.*

OCTOBER 2, 1937

WHEN I THINK OF SUICIDE I THINK ONLY AS AN end to sensibility. That is my disease, my only disease. That is what brings me near madness and that is what isolates me. I isolate myself. I find happiness only in the first flare of passion when it is new, when the man surpasses himself, is exalted, aggrandized, isolated, when the world and reality are pushed aside, man and woman confronted, united.

Then comes the world around the being one marries—his other selves, appearing in relation to others, a smaller, poorer, nearer, cheaper self. Then comes the spreading, expanding, and thinning.

Then comes the death of the personal self-relation. I ask myself insane questions: Did my love for Henry die a natural death, or a death hastened by either my abnormal sensitiveness, which makes life intolerable, or Henry's insufficiency as lover, friend, near one, personal human being? I get confused by my inacceptance of death. I say: If it is my fault I can become gay and indifferent. But I find Gonzalo. Yet now Gonzalo (since I love him) has the same capacity to hurt me. He goes from his political work to me, from me to the Dôme and friends like Henry's—or worse. The realm where we meet, touch, is small. His political work seems insincere (he is sincere but not the others), worldly, prosaic, immediate, empty of any great faith or élan. His café world is like Henry's.

Is there something wrong with me? I live too much in the same level, climate. Against all the reality of these men (the vulgarity of Rank, the ugliness of Henry's life, the emptiness of Gonzalo's head) I try to build a small inner sanctum (*Nanankepichu,* Shangri-la, the little house). And I am alone in the creation of an absolute. That is the solitude. Everything is against me, the outer world, the political world, cafés, the air of disintegration and idiocy we breathe. Every five minutes these two worlds collide. Henry brings Joyce, the showgirl, Fred, and Fraenkel to Louveciennes. Gonzalo is with me a short time and the rest of his life I don't like. This I can solve by work. I must work, or I will break my head against these walls. But work means the diary and the diary makes me suffer, to reread or to rewrite. So? I must find objectivity, distance, indifference. As Henry found it. How? Where?

Letter to Lawrence Durrell: I was thinking of all you had said the other day and I wrote pages *d'un journal désincarné*—meaning "disembodied." I thought I could disembody the journal, draw mysterious aphorisms, maxims, morals out of it. I mean for [T. S.] Eliot['s *Criterion*]. Impossible. I have two more numbers [of the *Criterion*] for you to read. I hope you will call soon. You were so accurate the other day.... I have a sort of prophetic hunch that, without any heavy responsibility, you might pull me out of my too dark worlds (do not fear this role, one's effect on others is beyond one's self or power to alter) and perhaps I will be the one to give you the courage of your strength, of exploding. You can talk all you want about the version of *Hamlet* you want me to write (and now I understand better that it was a prescription for sanity and painlessness you were giving me, for the great classical relief from terror and pain), but what I really understood is what you gave me—whatever that is, I don't want to dissect it, but I am grateful for it. There are no solutions, there are displacements. Something in you helped me to displace myself and I breathe better. Thank you. Perhaps [it is] the old idea of faith.

I never took surrealism seriously. Today Henry and others are beginning to see its falsity. The visit of Breton was the last confirmation I needed. Breton's attitude toward music, his hatred of it, his deafness, clearly betrays the intellectual *fabricant,* the man of the laboratory.

Henry has no sense of values. That is one of my sufferings: I see ahead of others. I see too clearly. The reaction against surrealism was born today.

My next vision is the literature that the revolution will give birth to. I will define it, I will lead men into it, I will point the way. I know what it should be spiritually. I am not deluded by the mass literature, by the masses waiting, or by the revolution itself. The literature it has produced is propaganda. Writers are blinded by the workman—as all poor artists are conscious of the public. They think that to write about labor troubles, factories, workmen, is to be universal. Whereas it all lies in the true unconscious content, or nature; in direct expression or sincerity; in trueness to the self, to the *nature* in the self, the abolition of the intellect as a guiding motivation, the end to the action-paralysis of the neurotic. The writing that breaks with the conventional frames of religious dogma (but unites with God), of the forms of marriage (but describes love of which marriage is one of its aspects, or expressions), that breaks with all conventions and leaves nature free, gives the great amoral creative laws of the artist, awakens in the people the self-discipline inherent and manifest in the artist, touches in each the self which by its sleep alone permitted the slave and martyr, awakened to a new psychological liberty—that is the writing of tomorrow. Revolution is only a symbolical burning down of man's fetters. But the artist must do the delicate individual *horlogerie,* the clockwork to put the soul in tune with the external revolution, or it will remain a gesture. The artist must help by mysterious routes of language to formulate and arouse that which the soldier and mystic have violently inscribed in the sky with flames and blood. Each cell of the soul fettered by its own weaknesses must be made to breathe, touch, and walk into a vaster world. A man enchained and liberated is still full of fears. The word alone will free his soul of fear. His chains are visibly broken, but it is the artist who has to open the new skies, chart the land this man never saw, open his eyes to the new air and space around him, and the possibilities of a new world. When writing itself bursts the bounds of repressions and hypocrisy—of fears and taboos, he will melt with a world that does not block his expansion, defeat his dream at every step. The poet must express not the real chains being broken or the acts of the revolution itself but cause the vision which gives man the strength to leap out of his fears. The revolution in fact, in reality, must be made with the men who handle matter. The artist must nourish and breed the invisible one, but not with the same language of propaganda, not with the same elements of reality. The spirit demands its own food, in other terms. It was never satisfied with a language of economics, of the factory, of the bureau, nor of intellectuals.

Larry and I walking around Parc Montsouris: "Your diary is really tragic, the most tragic thing I ever read, more terrible than Nijinsky. Henry loves you so much, too much almost...."

I had gone to Henry that afternoon rebellious over his impersonality, brooding the kind of storm which Larry's understanding dissolved, a storm against my own tragedy and for which no one is to blame. To be talking with Larry about the diary and Henry dissolved my pain and I felt the illusion reestablished. I rushed back to Henry ecstatic. Feeling near him—I danced around him. Henry himself had said once: "If you lived with me you would not write in the diary." I reminded him of this. I said: "Let me give myself to the diary, wholly." I believe Henry fears my portrait of him, so I told him what Larry said. I even told him: "If you were not so busy writing you could have kept me right here, but I had to flit about, being alone." Then I cooked dinner. Henry lit the stove. He set to work on *Capricorn* and I read.

I felt a great tranquility—my illusion: Gonzalo was there, hot and near—life. Henry was there, pale, and in another world. I remembered the night before—I could not sleep. Hugh was asleep at my side. I had burnt my eyelids again with the sunlamp and I imagined them growing worse, spoiled. I felt a kind of fever in my blood. The moonstorm coming soon. Life so difficult, hurting me, and I shrinking away and getting far away again because of the sickly sensitivity. Would I return to Henry the next day, the Durrells, the art world in which I do not altogether belong? Reality. The pictures of burlesque queens on Henry's walls. Sensual life. He writing about sex, blind to all but sex, writing like a maniac about sex, become animal, an animal madness. If I go on this way I will be all alone. I must close my eyes. I must not always rebel, discard. I create my own isolation.

Suddenly, abruptly, I felt God, as I felt Him at the hospital. I felt this God taking me tenderly in His arms, holding me, putting me to sleep. I felt protected. My nerves were unknotted. I felt peace. I fell asleep. My anxiety was all dissolved.

The winter comes, invading all with gray mists. The city is blackened, smoked. It strikes melancholy in me. I want to hide. That is it. I want to hide somewhere. Larry says: "The more you struggled, of course, the less you liberated yourself." But I should have answered: "Don't you see, if I don't struggle then I want to die. Struggle relieves me, gives me hope. As soon as I lie still I get desperate."

Moricand's talk is spherical, making enormous ellipses, to prevent anyone from coming any nearer to him.

Why do I always seduce my doctors? I walk into their offices quite humiliated by some affliction—and I spread enchantment and magic. Dr. Dausse, taking care of me, drops his injection needle to talk to me about Hindu philosophy and to insist that I see Le Vasseur to answer my desire for body expression. The room is filled with art, the dance, philosophy, literature, and magic. Poetry triumphs. The injection is over. And the doctor is cheered.

Le Vasseur. The body free of imposed techniques, encouraged to make its own gestures. I believe in intuition and spontaneity. Dancing technique sometimes hampers the individual. Of course, visionary eyes, and all he says corresponds to what I need: I cannot adopt a dance technique. I want to dance, just to dance, to move freely, myself. Let's try. Writing alone is not enough. I have to use my body.

I want really to live in seclusion with my lovers and writing and dancing. I have nothing for Henghes, no more strength, interest. I can't give more. I have to build a shell around my life, because now I am like flypaper catching people everywhere. I could people an island with those I ensorcell.

Today I took care of Henry, who has a bad throat. I push Henghes away. I adopt the Le Vasseur gesture work. I meet Gonzalo to drop into caresses.

Le Vasseur says: "Life is dynamic. Why do people want to stop its movement, out of fear?"

I'm going to dance away my fears.

O CTOBER 8, 1937

Y ESTERDAY MORNING WHEN HENRY AND I AWOKE and I discovered he was sick I stayed with him. At ten o'clock I went out to get breakfast food. I served breakfast and I went out again to order coal, to telephone Hugh and Gonzalo (Gonzalo was not at the office and not at home). I walked to *Nanan-kepichu*—the little studio—to see how the work is progressing. Came back to Villa Seurat with provisions for lunch. Meanwhile, at the same time, Gonzalo, moved by an obscure intuition, was looking for me all around here, he walked the same streets, and we did not meet. He did not meet me with my market bag full of food for Henry.

In the evening when I met him he told me this. I was amazed. I said: "You're very intuitive. I was at Montsouris but to see our little house, and how the work on it was progressing."

"It isn't intuition," said Gonzalo, ironically. "You're always going there, it's a question of hitting it right always when you say you have been there." But I felt a real shiver of fear and at the same time amazement. God is protecting me, there is no doubt of it. He does not want anything to happen to hurt anyone. But what shall I do? Changing quarters does not improve matters. On the contrary, the studio explains my presence in Montsouris.

I have never been able to describe the spiritual mental legend contents of certain nights with Rank, nor the creative mystery which made them possible. Whereas it is Henry's caresses, Gonzalo's caresses I remember, I cannot remember one single caress of Rank's. I know he possessed my soul for a moment by his penetration of it. The voluptuous joys I experienced were those of being completely understood, justified, absolved, as by a god. There were times during our last weekends when I did not want to see him anymore, when I went to meet him against all my desires. I used to arrive at Pennsylvania Station feeling clearly the rebellion of my body. I felt closed, my mouth felt disgust. I used to stand before the windows of the shops to delay the encounter. Once I saw one of Hugh's aunts passing. She did not see me. Another time a friend of Katrine Perkins. These encounters I made use of when I met Rank to justify the irritation which his intensity caused me. He always came out of breath, perspiring and nervous. His physical *élan* toward me was heavy, possessive, hysterical. I could not respond to it, and I would be reserved, explaining lamely: "I have just seen Hugh's aunt."

We would get into the train. It would be lunchtime. The soft Negroes served us, and among them Rank seemed like a graceless, inhuman animal moving inharmoniously. The Negroes served the food which Rank devoured like a stone Buddha opening jaws which could not taste, jaws of stone, to the huge offerings of the faithful. He always ate ravenously and as if he did not taste anything. A mummy. His body the color of death. But full of nerves, full of energy, and in my presence flushed with a momentary life that was not life but lust, appetite, desperate appetite.

My body was sullen.

He would always ask me what I had been doing during the week. And at this moment his magic would begin to operate because no matter what I told him from the most trivial: "I bought a bracelet," to the most important for me: "I am so happy, I got the dancer a job," or "I wrote a page on minerals for *House of Incest*," Rank would immediately pounce on this fact with a joy he did not have for the food and raise the fragment to a brilliant, a dazzling, complete legend. The bracelet had a meaning, the minerals had a meaning, they only revealed more clearly this divine pattern by which I lived in which Rank alone could see the whole tapestry. He would repeat over and over again: "You see, you see, you SEE." I had the feeling that I was doing extraordinary things. When I stopped before a window, and bought a bracelet, I carried in me the entire drama, past and present of woman's slavery and dependence and bonds. In this little obscure theater of my unconscious, the denouement which I brought about when I spontaneously bought the bracelet, urged as I thought by the color or shape of it, by my love of adornment, was more dramatic than I knew at the moment. Here before Rank in the train speeding to the beach, the whole journey, the waiters all seemed to be attending the mystery and the unraveling of its meaning! "You see, you SEE." Not only the bracelet, the lovely moment spent on Fifth Avenue was revived, intensified, but all I had done during the week was like a huge giant camellia of a hothouse flower show, fostered, precipitated by a continuous old *travail* of fever-hot creation with which Rank could trace down each minor incident of my life so that I felt at once like a marvelous actress who did not know how husky, how moving her voice and gestures had been, their tremendous repercussion, but also like a creator preparing in some dim laboratory a life like a legend, and now reading the legend itself in an enormous book, open, carried by many Negroes on slanting trays, served on silver platters, smoking on a fast train going to the beach, and this certainly was part of the legend, this man bowing over incidents, explaining, to marvel always at this miracle which had never seemed a miracle before: my walking along and buying a bracelet, as miraculous to Rank as the liquid turning to gold in the alchemist bottle. The more he talked, the more I poured out stories of all I had done, ensorcelled by the discovery that I had not only covered the earth with multitudes of little acts but that all these acts made so quickly could be illumined like a Host in a ciborium and worshiped for their significance, the very act of their flowering. I would find more little acts down the dusty streets of my enormous life, which touched up by the blue light of Rank's enormous beacon light acquired a new depth, a patina, a tone I had never noticed before. I was at the center of this like a princess of the Arabian Nights spurting forth jewels, exposing a pattern which Rank said was one of the most intricate and beautiful colored tapestries he had ever seen.

What game was this of colored lights played on the most insignificant of all acts? *Nothing was insignificant.* When I lied to Allendy it was not merely to conceal my bond with Henry, but to laugh at analysis, to mock it, to expose its possibility of error by proving I could lie without being detected. And Rank laughed, laughed at my games. Laughed because I would not make things too real so they would not die or turn to tragedy. This he had discovered, to explain my separations from him, my eluding, my sleeping alone, my ELUSIVENESS. He had found so many explanations: I liked play. I did not want tragedy, destruction. I was really a flame. One could not possess a flame.

This flame was rolling in a fast train to the beach. This flame, this valise, this impatient man, reading into my past, into my writing, into all my acts, unable to read that I did not love him, him, this man Rank.

The long sad boardwalk with its noise of feet on wood. Crowds. Discord between sea and voices, between wind and colors of movie advertisements, between shopwindows and sand. Discord. The crowd walking, chewing nuts, cakes, sausages, not breathing, the wind on dyed hair, the salt so bitter on this skirt of the sea's dance, trodden by houses, bold houses which should have been hiding, exposing so aggressively their common facades, open-jawed shops with loudspeakers deriding the hiss of the sea, the wind, announcing sales of furniture, of horoscopes, of dolls. Long boardwalk, a fair of monsters exposed without charge, faces of owls, rictus of walrus, eyes of stingrays. And their families. A hotel like a penitentiary fast covered to order with gold leaf and red brocade, filled with robot waiters. The sea there, discordant, rhythms broken by the radios.

The vast room of all people, anonymous. Everyone has passed, no one has passed. It is a sieve, a wax paper on which no trace was left. The boardwalk full of people has passed through these rooms with a noise of wood. The sea cannot enter. Too many curtains, waiters, bells, signs on the doors, too many mirrors, rugs, discordants, and Rank snapping many words and throwing cigar butts on the sand in jars. Out of the window the sea looks far off. So many Ranks walking out of rhythm with the sea. Soon the fluidic current will be established by talk, and incidents chained together will produce the semblance of a symphony that is only a semblance because it will vanish faster than music, it is only an imitation, it is chaining together with meaning what need never have been separated and should have been continuous like a symphony in the blood. When Rank seeks analogy and premeditation and exults because of the time he ruined himself to buy a statuette of a Byzantine Virgin, he was buying an exact replica of my face. Digging into incidents for a symphony broken by discordances seems to restore a flow between our acts which is only the flow of its meaning but which dies quickly like all the dissonances of the boardwalk being only footsteps carried away by the sea.

Underneath all this was the sea, was my nature which would not amalgamate with his, was my lie, was his blindness to the lie. He was embroidering, he was inventing. The music was not produced, there was passing of our lives as upon a delicate stage with new lights and new shadows, but no music was ever produced, no music issued. It was an imitation of the movements in life—a semblance of activity and revelation. It was a continuous dance around phenomena. And nature, life, the sea, was constantly surrounded and never entered.

The sea was there, in me, churning revolt. Ebbing back and forth away from touch. Hearing only—playing the game in space and eluding touch. The "you" in Rank was this man I did not want.

I liked sitting on the floor after dinner, Arab fashion. Once I laughed so much that I threw myself backward, lying on the rug, laughing. He came over and sat at my side. I saw desire on his face, I leaped up.

Illusion of rhythm given by similar thinking. Rank's philosophy and his own wisdom was mine—I had lived by it. I had lived a life which he alone could penetrate. This coincidence, perpetually explored, was what made our nights glow. His humor which was irony was the kind I shared. What I remember of this interplay in the darkness was a fusion of attitudes. And this alone caused the harmony. At first I did not feel his body. I felt only the passion in it. When this passion became hysteria, fear, clutching, then I awakened to his presence, his physical presence. He possessed my spirit and he tried to stifle me. And because he was so heavy, so obtrusive physically, I was not permitted, as I had done at other times, to take what I wanted only and dance away with it. Great understanding exists only in those who can momentarily efface themselves, become selfless enough to enter the other's feelings. Rank had this. But as I had equally the faculty to make the most selfless people aware of their own needs, desires, I awakened in Rank the demanding, voracious self, the self who did not want to die. "Before you came, everything was unreal. No woman loved me for myself, or was even herself. I created and invented them, and it was all unreal. I did not have to create you, I only helped you to become more yourself."

It was that night, at that moment, when I withdrew from his embrace on the rug, that Rank realized I no longer desired him. He fell into a depression, and lay awake all night. There was no open admission. I could not console him without admitting there was a loss to console him for. So I put ear stoppers in my ears so I would not hear him sigh and breathe heavily, and went to sleep.

OCTOBER 10, 1937

CONVINCED ALL UNDERSTANDING IMPOSSIBLE IN Henry. He cannot understand. We begin our argument on expansion, and he ends by saying exactly what I said in another form, he cannot deduce, he cannot see anything but what he feels for himself. We were expressing again the woman problem (he is baffled by my essay on woman's role in creation). I said Marika

Norden* made herself ridiculous in her confessions because she proved she was a woman who realized she could not suit her rhythm to any man's because she herself had no core to relate to anyone with. Theoretically woman always sits at the center of her being and brings the vaster peripheral activities into the center. I bring all of Henry's philosophies and creations into the core of our life. At the center are my intimate relationships: Gonzalo, Henry, Hugh, Durrell. I never lose sight of those who are on the periphery, do not confuse them with the center. But Henry has no core. I say to him: "I swung into your peripheral rhythms not to sit alone in the center, as all women do—lamenting. It is not natural to me, but necessary."

Henry does not understand this. He denies the reality of all this—but says at the end: "Man's impersonal world masks the personal." He is all confusion. There is nothing right or wrong, bad or good. This nonevaluation comes exactly out of the impersonal attitude: it does not matter who I pick up, who I listen to, everything is interesting, that is, abstractly to the artist, not to the self. I know it is that constant expansion, exaggeration, which thins out his work, empties it of meaning. It is a gallery, a set of types, crowds. Then he says: "We are freaks." I say: "We are not freaks. We are exaggerated men and women—we represent others only heightened. This exaggeration in you (now it is interest in Marika Norden's letters which are obviously cheap, false) is a waste. You are less whole than I am because of that. One painter represents many painters. Many painters represent less than one painter."

I am philosophically against his exaggerated periphery. It is the reason why Henry will never be read for depths but for types—for general experience. He cannot understand at all what I mean. The dehumanization. I have ceased long ago to struggle against this.

I love Gonzalo. Henry may give me the feeling of an enlarged world but by its enlargement it is empty of emotion, humanity, and drama. I entered it. I lived his rhythm. I expanded. But I returned. It leads nowhere. It is thin. His nonunderstanding is linked somewhere with his absence of values and his absence of meaning. Henry

---

*A Scandinavian writer, Megan Vogt, who used the pseudonym Marika Norden on her book *The Gentle Men,* published by the Obelisk Press in Paris in 1934.

is flow—but meaningless. It is dynamism, but sensual dynamism. It is nature. Not the soul. That I know. It is instinct but not feeling.

I sentimentalized Henry. I said his feelings were there, but inhibited, perverted, ingrown. I said sentimental things. The man who creates these books without soul is one with his books. I am his soul. But I work against his pleasure seeking, his Rabelaisian attitude, his receptive wax-reproduction of a whole world of people. That I hate. I won't go any further with him. Now I need not be so baffled by what he likes and seeks outside of me, caricatures of himself, affinities with his own vulgarities, lack of perception, he is as blind to values as he is to the shock of violently ugly wallpaper. He is of the people, and he is returning to the people, burying himself in the very world from which he sprang and which he has wanted to escape from. He never escaped this world, the streets he played on. He was born in the ugly and he will die in the ugly. I thought Henry the artist would swing himself into a new dimension. That was what June discovered.

Perhaps I am writing out of hatred for this man who could still today possess me physically when I am no longer possessed by his created world. I don't know.

He thinks I am talking about ethics, morals. I am talking about core. I'm talking about a center that keeps one faithful, gravitating around a center. What I protest against is not expansion but the exaggeration of it, the malady. Henry wants to get many letters, to meet many new people everlastingly, he is a manhunter, every clue is a scent for him. That is why his work is peripheral, and crowded—not profound. He puts back the street into it. It does not take so many people to say something. This is Wagnerian with all of Wagner's defects. After all, he is of the Wagner lineage. When he said: "You do the same," I answered: "I did it only in self-defense, to catch your rhythm, and be with you."

I am not doing it anymore. I am letting Moricand starve. I am pushing off the peripheral friends. I want to give myself more to those near me. It was like the time I went to New York to take care of my patients I didn't care about and left Hugh, Eduardo, Joaquin to their loneliness and sickness. The impersonal savior. The collective doctor. *Merde!* Nothing is vital or beautiful that is not personal.

Henry thinks he does not lose himself. He not only loses himself, his life as a man, he lost me. He will have to find me in fragments. He deserves to be pushed into a completely fragmented life. He will get a little protection from one, a little passion from another, gifts from one, tyranny from another. That ought to be his fate.

I may be unjust. Perhaps Henry works toward his periphery from a foundation of his work and me. I don't know. Perhaps the periphery masks the core. The woman who loves always gives the best interpretation. All I know is that I love Henry, even after his caresses, with a feeling of unsubstantiality and that I meet Gonzalo and I feel the man and I am glad he is only a man, a warrior. I have lived like an elastic distended by Henry's inflations and this dilation produces only abortion.

In spite of Henry's philosophy I believe it is this defect in him as a man which appears as a defect in his writing. The Wagnerian inflation. I don't believe it is a quality.

Struggle? Why struggle? One only struggles if one is enchained. I am not free. I am enchained. And in my diary I rebel. I must still be enchained by Henry. Or why should I be struggling?

OCTOBER 11, 1937

EVERYTHING LIES IN THE SELF AND COMES FROM the self, Elena's aloofness just as much as my overmultiplied attachments. Since I have known Elena, I have seen her reject life, companionship, exchange. I have seen her create opposing currents to all forms of attachment, resist all forms of lives, assert her independence, selfishness, not give herself, and then lament her empty life. She makes her life empty. She gives nothing. She only likes to enter someone else's life all ready made, as she entered mine, to satisfy her appetite, without paying. She asked Moricand to do her horoscope but refused to pay for it and alienated and estranged him. Then complains that he is not interested in her. She used Hugh and then laments Hugh does not love her. She sent for Eduardo only to ask him for astrologic lessons and marvels why Eduardo (who only wants to be given) runs away from her. She sends for me only to listen to all her troubles and the next day she is healthy and I am tired out and it has all blown over for her. She talked to me for three hours about the necessity of marrying or not marrying so-and-so, only to throw it all overboard the next morning. So I elude her now—when I have work to do or my own life to lead. She is a worthy opponent to Henry's using. So I throw off the chain of Elena's colorful reign.

What she envies, has not got, she cannot create. I am certain that with all the coincidences of Paris life (I did not meet Gonzalo for six years although we knew the same people) if she has not met Henry it is because she has not desired it or magically conjured the meeting, not because I made the separation. Her fate lies in her attitude, the nature of her quest. She does not say: "I want to give myself." She says: "I want to be protected. I want this and that. I want a brilliant life. I want. I want. I want to amuse myself. Enjoy life."

I feel free of all responsibilities toward human beings. I used to believe I ruled or created their lives. But it is not so. I have given Elena all kinds of philosophies, directions, orientations. She has not made use of them, of my knowledge. She is still living on crumbs. She wants me to feed her, fill her life with mine. It is too great a lucidity which arrests my life always. Yes. It is necessary to be blind. I see too much and it creates A PAUSE.

> *Letter to Henry:* I want to try and explain to you, Henry, how it is you make things so inhuman and unreal that after a while I feel myself drifting away from you, seeking reality and warmth somewhere.... You repeat over and over again that you need nobody, that you feel fine alone, that you enjoy yourself better without me, that you are independent and self-sufficient, you not only keep saying it regardless of the effect on me, but you never once make a gesture or a sign like a human being. I can walk in and out, I can stay away a week or a year, you never so much as telephone, or extend a hand to hold me, detain me. Everything in you pushes me away, your collective life, your constant life with others, your inca-

pacity to create nearness in relationship with a person, always with a crowd. I seek on the contrary to keep you at the center of my life, but you make me feel the very opposite, that you are the center of your life, with your work and then you marvel why it is a woman drifts away. My trip alone to New York was due entirely to this feeling you create in me, to this perverse thing in you which makes all your loves so negative and destructive. What a twisted, ingrown, negative love you have. When I read what you write about June now, I feel almost like laughing. You spent your life storming at her, criticizing her, attacking her, denying her self, her value, all she represented (and then you say you love, but what is love but the acceptance of the other whatever he is). You could have made me yield with a sign, but this sign you never made. Remember this: it was never vanity which made me seek to be loved by others, but the need of reality, of humanness. The need of expression and directness and worship one can put a finger on and say: there it is, it's a heart beating, if I move this person feels it, if I leave this person knows it, if I drop away they feel fear. I exist in them, that is life, there is something happening there. But when I walk into your place, I see the most expressionless face, the most vague, negative gestures, the most complete ghostliness. It is not enough to take a woman in bed, you know, human beings were given other forms of expression. I express what I feel, you go out of your way to deny, to blur and efface all manifestations of attachments of any sorts, you harp on the collective, on the principle of friendship rather than the friend, the general "cunt" world. I glance over what you were writing in *Capricorn,* and there it was, the great anonymous, depersonalized, fucking world. Instead of investing each woman with a different face, you take pleasure in reducing all women to an aperture, to a biological sameness. That is not very interesting, I say, nor very much of an addition. It's a disease. It is like a dog in heat. People get in rut, that is understood, and right. But man does not live in a state of rut. Your depersonalization is leading you so far, you are disintegrating so far that it all becomes sex, and sex is a hole, and after that death. Oblivion. My God, Henry, the only personal individual thing that ever happened to you was June, because she tortured you and so she finally was able to distinguish herself from the ocean of women. I am against what you are doing, I see you becoming the animal, like Nijinsky, and then insane. The way you focus on sex is a death obsession. I have pulled you out of this many times. You had such a primitive attitude toward Lesbianism, for instance, did she or did she not sleep with, that is all you knew. I gave you another conception of Lesbianism, the whether she slept or not was not the millionth parcel of what happened with June, to June. And now you are at it again, sleeping with whom, with what, how, and you think you are writing and living an apotheosis, and it is exactly the contrary, it's a downfall, it's a disease. That is where collectivity leads you. You are simply this: an Ego in a crowd. You are in the same danger of being an Ego in a crowd (the ego can only perceive a crowd, he cannot perceive an equal), that is the sign of the ego, because a crowd is a malleable thing, he can identify with or dominate, or dazzle (it is the opposite of relationship). I use your attitude toward me as an example. I am not making a personal plea. I am beyond that. Whatever that insufficiency in you that cannot keep relationship alive, I have got beyond lamenting. I made another life to supplement that. I have nothing to ask. Because I do not believe asking can change anyone. That is your way. Your destiny. But while I am next to you I will continue to shout for the ego and his equal, not for myself, as I say, but because I can see through that god, ego, self, alone-man principle and I will write about it, and fight against it, and every time I can awaken you for one day to the consciousness of another I will be glad for your life as a human being, as a man, one's life as a man is not in the collective principle, the crowd, it is in the friend, in the woman, within one's self. That you never acknowledge, you never make your gestures as a man, a simple direct man who is losing something, unless you are driven by a violent situation. That is why I was so happy that time in New York and wanted to return there because I thought it was New York, it was the only time you became Henry Miller a man, a human being, saying, holding, directly, for himself, pure drama, pure feeling. After that began again this vague world of floating art. And the key to that is Fear. You made an illuminating statement once when you said I brought all philosophy into you, and you said: "But that is dangerous because you can lose me. It's tragic to put Lao-Tse in me, it's dangerous." There you are; fear, fear of the immediate, possibly tragic personal relationship of which I am not afraid. But that is why you also evade tragedy, that is why you attain joy, you make the whole world the simple thing which we feel with acquaintances. We always say: we have a good time with certain people who don't mean much to us, but all of us agree that this good time is not what nourishes our life and those who have only this kind of ephemeral light contact with people, who have a continuous good time, we soon find out their life is empty, they get sick of it, they feel empty and without joy. Fear, I see that in you now, when you sleep, elude, evade, slide away, seek the cafés and the crowds. With you and me I don't understand, because there was no reason for our relationship to be tragic. None, as far as I am concerned. But it has become so for me because you do nothing to make it real, all you do is evaporate, dissolve, decompose it. Volatilize it.

Letter unsent. Pasted in the diary.

Hugh, because he is the man without defects, because he protects and forgives all things, is God-the-father. He was actually jealous of my abandon to God a few nights ago. He said: "I don't like that. I want to be God. I'm jealous."

Hugh is the ideal father.

I love him as such. When he leaves me I suffer. The foundation of my life is not my self. I have given this self to God-the-father and my lovers. I need both terribly because I give myself.

My lovers can hurt me because they possess me. God-the-father in me does not hurt me. I have given him all my faith. I sit here weeping because of my weakness, because I do not belong to myself and when Hugh leaves me I feel weak. I think of church and God to replace him.

This letter to Henry I never showed him. I wrote it a few days ago and when I saw him he was sick and I put it away.

The pause—due to fatigue. But all is made right again by a night with Gonzalo. Gonzalo in my arms and I am at peace. At peace in the soft human warmth of it. In sleep he is passionate, in sleep he turns and nestles into me. In sleep, blindly, he murmurs: *"Te quiero, chiquita."* He loves it when I pass my hand all over his body. He is voluptuous like a cat. He murmurs, sleeps, purrs. All human life is here, in the flesh.

Gonzalo dislikes the vulgar types of women Henry adores. Henry's taste for women is exactly as senseless as all his values. He has no sense of beauty, less sense of expression, and less still of contents. So I feel inside of Gonzalo as really his woman, loved above all. If I come running to him he feels my heart. He marvels at how wildly it leaps without breaking through, making a hole through my body. I marvel at his eyelashes. At the humorous way his cheeks swell out when he talks about contrition, attrition in Jesuit theology. He talks over and over again about his childhood. I know all his early life. He is the man who felt the sensuality of Solomon's song and was not deluded by the Catholic commentary: Christ's love for his Church.

Gonzalo's marriage between sensuality and spirit is like mine. In Henry they are separate. The sensualist predominates. Sensuality alone guides him. The strange thing is how we are forced into creating an unreal being if we are too aware of the other. Henry is himself because he is not aware of the other. I am too aware. It makes me unnatural. I cannot share my work with Gonzalo because it is all about my life and would hurt him. I have hurt him enough with stories about my Father, life with Henry, New York, etc. At the beginning I used to talk profusely—whether to enchant him with the fullness or to reveal myself, I don't know.

I need to live in exaltation because otherwise I fall into analysis. As soon as my life slows down I fall into analysis. Now when I have time I think about Larry. Larry has an understanding beyond his experience. But I feel that he is fluid. He has more values than Henry. But he is impersonal. The personal terrifies him. I want never to analyze again, but I do so to understand, and I seek to understand to be less hurt. Perhaps there is another way to be less hurt—without analysis.

Remember this, Anaïs (written at midnight): NO ONE IS TO BLAME. You are mad with sensitivity. You magnify everything. The smallest incident is enormous. It is your curse and your gift. But BLAME NO ONE. SCOLD NO ONE. No one is to blame for my unhappiness. I can never be happy until I care less. If I cannot bear the caring someday I will put myself definitely to sleep. This is my testament.

OCTOBER 18, 1937

THERE IS SOMETHING DEFINITELY WRONG WITH me. I am no better than June, Thurema, or Elena. Those women who so vividly, so exaggerately prowl in jungles of feelings, a chaos, no philosopher.

One morning I arrive at Henry's and find him reading a letter from "Marika Norden" who wrote *Gentle Men*. Henry never got interested in her or her book, published by his publisher, until Jack Kahane dropped the remark that [the writer, Hermann Count] Keyserling had praised it. (I had told him three or four years ago the exact value and weakness of the book.) Then he wrote to her. She answered that she didn't like *The Booster,* that it was not serious. Henry mocked her lack of humor. But wrote again. This morning he said: "She is a woman full of fire." She had sent a photo and written to please and interest Henry, taking up his playful tone, saying all he wrote was hilarious (tuning up her instrument to his key). Henry said that the photo looked like Greta Garbo and Marlene Dietrich together.

I said nothing. I felt there he is again, charmed by something of no value. I dominated my jealousy and tried to see what I could admire. I reread her book. I said to myself: Be generous, Anaïs. I wrote her what I thought of her. But Henry was piling up his enthusiasm, reading and marking her book (I interpreted all the underlining as sympathy). Today, when I arrived, there was another letter with another photo, a letter full of narcissim, describing herself, really making herself seductive. "I am dynamite, I am strong as a Titan, gentle as a lamb, full of courage. . . . Keep my letters well. . . ."

Then I blew up with jealousy and told Henry I wanted a man I could have for myself, that I was tired of being hurt by his unfaithfulness: "Now that I have accepted your sexual unfaithfulness, I also have to accept sharing you with all the artist women, besides your work, and with the everlasting shadow of June, with the world." No. No. No.

Henry was astonishingly gentle and wise: "Before, Anaïs, I wanted to possess, by taking, putting a fence around it. Now you see, I have learned that one cannot possess that way. I possess you only by what holds us together. It is not that I love less, but with more faith. I have suffered and it is true that I have got beyond fear of pain. But in a sense it is not true, and you know I can suffer—you know that."

"Yes, I know. But you got beyond pain not with June but with me, who wanted you not to suffer. I don't want to get beyond pain with someone else. And you cause me pain constantly. It is in me, I know, in my attitude. I am not quite where you are. I helped you not to suffer. I did not torture you. I did not want to. But you hurt me."

"Unwittingly, then, by my own honesty I show you everything. I don't feel there is anything wrong. As a matter of fact, you jump too quickly always. Marika's book, as a matter of fact, rubs me the wrong way. I'll show you how I wanted to write her really."

"You are easily enchanted, Henry, so easily deluded."

"But you know in the end I always see through sham. I want to help you not to get hurt. You say I do help you. Expansion isn't wrong. I can't see that."

Then I told him what I have come to believe. "Beyond a certain point it destroys the personal. I don't do it anymore because I don't want to lose you. It's like saying: 'I don't travel because I don't want to be separated from you.' These are like voyages. You say you won't travel because you don't want to be separated from me. Yet you're off to Norway now, and I can't bear it."

At this moment the thought of Gonzalo never comes to me. I have the feeling I am in one world with Henry, and in another with Gonzalo and that they don't touch each other, which is the exact opposite of what I am saying to Henry. So—does this mean that for people like us expansion can continue without destroying the core relationship? Henry made me feel this morning his love and attachment for me—to me. He felt me. I knew I could hurt him, destroy his happiness. Each time we have a scene I felt this—his attachment and how all else is appearance. He could philosophize—like an old Henry. I was the younger one with uncontrolled passions—fears. I can't understand—do I love him? This love that manifests itself only in jealousy. Yet I can forget him with Gonzalo. Oh, God, oh, God, I am confused. I cling desperately to Gonzalo, I want him to swallow me, keep me, help me. Yet only his jealousy and clutching hold me, his passion and then what holds me to Henry keeps on living, a vaster world, like an illusion, like art compared with immediate life, like a distant spell, a mysterious and difficult marriage.

I don't know anymore what is love. Love, I said, always was to give. Now I clutch at Henry. Love, I said, was not clutching, but I believe more in Gonzalo's because he clutches at me. I am all confused. What is faith? Did Henry clutch at June because he did not believe in himself or because he felt he did not possess June? Does Gonzalo clutch me because he feels he does not possess me, as Henry has without clutching? I don't know anymore. There is always this abyss of one's faith or lack of faith. Is our faith blind, or is our jealousy blind? Or lucid? Or clairvoyant?

I'm trying to unveil the mystery. Larry says Henry loves me. The world and Gonzalo say Henry does not love me. There is an immediate clutching love and an eternal mystical one. With Henry something eternal was created beyond our passion which outlives it. With Gonzalo all is immediacy, nearness. And sometimes it is the fear which triumphs—presence, physical awareness, rhythm. Sometimes it is the eternal one in space. Then, when Henry and I converge in this vaster span, the smaller one vanishes. I love the presence of Gonzalo.

But Henry during his voyages, his absences, his unfaithfulness, what does he leave our relationship in care of? In care of its inevitability, potency, its survivals, its eternality. I was Henry's victim—he did not want me to be. Just as Gonzalo is mine, Gonzalo who suffers from my greater life—what is not his—what is beyond him. Around the Gonzalo who sits listening to the election returns, counting the communist deputies, floats a woman who cannot remain here, at his side, at that moment—a woman who marries, in space, Henry's last writing on Abraham Rattner, who listens to his words and suffers only because this medium reveals a Henry so far from reach.

Now Henry makes the bed and says: "Let's take a nap. I need it after the shocks you give me. I'm a sensitive guy, you know." We're laughing. He says: "Are you sure you're all right? You won't go home and write me a lightning letter?"

"I'm all right. I only write you when I don't jump. If I jump it is all over."

And we took each other with the usual frenzy.

As I write all this I nearly weep again. And last night I was awake most of the night taking care of a sick Gonzalo. Feverish. Who does not like to be sick before me—who treats me like an idealized mistress, beloved—when I wanted really to shower devotion on him, sacrifice, serve, because I want to annihilate myself, hoping for peace, and because I love him so humanly. I love people so completely, I want to be everything, all things.

The night before I slept only with medicine, because Gonzalo had said at six: "I'm going home to get into bed. I feel I have a bad grippe." I know he hates it when I go out. He lies awake with jealousy. So at nine I telephoned him from home to say I was home and would stay home to please him. He was not home and I left a message. He did not telephone. I imagined he was out, drinking. And I could not sleep. I wrote a testament. Idiotic.

What can I do?

It is very strange to think that I have made Henry wise. I am the one who imparted to him wisdom and psychology and the subtle art of relationship. And now, when he gave me my naturalness, primitiveness, emotionalism, it is he who plays the paternal role. He talks compassionately like a father. Great tenderness. And suddenly I feel the depths, as people feel it in me who are at first (Artaud) deceived by the scattered, profuse, colorful, eternal aspect of my life. Take my letter to Henry—the one I did not send. Read in place of YOU, I; that is, read: I volatilize, decompose, make unreal, and I think we are getting nearer to the truth. But there is alchemy. Henry and I volatilize, Gonzalo and I make real. All this is what Marika Norden does not know.

OCTOBER 23, 1937

PITA AND DÉSIRÉE, THE MILITANT COMMUNISTS, Gonzalo's closest friends when I first met Gonzalo, were slowly estranged by jealousy and envy. Désirée never being able to dominate Gonzalo (perhaps to win him), Pita very fascinated by me, much to Désirée's insane alarm. Envy of the change in Helba and Gonzalo's life. Then came envy of Gonzalo's ascension in politics, of the printing press. Pita turned woman, began to scratch and hiss. He looks so feminine once Gonzalo said to him: "I'll lift up your skirts and give you a big spanking if you continue."

After this they were both given work at the Spanish [Republican] Embassy. Then began an insidious gossip campaign culminating in an open attack: Gonzalo is a fascist spy. He is working for the fascists. He receives money from Hugh Guiler, banker, fascist, he was given a printing press by Anaïs Nin, daughter of the fascist Joaquin Nin. It was a volcano. I offered to declare myself publicly a communist to save Gonzalo. We were both wild at the injustice and irony.

Suddenly all my playing again brought to a standstill before reality. I play with real dynamite, saying I don't believe either side, I believe in humanity, in giving, in love.

This happened simultaneously with my disillusionment with Gonzalo—the impossibility to amalgamate our spiritual worlds, art, and politics. His perversities, loving me with passion and jealousy only.

Wanting me estranged from my friends, alone at home, but just to know me alone, not to be with me. Just to calm his jealousy. A negative love made of fear and anxiety, not of positive elements, being with me, entering an art world, sharing, living WITH. He is full of secrecies and reticences, he hides when he is sick. I can't be maternal and that starves me. He seeks torments, I can't protect him, he prefers to console himself with drink. Again I wanted the impossible in relationship.

I reached a new peak of tragedy, then I threw myself into work. I shifted my position to a less painful one. I really began to work. I have found my way now. Beginning with what I wrote on Rank's talk right here. I went back and found volume forty-five to which it belongs. I inserted it. It means sometimes cutting out one or two lines of notes on the subject and substituting the real description. Again I found a few phrases scattered here and there about the analysis of one of my patients. Cross out scattered phrases and insert fine good solid pages of the patient's confession. I wrote today in a very natural, spontaneous way, very similar to the mood in which I write the diary. I only write what I FEEL like writing, but full, quietly. I also wrote about Fez. I feel satisfied.

Relationship, I mean satisfaction in it, is not possible for me. I am too absolute. I must work.

Today I shut myself in, saw no one, forgot Elena, forgot jealousies of Henry, or Gonzalo's jealousies, forgot people, and wrote. I take Gonzalo's visit tonight as pleasure, a delectation, not the fixed central vital point of my whole day. I am filled with contentment from my work.

Various scenes preceded my discovery of Gonzalo's perversion. Once I met him at six at a café. He told me he was very much depressed. I had been with him the night before and we tacitly understood he had to be home that night. But when he said he was depressed and worried by the treachery of Désirée and Pita, I said: "Let's have dinner together. Stay with me."

"No, I can't." I pressed him a little more, then desisted. After a moment he said: "You're not going to the Durrells'? When you go to the Durrells' I get anxious because they live so near to the Villa Seurat." I was planning to go to Henry's, but I answered: "No, I may go out with Elena and then I'll go home early."

"I'll telephone you later."

"Very well."

"I wish you would go home early. You're getting the grippe, you ought to get into bed."

"Don't be uneasy, Gonzalo, I'll return home early."

"I'm not uneasy now. Later sometimes, I begin to jump with anxiety, wondering where you are. You walk so fast, so fast, so fast . . ."

"Why don't you stay with me?"

"I should be home tonight."

I took the subway and went to Henry's. Henry was with the Durrells and the evening was devoted to his experience with a chiropodist he had gone to see for an advertisement in *The Booster*. Henry was in one of those moods I can't share, wallowing in a kind of humor I don't feel, a sort of broad American horseplay about corns, dirty feet, etc.* He and Fred had been there and had their feet done. What made Henry hysterical with amusement did not touch me. I felt Gonzalo in me, pleading in me, desiring to imprison me. Gonzalo's clutching mood covering me. I felt far from Henry's circus and hungry for solitude and Gonzalo. I left early. Once home I telephoned Gonzalo because he loves to hear me say: "I am home now." He was out. He had not gone home. He had stayed in a café drinking with a friend. Afterward he had walked around Montsouris, tortured by the thought that I might be there. He loves his jealousy, unreality, his

---

*The October 1937 issue of *The Booster* carried an advertisement by "Mrs. Baratta Alexander, Graduate Illinois College of Chiropody" under the headline: "Keep Your Feet Fit for Golf." The advertisement promised "Scientific Treatment of Ingrowing Nails, Bunions, Calluses, Corn between the Toes, Warts, etc. Electrical Foot Massage and Treatment for Fallen Arches." In the November 1937 issue, Henry Miller published his "How to Lead the Podiatric Life," a two-page essay on Mrs. Baratta Alexander, née Lavanda E. Alexander, in which he recommended her not only as "a trained surgical chiropodist" but also as "a trained guide with intimate knowledge of Paris nightlife," and suggested that "should you want to make a night of it with your newfound feet" let her be to you "what Virgil was for Dante."

invented betrayals. This cured me of my desire to submit to his possessiveness, another form of yielding. His corrupt, negative love, not being with me when he could have been, then indulging in a self-created suffering, too perverse for me. Desperately wanting me when he can't have me, and leaving me alone when I am free. A great shock, this. I turned to work. When Hugh left me, Henry and I liked living together. Not Gonzalo. Am I imagining again? Was it because Henry was free, and Gonzalo has a home, a wife? I made a scene. Nothing was clarified.

Meanwhile Henry is pushing me into prominence like a fanatic. He has set himself the task of getting the diary published. His essay has made a great stir. He was questioned by the *Nouvelle Revue Française*. He talks about me, writes about me.* "Poetic justice," he says. Truly generous and effective with his obstinacy and profuse talkativeness.

What man wants is this: to be passionately, wildly loved while he is there in your bed. And when he leaves to be relinquished, the bond broken. Intermittent wholeness. Woman has a continuity. An obsessional faculty. If I am happy with Gonzalo I do not care for friends. But I can make Gonzalo deliriously happy, and he will leave me and go to a café and spend hours with friends, who, if anything, are worse than Henry's, real derelicts, real imbeciles, like Fred. I can't understand this. Then he comes home to me and says: "The world gives me nausea—disgusts me. People are foul and dirty." He rages, and returns to them. When he comes to me and if I am not alight like a bonfire he says: "What is the matter? You're veiled. Don't you love me? What are you thinking about? Did you want to be with your friends?" If I am on fire then he plunges into this, and leaves me, as if this could be turned on and off like an electric current.

---

*Henry Miller issued a reprint of his essay *"Un être étoilique,"* from the *Criterion,* sent out several hundred flyers to solicit subscriptions for the publication of *Mon journal,* in "a faithful reproduction" as he announced in *The Booster,* and composed another, briefer essay, "The Diary of Anaïs Nin," as a possible introduction for the volume. (See, for instance, *Anaïs: An International Journal,* Volume 14, 1996.)

Last night we could have been together: He saw a comrade who offered him a bribe for political betrayal; an Argentine sculptor whom he constantly denigrates; a Peruvian friend who is as dead as a ghost; or Manuel, who is a neurotic exhibitionist described by Gonzalo as a *rat de bibliothèque,* a rat who likes to take down his trousers in the library.

I suppose I cannot understand this seesaw which is not necessary to me, like the woman who retires in Tibet to lead a holy life and comes to Paris regularly for debauch. I am always in the same climate. I am always in my world. And this isolates me. When I arrive at the Durrells' and find Fred sottishly drunk and gurgling like a half-wit, Edgar mentalizing like a machine without breaks, a runaway horse of abstractions, Nancy rebelliously cooking for them all, Larry enduring all, I say what is the matter with them? They won't select, throw out, resist, separate. Why? I can't yield. Everybody yields. Nobody cares. I can't get drunk, collapse, foam at the mouth, dribble. They all look tired, frayed, worn, stained, they lose their teeth, their hair, their potency. They rot while I look at them. Larry is being washed over, swallowed too.

I am tired of holding out.

Seeking to recapture the mental climate of world with Rank to be able to describe collapse of it. Hard.

Gonzalo missed his chance to possess me and hold me and imprison me. He could have. Racially he awakened female submissiveness, but he is too perverse to take what he wants. He did not make good use of his power. I feel now that I am going to scatter myself again! Perhaps seek destruction and death. I do not care.

I see that whenever I have come to an absolute and was ready to surrender duality to it, as with Gonzalo, this absolute proves an illusion and I am driven back to duality for satisfaction.

Passion alone does not make a world.

OCTOBER 26, 1937

NEVER WAS THERE SO CLEAR A CASE OF A GOAT butting a wall of human relationships until it broke its horns and then, turning its backside on it, it entered the royal field of synthetic grass to chew on the cud of creation. And what a relief.

I caught a convenient grippe from taking care of Gonzalo, stayed home for two days. Gonzalo came, all caprice, perversity, and flights (as soon as I hurt him he swoons with desire). What irony. First I am too emotional and primitive for a Henry become creative and philosophical, then I am too creative and wise to sink back into torture, anguish, jealousy, with Gonzalo. I see his mouth saying: *"Soy corrompido."* Corrupt? I am corrupt? That's what wrong with me. I am *not* corrupt.

And so: WORK.

Marvelous work: Rewriting volume forty-five (New York, Rank, Henry). There are in the diary so many flowers like the Japanese paper flowers which need to be placed in water to achieve their flowering. So I am putting all the closed buds in water: Hilarious confessions. Two pages on Fez. Pages on Rank's clothes, men's clothes. Pages on moonstorm. Essay on Rank's philosophy (poetic justice). Goddamn it, yesterday I wanted to destroy myself, maybe I'll destroy the world instead, out of disillusion.

I find peace.

I take man intermittently as he takes woman. When Gonzalo is in my arms I'm happy. When he is gone, I forget him. I enter my world alone. That is how man escapes from woman, tragedy, and all the human problems. They are right. I bury myself. Amen.

How I feel the diabolical alchemy, the exaltation spent on awaiting the lover, on expectation, on a caress, flowing into the pages on Fez.

The fire spent on remembering the nights, the temperature of joy, flowing into a marvelous canto to streets, a bonfire of words. I sit here alone tonight, detached, in a trance, like the trance of saints, removed from the world, inhabiting and caressing Fez and my mysterious sorrows. I don't rage or weep. I ascend spirals of metaphysical ecstasy. I sit on the tip of minarets, and this was the tongue Gonzalo took into his mouth, this was the breath which was hastened by the orgasm. Disillusion acting like the SAIL. Comes the wind of detachment and I leave the land, to caress Fez and breathe out words with closed lips—not the words given like a communion wafer into the mouth of the lover. Fez.

OCTOBER 28, 1937

YOU LEARN TO PLAY ON THE INSTRUMENT OF HUman nature, you get deft and adroit because unless you do you are shipwrecked. I let myself grow wild when Hugh was away. I let myself flow all around Gonzalo with a complete love, when he was sick I wanted to care for him, when he was worried I wanted to share his worry. I was shocked to discover that when he was free—he did not come to me. This cut my rhythm, threw me back again into myself. But listen to this injustice. Gonzalo so nervous when he is here at quai de Passy for fear of Hugh coming. So yesterday I said subtly: "I am free for both lunch and dinner. Hugh is busy. You can choose. I know you are uneasy in the apartment." He chose to come for lunch. Very well. He said nothing about the evening. I said to myself: Now we will see, Gonzalo, how perverse you are. I went out with Henry to the movies. Then the next day I said casually: "I went out last night." Gonzalo jumped: "What! You went out last night without Hugh. Why didn't you telephone me?"

That is all. I felt like some sort of spiritual detective. I had resolved something for myself. Gonzalo, like Henry, lived by caprice, contrariness, negativity, perversion, and chaos. Very well. I learned to say to Henry the opposite of what I meant, to see him take the other side and so say what I wished him to say. So I have to learn to deprive Gonzalo, elude him, so he will beg and yearn. There is a kind of logic in me which should rightly come from Henry or Gonzalo. The whims, caprices, instabilities, contrariness should come from me!

Letter to Father: I rejoice at what you tell me about your house, for you. I beg you never to talk about what you will leave me in your will. You see, I feel that what parents leave their children *afterward* is a barbaric and commercial invention. It is what the parents give now, share now with the children which is beautiful, what they can share together in life. When you will not be there, nothing will have any value for me, your house will seem hateful, because an object is nothing without the joy and human emotion and the feelings which animate it. I know it is out of goodness that you are always talking about what you will leave to me but I do not believe in this. I believe in it so little that I have prevented Hugh, for example, from buying insurance on his life. The fact that Hugh should work to pay during his lifetime to leave me something when he is not there repels me.

First of all, if something happened to Hugh, I wouldn't want to live and wouldn't want money. Everything he has would be shared during life, in life. I do not believe in planning for the future. I prefer that you should enjoy all you have now. Hugh's mother will die someday, after having made Hugh's life so difficult, and will feel proud to leave him something which he had much greater need of while he was young and starting in life. If I had had children I would have given to them at the beginning, not later. So please do not talk anymore about the future. It goes against my feelings on the subject. Enjoy it all, enjoy your house as much as possible, to the limit, and leave me a legacy of having known you happy. Let the house live and die with you. It is you and your present life and pleasure which interests me at the moment.

NOVEMBER 1, 1937

HUGH RETURNED FROM LONDON. MEETING GON-
zalo became difficult. I met him once after a
political meeting. He was vibrant, passionate. We walked hazily
through the street kissing. He is disillusioned with politics, the betrayals and retractions. He is foaming at the bit. His eloquence and
fire at certain moments could lead a country into a revolution. But
the French are sitting back, and Gonzalo is not placed where he can
talk to them. He is locked in his office, writing letters, and if he could
talk they would not understand his French. Even in Spanish he talks
through closed lips, for himself, cavernously. But if all could hear him
as he talks to me at night, the vehemence, the fire, makes me want
to throw bombs. Everything is right again as we walk, the night, the
barriers between us, the obstacles, the wild kisses. It was I who was
wrong, desiring Gonzalo different. Here is Gonzalo, ardently breathing out the fire of revolution, kissing me. My skull cap with the
luminous flowers fell off. What was I sorrowing about yesterday—
the change in my illusion and the clash against the real Gonzalo. I
was forming a pattern out of his promises: "I will print all your work."
A world together. But the real Gonzalo wants a revolution. Wants to
kiss me wildly and talk vehemently and drink abundantly, and sleep
in the mornings. Little idiot Anaïs—you're given a spiderweb and
you want to make a sail out of it and sail a boat. Where were you so
intent on going yesterday? All your life is like your quest for a boat.
Yes, my running through the *Exposition* to see again a lovely boat I
had caught a glimpse of when I walked through with Henry. A boat
with a spiderweb sail not made for sailing. And I was running
through, it was Sunday, the crowd was strolling, surprised at my
speed. I saw nothing, it was like a film, the crowd, the buildings, the
Arab I bumped into, passing blindly on my quest. A boat! A boat! A
boat! I want a boat. I want to get outside of the world with Gonzalo.

I don't like Gonzalo in a room. He is a demon, a pirate, an anarchist, he is thirsty for blood, his body is in a fever, he is made for war and struggle, for heroics. His eyes are ablaze. Lover and warrior. Anaïs, don't cling. At dawn he must put on armor. He will leave you for a Crusade. He is the lover of the myths.

Night of passion in a hotel room where I cover the lights with my panties. Dawn of acceptance. Furtive meetings.

Henry and I working on sending the essay and circular for subscription to the diary. Dropping with fatigue. Henry taking me after three days' separation and making the orgasm last so long I was in ecstasy. It's like an electric hammer blow, one, two, three. It is like a gong struck once, twice, thrice, or longer. The entire mystery of pleasure lies in the intensity of the pulsation. Sometimes it is slow, one, two, three. Three palpitations which seem to project a fiery and iced liquor through the body. If the palpitation is feeble, it is like three kisses without echoes. Pleasure, the little pocket seed of ecstasy, has not flown through the whole body. If the palpitation is intense it is slower between each pulsation. The pleasure is so exquisite I feel I cannot reach greater ecstasy, but then comes the second beat, these two electric flesh arrows touching off each other, and a second wave of pleasure falls over the first, a wave of liqueur spreading and touching off every tip of the body, and now the third, like an electric current traversing the body, a third rolling of waves, the flesh shivering in folds of silk . . . silk and fur caressing the body traversed by a rainbow of colors and lifted and rolled into a symphony. The waves of pleasure ebbing, leaving the foam of music. And the beat, the hammer and the gong can beat, once, twice, thrice, or more on certain nights. There are moments when the woman feels her body but lightly played on, other times when she feels she has trembled and vibrated to the utmost of her sensual feelings. There is this strange, thirsty, yawning womb with its mysterious walls, filled, entered, caressed, when the core of it, like a fiery tongue, flicks out at the male, flicks back and forth until it touches off the fiery miracle of the orgasm.

So many orgasms, orgasms of absolute abandon, orgasms caused by tenderness, by desire, by images, and orgasms paralyzed by anger, by timidity, by not wanting to give, by holding back, by fear, by mistrust. There are times when the day itself demands its orgasm—days of cumulation and unexploded feelings. There are days which do not end in orgasm, beings are disunited, the mind has a thought, the dream another dream, the body is asleep. There are days when the orgasm takes place in emotion, in jealousy, in suffering, in terror, or in physical pain. There are days when the orgasm takes place in creation, a white orgasm of exaltation which sends one like a rocket to the planets. There are nights when all the gongs of dream and feeling are melted into one lashing out of this female tongue of fire—once, twice against the strong hard male, and the sky is brought down over one like a blanket, everything is pulled down like a cover over this single, unique orgasm in the darkness of the woman. Revolution is another orgasm. Sainthood is another orgasm. They are made of wafers on the lip, or blood and wounds, experiencing while blubbering God, or dead words, in epilepsy or insanity. All pulsations leading to explosion, to a flood, to the multiple symphonies spreading into eternity, touching the sky where sky touches earth, earth the sky and the sky the skirts of planets, everywhere fire lashing tongues of flame licking for life, gongs of pleasure sounding church bells or death knells, communion bells inside the host inside man and woman, communion and orgy, revolution and paradise of liqueur spilling the same orgasm.

Gonzalo said: "You have the most extraordinary audacity. I love that. You're really reckless."

I have reached maturity as an artist. I can write well about anything. I see clearly the difference between analysis and direct presentation of the drama. I am inside now—I hate comments.

Here comes the moonstorm and the earth turns faster. Henry has news of his daughter.* She is a musician, she writes, and she is

---

*While married to his first wife, Beatrice Sylvas Wickens, Henry Miller's first child, Barbara, was born on September 30, 1919, and after their divorce in December 1923, his ex-wife retained custody of the child, with whom Henry Miller had lost contact since then.

attractive. He breaks down weeping: "I'm a human being, I've done wrong, I've done wrong."

"Perhaps you'll do for her what you never did for any woman," said Larry.

"No," said Henry, "tomorrow I will go on just the same."

He means playing, he means his destiny as a writer. To get a thing like the "Alf Letter" published means more to Henry than to send six hundred francs to his daughter. He is afraid of her needs. "What can I do when I see her, about her poverty?"

"You can make sacrifices."

"No, I wouldn't do that."

I had rebelled at the "Letter" about Alf, a trivial, farcical, foolish bit. And he had given it up.* Larry is putting up the money for three books, to become Kahane's partner, giving Henry the leadership. Larry kneels before me: "We will do you first." "No," I said, *The Black Book* first." He begs me: "Stand by me, to keep Henry from fucking himself, publishing small things right and left instead of big books."

I am deeply tired. I got Helba a new place, what she wanted, and a week later she has not moved yet from the damp, black, smelly cellar room to a new apartment overlooking a garden. Meanwhile I have debts, holes in my shoes. And melancholy. Melancholy. With the Durrells it is all sweet and not crazy. Henry is exactly like a madman who lives in his own world. Now and then he breaks down and becomes aware. He weeps. He weeps for me, for his daughter. The next day he is writing again. For a moment I felt: He is as much a victim of his destiny as we are. But it is only partly true. He is the victim of his destiny as a writer but there are many wasted, selfish, foolish things he does which have nothing to do with his destiny but

---

*In October 1935, with royalties from *Tropic of Cancer,* Henry Miller had published a twenty-page pamphlet, "What Are You Going to Do About Alf?," which somewhat farcically asked for contributions to send Alfred Perlès to Ibiza so he could finish a novel he was writing, and which was distributed free of charge. This "Open Letter to All and Sundry" was reissued in January 1938 and priced at five francs, without identifying the publisher.

with his amusement or vanity. He lives with admiring disciples who are all afraid to hold their own opinion, who flatter and exalt his megalomania. I suffer to see him sitting swallowing flattery. He cowers even Larry with: "If you don't admire Picasso there is a limitation in you." I wish I could be rid of the nightmare of my life with Henry, which is really the cause of my unbalance, for to try and keep one's integrity living with Henry is to be subjected to war, to pain, and absolute inhuman life. Yet I go there out of loneliness, for with Gonzalo I have only the moments of passion, a flash, a night of caresses.

Is the moonstorm enlarging Henry's craziness, his complete absence of values, taste, wisdom? Larry, at twenty-six, dismisses Marika Norden with immediate insight: "Cheap. A man's values represent his SELF. Henry is a mouthpiece, like an imbecile or a madman, of something that does not belong to him."

Moonstorms do not make me completely crazy. I am hanging on by a thread. I lean over at moments, I can still see what is true, right. But I am hanging on by a thread. At times Henry confuses me as he did June. His own confusions drive me to despair. The effort at hanging on, at holding him together by the human thread and by my vision wears me out.

Larry is there, balancing. I feel a relief in his presence, a saving solidity. But he loves Henry too, and he yields. "I don't want to spoil his enthusiasm. It is worth one thousand francs thrown away." One has to live intoxicated, not lucid. Or one suffers.

I return home battered. Gonzalo works for the revolution. Joaquin condemns me periodically. Hugh alone condones, accepts, understands, loves blindly. But when I get lost I can't turn to him. The truth is, what I hate most are my self-doubts, my faith in others which makes me falsify myself: I am going around selling *The Booster,* for Henry, I don't like it. It is vulgar and farcical, uneven, and strident. Then I feel guilty. I say: Perhaps I am too austere, too pure. I can't understand and accept. I'm in the wrong world, and that makes me doubt myself because I have faith in others. I believe really too much, I'm easily seduced, touched, I really believe and that is why I fall into abysms of doubt and then I need the father, the seer, a God. I want always to know absolutely. I am not sure except of what I feel. I'm ready to consider myself in the wrong yet my feelings tell me I'm right.

Love confuses one terribly, blinds one. To be right is to be alone. So I yield until I feel a rebellion choke me.

Stumbled on this note on Henry, made years ago: "I adore your courage, the pain it engenders, the struggle you carry in yourself. I adore your terrifying sincerity. I worship you when you mock, when you explode, when you tear apart. You are right: the world is to be caricatured but I know how much you can love what you caricature. How much passion there is in you. I do not feel the savant, the revealer, the observer, but always the passion, the flow, the curiosity." This I loved until the exaggeration of it became a very grotesque defect, waste, inflation, falsity. This note: "The obscure soft joy in the womb you inflamed." And again: "He writes me a letter which is like a brainstorm. His furies are at once sacred and disproportionate."

Met Gonzalo for a while in a café. Came home and felt that what saves me from insanity is my peaceful life with Hugh, Hugh painting gently, the cat sleeping, the soft lights. Then I feel that my fantasy is a fantasy, a fit of insane melancholy, and I slowly reenter a kind of convalescence. An hour ago the trees were black, the fog sinister, the river threatening, Henry crazy, Gonzalo a stranger with his talk of politics like Hugh's talk of banking, all petty intrigues, realism, manipulations, calculations. An hour ago I was estranged, dissociated. I struggle out of my world to understand the worlds of others. I get discouraged. I can't live in them. Then when I get inside of mine I am aware the lens deforms others. I go out again, for love, for compassion, to give, to yield, but *I can't give up my world.*

When Henry sobbed over his daughter I was not jealous. I love him in a different way, for himself and for his life again, not for myself. For myself there is no one who can give me what I need. Not what I want, for it is not my will or my ego demanding, it's the crazy, morbid, sick me, the Anaïs nobody knows, who is more to be pitied. If I need to be loved and reassured it is because I am not sure of myself, or my value. At the basis of my life is fear and doubt, yet I give faith to others. Gonzalo said: "When I'm despondent I don't like to see you. I hate to spoil the luminous atmosphere around you." I am alone with my secret. My only relief is activity, action. That is why I suffer when I give Gonzalo the printing press and six months later it has served no purpose. And that is why I can't be alone. I can't rest alone. For then I face an abyss, the abyss of my own lucidity. For I see too much. I saw how Gonzalo's jealousy was a weakness in his love, not its strength. I see Henry's incapacity to love deeply. His daughter cannot make him sacrifice a whim, a caprice. I can't bear the depths of my disenchantment. So I work until I'm worn out. Opium. I began tonight, thinking I can't call Gonzalo at *Paix et Démocratie* because I'm suspected of being a fascist spy, a dangerous woman. I can't call up his home because if he is asleep he does not hear and the concierge curses me. Then he gets angry if I don't call him. Hugh is painting with delicacy. His new passion is painting. I am indebted, harassed by money difficulties, yet when I ask Gonzalo gently: "Did you ever get paid for printing for *Paix et Démocratie?*" he answers: "No, I couldn't be bothered doing the accounts." Henry gives away books, booklets like confetti because it makes him feel generous. I sent out four hundred subscription envelopes to diary one. I go right ahead without fear of what Gonzalo will do when he discovers Henry is publishing my early diary. Gonzalo who promised me six months ago: "I will print all your work on the press" and whom I believed. The nine hundred francs which have come in are already spent. Hugh, who alone keeps me from insanity, is going to live in London. I feel utterly, utterly weak, as I did in New York. I pushed Elena away and the haunting overtones of jealousy I felt with her. Saying I am going to live in London. An edifice of lies. I know that I seem sane but that this world in which I find myself—enclosing a severe Father, a Gonzalo forever rushing into danger and destruction, a Henry whose life-juice evaporates in language, creation, and collective living—is not a real but a deformed world. I cannot see my Father as human, Gonzalo as a lover, Henry as human, because they are so only intermittently, and in between what they are leaves me always in an abyss of solitude. The moment when hope and faith collapse, when my illusions vanish like mirages. All my life is an illusion but you can't stand behind it and see because that is death. Tonight I feel that I stumble on mirages, but I cannot bring myself to the wisdom of not seeking an oasis, water, trees, beauty, repose. Why must I constantly create mirages? There are days when I know very well there is a veil between what I see and touch and myself. Why is it that what I know I cannot accept and continue seeking, stumbling, desiring? I know they are mirages of everything, but they are inside of me, inside of my very eyes. Why do I create, invent? Human life, failures, defeats, detours, limitations, chaos, explosions, accidents. Why do I constantly rebel against them and seek *Nanan-kepichu* and Shangri-la?

I am lost again in mirages.

Human life does not enclose me, hold me. It is metamorphosed by my dreams, my anxieties, my magnifying lens, my terrifying sensitivity. I see malice, persecution, hatred, and fear all around me.

It is true that a small thing unhinges me. Lately it was the question of humor. Henry said I had no humor because I hate Fred. Or he said: "Spanish people have no humor." So I fretted and thought: He means I am too serious. I can't laugh at all he laughs at. A small phrase can also set me right again. Today, after the nightmare of the weekend, I went to Henry full of charm, gaiety, activity, determined to overcome my defects. Among other things he said accidentally: "You've so much sympathy, that prevents you from seeing the humor. You're not without humor, you have more than humor, you have a natural gaiety." And I was satisfied. I can't bear to be deficient or I think I will be less loved. I have gaiety. No one but those who read my diary can detect the melancholy. I hide it well. Slowly I climb out of my inferno again. I go to Henry with new magazines dug out of Eduardo's mass of books, with carbon paper, new ideas, another subscription to the diary, exuberance and enthusiasm.

Tonight supper and night with Gonzalo. I do not want to become like [Hans] Reichel. Reichel's madness: "No one has ever told me: 'I love you.' I'm full of anguish, anxiety. Everybody is against me. You are hiding the wine. I'm sure there is more wine here but you're hiding it. I see you making fun of me. I can't find peace anywhere. Take me back *chez mes peintures.*"

Chez mes peintures, as if it were "take me back to my home, to my family, to my lover." Reichel clutching at people, physically, violently, so they won't leave him, for contact, always drunk, indifferent to his success, to the money he has made, afraid "the evening will come to an end." Reichel mad. Louise de Vilmorin mad. Understanding can no longer bring them back. They no longer believe—they believe in no one. No, I can be brought back with one word of love, one glance. I still have my faith in others. But the world in which I live I can never escape. The world of my own fantasy. I am a lucid madwoman, I know I'm wrong, I face each time reality and I am tamed again, reassured. But I cannot live without anguish, I dread the last cord snapping and that I should be like someone on a ship in midocean never able to land again.

Now I have to conquer the harm Gonzalo does me, unwittingly, by considering politics the most vital of all interests, and regarding my work as an adornment. All this has to be conquered because I should have faith in myself. I should be able to write, to live without approbation. The criticalness or condemnation I see in others is only a projection of my doubts. To rely on others' understanding, others' encouragement, others' worship, is bad.

I said laughingly to Henry: "And this applies to you too, for I notice you made all your women more critical, more condemnatory than they really were, including me. There are times, I notice, you interpret my silences as condemnation, whereas if you read my diary you will see how often I have yielded to you and accepted and approved. You project on your women all your guilts. Your guilt for all your nonhuman acts you project on me. I refuse to be your guilt garbage pan. I want you to know I have no accusation against you and when I have had one I have said it." (Which is true.)

Guilt certainly betrays all the men who seem amoral: Henry, my Father, etc. They are not really free of it. And I suppose I do my little atoning on the side too, in spite of my apparent recklessness, insouciance, and seeming amorality.

Mirages are those created by my own weaknesses. The deceptive ME, bewildered by my own elusiveness, duality, and treacherousness.

Everything becomes mellow again. I let Gonzalo be erratic and perverse. I am happy when he calls, happy when he is late. I let Henry inflate like a balloon, and burst into flames and when the pieces fall I pick them up tenderly. Very often, as [D.H.] Lawrence went back to Frieda, battered, Henry comes back to me, disillusioned with all but me.

Waiting for the master like an Arab woman! Oh, Anaïs, Anaïs, you bitch, slippery and volatile, walking, running, dancing between all these men, adoring and smashing, revolting and attacking, betraying with innocence—I can see as no one else does. I can adore, but I can't be resigned and passive. I want not to suffer. I want to enjoy them. If I love them so much I must love the defects. That must be the deepest love—acceptance. All suffering comes from the needs or the demands of the Self. To give this self away, to love, to yield, that ends all madness. I went to Henry today to love Henry. I washed dishes for him, I sewed the pillowcase, I cooked his lunch, I yielded to his mood. Tonight I will love Gonzalo, give him all he wants. When they turn toward work or politics, I will do my own work.

Since I live on illusions, on internal changes, on mysterious anguishes, I do all to create this happiness. One day after seeing the Durrells for tea, I was to go to Henry's. I needed to see and to touch Gonzalo—I rushed down in a taxi, just to get one kiss, one caress, and I returned to dinner with Henry and the Durrells full of gaiety.

Durrell calls my copies of the diary my black children—they are bound in black—I keep them in the Arabian wedding chest, violet velvet with gold nails. Lovely to see the *coffre* open, brimming full. And now this one will go to the vault—to be locked among other people's jewels and testaments.

Oh, God, what moods. Now I'm bursting with ecstasy. What a *montagne Russe!*

NOVEMBER 11, 1937

GONZALO ON HEARING DURRELL'S PLAN TO ASSOciate himself to Kahane and publish me: "Don't compromise with the fascist world. They will never accept you. Only a communist world will ever print you."

Hugh: "Don't send announcements to the bank people."

When I explode Hugh recognizes that he has been unduly afraid—that it is true, somehow or other, I "get away" with everything. I have loyal friends in the bank. I never hurt Hugh's reputation. People never harm me—they respect me, they are charmed. The fight against conventions, fears, publishers' vacillations. Plus fear and jealousies around me. Gonzalo is jealous of Durrell, feels I live in an art world, for I substitute Durrell in the stories of all activities of Villa Seurat—the magazine, introductions, etc.

Negative love. They *do* nothing, but as soon as I act, they criticize out of jealousy. They do nothing actively, positively, but they oppose my activity.

Hugh helps me, gives to me, frees me—has not sacrificed me to the bank life—but publication terrifies him. Actually, he has nothing to fear.

The day began beautifully, with Dorothy Norman of *Twice a Year* accepting both the "Birth" story and the "Woman in Creation" essay, and saying she has a great admiration for the purity of my work. But it ended in a violent quarrel with Hugh—with justice at the end, Hugh admitting his fears unjustified. At the bank I never hurt him, winning the most moral and severe of them all, Walter Wolf, who respects me, and I freeing Hugh of guilt by reminding him of all he does do for me as an artist, permitting me an individual life. But with all these struggles I'm broken. Henry and Larry are the ones who give me impetus and activity. The activity Henry has created is extraordinary. He lives in a whirlpool—drawing everyone to him. I am to edit a number of *The Booster* of women's writing. It is out of our discussion one night, Henry, Larry, and I, that the "Woman in Creation" essay was born. Larry has written a voyage through the womb which is unmatchable.* We're rereading [Rank's] *The Trauma of Birth*.

Thurema is walking the streets selling my perfume "Azul by Inda." We write each other passionate letters.

Gonzalo's activity, politically, is increasing, because it is a *lost cause*—and it is his nature to defend what is weak. I feel communism weakening and I fear for him. In the dark, we quarrel, too, because he said: "To think a year ago I was the most insouciant, the most happy-go-lucky being. And now I can't sleep with worries, with the plans and ideas I have." And I couldn't help saying: "I wish I had known you before!" I can't get passionate about revolution—and I'm afraid for our love, his life. Then suddenly I take his head in my arms again and I forget all that separates us—all but the love, the love. I am learning to surrender. In the morning I surrender him. I don't telephone. I wait, until he comes again. There are moments when I feel that in spite of Henry, if something happens to Gonzalo I would want to die with him because he is all my human life, he is feeling, emotion.

---

*The December 1937–January 1958 issue of *The Booster* was subtitled "Air-Conditioned Womb Number" and bore on the title page the note: "The Labyrinth/The Plinth/The Nth/By/The Womb Sextette." It contained Anaïs Nin's "The Paper Womb" (reprinted in the 1940s as "The Labyrinth"), Lawrence Durrell's "Down the Styx," and contributions by Miller, Perlès, William Saroyan, and the mysterious, pseudonymous "Le Huitain." There is no indication that Anaïs Nin acted as the editor of the volume, which names Alfred Perlès as *"Directeur et Rédacteur en Chef,"* and Betty Ryan as *"Secretaire de Rédaction."*

NOVEMBER 13, 1937

*J*UST AS I LOVE IN GONZALO QUALITIES ALTO-
gether lacking in Henry, Gonzalo loves in me
qualities Henry is indifferent to. Gonzalo is deeply stirred by my
character, my integrity, my courage, my independence, the way I oppose those I love in spite of my slavery to affection and feeling. He
sees I side with his communism out of love for him, to give him
strength—not for myself. I do everything for human reasons—yet no
one can stop my honesty in writing, my fearlessness.

Henry and I sit watching a film on China in which is revealed
the great resignation, passivity, sense of the eternal—annihilating *personal* sorrows. I see Henry's attitude. His face is like theirs. It is their
solution to life—resignation, acceptance, indifference. That is not my
nature. Gonzalo and I have the same nature, the same restlessness,
anxieties, need of action and drama, combativeness for lost causes,
sleeplessness, fire—we snort fire! In politics all his strength comes
out—his vehemence. He is whole. It is *his* creation, his fulfillment. I
must stand by him.

When a desire is blocked, crossed, most people react with philosophy. I react with violence because it is not merely a whim defeated,
a wish that is snuffed out, but a piece of life that is killed. Since I
saw the little studio I thought I could have, I lived in it for days: I
pictured how it would look, how it would feel. I fitted myself to the
shape of the room, to its temperature. I modeled my new actions
according to its design. I moved in the room. I worked before the
window giving on the little garden. I heard the trees swinging, I saw
the sky through the top window. I lay down in the place of the bed
and was warmed by the fireplace. I waited for love on winter nights.
I wrote, I danced, I slept in the place. I took a shower, I cooked in

the dark little kitchen, I left my key under the doormat for the *femme de ménage*.

When the place was denied me, a life was killed. It was really a murder of something alive. I was in the place, living there. I had moved from my other home.

Tonight I no longer live in quai de Passy. I have detached myself from it. From its expensiveness. I come from the rue d'Odessa, where I have already arranged the furniture, where I slept in the alcove lined in black velvet, studded with colored stones. I come from there. I have walked because it is near Henry. Desire thus so violent, being actually living, not imagining, that all defeat, rebuff, change becomes intensely difficult. That makes acceptance almost impossible. The imagination rules the life, not reality.

My moment of happiness, of serenity, comes when I am alone in the oriental warmth and velvetiness of my room, protected by fur, velvet, and colored stones, lulled by textures, colors. There, I rest. With the diary on my lap. I don't like this little book—it is narrow and stingy. *Je suis a l'étroit.* I want to finish it quickly.

Visit from David Gascoyne—only twenty-one—a child prodigy. I don't know his work, only his reputation. A mystical, poetic boy, but bound like the dead Arab by multiple white bandages. He leaves me his diary, full of reticences and evasions. I give him diary volumes thirty-one, thirty-two, thirty-three. Can I light the fire in him?

All I can do is remember my night with Gonzalo. How he places his head, his hand, his legs. The beat of his eyelashes against my cheek. His voice when he says: *"Ay, qué rico, chiquita. Ay, qué dulce."*

NOVEMBER 15, 1937

So I overcome my fears for Gonzalo— because fear for those we love weakens them. I give him all my strength. I seek to understand what he is doing. I let him talk. He is ablaze with independence, with courage. It is as if he alone, by his passion, were fighting the disintegration of the Party. He brings unity, he radiates force, conviction, and personality. I have lost my fears for him. I nourish this power. No one will ever know that I nourished the revolution, served it—by awakening Gonzalo's force. When I remember the Gonzalo who entered Roger Klein's little room: A startling figure—disquietingly dark and fiery. But drunk. Drunk and dispersed. And his meeting me was like a shock. Gonzalo's first appeal to me was: "You are a great spiritual force." I must be true to this. I aroused him from his drinking and wasted Montparnasse life. I aroused him without knowing what it was he contained. If he is the One Man who can unify communism—well, that is his Karma. Perhaps it is my Karma to inflame great revolutionary forces: Henry in literature, Gonzalo in politics.

And now Denise Clairouin tells me: "I gave the diaries to [Maxwell] Perkins, of Scribners. He was interested. Instead of giving them to a reader, he took them home and read them himself. He was thunderstruck. 'What a curious, extraordinary woman.' He wants to see an abridged copy. Go to work."

And I face my greatest problem. Just when people want the diary *as it is*—as a diary—I have begun to transform it! No one can tell me what to do. I have an artistic need to transform. Everything I touch I must rewrite. What shall I do? And the human problems! How much can I reveal? Hugh might never read it, he only reads what I put in his hands. But Henry? Is cutting what the censors want me to do, to cut enough to preserve Henry's happiness! Oh, God. Duality. I work feverishly on forty-five—the transformed one.

Because of Henry's description of the whalelike diary, Larry calls me "the Whale." And signs himself: "your ever admiring limpet." I had to ask Hugh what a limpet was.

I suppose I'll end by chucking my whole art life (publication) for human reasons. I will never break down like Henry and weep: "After all, I'm a human being, and as a human being, I've done wrong!" My breakdown will be different. Someday I'll weep and say: "After all, I'm an artist, and as an artist I've done wrong—I acted humanly."

Artist. I want to do Louise and her brother's better than Cocteau's

Enfants terrible. I want to do June better than Djuna Barnes's *Nightwood.* I want to do Artaud better than Carlo Suares's *Procession enchaînée.* I want to do my Father, Eduardo.

It is Rank I'm doing now, fully. I no longer care about truth, exactitude, veracity. But what a load: My own spiderweb, immense around me. And so much pulling me away: Spain, revolutions, Gonzalo, Helba's needs.

I feel warmth for Larry, a kind of love. But none for Gascoyne. He leaves me cold, in spite of his suffering. He is a prisoner, he is much like Eduardo. The sound of chains rattling disturbs me—but I have no desire to break them. Am I getting possessed like Henry, by another destiny? Am I really becoming artist? A *force de désillusion,* of personal abdications. When I lie quiet, patient, gentle toward Gonzalo's erratic ways, Hugh's pessimism and realism, Henry's caprices, it is because I'm pregnant with something else. I come out of my cave to love—only to love. Sunday, it was astonishing. Hugh had something to do, so I divided my afternoon between Henry and Gonzalo. Henry got me into bed and took me exactly with the wildness of our first meetings and I abandoned myself wholly. I left him asleep. I met Gonzalo at the café. I thought: I will be empty of love. But I wasn't. When Gonzalo got up to light his cigarette, I looked at his body and felt the deepest vibration, as if part of my own body, my being stood there, tied to me, bound to me. I could have given him the most frenzied caresses.

NOVEMBER 20, 1937

AUDACE. HENRY INCITED BETTY RYAN TO EXHIBIT Reichel's paintings in her studio on the ground floor of his house. Announcements were sent out. Reichel's paintings sold. Elena somehow never heard of it, and I was sure she would see it and then go up to visit Henry, or even see Henry right there, he was so often in the place. I told Hugh about the exhibit because I knew he would love Reichel's work. He announced he would go with Carteret on Wednesday afternoon, about 5:30 or six. At six I had a *rendez-vous* with Henry. I could not let him know—I did not try to. At 5:30 I walked right into 18 Villa Seurat. I was ready to meet Hugh on the way and ready to say: "Hello! I was looking for you!" But I did not meet him. I tiptoed to Henry's studio. Passing Betty Ryan's studio, I heard Hugh's voice. I went and saw Henry, agreed to meet him at a café, left him, and walked right by Betty's place again and had dinner with Henry in a restaurant nearby. We took a taxi to go to a movie. Hugh was exultant over Reichel's work. He wanted to meet Reichel. He promised to call again! He chose an evening I had promised to cook for Henry. I could not market. But Henry did, and we had dinner right there together, while Hugh, Reichel, Betty, and Carteret went out for a drink. And Hugh had dinner alone in the Café Zeyer.

Everything divides for me into warm or cold. Cold people who never act from human *élans* but always by their instinct of self-satisfaction, fulfillment: Elena, Henry, Louise, June, Father. Warm people: Thurema, Gonzalo, and I. I *have* a cold side. I live for myself but not to the point of sacrificing others. I am capable of sacrifices. The cold ones are incapable of *sacrifice*. My whole struggle is to balance them. People feel this and that is why they forgive me, help me. They do not consider Hugh ridiculous or ridiculed by my tricks. Nor me cynical.

I feel innocent and protected. I feel Hugh protected because I want him to be. Elena says about herself: "I am passionate but cold—and selfish."

My Father the same. He is disconnected from all sympathy. He wants to hear only agreeable things, to pursue his games with one thousand photographs of Switzerland!

Have gone to work on abridged edition of diary. Will give this and then start my *art* work, my Proustian creation.

Elena is changing the curtains of her bedroom. Gonzalo is working underground for the revolution in Peru. Helba is sitting like the inmates of an asylum doing nothing for hours or sewing rags. Eduardo is visiting Italy with a boy lover. Henry is writing *Tropic of Capricorn*—as Larry said: *"A new dimension without emotion."* Henry's creation is exactly like an insanity—all experience disconnected from feeling, like an anesthetized savage. Soul injected with ether. I ask myself at night: *Why* is it I do not get cut off from pity, sympathy, participation, emotion in spite of the fact that I live out my dream, fantasy, my *"vision intérieure"* without wavering, without interruption. I dream, I kiss, I have orgasms, I get exalted, I leave the world, I float, I cook, I sew, I have nightmares, I follow a gigantic creative plan, I compose, decompose, improvise, I write in my head, I listen to all, I hear all that is said, I feel Spain, I am aware, I am everywhere, I burn with Gonzalo, I am open to wounds, open to love, I am rooted to my devotions, I carry an obsessional current of storytelling, I am writing my own story but I am never separate, cut off—never blind, deaf, absent. I hold on to the dream which makes life possible, to the creation which transfigures, to the God who sustains, to the crimes which give life, to the infidelities which make the marvelous possible. I hold on to the poetry and to the human simplicity. I write about the labyrinth, the womb, Fez, and I carry electric bulbs for Gonzalo's house.

Larry is sitting cross-legged on a chair like a soft blond Indian with a catlike suppleness and writing with a branding iron.

A day and night: Old Lantelme comes on his regular twice-a-week visit, saying: *"Elle est vivante! Je viens me réchauffé."* He tells me the latest joke, laughs, drinks a glass of wine, takes money. I give him something to sell for me, my amethyst engagement ring, the riding boots, the evening dresses I don't wear. Gonzalo needs money for a revolver. At twelve, the Joneses arrive, talking about their visit to Spain, the terrible suffering of the refugees, but *they* ate full-course meals in the hotels, and Hemingway, when he is not taking notes at the front, is hunting pheasants on abandoned Spanish property, and fishing. Hugh talks like a somnambulist about politics, in a monotonous voice, without animation, in a funeral orison of sound facts which sound as unsound to me as the statements made by hysterical com-

Anaïs Nin in St. Tropez,
late 1930s

HENRY MILLER

wishes to announce that by March 1ˢᵗ 1938, failing a world war or a collapse of the monetary systems of the world, he will publish from Bruges, Belgium, the *first* volume of Anais Nin's diary

MON JOURNAL

in the original French. This great work, which is now in the 54th volume, was begun at the age of eleven during the voyage from Barcelona to New York.

The edition is limited to 250 copies numbered and signed by the author. The book will be printed by the Imprimerie Ste-Catherine on this paper in this type of a format exactly this size. It will include two facsimile pages from the original *cahiers;* the cover design will be the author's own horoscope.

The price will be 100 frs. for France, one pound for England and five dollars for America. For other countries a corresponding rate based on the dollar. Checks or money orders should be made payable to the publisher, Henry Miller, and addressed to him at 18 Villa Seurat, Paris (xiv).

The flyer announcing Henry Miller's intent to publish, by subscription, Anaïs Nin's early diary

Henry Miller at a Paris café

Jean Carteret on board
La Belle Aurore

Gonzalo Moré on the beach at
St. Tropez

Thurema with her harp

Dr. Allendy in 1938

Joaquin Nin y Castellanos,
Anaïs's father, in 1939

munists (none of them seeing the truth, all of them deluding themselves equally). At three, when they are gone Gonzalo comes for a moment only because we have not seen each other for two days, and I give him the last copy of the *New Masses* which Walter Lowenfels sends Henry! At four, Madeleine Masson calls me up in a masculine voice. I have seen her only two times, but she says: "Darling, I must see you. I have left my husband. I'm very happy now. I have so much to tell you. When can I see you?" At five o'clock, Gascoyne comes to see if he can catch his own image in the pool of my understanding, the volumes of the diary he read have enlarged the space of his prison. While he is there I get a call from the secretary of the Comtesse de Vogue: "Can M. et Mme. Guiler come to dinner Saturday evening at 8:30, *en veston?*" I thought this meant evening dress and I thought how I have none to wear, and anyhow, damn it, I have broken with that world, divorced it, I don't want to go there. It's unreal, it's worthless. I'm dogged and stern and full of my work, of people's poverty, and strange occupations, and I'm tired from nights of caresses, dim caressing talks, a deeper, darker world which makes the salon look like a candy shop.

Henry telephones: "We got a subscription from André Maurois, only he says he doesn't want the entire fifty-four volumes—his house is too full of books."* In between I arranged all the diaries I have to edit in boxes, without bindings, so I can plunge into this sea easily.

I meet Gonzalo for dinner and we go afterward to a hotel on the rue Vendôme, a block away from where I first went to Henry, a hotel where no papers are asked because they receive members of the Party. One of our neighbors is a Russian captain, friend of Gonzalo. We hear him come in about ten, cough, sitting alone in his room, while we are drowning in a cavern of warmth and fervor, desire and tenderness. Gonzalo is afraid I am tired out by his fitful, capricious sleep, his insomnias. He falls deeply asleep after our caresses, in my arms, so I cannot move, and I can't sleep because he breathes so heavily. Then

---

*In his subscription solicitation, Henry Miller had mentioned that Anaïs Nin's diary, of which he planned to publish the first volume, had meanwhile reached fifty-four volumes.

about midnight when I am falling asleep he wakes up and we talk, he frets about not being able to go to sleep. About two o'clock I get desperately hungry and then he has to get a sandwich and a drink for himself. Then we fall asleep. At dawn he sometimes awakens again and smokes. I feel him awake and I awake. He goes heavily to sleep at eight when it is time for me to leave to arrive for Hugh's breakfast. And he can't go to work until noon. Having breakfast with Hugh I get a subscription to the diary, and an insulting letter from a book collector, Ben Abramson, saying *House of Incest* means absolutely nothing, what the hell, "it's Joyce without passion and Gertrude Stein without ancestry." Hugh tells me about his new work, the Egyptians he has been with, the problems of Carteret, who is so much like me, who takes Hugh through the planets. The walls of Hugh's room are covered with his own paintings of whimsical animals, all of them with broods, one whale covered by parasites, one large snail with seven little snails, a mouse laughing in the corner, a black peacock, a mocking fish. Joaquin comes, the Nin melancholy in his eyes. We are planning and calculating for his trip to New York with Mother. He picks up the Spanish books he loaned to Gonzalo which I cannot read. When he leaves I write to Eduardo that Hugh's trip to Egypt is canceled. Eduardo can come here for Xmas and we will use his place in Antibes. I work all afternoon.

What a struggle against outward disruption and interference. Janine [the maid] grumbling because there are not enough dishes and all the glasses are broken. The theme of childbirth does not interest the Soviet *New Country*. Elena saying: "Now that you go away I will be completely alone." Clairouin saying: "I don't agree with you. It is the document they want, without any changes." I sprinkle patchouli leaves over the lamps. The radio gives me music while I number all these pages of the diary and ask myself: What shall I cut? Just cut out the deserts, and cut what may hurt Henry. Hugh, I hope, will never read the diary appearing under another name, but Henry is sure to know. I am faced with the audacious, the bold dynamite-package I threw myself when I gave the diaries to Clairouin. I can't pull back. Put on the velvet dress for the Comtesse de Vogue—and sit on a white satin sofa.

NOVEMBER 26, 1937

GONZALO, ALWAYS IN CAFÉS, ALWAYS OUT WHEN not at work, so for two days I had dark resentment against his volatilization, which he laughs at because he says I have no cause for jealousy.

My Father, *sur un ton enjoué,* visits me and delivers the customary lies in tissue paper and red ribbons: "I have to train this singer—she is Norwegian, wants to sing Spanish songs. She is so cold. I have to blow heat into her." I know he is filling her with other things, and that the notes she utters are probably not the one she will sing at a concert.

All day I paste false names on the diary MS and I can't see anything to cut out except: 1. horoscopes, 2. constant *analogy* between past and present—a bore.

We love so much of the past in the present. Every day as I work I fall in love with all that Henry was—and I know it is not the same—yet once a week we dive into our dark sensual world and I find the same centi-penis, the same marvelous nonchalant lingering, relaxed, fulsome visit into my womb *étoilique.*

The Henry before was humble and unsure. The Henry of today is sure and slightly megalomaniac. I yield to the pleasure of his bullying me, a stubborn Henry doing wasteful, foolish things even *for* me, always sending subscription blanks, letters, and books to those who refuse to answer him! Always talking about China and wisdom: "I fight less," he says, after an evening during which he has said the most brutal, the most contrary, irrational things to a young English girl.

I no longer rebel against Fred—or people coming to eat. I feel their loneliness. Edgar. I cook vast pots of savory *poule au pot*. The

Henry of before passes like a lantern slide over the Henry of today. As the Hugh of Richmond Hill passed over the Hugh of the present.

Je voudrais être toujours au commencement de l'amour, I would like to be always at the beginning of love, when the flame is so strong that all the differences, all the hostilities, all the defects, are burnt.

Gonzalo said in the night: "I never loved anyone who did not love me. I was a *sourcier*—I looked for water."

His idea of love is rhythm. Love a rhythm, not a collision. There are two loves. One is all shocks and dissonances—another rhythm.

NOVEMBER 28, 1937

*I*N THE COMMUNIST WORK THERE IS SO MUCH suspicion, *médisance,* slander, gossip, calumny that my indeterminate political color is a danger for Gonzalo. So I am ready to assume the role of communist for Gonzalo's sake—but at the very moment when I see through Gonzalo, that it is just another form of tyranny, of narrowness, and a *lie.* They consider Allendy a doubtful communist because he publishes an article on sexuality in a magazine. They call it "exploiting the bourgeois appetite." They ostracize André Gide for telling the truth [about his trip to the Soviet Union]. I fought too much for truth, for a spiritually honest life, for human living, to pass from one battle into another—from one narrowness to another. Lenin is as much a dictator as all the others.

Communism—what a farce. I stand alone. I stand only for life and for truth against *all* laws. Forever and forever. Against all forms, all disciplines, all orders, all rulership, all government. I stand for the truth, the soul alone, free, never bowing, never submitting, never bound, never in servitude. No Mass going, no marriage, no money slavery, no dependence on anything—still less of the new tyranny of communism.

"All correspondence opened, all telephone calls intercepted," *El partido*. God. One hears the knouts. And each man who acts as a man is killed. Every day executions in Russia. Yes. Tyranny. Yes.

DECEMBER 1, 1937

GONZALO SAYS JUSTLY: "YOU HAVE TO LOOK BE-yond the defects, the discipline. To make a new world demands first of all destruction and severity. The men of today will be sacrificed, the individual will be sacrificed but for a new order in which everyone will have what only the strong ones have today. You had the strength to expand in spite of the bourgeois world. But what of the weak ones? Those who cannot, who succumb."

This argument always touches me. The weak ones. Those I help every day, trapped in morals, traditions, or hunger. I wonder.

He does not believe in character—the unchangeable character of man. I guess the strong ones, spiritually or physically, can always take care of themselves. And I suppose the weak ones can be given a better order to live in.

This talk happened at night, in our bare hotel room. I can always see at these moments the Gonzalo made for such a sacrifice of his individual life to an ideal—a Utopia. He is sacrificing his gypsy nature, plying himself to the discipline. Sacrificing his Bohemian life, his aesthetic leanings, his pride, his independence. His conflict is how to harmonize his individual way of working with communist discipline. He is on his own now, unifying the Peruvian elements, only partly tied to *Paix et Démocratie*. I see the revolts and conflicts in him, against injustices and errors—as in an army—but he surrenders this to a bigger Cause.

I had once the desire to psychoanalyze the entire world, because I thought it was a liberating factor. But this is a slow, impossible thing—an individual remedy only. Perhaps the other, external change, may be more possible.

However, I have other work to do. My work is individual. I have gone too far to make this serve a far-off Utopia. I believe now in my own value. I must live this out to the end. But I believe in my own destiny which is not to sacrifice myself to others by my death, but by living. I no longer belong to myself to give myself away—I am a symbol. I cannot serve anything that demands obedience, silence, sacrifice. I am not made for an army even if this army may eventually free the poor, the meek, the weak.

Monday morning. Gathering my papers together, a 1920 diary, paper, carbons, letters to show Henry. I saw first of all David Gascoyne, who is poor and to whom I am giving work. He lives in a real *Sous les Toits* room, low ceilinged, a garret with slanting windows. He gave me Pierre Jean Jouve [to read]—a new world, new dreams, a new poison, new drug.

Then to Henry's to a lunch of news: Denoël and Steele planning *Black Spring* in translation. Manuscripts accepted. Flattering letters. Subscriptions to diary. November issue of *The Booster*. Before, we always talked about writing. Now it is always publication, realization. James Cooney of Woodstock, New York, starts a new magazine [the *Phoenix*], appoints Henry "European editor," accepts my "Orchestra" fragment, speaks of doing all my diaries on his hand press, one by one, and had a dream of me, without knowing me.

Henry and I get into bed. The little bell of burning mercury rings so many times. Henry has a way of installing himself with such leisure and thoroughness—the most slumbering layers awaken to a frenzied palpitation.

He falls asleep. I have to run away.

After dinner Hugh and I have to call on Pepin, Alta Gracia, Father and Maruca. Father looks rather like a gazelle, reposing in an upholstered bourgeois world, with many cushions, and a portly wife. He is getting old, talks less, has no rebellions, no fever.

At eleven we leave, bored, and I let Hugh go home alone.

I meet Gonzalo. A passionate Gonzalo. And in me there is an inexhaustible emotion.

So many layers of the being. I feel Gonzalo possesses me as a woman might—that is, not with that ultimate act which solders man and woman but by voluptuous, external caresses, a *fleur de peau.* No woman can ever arouse in another woman the deep savage incredibly profound shock produced by the man, the very foundation of the flesh rocks, it is a moment of delirium.

I want Gonzalo to reach this female dark orgasm center. He has now and then, but not as violently as Henry. I want to yield to him.

D ECEMBER 4 , 1 9 3 7

*M*ARGUERITE SVALBERG COMES AFTER NOT SEEING us for a year. Looks at Hugh's paintings and finds him getting at last reincarnated. *"Plus vivant."* Hugh has only integrated this year, with painting and with Carteret's friendship. When Hugh left, Marguerite said: "And you, you have changed enormously. You are *centre.* I feel you have surrendered many things, are sad but whole and strong. Some disillusion has thrown you back into yourself."

"Into my work," I said.

She looked at Gonzalo's horoscope: *"Ça colle merveilleusement, sensuellement, mais il y a des dissonances spirituels. Vous ne vivez pas sur le même plan—il n'a pas la même qualité d'esprit."*

Marguerite's phrases hurt me, like fortune-telling—corroborating my fears. Under my *birth as artist* what a tragedy. How each day it becomes more and more difficult for me to *meet* Gonzalo. All our feelings cannot bridge the abysses. Each day he is more of a realist. Marguerite had seen him at the big party I gave. Said I fell in love with Gonzalo's madness, the poet in him—and this drunk, poetic gypsy Gonzalo is becoming a prosaic professional revolutionist.

With sadness I read Pierre Jean Jouve, intoxicate myself with *Dans les Années Profondes.* What a potent drug! I float again. While people come—Lantelme, my Father, Gascoyne, Maruca—I write the first part of the "womb-labyrinth" piece. I cannot explain to Gonzalo that I am making a revolution, a spiritual one, all by myself, with my writing.

Pierre Jean Jouve, and Carteret. Carteret's home. At the top of an old house. Before we enter he has seen us through his periscope. We enter a dungeon, a black-burnt hallway with glowworm lamps. We enter a cave of red hangings, fireplace, shadows!

L'antre du voyageur. We entered Mount Athos, Canary Islands, Hungary, Lapland. I sit on reindeer furs, on tiny Russian chairs. I pick up a spoon from Mount Athos, carved of wood, framed in the handle, behind a lattice of fine wood lace, colored metallic paper. Hung on the wall a mushroom shaped like a *bénitiers des poisons,* like a toadstool. The frail Hungarian instruments vibrate on the wall, the heavy Lapland boots hang ready for hunting. A Turkish rug is ready for flight through space, books hung high, as a sea star, a knife from Greece, incense, bottles filled with water from the Black Sea, the Aegean Sea, north pools and rivers, stones from the mouth of a Canarian crater, lava, seashells, human bones, a skeleton, a hat from Manila, Russian wooden cups, shawls, a dress from Ibiza, a whip, bird's down from a nest in Constantinople. When he opens a valise it is Lapland opening, furs sewn with the nerves of the animals, antlers like tortured giraffes, stones, dried lichen. It is China with a cottoned celestial blue blouse, it is Bali with colored handkerchiefs. Lamps are covered by medieval iron hats. A little book lies open on a diminutive book, a Chinese book. The pen in the inkstand comes from Russia. Cigarettes from Germany, from India. Hashish, opium. A book on torture is caught in one of the antlers. A dried root lies twisted. Dried cactus is glued to the window. A dried fish is glued to the mirror. Three candles burning. The small, delicate instruments are playing. A colored crystal ball swings from the lamp. Beer glasses from Munich are encircled by little peasant dolls. Necklaces hang with rosaries, with belts, with Chinese manuscripts and dried mint. Stones and dried bones, the tiny skeleton of a bird, a Lapland fur hat with four corners, a painting of a woman naked, laughing savagely because a pig has eaten a child's head. Valises open spill erotic postcards from Morocco, veils, slippers. On the bed lies a Japanese hat, a Tahitian skirt, and in every corner I feel Jean's fantasies spiraling from every pipe, even from one made of a lobster's toe! I would like to lie down with him and take opium. His eyes are full of the marvelous, widened by wonder and faith in miracles. He is a young magician. He can disguise himself. He can dream.

He laid the fur boots for me on a little chair. I knew they were for me. I took the bird down to make a small cushion for the Lapland crib. Objects like the cave of Ali Baba—not one without meaning and life. Spoons, pipes, silks, books, stones used for Black Masses. Magic Chaos. Prestidigitation of all the voyages. Out of his pockets come evocations. Out of his valises the earth and sea. Out of his eyes faith and the dream. His mother smashed his violin, his joy, his life, the music in him. He seeks it. He digs. He became an archaeologist of his own soul, he probed and categorized to tap again the source of the music killed by his mother. He reads handwriting, astrology, analysis. He conjures. He prays. He is possessed with wandering, with forgetfulness, timelessness. He gives himself away beyond retrieve, gives, travels. He lives in a haze. In a labyrinth. His game is with fetishes. The water from the Black Sea is in this bottle, in this room. Into a room he brings back the universe. The piano and the instruments on the wall are muted. But the music is in him, flooding the place, it vibrates, every object in it vibrates with it. I want to sink into the harmonies concealed in the shell of his misery. He is wandering outside, yet in every object around him I could place my ear and hear the sea his mother could not kill.

Pierre Jean Jouve has seized moods, sensations, reveries, and revelations captured by no one else. A new world, hung between bestial desire and hallucination, between perversity and analysis. Open-eyed passion again, stricken with death each time.

Jean. Jean Carteret talking to me about the problem of politics. Understanding, he alone, what I feel. The human, the natural communism in me. The clash with realistic communism. My individual world keeping me. But everywhere, a realistic expression of communism—realism. I am ashamed of dreaming, tempted to abandon my individual world *and* my cosmic world for what seems to be the manifestation of a collective world. Yet absolutely unable to abandon it. With all my love of Gonzalo, with the suffering of people touching me as it does, I cannot participate or act in this communism. Neither can Jean. We both feel the life pull. We are connected with the present. Our dream does not take us away from human immediacy. "But," says Jean, staring into space, "this is not the expression of *our* humanism, our humanity, our communism. This is a practical, utilitarian, concrete, factual, realistic manifestation. That is why we cannot enter into it. It is not a selfish individual life which pulls us away, it is another *level of life. We live on another level.* We have to act on another level. We are not escaping, we are not dreaming an opium life, we are dreaming the dream of life itself, a cosmic life, a Neptunian life. Our action is on another level."

For these words I was grateful to him.

"We are living in a realistic epoch, an epoch of concrete details, of economics. We are not of it."

From that moment on, I understood my poetic world, my work of which I have felt ashamed (while yet unable sincerely to abandon it), living true as usual to my strongest feeling as the right one for me, but, as usual, with human scruples because I am in contact with suffering. Yet I could not make a single gesture toward action for Spain. All I hear around me is gossip, details, stories of errors, injustice, chaos, of propaganda. Yesterday at Father's: "We must use the Nationalist Musicians for propaganda as the communists have done with their musicians." The artist is used for propaganda as an accessory to the army.

I cannot act otherwise. In my supreme wisdom I gave Gonzalo strength to fulfill his destiny. But hearing Jean balk was marvelous because I feel alone. True, Henry has the same attitude, but in Henry the self-preserving ego instinct is so blatant, he is so far from dynamic contact with the present that he represents still another kind of isolation. He has his work. But I live not *only* for my work, and the human problem torments me.

Jean looks luminous. He delights me. I love where he lives. I feel a kind of love for him. We talked until late, and the world seemed so marvelous, in contrast with my Father's world, Gonzalo's world, that I was ensorcelled.

At night I had a dream: Jean possessed me, so powerfully, and he said I knew nothing yet of what possession *could* be, I was inexperienced. *He knew of a greater rhythm.* I abandoned myself. But very soon he gave me the key to his room to give to another woman and sent her a message to come through me.

The cruelty of this overwhelmed me and yet I awoke with a feeling of magic about Jean, of warmth toward him. I know that he has had many women, that women do not resist him. Allendy is analyzing him. Allendy was attracted to him for Jean could be his son—the *poet* in Allendy who was stifled.

Hugh, during such an evening, is deeply disappointing. He utters banalities, clichés. He talks like an empty man—an automat. He is lost. He loves Jean as a spectacle. He does not talk Jean's language. He appears absolutely as an ordinary man. Why I have always believed in Hugh in spite of his ordinary, obvious platitudes, I don't know. He receives. I say to him: "Why don't you compose your talks as you do your painting, think of it, feel it as a creation. Either say nothing or say what approximates your feeling." Hugh talks like a wife repeating what her husband says. He is not original. He is a reflection of me.

I have eluded Jean. He was Hugh's friend. I did not want to enchant him. But even absent, Jean felt me. Jean worshiped me. I was terribly afraid Hugh would be exposed, Hugh would become the channel, the transmitter for the fantasies of Jean. Hugh would pale and shrivel. And I did not want this. But last night it happened. I feel now that I want to go to Jean's place once and smoke hashish with him.

I rewrote the "womb" piece. It is not good. I am tired and harassed by visitors. I don't sleep enough. *Life* seems marvelous again. I always have the courage to live by what I believe, but I get sad and desperate to be alone. I have been for the first time, for two days, unfaithful to Gonzalo—because Jean *was* the poet for me, he was the dream.

DECEMBER 8, 1937

*T*HEN I WENT TO GONZALO, AND AFTER OUR CA-
resses in the dark, we talked. When I touch
his communism it is so pure, so whole. He resists my attacks with
such force, he talks so *above* the weaknesses and vulgarities of it, with
such a vision. He says such true things: the literature, the metaphysics,
the philosophies, they were never effective without violence. Violence
was necessary, inevitable. People would not change their lives or free
themselves through Nietzsche, or psychology, or art. The revolution,
the violence was necessary even to establish religions. The art, the
poem, the novel incite men to act. The act is necessary.

I come out with two definite feelings: 1. I must hasten the crisis
(even Jean said: the only remedy is to *hasten* the revolution, so it will
be over, and we can go on). 2. I must keep Gonzalo because his
strength and unity lie in the act.

How? There are ways. I can get money from Rebecca [West] for
Paix et Démocratie. I can mail secret letters from Italy, England,
America. I thought of the first today. The mailing of letters I offered
to do when I heard all mail from France was censored in Peru. Now
that these things are definite in me, I feel relief. I believe in communism. I will help it in my own way and through Gonzalo. I *believe*
in his communism which is so pure that it filters right through the
falsities and errors actually made.

Then Renatta Bugatti came like a storm—a storm with the head
of a Roman soldier, and the intelligence of a Sphinx. A storm controlled by a tremendously full head. We talked like two cannons—
aiming each one always at the center of the being. It was wonderful,
breathtaking. She was surprised by my "delicacy" after reading my
preface to *Tropic [of Cancer]*. She marveled at my hands. I at her

force. Such a force that I remember hearing her play at the Salle Pleyel thirteen years ago, I remember the suit she wore, her head.

I do love these outsized women. I love directness, instinct, passion, and dynamism above all. I get a great exaltation from such women. I hurl my own strength at them—it is a bout, *un corp à corps*. I left her feeling such strength that I pressed my closed fist against the taxi as if I would break it open. Strange, these women who terrify men, who devour or efface or destroy them, are the women I can handle. I do not have to disguise myself as I do for man. For man I have to act with hidden strength, indirectly, subtly. Women I face in the open. I have not yet met a man who gives me the feeling that I can strike him, oppose him, hurl myself against him, without hurting him.

What a honeycomb of friendships. David, Renatta, San Faustino, Elena, Jean, Edgar, Betty, reconciliation with Fred, Larry. Larry, I don't know why, has diminished. He abandons himself to the flow limply—does not retain his color, form, voice. He looks like drift-wood—too long in water. I look for the eyes—they are faded. He fades.

DECEMBER 10, 1937

I HAVE ENTERED AT LAST THE SECOND DREAM WITH Gonzalo. I have entered the dream of communism—I have entered into its essence, the *first vision* of it, its purity. Through the wholeness of Gonzalo I entered that mystic core of *my* own communism, exactly as I took only the filtered essence of psychoanalysis, of astrology. I entered the poetic structure, without the dregs and without the decomposition that follows all dreams. I jumped over the decomposed, the dying forms of communism into communism pure.

Because of Gonzalo's wholeness, I saw another way of living out the desire that *others* may live—another form of giving. To give *individually* becomes increasingly difficult and discouraging. To give individually means to be submerged, killed by the endless needs of others. One must give collectively.

This is how it is done: You meet Mr. Ben Protter, who is straightening out Mr. [Edward] Titus's affairs and who gives you copies of your book on Lawrence in payment of royalties. You take your tentacles out of your handbag, your antennas, of which you place one part against your ears and the other on the chest of your patient. The pressure says: a communist. So you put your apparatus for the deaf in your ears (as normally you would not catch the sound of economics, crisis, collective running of factories) and you listen in. Then you talk about *Paix et Démocratie* with lowered eyes, admitting delicately it is an anti-fascist organization, and insinuating the potential revolutionary intention contained in its elegant *coffres* on the Rue de Lille. The man warms up with the cause fever. His eyes shine with high tension. And you exchange propaganda. You file his name in the boxes.

Then you tell Gonzalo: "I have another address for you, a possible member."

I walked away in the soft rain. The doctor had just said: "You are very pale." I was looking for a shirt for Gonzalo. I carried the string with which I had measured his neck. Gonzalo's neck. A shirt for Gonzalo. A church bell was tolling. I stopped. It was strange, this grave gong sounding through the agitiated city, city of nerves, wires, horns. I was one with the church, the bell, and not with the city. I was apart. In this vaulted dark silence in me where only large, deep notes sounded, only prayers, only the marvelous, shone the white Host of communism—a separate holy communism as it must have been in Russia. No connection with the talk with Mr. Protter. A world of great arches swung over vast spaces, there I lived with the sound of church bells, everything communion, everything with shadows around it, people isolated by their communion with God. This was the avenue des Ternes, with shops for *sports d'hiver,* where I sought the rough, coarse-textured shirt that Gonzalo likes, rude and simple, loose and nonchalant. Tinsel for Christmas. Rain. "You are very pale," said the doctor.

Il sagit de vivre sans étiquettes. Renatta asked Jean: "What is your occupation?"

I answered: "His occupation is to walk through all of them, *en état de transparence,* to live only in the essence, and in the frame of none."

Sitting at the table, Renatta before me, David at my right, I feel sexually aroused, sensitized. All my feelings taper into this nest which moves like seaweed—imperceptibly but stirring a current. At this moment I feel Jean's presence so sensually I no longer hear the conversation. I know he feels me.

I have again the desire to enter a lion's den. I am absolutely free of fear and anguish. I stand at the center feeling everything, my love of Henry, of Gonzalo, of Jean, of the world, of *all.*

"Your obsession to confront a lion," said Jean, "comes because you have so much of the *dompteuse,* the lion tamer in you."

Work on diary. Names changed. Cuts made. Work on sending MS to magazines, answer to requests. Correspondence regarding sale of my books, distribution. Work for Thurema's perfume, letters, sending announcements. Work for Gonzalo to get money, adherents, the participation of psychoanalysts. Work for *The Booster.* Getting ads. Subscriptions. Correspondence enormous. All the multiple services rendered to friends, hospitality to whoever comes alone, who is lost.

I am impelled to charm, to seduce. Placed before a person I unfold, open all my bags of tricks, innocently. I act by a compulsion to enchant even when I don't want to. Afterward I'm surprised when the person wants to see me again (if it's someone I'm not interested in!).

Villa Seurat. Tension. The tension broken, relieved by sensuality. The sensual feelings of the week all poured into fusion with Henry, the orgasm with Henry. All the caresses given in space to Jean, all the caresses given to Gonzalo, poured into the orgasm with Henry. Yet I felt the orgasm with Gonzalo, but not as strong—feel it more when we are half asleep and he more relaxed. The great secret of sensuality is relaxation. I think the high-keyed ones miss fulfillment, the hypersensitive, exalted people like June, Gonzalo, and myself are the ones whose tension is too high for pleasure. Henry brought me back to an earth rhythm, a plant slowness. Gonzalo relaxed with me and found enjoyment. He could never stay all night with a woman, rest in her. With me he does. Strain. All strain defeats life.

One could say hysteria comes because of unfulfillment, but that is not so. Hysteria is latent in all artists, strain in the neurotic. It makes fulfillment impossible.

When I visit Elena I ask myself: *Is this clairvoyance* or an obsession I feel? I keep imagining *Henry* there. How he would like the lack of good taste, the certain vulgarity about Elena's face. The prints, the big homely bedroom slippers, the blue colors instead of my oranges and black. Going to her place has become intolerable. Our personal relationship goes on: a comedy. She feels I understand her. I do. My fear does not devaluate her. It comes from my appreciation of her large, "moving picture" beauty, her intelligence and colorfulness. She feels I create her. I do. Only I do not let her enter the magic current of my life. The few fragments I offered, Moricand, Jean, Eduardo, Joaquin, Helba, Gonzalo, she made no link with because she does not love. She sees only the defects. She sees *only* what they take and not what they bring. Jean said: "I see her as a woman standing beside an empty dress and she cannot get into the dress." But she mocks his beard, his bad taste in dressing, his timidity in society.

My fears come because I find her so fascinating—so highly colored, capricious, emotional, stormy, violent.

I believe it is not *unfaithfulness* which drives the *grandes amoureuses*—but that when you are highly sensitized to love, when you vibrate deeply, sexually, bodily, when you love passionately, then it is like a current in the body which, being perpetual, creates a warm contact with all. I feel so many people physically, amorously, because I am in a state of love, like a mystic, and it is greater than myself, it is immense, the overflow. Just as activity creates activity, energy creates energy, creation leads to creation, so passion creates more and more capacity for passion. The being is enlarged, its capacity highly increased, and you have the answer to the amorous expansion of all born LOVERS. That is why the word *infidelity* means nothing to me.

DECEMBER 12, 1937

DEEP MYSTICAL JOY IN SACRIFICE, IN OBTAINING Allendy's support of *Paix et Démocratie* rather than his subscription to my diary, in listening to his confidences: "You tell me you are feeling old. Well, the day you wake up with that feeling again I will accept your ever-renewed invitation to sleep with you and I will show you you are not getting old!" Not to arouse his despair I always refuse his invitations by saying: "*Je suis une femme frigide.*" He asks me: "Are you happy?" I say: "I am philosophic. I live with the relative—I work."

Came home and danced to the radio. But seas of emotions heaving under my feet. I feel a tension which could shoot me to the moon— a *bolide*—or cause a war. I could weep and commit murder. I want to be hypnotized, anesthesized, insensitized.

DECEMBER 15, 1937

GONZALO AND I MEETING LATE AT NIGHT. The hotel room. Gonzalo takes me and lies back satisfied. I have not felt the climax. I feel like biting him, like devouring him. I bite his shoulders and neck. It gives him pleasure. He shivers with pleasure. He bites me gently. He begs that I bite him deeper, hurt him. I bite him as hard as I can without wounding him, tearing the flesh. He falls asleep vibrating under my caresses, murmuring about bliss and joy. I cannot sleep. I think of Jean. I picture Jean hypnotizing me. I lie on the red cover of Jean's bed, on the reindeer fur. Jean hypnotizes me but passes his fingers between my legs softly, very softly. Jean's fingers arouse me. The flame comes—thrusts me twice. I fall asleep.

Next evening. I am sitting in Henry's studio. Henry has gone to the bathroom. I hear a woman moaning next door. The walls are thin. At first I think she is sick. I sit on the divan to hear better. I hear the rhythmic moaning, dark and guttural, of pleasure, the inhuman, dark moan of the animal. Ah—Ah—Ah—crescendo. I feel her pleasure. I hear the man's beast voice, voice of effort in rhythm with his pushing. Between my legs I feel a tremor, a heat. I feel their pleasure. I imagine the scene. I would like to see if she is dressed or naked. The man moans like Henry. Low animal cries. My sex trembles with pleasure. When her moans get louder and quicker and when together they almost cry out at the climax, I feel the pulsation, the orgasm.

Just when Henry is returning to the studio, a quiet Henry talking about Thomas Mann. He says: "You look sleepy." I am sitting there, dazed by what has happened. Henry and I get into bed. He reads to me. I fall asleep.

Morning. Turkish bath. Lunch with Elena to whom a *voyante* has said: "You will go north, you will cross an ocean, and find love and money." And four days later Ansermet renews his invitation for her to go with him to Norway, not to London. She is renting her apartment. She tells me I have done so much for her, given her life. So I work miracles despite my jealousy. Apart from my jealousy, I like Elena because she plays with things. Together we remove things from their tragic plane and we volatilize them. They all assume colors, like dreams. And we tell each other things, intense and vivid, exactly as people tell each other their dreams in the morning.

Then Renatta Bugatti playing—her mask tortured and tense. As she plays I hear the man and woman in her moaning as they rhythmically push against each other. I hear Renatta entering into the piano, possessing the music. It is a sexual bout but in the end it is defeat. The melody does not rise. Her will cannot accomplish what the man and woman of last night accomplished, a moment of pleasure. The passion is of blood and nerves in her, not of catgut and ivory. The *coffre* she pounds into is her own body, with a male violence, and the mask, the mask is of the one who reaches neither the orgasm nor sainthood. No music rose or passed out of the window. It was too heavy with blood and unspilled juices.

At the Stuart Gilberts, talking with Denise, who asks me: "And that work on the diary, how is it going?"

I answer briskly: "It is going." But the truth is I cannot do it. Every day I do *other* work, I find pretexts for postponing.

December 18, 1937

*P*USHING MYSELF TO VISIT HELBA IN THEIR NEW place. She has been continuously ill. She comes out looking like a bedraggled gypsy, unkempt hair, wearing a man's shirt, and over this a kimono made out of a clown's red robe which she dyed black. Her face is yellow and old. But my pity is exhausted, for it is all due to stupidity, ignorance, and self-destruction. My doctor was taking care of her, but she believes in no doctor and keeps changing. She kisses me ardently and says she is beginning to feel better. But I am not eager to stay. It is like visiting a tomb, a mortuary, or the morgue. I am really angry at her will to die—and she drags Gonzalo into anxiety, fear, dirt. It is a rivalry between life and death. I even hate her disintegration, it is not even a tempestuous suicide. It is a rotting away.

A few hours later Gonzalo throws himself on me, but there is no semen in him. Much of my nervousness with him comes from the many times he wilts and dies inside of me, murmuring: "There is nothing inside—that has often happened to me."

This insecurity about Gonzalo's potency—the knowledge that he has less semen than anyone I know—fills me with uneasiness. And he does not accept it, which makes it worse. He *wants* to possess me. He tries over and over again—and at such moments my own desire dies completely. I felt depressed. I felt life ugly and monstrous. Over our heads an apache couple were talking in bestial tones. The shabbiness of the room overwhelmed me—the disillusion in Gonzalo.

Today I awoke with a bitter taste in my mouth. (And all the talk now about Gonzalo's work—the press.) I wanted to find again my unshatterable dream with Henry. I went to see him—and there it was. Talk a creation, and sensuality potent. When people cease to murmur like human beings, when the beast voice in them cries, when they forget who they are, then it is the sensual fusion, then it is the marriage of the instinct. I came away quiet, but profoundly sad.

DECEMBER 21, 1937

FAUSTINO LENDS ME HER APARTMENT. GONZALO and I arrive and he looks like a lion contemplating a lettuce leaf! But I light a fire to give the place life. And we get into the downy bed. The light behind us filters into the bed and exposes Gonzalo's bronze penis hardening against my luminous leg. I say: "We ought to be chaste for a month." But Gonzalo takes me. He frets like a child: "I will not be able to sleep. I did not sleep all last night." I caress him hypnotically until he falls asleep. And I dream back to the loveliest moment, before we came into the room. A cold freezing night. Gonzalo and I in the taxi. The windows clouded with frost. Gonzalo was cold. I opened my black fur coat and he put his head on my breast. He made himself cold. I was so acutely happy, so happy to be holding him that I thought: My God, the strongest love in me is maternal.

I write to remain close to Gonzalo, to the feelings he gives me. I write on the table at the Villa Seurat, while Henry sleeps and I watch the *poule au pot* boiling generously. I write as one sits by the fire to get warm and remember. It seems like a dream, at moments, when I am too swiftly carried by the current, the trip to Santa Margherita carrying important letters to mail for Gonzalo.

His dream out of his anxiety for the risk I run: I was in a prison. But the prison was like a church. It was very beautiful. The bars were very large as they are in old Spanish churches. A woman was sewing beautiful things for me on the other side of the bars. But Gonzalo could come in and out.

Henry is asleep. The kettle on the stove is whistling, the *poule au pot* is boiling. Elena and I said good-bye with electric green-eyed sincerity. A toy is taken away—one of the dream personages, a large de Chirico woman against a blue, blue canvas, half statue, half movie actress, an Amazon, a Greek statue of liberty and plenitude, but afraid of burglars, and pouting with selfish sighs and wishes, with envies and appetites, with demands.

She takes the subway at Passy to go to Norway and rents her apartment to Eduardo through my inevitable *élan* to solve others' problems and help them to live. I am a factory, a chess player, and at times I have the feeling I am the one holding all the strings. That is why at other times I want to be hypnotized, or become the victim of the Italian police. Maybe I will *rest* in jail!

JANUARY 10, 1938

QUAI DE PASSY. TRUNKS PACKED. CURTAINS DOWN. Rugs rolled. Books in boxes. Division between what is going to London and what is staying here with me.

The first thing I feel as I open my diary is the tear from Hugh, the pain of change. My guardian angel, my young father, my fixed stability, my protector, my brother, and my child. A deep pain. Nothing *replaces* him. Nothing takes his place. The life with Henry is different. The life with Gonzalo.

Behind the shock of change and disruption lie many layers. Peaceful days in Santa Margherita. Rest. Strength. The electric current when Jean and I kissed good-bye on the cheek. I felt his intensity. There is always lightning in his eyes. Jean's great love for Hugh exactly like mine. *"Il est l'homme diamant."* We are walking in the rain, after Hugh's departure, feeling lost without him. Moment of weakness shared, understood. Jean sad. We kiss again on the cheek intensely. I go to Henry. But I dream about Jean. I am in Jean's apartment (he had offered me a room in his apartment). I experience an extraordinary joy, a bliss, an ecstasy. I see only light—a High Place. Jean has been washing my stockings!

A marvelous, warm, sensual night with Gonzalo. I fixed my room as if nothing were packed. Candlelight. A dinner on the little black table. Warmth. Voluptuousness. We lie in bed asking ourselves why the candles tremble so. Gonzalo says: "They are anxious." Gonzalo is luminous again, washed of contingences, and in a mood of understanding. We are in the dream again. Yet strangely, mysteriously, my imagination follows Jean, feels Jean. I am jealous of an Italian woman whose masterful driving he admires. And Jean, of humble origin, is dazzled by the aristocrat, afraid. I dazzle him. I am taboo. I am the wife of Hugh. But each time he sees me the dream asserts itself and we talk one language, and we talk with a vastness, a limitlessness. He understands me and my life absolutely. He has the key to me. I to him. I see him untrammeled, fluid, free, magical. I cannot see the present chains which arrest him, block him. I see him free, with a wide, cosmic rhythm.

Slowly the weakness left by Hugh's departure healed. He will be back in three weeks. I plunged into the enormous labor of the moving. I cook for Gonzalo, and for Henry. I got rid of Janine the maid. I deprive myself, to give more to Henry, Gonzalo, Helba, and to Jean. I feel no pain of sacrifice. I enjoy the giving too much. *Je me dépouille.* I simplify—simplify. I send the best we have to Hugh. I keep the chipped plates, the odd towels, the unmatched sheets, the old dark furniture. I send the white, the new to Hugh. I return to my somber Byzantine possessions—the Arab bed, table stools, the large working table, the black bookcases, Byzantine lamps. I reduce. I throw away. I weed.

In the rain, I look for a hotel. I write to Hugh all day, in bits, here and there. His voice over the telephone keeps him near. He is the man without fault, without weakness, without treachery. He loves his naïveté, his integrity, his faith. *"Il m'accepte."* No one gives me what he gives me. As soon as he leaves I feel the terror and tragedy of life.

Today I wear my suit, I work, I arrange. I am consoled by the strange liberty.

Against disruption I fight with order. The whole moving was done smoothly—highly organized!

JANUARY 12, 1938

*D*AZED, DAZZLED BY MY FREEDOM. NO ONE AT home waiting for me. I sleep until I wake up. I leave the apartment. I can lunch where I please. I find a hotel on boulevard St. Germain in front of Les Deux Maggots. A marvelous quarter. I eat for six francs in a vegetarian restaurant with Eduardo. I pay for my room, twenty-three francs. I am very careful so as to have more to share. I am writing for the last time in quai de Passy. Gonzalo will come and sleep. I am full of joy.

He helped me find a room. A red one, a *"coquette"* red—very simple, but warm. I have a religious feeling, I am integrating myself. Living with three men was shattering me. The tension was too great. Now it is intermittent. When Hugh comes I'll be with him and absent for Henry and Gonzalo. In between I am so free. What a pleasure, this freedom. To roam, to eat anywhere. Neither Gonzalo nor Henry exert any control. Henry is gentle. I feel a great peace, a joy.

What I seek is the *vie féerique,* where all things happen as in the dream. Not comfort but the smoothness of magical happenings. Not luxury but the stage illusion of beauty. Not security but the drug effects of harmony. Not order but the unreal arrangements of objects as in the dream. Not perfection but the illusion of perfection. Not clock time but the instantaneity of miracles. Not labor but the realization of all wishes. Not service, but an immediate answer to all formulated desires. Not peace but the sequence of the dream. Not absence of death but the eternal life of the dream. Not rebellion against change, loss, death, passing of time but the quest of the eternal in every moment. The transfusion of blood into the dream. The dream includes violence, murder, pain, torture, and death, but no *end*. In the dream one never touches bottom even after one dies.

Hotel Acropolis, 160 boulevard St. Germain, room fifty-five. I was face-to-face with my work. There was no more evading it. I began to work on the very morning of the fourteenth. And today I'm finished with the cutting out.

I liked my rhythm. Two or three hours of work in the morning. Lunch in the little restaurants around here, either with Eduardo and Jimmy, or Gonzalo. I went once to lunch at Henry's, but I found Fred there, and I didn't try again. Two or three more hours of work. Coffee at the Café Flore with Eduardo or chance meetings with Gascoyne. Life free, easy, always impromptu. More work before dinner. Evenings at Villa Seurat or with Gonzalo.

Last night my rhythm broke because Larry, Henry, and I discussed the reality and the problems of the diary publication. (With ambivalence, I have tried both to uncover the secret and to hide myself. Henry's essay in the *Criterion* gave me away.) The conflict was so violent I got sick today—I lost my *élan*.

I was quite happy until today. I feel poor, I no longer take taxis, I eat for six francs, and I find it all good. Good for the artist. Life reduced to its simplest basis. Hugh telephones.

I respond fully to Gonzalo.

But Henry and I are separated by a hard, dissonant mood in him, a completely egotistical, inhuman mood, because he is not writing. I was beginning to feel a kind of ascetic joy, the joy of work. I wanted to go to church. Gonzalo alone, at night, could restore me to warm, sensual life.

I must go on.

The *reality* problem will be solved afterward.

Dreams: An African—or a Hindu—all covered with jewelry, gold, elaborate headdress, studded with stones. My mother, who is very old, falls into his arms, asking for his love. He repulses her. He loves me. I take my mother in my arms to console her. I look at him and say: "Couldn't you do it—just out of pity?" But he is inflexible. He mounts a high tower. I look up at him. He throws down a knife which pierces the lower part of my stomach. It does not hurt. I am to dance with it, to dance ecstatically. He will pronounce on my dancing.

A man whose profession is to kill cows, to cut them up in little pieces (as I saw cows cut up on board the Spanish ship coming from Barcelona). But he does it giving them an injection first. I am relieved.

Another dream of love about Jean—kissing without touching the lips but intensely, desiring.

Gonzalo's delicacy. I gave him all I had for his rent. It was not quite enough to cover extra charges. I didn't know it. I was without money, and had written to Hugh. Meanwhile we shared the little I borrowed from Eduardo. Gonzalo never told me about the rent shortage (I would have found it somehow). He did not dare face his *concierge* the next day without it. He slept in an armchair at *Paix et Démocratie.* Suffered. Suffers from the sacrifices I make, whereas Henry never worried much. I discovered it by myself.

JANUARY 22, 1938

*H*ENRY, THROWN BY HIS NEW WRITING INTO SPACE, cut off from all of us. Pale. Cold. Mad. I walk the streets with a *human* despair. Henry says: "I suffer like an animal. I'm like an animal. No one can help. No one is strong enough."

I walk the streets, dreaming of his work, of his orientation. I know what he is doing and how it surpasses us all. I am aware, as one is aware of the sky. But the woman suffers. "Perhaps he doesn't love me anymore."

I'm not schizophrenic. When I feel the earth opening under my feet, I turn to human beings. Henry is not there. The moonstorm is coming, mounting like a fever. Gonzalo is not in space. He is here. Like a flame. He is jealous because Hugh is arriving. His mouth is wounded. It reveals the torture. We kiss desperately, parting at the corner of the street as if for a long, long voyage. A beggar starts playing on his mandolin. Gonzalo and I were walking toward him. He was not playing then. I looked at him. I knew he was going to play at the moment when Gonzalo and I would separate on the corner. And of course, while we kissed the mandolin began to play.

I mailed my letter to Henry, telling him what was happening to him and that I was waiting, I refused to be pushed away. I was here for his return to earth (I feared his insanity). His equilibrium is tenuous. He has such a grandiose idea of himself and at the same time such doubts. I feel such anguish over all that befalls him. Anguish over Gonzalo, but in another world—reality. Violence. Physical danger.

My work is at a standstill. The blood is in my ears. My body is painfully alive. A passion for Gonzalo that makes me leap and burn. Henry's last kiss on my mouth because a phrase in Jouve untied the knots in him—and when I ran over to him he was ready to write again. He was happy. I came just as he had finished my letter. We kissed.

Hugh—the sexual hatred of him—and when the sexual nightmare is over, the deep tenderness. He brings back two paintings.

I have such a strong feeling of the *earth turning*. Everything is in motion.

Then suddenly it ceases turning. And it stands still *upside down*. Everything is reversed. Because I am sitting the next evening waiting for Gonzalo at the Café Flore and he does not come. A man, a few tables away, is mocking Artaud, who is locked up in St. Anne, parodying his speeches, his fears, his *délire de persécution*. I walk up to him and say: "It is you who should be locked up, not Artaud."

But what has happened to Gonzalo? It is nine o'clock. I have not eaten. He said between 7:30 and eight. It is raining. I run back to the hotel. Hugh and Jean are already gone. They got tired of waiting for me. I don't know where they are. Gascoyne comes into the café. He is drugged. Eduardo comes. He has a headache. He is far away. Jimmy's whimsical Irish fancies can't bring him back. What has happened to Gonzalo? I pick up the newspaper. Once he had said: "I picked up the paper and saw on the front page the photo of one of my best friends—murdered the night before by the fascists." That is how it could happen. Gonzalo could kiss me one evening on a street corner and that very night. . . .

I dragged Eduardo with me. I looked for Gonzalo in all the cafés where he goes. I measured my anxiety. I said to myself: He can't be dead. I would feel it. He may be sick.

It is drizzling. In the Coupole a friend of Eduardo's stops him. "Don't stay around here, Feri wants to kill you."

Eduardo and I sit in another café, talking about Feri and June and Weidman!* No, nothing has happened to Gonzalo. I hate to return to my empty room. The moonstorm is wearing me out. I am in a fog, and in anguish. When I get to my room I can't sleep. I want Hugh to come. He alone can take my anguish away. I can't sleep. I hear voices in the street. I think it is Hugh and Jean. I lean out. It is two apaches talking on the street corner. I remember waiting for Henry in New York. Lying on my bed I have a feeling that I am crucified. I am pinned down by pain again, caught, trapped. I cannot free myself. Anxiety. Pain. The world still seems reversed, arrested. The noises of the street immense, deafening. Suspense. What has happened to Gonzalo? I can't protect him, nor Henry. But Henry is never in danger of dying. I am pinned down to my bed, and I can't sleep. I can only imagine: Diaz, assassinated last night. Three bullet holes. Gonzalo's body. I am going crazy. I think when Hugh is not here I am crazy. Everything looks *queer*. Everything looks abnormal. The café. The streets. The people. As houses look just before an earthquake. Nothing has happened to Gonzalo—I can sleep. I will try to rest in God again. Then Hugh comes and I can sleep. And the next

---

*Apparently, Anaïs Nin is referring to Roland Freedman, one of June Miller's lovers, who, according to rumors circulating, had hanged himself after she left him.

morning I carry a letter to the little café where Gonzalo goes. No telephone. No Gonzalo. Hugh and Jean go to an exhibit. I am too tormented. I will go and see Henry. I take the subway. On the way I remember Henry has an engagement with Kahane and the Durrells. I return. I decide to walk to the café, to see if Gonzalo got my letter. Yes, they tell me, he got it. Then he is well. He came. But why doesn't he call me? Did he see me go to the Villa Seurat the morning before? Just as I left the café Gonzalo *felt* something, left his work, and came running after me! He had been sick at home—no telephone. Today he had called up and the hotel had not told me. Joy. We sit in a little café. I am breathing again. I walk back to the hotel. I pass by the church. I enter. I can't pray but I feel a deep, strange purity in me, a kind of holiness. In front of the door an automobile is burning. The firemen are working on it. I did not stop to watch. Inside the church, what calm, what a haven. The world, like some broken wheel, the world, like some machine that was jammed, the world began *slowly to move,* to turn. The world, or my blood which has ceased flowing, which had turned black with anguish last night. And this blood, this blood I hold with a piece of cotton inserted into the vagina as the dancers do—nothing showing outside, no belt and no bandages, which I hate. I was walking between Hugh and Jean and the little piece of cotton, too wet, slipped out, lay on the sidewalk. Hugh saw my distress. I pushed his elbow and said in English: "Pretend not to notice please." When they left me and I walked to the subway I saw an *agent.* I thought he would arrest me.

JANUARY 24, 1938

*H*UGH ACTS LIKE A HUNGRY LOVER. I FEEL GUILTY for all I make him suffer. Guilty. Deprivation. Alone in London. I say it is to heighten our life. Separation and pain, the pleasure of rare meetings. "I am your mistress." No home, no stability, no continuous union. "Adventure. That is how love is sustained, kept wonderful." Hugh obeys. "You'll swing from London to your adventure here." Docile. His feelings are pent up. He lives as Gonzalo and Henry do, without a wife. Though I have fabricated this to justify my staying in Paris, it works by a miracle, as I invented it. Hugh feels the heightening and likes it. Feels the intensity, the cruelty, the inhumanness, and the wonder. Jean and I throw him into this life of hazard, chance, intermittences, changes, variety. In the confusion of my three lives all my tracks are lost. No one can detect, catch, follow me. Naturally, I love Hugh more too. I am deprived of his great healing power. I risk losing him. I feel his departure. My own feelings are awakened. His departure really hurts me. Our pleasures are marked by their shortness—accentuated by their ephemeralness. Curious life. Treating Hugh like a lover who has no right to my continuous presence!

JANUARY 27, 1938

MY MADNESS—THE OPPOSITE OF SCHIZOPHRENIA, which is *separation*—is different from Henry's, Artaud's, Helba's, or Gonzalo's. It is as if by my fluid quality, my identification, my love, my pity, I were like water, and constantly *my* lake or my *sea* flows into another sea and creates confusion. For example: When I was loved by Rank, and I recoiled from him, I thought my recoiling resembled Henry's recoiling from me. *Because* of my doubts. If I said to Rank: "I don't like to live on an island alone with anyone," I immediately thought how Henry said this to me and did it mean he did not love me? *Because* Henry loved June, I doubted his love for me. But today I confound my love for Gonzalo with Henry's love for me. I see Gonzalo, the reality, winning over Henry, the past Henry. I believe more because I identify myself to Gonzalo and the way I feel toward him to what I imagine Henry felt for me. I cannot keep feelings separate. Henry expressed his love of June by a hatred of June—attacks, demolitions of her. Hating all she did, was, wore.

And with me he often says with great hate: "I hate the tropical climates. I hate the country. I hate red, orange, black."

And I feel: I am the tropics. Louveciennes was the country. Red is my color. He hates me. Then I get utterly confused. Gonzalo's words of love and desire in Spanish reawaken my Father's words. Everything seems mad. Now that I am sensuality and passion to Gonzalo, I think his ascetic fraternal mystical love for Helba is stronger—his pity love—because it is like mine for Hugh! And this, for me is the *labyrinth*. Identification. My identification with my Father. Projections. Myself in June. Myself in Gonzalo. My Father in me. My girl self in Helba. Myself in Thurema. Loss of confidence because June was more beautiful. But now I'm the beautiful one, and I think: the more sick, the uglier, the more pitiful Helba is, the more loyal Gonzalo is. I am his passion—not lasting! Now I see in Jean the brother of Hugh, his double, and I love him. But I see, too, *my* brother—in Jean my young Father! A young Allendy.

Is this a deep psychological truth and shall I explore it deeply, to its limit and make it the basis of my Proustian edifice? Is it at the basis of life—this madness of analogy, of interchanged souls, identities? Hasn't Henry become more me, I more Henry? Does love mean just that—this growing *into* the other, this interchange of souls and feelings? Not an abyss then, but a new world. Not a madness but a deep truth, a principle moving us, our inner fatality. We do not act as ourselves. We act. We are possessed. There are the multiple mirages of the personality. Or is all this in Proust?

Illumination of January 30. Evening—9:30 to 10:30: To smash the frontier between dream and reality in order to be able to publish everything. To say it is a *dream*. To me it is the same. I never wake up. I will say it is a dream. I will start with dreams and *write* everything: analysis, sexual experiences, incest, sacrileges, erotic fantasies, desires. Without frontier. It is a dream. People will fall asleep with me when they read, Hugh, Henry, Eduardo, Miguel, Rank, June. I will drug and anesthetize them. They will fall asleep all around me. *They won't know.* I will create the climate, the decor, and since there is so little difference between them, for me they are One. I will thus elude the great *conflict*.

Reality of pain for Hugh, Joaquin, Henry, Eduardo.

I will protect them all from reality.

I remember always the formula for the "Black Tulip," which I invented when I was fifteen. I found symbols, I invented signs, a language, and wrote a page. Naturally, it meant no more to me than anyone else. I had invented signs without keeping the key to their meaning. Anyway I didn't know what elements were used to produce a black tulip. It was esoteric, but for me too. Indecipherable. A mystery.

FEBRUARY 2, 1938

I HAVE NEVER BEEN AS HAPPY. WITH HENRY, Gonzalo, my work. I finished the main cutting of the diary today. One night Henry takes me and I respond fully, and the next night Gonzalo and I get into a frenzy of enjoyment. And there is nothing the same.

I imagine this: My Father has taken me up to the attic room to spank me. He takes my pants off. He begins to hit me with the palm of his hand. I feel his hand on me. But he stops hitting me and he caresses me. Then he sticks his penis into me. Oh, I enjoy it. I enjoy it. In and out, in and out, with ass exposed, my pants down, he takes me from behind. But my mother is coming up the stairs. We have no time. I clutch at him, suck him in, palpitating. Oh, oh, my mother is coming up the stairs. My Father's hands are on my ass—hot—I'm wet—I'm eager, eager. Open, close, open, close. I must feel him all before she comes. I must shoot quickly—stab, once, twice—and I have a violent orgasm.

I believe this really happened. I do not believe my Father penetrated me sexually, but I believe he caressed me while or instead of beating me. I remember the attic room where he took us to beat us. I only remember with sureness a time I wept so much he didn't have the courage to beat me.

This fantasy at times, I feel, means it is not Gonzalo who arouses me. Yet I do desire him violently—and I prefer a night of his caresses to Henry's. He does arouse *me*, but not so much the beast in me. Gonzalo says exactly what my Father said to me in Valescure: *"Ven, chiquita, ven, chiquita."* The curious thing is that my real Father taking me in reality did not give me any pleasure, but this fantasy does, and that it has increased my enjoyment of Gonzalo to such a point that I am able at times to enjoy him without the fantasy.

At the same time I feel a marvelous warmth in the presence of Jean, a keen exultancy he feels too—only he is not aware. I am not seducing him coldly, but I am more aware of all he feels. Every time he sees me the blood rushes to his face. He then falls into a dream. At a certain point during the day, if we meet, it is like an arrow meeting another arrow and the whole world focuses on that electric collision. He needs this—his life is dilated, dilated to the point of abortion.

He seeks me out for lunch or on his way to the Sorbonne. I walk with him. The restaurant man says to me: "The young man who looks like Christ was here looking for you." He comes to read me what he writes on horoscopes or handwriting, his conference on Lapland. He writes vividly. He is full of life, curiosity, wonder. He lives by miracles. He is floating in space, in vast reveries, but his body is warm—no planetary temperature. Fire.

Tonight Henry is busy, and Gonzalo can't come because he was here last night, so I am going out with Moricand and Jean. Moricand is writing a book called *Histoire d'un peuple devenu fous.**

At the bar of the Martiniquaise, next to my hotel, Gonzalo and I were having coffee. It is a smoky place, where the phonograph plays dance music constantly. It is full of *souteneurs, macros,* lesbians, Negroes, prizefighters. I like the atmosphere. It is absolutely dense, inert, dark, dissolved. Gonzalo meets two of his friends, the ones he

---

*There seems to be no record of such a title published by Conrad Moricand, though he left a number of unpublished manuscripts, among them *Le livre des singularités* and *Singularités de l'histoire de France,* which deal with the follies and paradoxes of history and religion.

used to go around with constantly. Malkine is stupefied with drugs, his face is haggard, his eyes sunk, his eyelids swollen. Gonzalo is startled by the disintegration. He no longer understands this dying in life, this feeding of the funereal worms. He is far from his friends. I ask him: "You were drawn to death, to disease, to destruction before?"

"Yes, I was, but not really—I'm more drawn to life. All that was literary. It was not the real me."

They talked about Artaud, mad with syphilis.

Gonzalo is far away from death—he is soaring. He is full of activity, of energy and fire. Helba says: "Anaïs changed you." Without words, without intention, without analysis, without premeditation. I did nothing. Gonzalo and I—in contrast to the constant verbal diarrhea of Henry and his friends—know the long, rich silences of being. I have been *silent* with Gonzalo. I have loved him. He knows very little of my ideas, only the poetic fragments of my work, nothing about analysis. But he is unusual—he has antennas. Sensitive antennas.

All these changes are mysterious and *beyond* me. I change too. Gonzalo transmits his gypsy ways, his nonchalance, his Bohemian recklessness. I swing *with* him into a musical disorder of strewn clothes, spilled cigarette ashes, indolence, into regions of chaos and moonlight. I like it there. It is the light of the earth womb. And the silence. The silence is the most beautiful expression of Gonzalo. It is like the silence of animals. The body is alert, the senses, the instinct. The mouth is silent.

His mother used to say: "You don't caress like a boy, you caress like an animal."

The desire to live the experiences of the loved one—Hugh living experiences like mine (talking all night, walking through London) and remembering me at the moment. I living out now Henry's poverty, Helba's, and Gonzalo's. Giving so much that I often find myself without a cent. Going to the pawnshop. Thinking of Gonzalo having been there, having been poor. Henry living out my "analysis" of people. Moricand and Jean understand this. By compassion, by great love, by communion one reaches the *dédoublement* of the mystics. In sorcery this is dispelled by the reintegration into the self. I do this by creation.

FEBRUARY 7, 1938

STORM OF JEALOUSY FROM GONZALO BECAUSE I went out one evening with Moricand and Jean and the evening was so marvelous, so luminous, that I was still aglow the next morning. Gonzalo the next night dark and destructive, saying he wanted me to live more austerely, that he himself was devoted only to me and his work. His instinct was not so blind, for I have been a little intoxicated with Jean.

Gonzalo says he feels the need of an austere life, devotion to his communism. He brings out in me my own austerity. He has returned to the mystical discipline of the Jesuits—for communism.

When he flares up with jealousy I weep. He doesn't know why. He came back the next day three times to try and tell me he had been very unjust. But what I really weep at is mysterious.

Moricand and Jean see me as the magic being—the Angel. Jean, when he can't write his dreams for Allendy, sleeps with *The House of Incest* next to him and finds he can write and remember his dreams if he writes them into my book, placing the page over my writing. He comes to a café near me to write his conference. Moricand is cured of a violent headache.

"Eduardo," says Gonzalo, "looks made of ammonia and salt." "Moricand," he says, "looks hypnotized."

I made the cuts in the diary *so that Henry could read it.*

Gonzalo would be killed by it: the love for Henry revealed, and the *impudeur,* the shamelessness, the completeness of revelation. But he won't read it. I respect the mystery in him. Half of Gonzalo is in darkness. He does not formulate, does not live naked. He says, "I'm not a pagan." But my diary is as naked as a pagan (though in living I am not naked, not a pagan, that is true).

Dream: Our city is invaded. We are to be massacred. The old, fat Chinaman, the leader, is smiling. One of us says to gain time: "We have a machine here to measure the quality of the mind. Would you like to be tested?" He consents. The machine looks like a permanent-wave instrument. One of the iron balls is applied to the Chinaman's forehead. The man looks at the indications and frowns expressively as if saying: "Not good." The Chinaman is crushed. But he looks at me and asks: "Do you think the machine is right?" I say: "Not at all. It was a farce." And in the dream I know that thanks to this phrase we will not be massacred as we would have been if the Chinaman had lost his faith in himself.

FEBRUARY 8, 1938

*D*REAM: ELENA IS THERE. I AM AWARE THAT I HAVE kept her separated from Henry.

Walked with Gascoyne along the river. Feverish with five hours of work on the diary, to the accompaniment of *L'Oiseau de feu*. Restless. Would like to go out with Jean because I'm ready for explosion, for ecstasy, music. Would like to get drunk with Jean, drunk on all kinds of things, silences, fancies, inventions, games.

Gonzalo, hold me, hold me, hold me. Can no one hold me, keep me? I feel at times as impossible to *hold* as music. *Je m'échappe.* I escape in space, fluid, beyond all walls, all doors—*L'Oiseau de feu*. Perhaps I could silence this *firebird* swelling my sails with blood winds, fevers, but even the Seine today was restless.

FEBRUARY 9, 1938

*D*REAM: *LE NÈGRE IMMENSE.* PAUL ROBESON TYPE. Wearing an ermine hat and a cape. The woman who was constantly betrayed, who suffered too much. *Le Nègre Immense* decides her suffering is unbearable and that we must kill her. He leaves his ermine hat and cape in a closet so as not to be identified. The assassination takes place behind a curtain. *They* all go at her. I hear her last moan. The *Nègre* comes out and gets his ermine hat and cape. Later the doctor, who is young and small, slides down the banister of a deep deep stairway, playfully. I am leaning over and watching him, because one of his fingers is in a bandage. He falls off. Another man, who wants to show he is more agile, does trapeze work on the banister, but he loses his clutch and falls down many many floors while I scream. The atmosphere of the assassination was theatrical, but the stairway accident very real. The two incidents were related. I knew they were related in the dream but cannot remember why.

FEBRUARY 15, 1938

*T*HE NIGHT HUGH WAS ARRIVING, A HALF HOUR before, Jean came for a moment. I had taken a bath and was wearing my nightgown and a red velvet kimono—as Hugh likes me to receive him. I was playing the *Firebird*. When Jean entered I felt my whole body warm. *He is suffering, it is his suffering which has roused me,* I thought, while he talked to me, while I talked to disentangle the knots of his life. He talked, but a little dazed. As he left I offered my cheek. A great *"trouble"* came between us. A brother, a brother, but oh too much warmth, and when I feel the very delicate bristle of his Christlike beard I am stirred. He went away as if hypnotized, dazed. I danced in the room. You bitch, you bitch, you bitch. Unless you love him do not radiate this warmth. Close yourself. But I have no doors to close on ecstasy. I wanted to dance with Jean, to dance with him. I wanted his nearness.

The next evening we had dinner together, Hugh, Jean, and I. I suggested we go dancing. We went to the Bal Nègre. Immediately Jean was paralyzed. He is afraid of dancing, he is afraid of his instincts, he is afraid of me. And I tried magical ways to lure him into the dance. But Jean could not dance. He was awkward. He was afraid. He is afraid of me. When he first held me he was trembling. He was cold. Does he feel what I feel? A joy, a joy at being near. He is too afraid. But I would make him dance. I said to him: "Are you sad, Jean, do you want to leave?"

"I'm not sad, but I'm blocked. My whole past seems to stop me. I can't let go. This music—I feel as if I could inhale but not exhale. I'm just constrained, unnatural."

"It is my fault, Jean. I felt so much that you had my rhythm, that I wanted to dance with you. I feel dancing is necessary, natural."

After these words, suddenly, the tension in him loosened. He held me very close, and I felt the current passing through both of us, waves of intoxication, but intermittent, broken by his fear. I did not ask him to dance anymore; I danced with a Negro. We left. Jean was talking about all the knots, the fears, the paralysis in him. I felt: the miracle has not happened. I will free him by a miracle, not with words, not directly. What he suffers I know. I suffered it once. But I *know* the free Jean. I want Jean free. But, Anaïs, you bitch, you do it with love, you will kill him. You're drunk but not with love. He will be drunk with love. He has not known anyone like you. You know that.

A moment of ecstasy.

And morning. Jean is here. We wanted to visit a *péniche,* a houseboat I saw advertised. We couldn't. We had lunch. I feel immense waves of tenderness, I feel like enfolding him, protecting him. It is a love, but be his sister, a passionate sister. I went later to see the houseboat alone. I will only describe it if I can get it. Strange coincidence.

It lies next to old *Nanankepichu.* It is for rent. Saw Gonzalo only for a moment. He has been ill. I seek to smell his hair in the café, to find him again. Gonzalo is there, in me, intact. I breathe his hair. He is nearer, nearer than anyone, entangled with my body, inside of it. We are in a kind of dreamless forest. Gonzalo has the body of the *dream.* Each gesture, each breath, each glance is that of the languid or violent forest animals. A dreamless world. Being.

I was glad Jean felt the core. He is so confused, dispersed, lost that he needs this. Gonzalo passes while Jean and I talk for a moment in a café, and he looks like Othello. Othello. Dark with jealousy. If you are *one* with the loved one, you can't bear his jealousy. It is your jealousy. I can't bear Gonzalo's jealousy. When he rages at Jean's presence I resent that the Gonzalo who dreamed, whom I first knew, who slept with me in *Nanankepichu,* was buried under the Gonzalo who works at a *real,* realistic communism. In reality. In the world. In the present. He buried his drawings, his writing, his reveries, his ec-stasies, his gypsy ways, his drunkenness.

I am luring Jean away from the Sorbonne, from the Psychological Group, from Montparnasse, into pure poetry.

But none of this has to do with my love for Gonzalo. I don't want to lose him.

Jean looks like Christ. But his mouth is thick. His ears are very delicate and small, like Hugh's. Elena overlooked him because he wears impossible clothes: the black formal suits of the *petite bourgeoisie,* of the provinces far from Paris, or highly outrageous things like the yellow foulard of the apache, a woman's ring, a dark Russian-necked shirt or a French bow of black-and-white stripes. He dresses like an old French actor from the provinces, or a horse-race man with check-ered trousers and spots! He loves zippers on his pockets, even on his trousers. I said to him: "Are you afraid of the buttons bursting open?" His pockets are full, inexhaustible. He carries books, photographs, notes, magazines, pipes. He is like a heavily charged snail. His eyes are terrifically innocent, yet he likes and attracts *louche,* underworld people. He lives always late, late for everything. Cannot finish, realize, fulfill. An overcrowded, chaotic life. Every day new explorations, new appetites, new enthusiasms. Everything is interesting. He has Henry's fieriness (born under Aries too), Gonzalo's jealousy and chaos, and my imagination. He is united to Hugh by his candor and is in need of Hugh's faith in him. ("He gives me strength.") He writes letters he never mails, promises visits and never arrives.

But Gonzalo has initiated me to this world of unkept promises, of Russian plans, of creation by words. Gonzalo says: "I will fix your radio. I will show you my writing. I will bring you paper. I will come and wake you up in the morning. I will take you to see this dancer. We'll go and visit boats together. I'll write you my impression of *House of Incest.*" Already I do not believe it. I have learned not to believe, not to await, not to dream for fear of disillusion. For I execute *all* my reveries, wishes, words, promises, plans. The wildest, the lightest. A wish for me is not a game: It's a creation. If I lie on my bed and dream of the pointed seashell necklace I could sew on my black dress (the same black dress of my first trip to New York, three years ago) I get up and sew the seashells. I come out with luminous *nacre* flowers on top of a little black velvet skullcap. And Jean marvels: "These flowers—marvelous—not like other flowers—incandescent—sea flowers. The crown of a queen too." Whereas Henry does not *see* the flowers. The flowers are strange, not understandable, significant, natural, a part of me. He would prefer I did not wear them in Montsouris. But I don't care about Montsouris. I don't care about the café woman's glare. I am not living in Montsouris or *for* Montsouris. I come from somewhere else. Haven't you noticed, I do not *wear out* my clothes. It takes me years and years to wear them out. They hang in my closet like costumes of a stage play used only for the performance, not for or by life, living, the private, personal life of the actor.

It is only the ecstasy I would like to live over and over again. The moments of ecstasy with Henry, June, Artaud, my Father, Gonzalo, and Jean. That moment during the dance, moment of oneness: Jean's slender, tall, sensitive body, rigid at first, then full of currents, but straight, not lascivious. As Gonzalo was straight. Men of love. Not animals.

FEBRUARY 15, 1938

I PICKED UP A NEWSPAPER IDLY AT THE CAFÉ Flore and looked over the advertisements. "*Péniche*. Houseboat for rent. Two thousand francs a month." An impossible sum. But I went to see. Gambled. Said one thousand to the man. Eduardo and Jimmy saying I would have rheumatism, Hugh that it would be dangerous. Yesterday the man did not telephone. Today at nine he awakened us. "Your offer is accepted." I went with Hugh and Eduardo. I signed the paper. I'm wild with joy. I was dancing toward it. It lies next to *Nanankepichu!* The place where I was very happy, deliriously happy with Gonzalo.

It is homely from the outside. A shack house on top of half of a *péniche*. But I love it. The little house part is gray. The prow is thick, wide. Little door. To the right is the studio. Skylight window pointed. Little windows all around. Down the stairs. Another large room full of little windows. Kitchen with big coal stove, which heats the water for the bathroom and radiator. Bathroom. Foyer. Small servant room. Tiny room for trunks. A little electric battery to make electricity.

Marvelous. The river all around. Feeling of *partenze*. Eduardo and Hugh were dazzled. Hugh who has been planning to make his studio look like a boat said: "I'm jealous."

I'm delighted, wild with pleasure. I am near Gonzalo's office. I am near this quarter I like so much, near my favorite restaurant, La Petite Marmite.

I wrote on the title page here: *"Les Mots Flottants."* ("The Floating Words.") I had to find a houseboat for them!

Pétillant, sparkling talk with Larry who writes me: "You are sweet the way you spread your wings and we all climb under them for help. I don't know how you do it. You must have the wingspan of an albatross." Gascoyne writing a poem to me, "The City of Myth."

Hugh saying: "This life is more exciting, more adventurous." We shopped for his studio in London.

Paulina 1880 by Jouve put me into another trance. I read it all throughout a busy day, in the subway, in the café, on my way to Henry, on my way here and there, while my hair was being washed. It has this epigraph: *"L'amour est dur et inflexible comme l'enfer"* ("Love is as hard and unbending as hell") by Sainte Therese d'Avila.

[F E B R U A R Y   2 8 ,   1 9 3 8]

*T*HE STATE OF EXTASE *IS ALMOST CONTINUOUS IN* me now. It may be what Moricand calls *"l'état de grâce"* in me.

When Larry made a vivid description of Anna Wickham, her enormous body, mustache, hair in her nose, heavy paw hands, her voice, I said: "She must have hair inside the womb, too."

I always write a title on a diary volume before I write in it, and it becomes a prophecy. *"Les Mots Flottants"* led me to the boat *La Belle Aurore* on the Seine. I sit here Monday, February 28, in the upper studio. The boat is rolling gently. The Sunday we moved it to be near the stairs of the Pont Royal, I telegraphed Gonzalo to come but the *pneumatique* didn't reach him. It was Jean who sailed at the prow while Hugh and I stood on shore to help with the ropes. Prophetic? I gave Gonzalo the keys with a feeling of surrendering to him, gave him the keys so he would feel he possessed the boat and me—and access into my life. I slept with Gonzalo here secretly, seeking to recapture *Nanankepichu*. While Jean and Hugh were at the movies and Hugh did not know yet the boat was already filled with furniture and livable. But Sunday when *La Belle Aurore* sailed a few yards down the river it was Jean who stood in the sun, the opposite of Gonzalo, luminous, with his pipe, his dreams, his Christ face and beard, his earthy energy, his will, too. The old sailor Mathurin was blocked by difficulties, but Jean and I surmounted them, domineering and willful and tricky, both of us.

Saw it Sunday.

Signed Tuesday.

Moved Wednesday, February 14.

Slept in it with Gonzalo Friday, February 16.

Saw it with Hugh, February 17.

Moved it to the stairs Sunday, February 18, with Jean. Slept in it Monday.

When Moricand came he was sure I was smoking opium. Associated the boat to drugs. Always thought I took drugs and that *House of Incest* was the product of drug intoxication. He realized after I talked that I was naturally drugged. I have all the states, moods, conditions caused by drugs.

After the night we danced together and Jean was frightened, I had ceased to feel exaltation in his presence. But that Sunday night when we finished our afternoon's work and rested on my bed, Hugh, Jean, and I, and Gonzalo arrived, I felt Jean's jealousy.

Jean wrote me the first letter to arrive in the little letter box. Then he came to get Pepe, the cat, on his way to London to stay with Hugh. I had to leave hurriedly. Henry was waiting for me. Jean said he would come along, to talk to me. The buses were full—*complète*. We took a taxi. I stopped at the rue des Artistes. I kissed Jean on the cheek as when I left for Italy. I felt suddenly his turmoil, his mouth seeking mine. And we kissed hungrily, furiously. I tried to leave him, but I looked at him. He said: "I knew this would come, and I was terribly afraid. I am no longer afraid. I am dreaming." Then I offered my mouth again and closed my eyes. I did not say a word except when he asked me: "When will I see you?" Then I remembered everything, Gonzalo, and Hugh waiting for Jean. I said: "When you return." I walked down the rue de la Tombe-d'Issoire dazed. Fortunately, Henry was in bed with a cold, drugged, silent. And I could go quietly, silently about preparing his dinner, taking care of him and fall asleep by his side, early.

I was not happy. You bitch, you bitch. Gonzalo had taken me the night before. I passed my hand between my legs seeking the odor of Gonzalo. I smelled my fingers as if to chase away the spell of Jean. Gonzalo, Gonzalo. Hold me. Hold me. But it is too late. The poison is in me, the poison of the kiss.

I thought during this week that Jean is away I could build up resistance because this with Jean is not a game. Jean's nature is deep, and mine I can't trust. But Jean, God, Jean can take me too far.

Unless there is in Jean himself some fear, some paralysis I cannot hold back. Strange, I don't feel I can be pulled away from Henry, but from Gonzalo.

Nanankepichu is in danger. So lovely. So beautiful the bedroom, low ceilinged, with beams, with tiny trellised windows. The Arabian bed is made for it. All my things are made for the boat. Gonzalo is made for it when he lies asleep, his black hair wild, his wonderful high brow so dark, his hand closed like that of a child, and at the same time when he awakens, so strong his body that he frightens all the little Frenchmen, even the *pègre,* the crooks hanging around the boat. The seduction of Gonzalo is a seduction of silence, of the realms before language when man was closer to the animal silence. Gonzalo was only a poet and eloquent when he was wooing me. Now it is all underground, in the silence. And in the jealousy. He came to sleep on the boat one night I was not there. We had agreed not to meet and that I would sleep at the hotel because he was not certain to be free and he didn't want me to sleep alone on the boat (I was with Henry). At six o'clock Jean had come to get Pepe. I had purposely told Gonzalo Jean was coming, to show him I had nothing to hide, to reassure him. I left my cigarette stub marked with rouge in the same ashtray with Jean's. Gonzalo, alone, studied the position of the stubs and decided that Jean's being over mine meant it was laid in the ashtray with the right hand passing before me, *over* me! This is curious in view of the fact that although Gonzalo was wrong about the cigarette, that very evening Jean had kissed me in a way that I remember constantly.

Today, the first quiet day on *La Belle Aurore*. Moricand came, or as he calls himself at times, *"le Mohicand"*—the last of the Mohicans, or the White Indian. And while we talk in the candlelight he suddenly takes my hand and kisses it adoringly and shows all his sensual upheaval in his face. I eluded his attempt to caress me, and adroitly made him feel I did not respond to his emotion.

"I am so poor in everything. I care too much about you to lose you to my clumsiness. I am very worldly. I would like to know your earthly life. You are the most real and unreal of women." We went out to dinner gaily and he showed me the bookshop where one could buy real incense from Africa. He promised to bring me a revolver.

Joaquin [after his concert] cables *"Succès sans précédent."*

MARCH 1, 1938

Moricand brings me a revolver, incense, Léon-Paul Fargue books, a poem of Max Jacob about a houseboat. We light the incense. Gascoyne brings his melancholy and oceanic eyes. Gonzalo brings his jealousy and somber eyes. They bear gifts and the boat enchants them. The boat takes them away on mystical voyages. In my bedroom at night I am in a medieval galley because of the little trellised windows. The Byzantine lamps swing now like incense holders. The shutters strike against the window violently like the wooden wings of a giant seagull.

The dark, prowling vagabonds are outside. The fire burns in the stove. I write in the Day Room, the upper skylighted studio. Daylight. I sleep in the Night Room—somber and luxuriant. I am surcharged with violent dreams and sensually so open that I could open my legs to Moricand, a continuous sensual vibration. The night with Gonzalo seems prolonged without barrier, it is a fire burning, I cannot close or become cold. All my dreams are dreams of voluptuousness, of abandon, of contact.

Moricand is perverse, full of ruse and destruction. He has frequented the somberest people, the killers, the sadists, the prostitutes, the young boys. He has used this revolver he gave me. When I held it in my hand I realized death. With this I could kill. And it seemed incredible, terrible. Death. To kill. I have never dwelt on death except out of jealousy. I have wanted to kill. The revolver fascinates me. As Moricand's story of the flower produced by the sands of the desert, a kind of petrified dust rose as I had imagined in the "mirror" story. Moricand penetrated *The House of Incest*—completely.

MARCH 3, 1938

CLOSE TO GONZALO AGAIN, SEEKING CLOSENESS, unity. Our life on the boat enchanted. I cook dinner for him. We get into bed. The seduction of Gonzalo is infinite—his voice, his eyes, his body. When I see him walking away I experience a desire for him again. I wish Jean would not return and destroy this—this purely human nearness, this closeness of feeling.

"*Chiquita,* I lit your fire and filled the tanks and bottles of drinking water. I will come at twelve. Very eager to see you."

MARCH 3, 1938

RECEIVED WITH RED CARNATION OUR [FIFTEENTH] wedding anniversary:
"ETERNAL LOVE, HUGH"

MARCH 4, 1938

WHEN I TURN ON THE TAP IN THE BATHTUB, IN float a suicide or two, or a few drowned kittens. The rain falls into my letter box and the letters look as if my friends had been weeping. When I have washed a pair of stockings the tank is empty and when I have made coffee the coal is finished. When I'm short of money I can fish, or I can fish for wood when there is no fish. I get all the sun, the air, and coal dust from the *remorqueur,* the tugboat. My friends have given me three revolvers.

Dream: A woman has only one eye. I operate on her and give her two eyes. But the woman is also myself.

What is similar between Gonzalo and me is *angoisse* over the loved one, fear of loss. I used to fear losing Henry during a two-day separation. Mondays, after weekends with Hugh, I would rush to Henry in a state of anxiety and would be reassured by the mere sight of him. I would have liked to see him every day.

Gonzalo has this after my evenings out. He suffers each evening I am not with him. It is Helba herself who tells me that she knows when I am out with friends because then Gonzalo gets somber and irritable. It is Helba who tells me how jealous he is, as he was not over her. She has truly sublimated her jealousy into love. It is strange that the day I rode in the taxi with Jean we talked about jealousy, how it could only be overcome by love (my love of June). Jean was telling me that is how his jealousy develops—into love. How the first woman he had loved had not loved him but his friend, and Jean had gone as far as lending them a room in his apartment when they had nowhere to go for their lovemaking. We talked about jealousy being the most terrible of all tortures.

Helba is truly a saint now—absolutely and incredibly selfless, saying of all women for Gonzalo to have she preferred me. That Gonzalo had never *fallen in love* until he met me. That women all pursue him but he eludes them.

She really loves me. Talks about what she would do in dancing with my hands, how she could create "mystical" dances for me, unreal ones. She is really a saintly character. Her illness separates her from all the human passions. I feel protective toward her. She hides in my arms like a child.

MARCH 5, 1938

*T*HE CURRENT IS TOO SWIFT. I HAVE NIGHTMARES of storm-tossed boats. I awake and find Hugh's letter in the little box. Helba comes, weeping with pain. Nancy comes alone and looks at the boat quizzically. Nancy is practical and realistic. She is Larry's ballast. Nancy said that she found my diary "a straining for sensation." Nancy, deep down, is against me, but she doesn't know it. She thinks what I do is done for effect, for its effect on others.

Novalis words: *"La vie poétique est le seul absolu—la seul réalité!"* ("The poetic life is the only absolute—the only reality!") That is what it is. We have escaped the fatality of the historical time, the tragedy of daily life, the astrological predictions, the racial taints, political dung, the newspaper catastrophes, into the *vie poétique*—the eternal. Henry, Gonzalo, Helba, Hugh, Jean, and I. Gonzalo is occasionally washed ashore by his immediacy. The newspaper in his pocket, his contact with political men, his work, break the bubble of the *vie poétique*. Hugh is swimming fully into it, creating his *own* place as he likes it (not for the bank), cooking for himself, painting, liking the restive flavor of adventure. Jean will soon break with the Sorbonne and psychological labels. Moricand swims in it but with feet in lead boots of fatalism and neurosis. Larry's English fear of anchorless engines stalls him. One must not be afraid. One must know how to float as words do, without roots and without water. One must know how to navigate without latitude or longitude and no engine. Without drugs and without impediments. One must know how to breathe like a wind instrument.

The tragedy depicted in a novel such as *L'Ouest rien de nouveau* [Erich Maria Remarque's *Im Westen Nichts Neue*] cannot befall us. Our war is on another plane. As Larry put it: "My God, Anaïs, you're always opening new trapdoors." I will not be caught. I open trapdoors on the infinite. As a child I noticed that certain voyages move toward a horizon which was never touched, attained. The slippery, evanescent, invisible contours of illusion. When words and feelings learn to float they have reached the poetic *"mouvement perpétuel."* To float means to be joined to the cosmic rhythm. The absolute means the pulsing moment of rhythm. It is while floating, abandoning myself, that I suddenly became tied to the cosmological system. I let myself be pushed by all that was greater than myself, love, pity, creation. I floated thus into unity. The boat is carried by something, by a water many times deeper than itself. I am in the current. I fear no *accrochages,* no sudden dislocations or rheumatism. I am perpetually oiled by faith.

Helba asks me: "How have you done it that your husband is still in love with you after fifteen years?"

The studio is the solarium. It is pierced, saturated with sun and light. It is a bower of light. The bedroom is the mystery. The bower of night.

I sit in a café waiting for Henry, who is visited by Keyserling's son. The boat is dark. Jean will soon return.

Novalis: "Poetry is absolute reality." It is the core of my philosophy. The more poetic a thing, the more true.

"Chiquita: I lit the fire. See you at half past ten at the Café Terminus. I came at seven, at eight, at eight-thirty, and at nine. I left you a note. Afterward I went to my place to eat and came back at ten P.M. I waited until quarter to one. I am so upset that I can't sleep and am going home. *Ciao."*

taking astrology lessons because he doesn't believe in astrology. Until I prove to him he believes in *"coïncidences poétiques"* and seeks merely to be fecundated by new images. "It isn't astrology I want you to learn, but to enter new images, new food."

Moricand wanted disciples. Both of them now are fast and feverishly fecundating each other. Moricand has found the brother of Blaise Cendrars. Henry a new perception of his own work, which his friends never gave him.

Jean says I break all the chains around him. He relieves the pain I feel at Gonzalo's clumsy ravages in my mystical or art world. I am weak because of my love.

Every time I remember Gonzalo coming in like a murderer, shouting: "You, of course, can't understand, you live in the moon. You would like me to take Eduardo's attitude, I suppose. What right have we to caress at this moment?"

That all this coincided with Hugh's long stay, and that even this Gonzalo imputes to the "bourgeois world" against which he holds so many grudges, makes me feel that Gonzalo is a Catholic victim of guilt, of his own impotence to create a world as he wants it.

I have created the world I want, which adds something to the world's possessions.

If one does not believe the world can be reformed one seeks individual perfection. The boat is transpierced with sunlight. "Of course," said Jean, "this boat is yours. No one can take it away from you. It is a symbol for the world."

I called it "Noah's Ark."

And the deluge is politics. It is the undertow of wholesale treachery, division, of collective hysteria and will to die. They are not dying for an ideal.

Jean makes me feel guiltless because I am not turning away out of indifference or egotism, I have never refused the gift of myself, my mystical participation and my suffering for the world's suffering— but because I believe only in this that I am doing, because for each one to do what he is fitted for alone is pure.

MARCH 22, 1938

*I*N THE DIARY I DO ALL THE WEEPING, BUT IN LIFE I am strong. I saved Gonzalo from his despair. I balance the tragedy, horror of politics with my life above the clouds. If I were *in* it, I would not have the strength to do it. I clambered out, I sat at my table and wrote. I saw Michel Simon, charmed him and saved the *péniche* from being sold to somebody—lost to me. The sun helped me. I began "Chaotica" yesterday morning.

Hugh left. Gonzalo came—changed. One thinks the love is killed, altered. It only becomes more *human*. Imperfect. If it survives the reality, it endures. So I found Gonzalo again, lured him back into life, desire, energy. Today he said: "Coming here to your boat is like an oriental dream. It takes me away from the horror of Vienna."*

"Would you prefer it if I were in the action, Gonzalo, like [Maria Teresa Leon] the wife of [Rafael] Alberti?"

"No. I love you more for this."

Could it be true, by keeping the dream alive, I keep everything alive?

I didn't write about my visit to Jean.

When he returned from London, after the kiss in the taxi, he came one morning, and I promised to go and see him one afternoon. I wanted to, and I did say: "Jean, we love each other as brother and sister." But there was this tension between us, this electric storm. He began to kiss me. I knew then I didn't want him. This was not the Jean I desired. His body was alien, I could see its defects. It was a

---

*The annexation of Austria into the Third Reich, the *"Anschluss,"* which had been welcomed by many, signaled the beginning of the crackdown on communists, Jews, and sympathizers of the Spanish Republic, since Nazi Germany was supporting General Franco.

feminine young man, afraid. His shoulders were small. But his desire was ignited—and I submitted, not for myself. I felt no pleasure and no desire. He bathed in a feeling of ease and of an opium dream. He said: "It is marvelous. You know, Anaïs, I was afraid. I couldn't eat for two days. And now it seems simple, so sweet. You have made me a great gift. I feel I have nothing to give you."

Jean lives in the dream. He seduces by a mirage, a mystical magnetism. Perhaps sensual for other women. But I did not feel him.

Tenderness flowed through me. Jean was a brother, a twin. We think alike. And again, thinking alike brought no blood answer. I knew this would not be tragic because it was not real. When we met again with Hugh, there was no more tension, drunkenness. But he was very ill with guilt—castration. And he came to the boat and Hugh and I took care of him. He got well. The three of us dreamed together, talked. Jean is my echo, my double. That is why Hugh loves him and he loves Hugh exactly as I do.

Jean left with Hugh, and it was all dissolved like a mirage, leaving the twinship.

Then I made an effort to meet Gonzalo's thoughts. His mysticism is religious, not cosmic. And his Marxism is terrestrial, concrete. He and Helba, who come from the magic mountain, do not believe in magic and have no faith except in physical, material things. They are spiritual and yet Gonzalo cannot see the psychic illness of Helba, nor of the world, the soul disease that no revolution can cure, no violence. Violence is holy—but not without inner meaning. Gonzalo is spiritual but not transcendental. He has the Spanish *realism,* so has Helba. So I tried to transcend Marxism, to discuss it as an incident in the eternal evolution. I tried to make all things fuse. If one rises far enough there are no contradictions but an equilibrium, and *all* profound things marry if they meet far enough from their expression, manifestation, realization. We get lost in details, as we get lost in the appearance, external traits of people. We lost the vision. Gonzalo understood, and I try to keep this pinnacle, so that the differences between us do not shatter us again. Gonzalo needs me, I know it now. He would kill himself, with his blind rages and rebellions.

I must understand his action, too, *as a rebellion against reality.* Before, he escaped into drunkenness. He was never satisfied. Now he rebels with a desire for reform and change. It is in keeping with his *immediacy* that I love so much. His *presence* which makes our moments of love so marvelous. When I think of Gonzalo I always think of our moments of love.

Jean. I have learned, because of Rank, that the sameness of rhythm of thought and attitude is *rhythm,* but not love. It's narcissism, but not love.

MARCH 23, 1938

I HAVE CREATED SUCH A POWERFUL DREAM against death, anguish, that I am drugged myself. I can't work. Last night Gonzalo came about eleven. All the candles were lit in the large bedroom, all the lamps. The incense was burning. I wore my red velvet robe. Gonzalo came from seeing a friend who is dying. But he lay on the bed and buried his head on my breast: "You make me forget everything. You are like a drug. This forgetting is a treachery."

This forgetting is your strength.

Gonzalo. Helba says: "In Lima everybody knew him. He worked in his brother's newspaper. But they all thought him crazy. I didn't at first. And once, before I left Lima, where I was earning a lot of money, I decided to give a farewell recital. I let him take care of the details. He engaged a very large and expensive hall. He was to have the announcements posted, programs sent, etc. I arrived there to dance, I got dressed, and the hall was empty. Someone came in and said: 'They are pasting the billboards on the walls. It is nine o'clock! Too late!' I lost a lot of money. Another time he made up the programs and sent them all out. But nobody came. He had forgotten to give the name of the hall."

Yet what a great tender charm in his face, what seduction in his manners, what beautiful expressions in his eyes, what passion, what fervor in the voice when he read César Vallejo's poems.

Gonzalo has a *psychic* knowingness, a divination which does not endure.

I was saying to him: "I think Hugh is getting more and more to have a life of his own, his own individuality is coming out." "Not at all," said Gonzalo. "If he were free of you he would not be busy buying minerals, your stones, for himself."

It is true, Hugh has duplicated our lives—chosen to live with my colors, my marine atmosphere. Has bought seashells, taken the fishing nets we bought in Santa Margherita, and was surprisingly, unexpectedly, selfish, taking all this for himself, to duplicate what he is losing.

Poor Hugh. He played the analyst, too. Finally, he loved a friend who resembles me, and who resembles Gonzalo and Henry in his fantasy: bohemianism, irresponsibility. Poor Hugh.

Henry sent this "Biographical Dope" to a British editor: She is thirty-four now, married, under another name of course. Born in Neuilly, France, lived as child in Belgium, Germany, Spain, then to America, as my essay recounts. Back to Europe again about the age of twenty-one or so, and has remained here since. Speaks and writes French, English, and Spanish fluently. Was also a dancer. Has been a practicing analyst with great success, but finds it bad for art and has abandoned it. She is the daughter of Joaquin Nin, the pianist and composer, also the sister of Joaquin Nin-Culmell, pianist and composer, whose compositions are known at Oxford and Cambridge, where they were published. She is also quite beautiful, a Neptunian type, one of the very rare Neptunian types, according to astrologers and psychoanalysts. Has a character which is almost perfection itself. Is the most intelligent woman I know, intuitive, sympathetic, plastic, mobile, alive, alert, and capable of making a success at anything she tackles. She is of mixed blood—Danish, Cuban, Spanish, Majorcan, Greek, Arabian, Basque, Phoenician.

MARCH 24, 1938

YESTERDAY THE KIND OF DAY ONE FEELS BETWEEN the legs. I could not work. The boat was too beautiful. I wandered out. I saw a Hungarian gourd—made of horse fur and leather. I desired it insanely, for Gonzalo to drink from. I got it with great joy.

Yet when Henry came to see the boat (his visit was spoiled by my fear of Gonzalo coming) I said to him and I felt this: "I would like to buy the boat and you come and live in it. I would give up Hugh and we could always manage to eat, if we had no house to pay. Would you like that?" Henry seemed so gentle, and he liked the boat so much.

I felt badly. I wanted peace. The anguish I feel when I am with Henry—lest Gonzalo see me. My early rising at Villa Seurat and rush back to the boat for fear Gonzalo has come early and seen my bed not slept in. I say to Henry it's because I would lose the maid. She would be afraid to stay nights alone. She thinks I sleep on the boat. So I must arrive before she gets up, get into bed, and call for my breakfast.

I say to Henry not to come to the boat because Hugh has left Gonzalo and Jean in charge of the pumps and the electric power motor and they come at odd hours and would tell Hugh. I say to Moricand not to speak of Gonzalo to Henry.

Letter to Gonzalo (after our scene—not shown to him).*
Now you ask me what's wrong. What's wrong is that you have robbed me of all desire to live, all enthusiasm and interest in life. I have to realize that you are following your destiny, which is not one of life but rather self-sacrifice, detached and

---

*In Spanish in the original.

separated from both you and me. What's wrong is that I now have no reason to live. My only reason for living is you, and yesterday I had to give you up to the thing you have chosen as your *only* passion and reason for living.

We tried to be one. You have broken away because, like all depraved Catholics, you carry within you a death wish. While you fight for your ideal, you are a force of creation, of spiritual life and faith. But the day you say that you want to die because you can't achieve your ideal, it isn't a creative ideal that makes you want to die but rather the curse of Catholicism that always leads toward death.

MARCH 25, 1938

I HAVE FOUGHT MYSELF BACK INTO BEAUTY. A DAY of perfection and enjoyment. I left Henry early. Albertine, the housemaid, with a gift for silence, gives me break-fast. I work in the bower studio, bower of light. The day sucks me out of the boat. Wandering. I found knives with handles made of tree branches. I sold my Claude Farrèrre books on the quays to purify the bookcases. I ordained my Noah's Ark into order. I took a bath, the first one. I told Albertine she could go out tonight. I am wearing the black satin negligee and a little coat of green with gold embroi-dery, a heavily ornate coat I have had for fourteen years. The negligee of Louveciennes has been brought here—the feeling of a house all of one's own. I was happy today because according to the new arrange-ments I am buying the boat with rent, if I stay long enough, and yet I am not tied to it if I leave, anytime, then it is just rent. I may own it, but I am not bound. That is how I like it. I write Hugh marvelously warm letters. I write Marika Norden because her rebelliousness touches me. I quote from Lawrence for her: "Everybody wants to destroy me because they feel I don't conform." I send her my books. I write Joaquin about his great success in New York. I cling to all this, this order, this beauty, as a nourishment. I am very simply happy. My taking the suffering of the world into me, as I did as a child, does nothing for the world. Creative men were never sentimental. Keyserling writes this well, saying they accepted creation and destruction. All I can do is add my creation to the death balance of the world.

Gonzalo comes to rest, to sleep with his head on my stomach, his hands closed like a child's. I write Henry, quoting for Edgar Keyserling's attack on Rudolf Steiner with whom Edgar is obsessed.

Elena I *desired* away, and though I wrote her a letter, she has vanished. The river offers its changing moods. I lose myself, my pain, my anguish, in the beauty of the room, the succinct beauty of it: the wood depth, the carpet, the royal bed. Outside I wear simple things. I really own very little, only what has meaning. When I am happy it is so rare. I need to dwell on it, to contemplate it. What a hunger, a craving for beautiful things. I even ask myself if I am pregnant, the need is so violent. I lie in bed writing in the diary.

MARCH 26, 1938

GONZALO TALKING ABOUT HIS FRIEND, A REVOLUtionary leader in Moscow: "He's writing desperate letters about his wife for me to try and get her out of Barcelona. This is no time to be obsessed with one's woman. He has other, greater, things to do than to call out to save his wife."

Gonzalo about another friend writing him: "They are all too sensitive and too emotional. I wrote back a hard letter. This is no time for softness. That is what is called bourgeois individualism."

I write to Thurema: "I am no longer happy with Gonzalo. The period of happiness is always short. One goes on loving but it is not the same. I have lost my faith in him as a man of feeling. Politics are hardening him, making him impersonal and devoted to an Idea, as

Henry was devoted to his creation, and Joaquin to his music. So far as happiness goes, that is ended. And I have only you to feel with. . . ."

MARCH 28, 1938

*H*ELBA CAME. SHE BEGAN TO TALK OF GONZALO'S changed ways, his aggressivity, violence, boasting of necessity for brutality. I began to weep. Then she rose above all this that baffled me, and it was she who explained to me: "Don't be hurt, Anaïs—it's all talk. It's all because he is so sensitive and emotional. He is trying to pretend to be *hard*. It is not real. It is all talk. Gonzalo is too soft. But you see, it's a defense. In politics one must not be soft. Gonzalo was born *'equivocado,'* mistaken, born to blunder. He has always been on the wrong road—always. He is blind. He is like an animal. He is a child. He is not intelligent or philosophical. He talks foolishly. You and I live on another plane. One can't talk to him. If I talk to him about the errors, the Puritanism, the tyranny of present-day communism, he calls *me* a fascist. He says he will shoot me with his own hands. It's ridiculous. Don't cry. He's a little crazy. You must analyze a bit, you mustn't get confused and hurt."

Helba so wise, and I, because I have been naive and believed Gonzalo, was suddenly lifted out of my despair. She added with amazing insight: "At the bottom of it all there is jealousy. Yes, I have noticed Gonzalo is insanely jealous of you. He doesn't want your writing known because he feels if the world knows you they will love you and take you away from him. He wants to become a Lenin out of pride, to be something for you. He doesn't want to be a nobody, because of you."

"My god, Helba, I love him as he is. I don't want him to be a Lenin."

"You can't help it now. I have seen how jealous he is. When he comes home and kicks Elsa, fights, becomes violent, I know already that Hugh is here in Paris. I know when you are out with friends by his mood."

And then, bowing her head: "Don't let anything bad happen to Gonzalo. I would die of sorrow if he were shot."

I translated my "Birth" story to her. She kept her head on my shoulder, kissing me, saying: "I have never seen such a realistic incident lifted to such a noble, spiritual experience."

When Gonzalo came back to me, the change in me was made. Gonzalo had to be protected, guided, his violence directed so it would not destroy him. I must not mind his violent, terribly stupid words, his inaccuracies, his obscurities. He has days when I can reach his spirit, and he *sees,* but this is unrelated to his passionate, blind rages. All I can hope for is that in the obscure realm of his consciousness my image, my love, may act on him to prevent his death. Perhaps in a moment of despair, frenzy, panic he'll come to me. But I must not become blind with him. His words, violent and aggressive, always blind, enrage me. And then we quarrel stupidly, as June and Henry did.

Again I am not permitted to live out my feelings as a woman, I must be seer, guide, I must be the inner structure Gonzalo lacks, *his* balance, his eyes.

For Hugh, for Henry, for Gonzalo.

There are moments when I feel I love Joaquin in Gonzalo. They have the same nature. Joaquin was the same when he was a child. And today each time he opens his mouth it is to say something chaotic and unwise and untrue. Such is Joaquin today and that is why all our talks end in tragic frustration.

Gonzalo has the power to affect my feelings directly. Even if what he says is obviously *obtuse,* it disrupts me. I know he talks against astrology, literature, because of jealousy of Jean, Moricand, and Henry. I know he violently attacked my being published by Durrell because he sensed Henry behind Durrell. He has to kill my joys if they do not come from him.

Helba. What a rare scene, Helba always helping me to believe in

Gonzalo's love so that I find the strength to help Gonzalo. I have no strength if the demon of *doubt* possesses me. Gonzalo's talk about his political destiny being primary, vital made me doubt. Helba shows me the twisted way his love manifests itself.

"He adores you, adores you. I have never seen Gonzalo so in love."

So when Gonzalo came yesterday, unconsciously penitent, I received him with serenity, the serenity he needs. He put his head on my breast and went to sleep. And I smelled his hair, watched him, pouring love all over and around him. When he awakened he asked me: "Did you sleep?" I answered: "I was too busy loving you."

"Yes," he said, "that is why I slept—I sleep on your love."

The people who feel afraid of Gonzalo are right. The demon in him is the darkest of all of us. Helba's demon is in her dancing. Mine is the demon of doubt. But Gonzalo's is violence. Henry's demon was captured in his work, caged in.

MARCH 29, 1938

WHEN JEAN LEFT THE BOAT WITH HUGH HE ASKED: "When will I see you?"

"You say when—choose the day astrologically." He said: "Saturday or Tuesday."

"Saturday Helba comes from the hospital. Tuesday I'll come."

I didn't want to. I don't love Jean with desire. After I was with him I wanted to wash my mouth, my whole body. I didn't like his blood in me. The day came like an eclipse of the sun. I prepared myself to say to him: "I feel you as a brother—let's not be lovers." I did say it. But he was burningly passionate. His desire was contagious. No love, I didn't want to kiss him, I felt like a whore, sexually stirred by the other's desire. When I refused his caresses he said: "I'm going to take you today. We'll have no regrets, and then we'll see. But I want you today."

I lay on the reindeer fur, naked. I was superficially stirred—but

I didn't feel him completely. I felt I was giving him this, an illusion.

Afterward we talked about him. He said: "This is the first time I have had a real woman. When you came I thought: *Enfin, une femme!* Always before it was women who were inferior to me."

He sought tenderness. It was hard for me to give it. I didn't feel it.

We both noticed how outside of the world this was, we didn't feel any bond, any alteration in our life. An opium dream. I liked him better when he was dressed again and we were walking very swiftly to the boat, after hunting for the lost diary—for I have lost the diary of my first year of marriage. David Gascoyne lost it by what seems to me an act of sheer stupidity. When I went to fetch it as we had agreed, because he was leaving for London (he had been typing it out for me), he decided an hour before to mail it, without registering it even, a crazy destructive act for which I curse him. And I am trying to find it. I feel the loss terribly, like a fragment of my life itself. The diary is too human, too close a thing. The loss of it is like my own death.

I arrived at the boat at eight, a little before Gonzalo, and I felt only this: the reality of Gonzalo, the unreality of Jean. The reality of Henry and the unreality of my Father and brothers. I asked myself: Is it incest again?

I am older than Jean. He asks me naive questions. He is always in a panic when women court him, but never has the audacity to do the courting. He has a diminished vision of himself. I heard all this with a feeling that I had lived it before. My soul is tired. I am traversing roads already known. Jean's timidity. Jean's feminine nature. Fear of being brutal with woman. Excess of sensibility and romanticism. The need to live out certain things to prove certain things, to assert one's strength, to rid one's self of doubts, fears. "I do not believe in myself. I never thought a woman like you could believe in me."

Perhaps my soul is tired. Tired of feeling. Jean's is not tired. For the first time I feel I have had many lovers. Jean is barely thirty. I am lying down naked and unpossessed, saying all he needs to hear. But it is not real. I am far away. This is only a respite from the deep anguish over Gonzalo's fate. It is an afternoon in the Chinese theater. Jean is showing me his boxes full of objects. Jean is cleaning his narghile. We are lying under two crossed swords. Little stage lamps everywhere: the dream. The little lamp with the red dragon. Red color everywhere. There are moments in the dream when everything is made of cardboard and feathers. Jean and I are standing by the fireplace. He runs his hand inside my skirt, seeks my sex again. I feel drunk, sexually drunk. There are things I cannot live anymore. That is how Henry must feel. Motifs repeat themselves. That is why one love is more than many if deeply lived.

I reenter myself, but there lies the nugget of pain. Fear and loss. Henry will love his daughter. Gonzalo is in danger of death. Jean, I ought to be grateful. For one afternoon you kept me in your room without suffering. No jealousy, no possession, no drama. He is timid. He does not want to disturb my life. He accepts the husband, the lover—all. He is humbly grateful. No weight.

APRIL 3, 1938

GONZALO QUIETER. I LIVE THE LIFE OF A SPY. Spies do not live *with* their fear. The risk and danger *is* their climate. They live in tension, of course, alertness, wakefulness. Not trembling. That is how I live. I am aware of the danger but not afraid. Hugh might discover all. Gonzalo might discover my life with Henry. Henry might discover my life with Gonzalo.

When Moricand gave me the revolver I immediately gave it to Gonzalo because I knew he was always in danger because of his work. Yet at the same moment that I wanted Gonzalo protected, I knew I was risking my own life because I know Gonzalo's violence and if he ever met me in the street with Henry he would not hesitate to shoot.

Analogy in philosophical thinking is good, but in neurotics it leads to insanity because the premises are false.

I do see an analogy between Gonzalo and June. It is not visible to anyone else. On morbid days I carry the analogy to great exaggerations and I identify myself to Henry and his suffering with June. Henry saying: "June was always so confused. She had no intuition. Everything she touched would be botched."

But this is not true of Gonzalo. He is faithful, he satisfies his love of intensity in politics. He does not torment me except when he torments himself.

Helba's story: Her father ran away from her mother and she never found him again. He took away her two brothers. Left her with the mother who hated her. At seven she was placed in a convent of orphan girls. It was situated in what had once been a prison. The nuns who entered never saw the street again. There were no windows on the street. Only *vasistas* on the ceilings. They awakened at five in the morning with a nun shouting: *"Viva Jesús."* Then mass without breakfast, and uneatable food. They were only allowed to urinate at certain hours. Helba could not urinate when told, and would then feel the need later during class. She was so panicky about feeling the need during class that she would urinate when the nun called her to write on the blackboard. The nuns said she was possessed with the devil. They punished her by having each girl braid her hair very tight, all over her head first, and then the nun would take all the braids and tie them harder together and leave her two days with her hair pulled this way until congestion followed and Helba fainted. Helba felt a great need to urinate during the night but that was not allowed. She would stealthily get up, and in desperation, urinate inside the boots the girls wore, different boots each night. In the morning the girl would find the boots full of urine, and all shriveled and swollen, unwearable. The nun spied on her until she caught her. She had her stay all night in the cave of the church where the dead nuns were buried, tied to a stake, and Helba shivered with cold and terror until big black spots appeared all over her body and face. From there she had to be taken to the infirmary. The girls were not called by their names but by numbers, like prisoners.

Helba discovered that by putting a piece of black paper behind a window it made a mirror. She called all the girls' attention to this and these girls who had never seen a mirror all wanted to see their faces in it. The nun caught them and said it was a mortal sin. They were flogged on the tips of their fingers.

They were bathed wearing their long white cotton nightgowns, and passing the soap over this nightgown. They had lice in their hair and all kinds of diseases.

The nuns while flogging them would keep muttering: *"En nombre de Jesús, en nombre de Jesús."*

The mother did not believe her stories, she said Helba must have been very bad to get such punishments, and the nuns told the mother Helba was possessed.

Her hysterical screams all night when locked in the tomb of the nuns.

Two years in the convent.

APRIL 5, 1938

GONZALO SAID: "ECUADOR AND PERU ARE NEARER the moon. And high up near Titicaca, fourteen thousand feet high, we were still nearer. The moon is so immense it frightens the white men. And it appears with a blood red halo; it takes half the sky and everything is stained red. My brother would go crazy at every full moon."

He told me about the bird they hunted down, whose life was so enduring that after they shot him, to kill him completely, the Indians tear out two of his feathers and plunge their hard tips into the back of his neck.

He told me about the very long-beaked bird who only fed on brains, who sucked the brains of animals and dead men through the ear.

Killing ducks in the marshes—losing his boots. The tamed eagle who stayed on the roof and was fed chickens. Among the lambs, one male is castrated and sent among females to warm them up, to caress, excite them in preparation for the male who doesn't trouble to *court* the lambs.

Big formal dinners at an aunt's house on Sunday with the priest, monsignors, stiff dresses. Masses and prayers in the house. The rosary in the morning told by Gonzalo's mother for the entire household. Ancient atmosphere of sixteenth-century Spain overlaid the Indian life. Eating wheat cooked by hot stones. Indian servants. Scotch father teaching his three sons how to run the *hacienda*.

Gonzalo at seven suffered a cerebral hemorrhage, congestion, nearly died. At twenty double pneumonia.

I see so well in him the twilight moods, the contemplative, meditative trance. And I like it. We lie silent for hours. The trance caused in his country by the immensity of nature. So immense it gives sadness and loneliness. So shabby and meager, Europe seemed to him like a toy. A toy moon.

While he talked about the moon I invented this for him: "People take sunbaths, but they never take moonbaths. I have taken moonbaths—naked."

This is in part true. Although I had always heard that the moon was dangerous, in Richmond Hill when I saw the moon I would lie in bed where it shone through open windows and lie bathing in it, never feeling the harm. And in Louveciennes I sought it out.

Last night Henry and I went to the movies to see Luise Rainer, whom he likes so much. I thought he admired her because she was a little like June, and I was sad. But when we came out of the movies he said: "She has wonderful gestures and bearing, such a gracious way of carrying her head, such delicacy. She is very much like you. Her gestures are so light, like the wind almost, and she moves so beautifully. You and she have a great deal of affinity. There is in her face at times a deep sadness, not called for by the part. A tremendous sadness. That is what you have. It's queer. You are all light, all gaiety. But if one catches you unaware one sees a tragic face. That has so much greater charm, this acquired gaiety, than a gaiety one is born with. It's something you fought for. One feels the luminousness and at the same time this tragic feeling, a mysterious dual character."

I fell asleep very happy. I felt Henry has never understood me as well as at this moment.

APRIL 15, 1938

GONZALO LOST A FRIEND [CÉSAR VALLEJO] HE loved for twenty years. Helba was in the hospital. His suffering I took into myself. The anguish only ceased today. Helba is home again. Gonzalo's friend is dead. For three days I was caught in his suffering.

I went to see Helba at the hospital of the poor. Came back with visions of horrors I had seen. Sat down and wrote the most beautiful of the pages on dreams in the book of dreams now called "Chaotica." Pages on the nightmare. The book is growing.*

Traversed a period of frenzied love and pity for everybody, for my Father, for Henry, for Gonzalo, for the whole world. All stirred, in a turmoil of giving and sacrifice. Feel hopelessly crucified by my participation in the lives of others, my devotions and attachments. Take refuge in work—creating. In this book I enter into the dream, under cover of it I tell everything I want to tell.

What familiarity with the dream. I install myself in it. I have neuralgia all over the body from tension. Hugh is here, but he weighs on me like a chain. I look out of the window and feel imprisoned, and I live in dread of his desire, which is loathsome to me.

I feel he can never give me enough for this moment in which I yield to him physically with physical hatred of him. Poor Hugh. Unaware. The comedy goes on.

---

*Anaïs Nin used "Chaotica" interchangeably for a number of projects, including the "Father" story, which eventually emerged as "Lilith" in the first edition of *The Winter of Artifice*, and was later given the title of the volume. She also sometimes referred to the Barbizon Plaza in New York, where she met some of her patients in 1934 and 1935, as the "Hotel Chaotica."

APRIL 19, 1938

*J*EAN DID NOT REMAIN OUTSIDE OF THE WORLD with me. He began to brood on his not having conquered me, on Gonzalo and Hugh—on my not being completely possessed.

"Tu n'est pas fixé sur moi." "You are not focused on me." I tried to keep playing. I said: "We're so alike we can't fall in love, because we don't trust each other. We are like two magicians who know each other's tricks. You are Don Juan and you remind me of my Father. You want to be loved. And I want to be loved, and I feel distrust of you. I know you're fluid, vaporous, treacherous. I saw *you* were not obsessed with me but with a thousand things besides! I wouldn't think of marrying you! But (this I said with sadness) there is always a curse on the love of people who are twins."

"I want a woman *smaller* than I am so I will fill her and she will only love me. You love so many people. I feel inferior to you, because you have a personality, a work, a crowded life. I'm afraid of you. Falling in love with you is fatal. *Je me defend*—by my adventures."

I don't want to say brutally that all this arithmetic vanishes before true love, and that I don't love him. It is humorous, the two narcissists, the two without confidence, the two who need great *proofs* of love, the two who cannot endure this great suppleness, airiness, who need to be *solidly* loved, confronting each other. No doubt we seduce and charm each other, but we don't yield to love. I am already too much in love with Henry and Gonzalo. Jean is too young, childish. I am playing with him more than he with me. I enjoy the mystical relationship. He looks like my Father when my Father was thirty. He is the seducer, generally, not the seduced. And I, outside of Henry and Gonzalo, have done nothing but seduce without getting caught. Jean can't catch me. He tells me about his adventures. He is lonely. He had dreamed of taking me away from everyone, marrying me! He

244

cannot stand the space, the open doors. He needs a great love. What I gave him only adds to his lack of confidence. I only added a game of shadow. I only gave him enough so that he can't fall in love with other women! Just enough to poison his adventures. He compares everyone to me. I am the only one who has the key to his being, who knows the secret of his anguish and how to dissolve it, who can arouse his desire.

In a frenzy of irritation and hunger he took hold of me violently when he was leaving and kissed me crazily, bestially. And I was unmoved. I felt diabolical. Of the two, I am the more diabolical. I laughed when he left. To disturb, taunt, and play with Don Juan without being caught—that I enjoy. Here is Don Juan. Women never resist Jean. He has a power over them. So has Gonzalo, so has Henry. So has my Father. But my *real* loves are too real. Henry possessed me wholly yesterday. And Gonzalo at night. And Jean came between them, and culled only the teasing.

A PRIL 23, 1938

I WORK DESPERATELY ON "CHAOTICA," PLUNGING into the dream, while surrounded only by the needs of others, by constant problems: Helba's sickness; pay their rent; give to Moricand; pay Fred's room—money for gifts never enough. Reality strikes at me every day, heavily, limits me, impoverishes me. I feel spiritually undaunted but religious. A stern life, without gaiety or beauty. I sometimes go to beautiful places, to breathe the luxury and the indifference. Instead of more I am getting less and less indifferent. I am moved when Jean says: "I would like to *bathe* in love, to wallow in it."

Henry alone, at this moment, seems marvelously the Happy Rock. Chinese. Full of joyousness and activity, and wisdom. I bathe in his Chinese philosophy and the richness of his fantasies while Helba and Gonzalo pull me down into caverns. Gonzalo thinks of death even at the moment of sex. He listens to his heart beat after the tumult of possession and thinks of his friend who died: And suddenly the heart stops beating. I get no more life from him, only heaviness and darkness. I have to carry him, breathe into him, animate him.

*J*EAN COMES, PARALYZED, SUFFOCATED, NEUROTIC. I give myself the spurs and talk as an analyst, with great force and acuity as when I was in New York. I shake the very roots and foundation, show him how all his activity goes into elaborating, expanding his neurosis, making a marvelous venomous flower of it. With what complacency he describes his condition, elaborates, adds to it. How he confused Allendy in a maze of talk and richness of material to win over him spiritually (as I wanted to win by my lies). How he creates this labyrinth so no one will really know or cure him, to elude himself the simple *roots* of his malady, the simple conflict between instincts and fear of life. How he destroys the very loves he courts, destroys women's primitive *élans* toward him (directed at the sensual Jean) out of fear and then laments he is not loved. How he wants to play the young magician and seduce others and then complains no one knows him. How he can't write because he aims too high and can never be simple. How he dreams life with analysis, shattering every spontaneous act to bits—how he exerts a tyranny, a moral punishment over his desire.

"Your anxiety is not only just doubt of others' love, but doubt of reality. It is the Neptunian anxiety. Neptune makes fluidity, the dream, the mirage, and the Neptunian needs to be *incarnated* in his love. He lives through the *body* of the love. Through his capacity for 'decorporation,' transformation, elusiveness, he makes everything seem a dream. He can remove himself so much, live in a mystic world so remote that he seeks the warmth, the body-assurance, the incarnation in the sincere primitive love of the other.

"You have fallen in love with Liliane's sincere, human love for you. Stop reasoning and analyzing and destroying what appealed to you. You need the reassurance of being loved steadfastly because you float so easily, you are so easily cut off."

I jumped on him when he began again his fine images: "You see, other people are sewn naturally, loosely, with a space between the stitches to breathe. I am sewn so tightly, with so many stitches overlapping, that I suffocate. I think of not one but a million things at once." I said: "Stop! The artist in you is enjoying the description of your condition, but it is your way of eluding the core, the issue, perpetually. Everybody gets involved, enmeshed in your evolutions. But that is how you elude the cure. You're creating a neurosis and have become incapable of the *acte simple*. You don't permit the simple diagnosis to take effect, you immediately rush into volatilizations, inflations."

While I talked I understood too why there was no love possible between us: I leave the earth with him. We could caress each other until death from fatigue and we could not make this a human love. I can only feel his mobility. Yet there is a Jean who could be attached by his need of devotion, but I am not today the woman who can give that. I have only found my life possible in expansion and duality, in a rhythm between two men. I suffer too much when I live in *one* love.

Henry and Moricand, discussing *colors,* discovered that Henry's color was the philosophic yellow, but when discussing mine Henry said, very justly: "Anaïs's is a *vanishing* color. She has no determinate color. She only comes out when the atmosphere is propitious."

It is true. And it is true I think of love as a rainbow, too, created by the atmosphere and vanishing. The indissoluble tie of love, its strong earth roots, which I can see in my love for Henry, and now of Gonzalo, the bond of instinct and blood and emotion, do not serve against this outer mirage appearance of the moods of love which I take for a miracle. *Se me promene trop souvent dans les coulisses de l'amour.* If I tire of Gonzalo's passion for sentimental, banal, political platitudes, and feel entranced again by the immense, eternal, Beethoven world of Henry, I see my love of Gonzalo pale and it appears dead, as I once thought my love for Henry dead because the passion of Rank burned all around me. This death is not real. But it happens when the life of mystical colors, of mirages, predominates, and every day the life of the instinct has to conquer the delusions and reassert its human rights. Every day the caress of the loved one must destroy the spiderweb of moods. When I say: "My love for Henry is dead," this is only produced by a profound naïveté and fidelity, sincerity, because no one else would take a spiritual mood for a permanent reality. Neither Henry nor Gonzalo *believe* in these delusions—for them only the human reality exists. I understand now why Henry laughed. I understand why my love for my Father, who has the same nature as I have, was tragic. And why when I met Jean I was not deluded. I will never again (as with Eduardo) mistake the mystical connection for the human.

Faced with Jean I recognized a nonhuman connection. I saw in him my Father's narcissism, his Don Juanism (the need of conquest as proof), his incapacity for love, his digestive childish appetite for everything, his infantile egotism, his incapacity to create, only to analyze. When I walked up the rue de la Tombe-d'Issoire I saw myself in a mirror. What I saw was *Jean's hair*. Exactly like mine, very fine, light, brown with red in it, and growing the same way, falling the same way, with the two unruly parts over the temple growing straight up, obeying no comb or curling. "A sign of independence," he says.

Henry said: "I hear sadness in your voice."

I saw in his mirror that I am thinner.

Henry said: "I didn't ask Lowenfels to stay because you were coming and I know you don't like these big talkers." I escaped a diarrhea of talk. The diarrhea of commentary, reiteration of verbal mania, which makes me yearn for Gonzalo's primitive, unreasoning, unformulated nature.

Henry is more fragile than he was, paler. He feels the cold. I want to take care of him. He has moments of protectiveness for me. He is more and more delicate, Chinese, with a marvelous joyousness.

APRIL 25, 1938

Wrote the pages on the whore—rubens woman in the dream book.

Hugh is in London, after staying much longer than he intended. The struggling to separate himself from me, from his identification with me, makes him exaggeratedly egotistical. His idea of individuality is to thrust his slightest drawings before the attention of everyone, whether they respond or not. He is equally insensitive to all but his own discovery of an ego, awkwardly so—like a bad actor. When he was passive, blind, silent, selfless, the limitations of his character were not apparent. Now that he is dictatorial and is creating an ego, I have to listen to the most imitative, repetitious discoveries and platitudes. Without his goodness and selflessness, Hugh becomes an absolute stranger to me. He was my echo—he was the one always agreeing, absolving, accepting, justifying. The self in Hugh I don't like, for it is still an echo of a million personages. He takes the colors of Jean, or of his English friends. And his positivism is strained, insensitive, unsubtle. He repeats everything but in stone. It becomes stone in him, granite. It still lacks life. I know I am cruel to him. I can only act passively in sex. It is all I can do to control my sexual hatred. His efforts to affirm himself and blind himself to my no longer belonging to him, to accept the delusion I nourish in him, are tragic. But I feel hard. I cannot yield. I cannot go and stay in London. It is suicide. I know I am pushing him away. I may lose him. His love may someday turn into hatred and rebellion.

My whole resistance lies in the sexual act. This turns my tenderness and devotion into hatred. And he forces it on me. He is absolutely blind to my evasions, resistance, indifference. He is full of erotic caprices. He has to take me as soon as he arrives, and a minute before he leaves. That is where *he* is cruel, in his autocratic forcing, overriding me. When that moment passes, all is well again.

MAY 1, 1938

*A*N IMPORTANT DATE. I SAY THAT IN WRITING THE dream book I walked into an impasse, because I have to be *true* to the dream and I could not include what happened outside of the dream. I wrote fifty pages of pure dream and found myself faced with the book to give to the Villa Seurat Series—the book already advertised as *Chaotica* to follow [Durrell's] *The Black Book*, and Henry's *Max and the White Phagocytes*. Henry and time pressing me. Being signed with my real name, it could not be the diary.

While working on proofreading of *The Black Book* with Henry I *saw* what I could make of the New York volume (forty-seven—second trip [in 1936]) by a few transformations and depersonalization. I was in a fever. After two hours of proofreading I rushed back to the boat and wrote fourteen pages outright, without a moment of hesitation. I've got it! Anaïs gets properly disguised, all means of identification destroyed.

MAY 2, 1938

*W*ROTE TEN PAGES STRAIGHT. THEN SHOWED IT TO Henry. Great shock because he found it confused, unnatural, false. He fought for his judgment. I wept and defended myself. A personal element played because Henry suspects all the experiences I describe are mine, and I deny this.

I gave my saintliness to "Elizabeth," the incest to "Miriam," the frigidity and adventures to "Djuna." The analyst is a composite of Rank and Allendy.* But Henry stuck to his feeling.

I am deeply puzzled. Henry and I first differed radically in our opinion of Jouve. I am doing something closer to Jouve than to anyone. Am I simply taking a different route? But Henry can't be wrong because he merely says: "It is unnatural," and I know that as soon as I step out of the diary I am not natural. Here I *want* to be confusing and mystifying.

I feel very emotional, because I can't publish the diary and I can't write a novel. I feel blocked. However, this morning I gathered myself together and went on—I must go on. My joy, exultation, were killed. I labored—but I went on. Perhaps I will get more natural. I must get natural outside the diary. I wrote ten more pages today. I'm tired and sad.

Moricand once said, standing on the *passerelle:* "How I would like to know something about your earthly life. Even looking at your horoscope, I suspect many things but I know nothing for certain. You're the most unreal and most real woman I have ever known. But you show me only the angel side, alas!"

AUGUST 1938†

*I*AM LYING IN BED, IN THE BOAT. IT IS FOUR o'clock. A dark, cold day. The valises and the trunks are filled. The black cats are leaping around me. The mousy maid is washing the laundry for the last time. This is the end of the water dream, of the flow.

*The analyst composite emerged eventually as "The Voice," which gave the title to one of the three stories in the original *The Winter of Artifice.*

†In the transcript of the original diary, volume fifty-eight, page 31, there is an unexplained jump from the date May 2, 1938, to "August 1938," which seems to indicate that Anaïs Nin did not keep a notebook during this period but subsequently recalled certain events under later dates.

I was finishing my book *Chaotica*, fusing together the transformed volume forty-seven and fifty pages of dream. I wrote one hundred pages or so of wonderful hectic confessions—a mystical, sensual book. Henry was satisfied I reached naturalness.

My life on the boat was a dream. The sun was shining. Gonzalo came often. I fell into a whirlpool of violent admirers. Renatta Bugatti wanted to see me all the time, all in a fever. Waldo Frank came, pouting, sighing, childish, sticky. Henghes came to see if he had died in my eyes. Moricand. Helba in the afternoons. Everybody jealous and desirous and I gay with vanity, diabolical pleasure. Gonzalo and I would awake in the morning to the sound of Renatta's heavy masculine footsteps in the studio above. The housemaid would say: *"Madame est sorti."* Renatta left furious notes: *"Vous avez encore fait la noce. Vous n'ete jamais chez vous.* You ephemeral nature." Gonzalo and I laughed at her. Her notes: "Come and kiss me good-night tonight."

Then a note from Maruca: "Come immediately to see me. I am divorcing your father."

Her eyes opened—her rebellion—hatred—death of her love. I must go to Switzerland. He threatens suicide. I never believed in the suicide. But she wanted me to make him understand she would never forgive, never return to him. He must arrange a new life. I went, more to protect Hugh and myself from being burdened with him, to make him accept Maruca's modest help, to prevent the catastrophe from spreading. I felt absolutely hard, indifferent to my Father. Felt he deserved all this for his egotism. Went to Caux, where I went once alone when I was unbalanced by my meeting with Henry and June. Went coldly. Persuaded him to return to Paris that very night I arrived to plead with Maruca. Traveled all day thinking I must prevent my Father from becoming a burden, to protect my own life, my lovers, my husband, Joaquin, from this cold, egotistical monster. Already he was saying: "You should throw out all your protégés and take care of your Father."

No. I was adamant. Hard. Cold.

We traveled back that night.

Maruca would not see him.

I let him act out his despair, let him talk of suicide. He spent that day and night at the boat. I consoled him mechanically, said all I was expected to say. No more. Felt nothing.

I let him sleep in my room, in my Bohemian room. He opened his luxurious valise in my old, fairy-tale room. Bemoaning only the loss of luxury, of pleasures, of a wife he had formed to serve him like a slave. Never a moment of true, deep human sorrow. Every word a selfish one—a narcissistic one. Talk crapulous when angry. I saw all his moods. Was utterly convinced of his soullessness, vanity, shallowness, feebleness. He only wanted to hide under my protection. Thought of me as another servant. But I made this clear: I was not going to take care of him. And I didn't. I pushed him off, out of my life. He fell asleep—a stranger. I went upstairs and went to sleep on the couch.

About three A.M. I woke up and heard Gonzalo's voice in the bedroom! He had come, out of a blind jealous instinct. Late. Even a little drunk. I had not heard him. He had walked right into the bedroom, turned on the light full on my Father. My Father jumped with fright. Gonzalo excused himself. I called out to him. He came to the studio.

"Oh, *chiquita*. You're here. I was afraid. I'm relieved." He kissed me. Was reassured. Put his hand between my legs and found I still had my pants on. He took them off, caressed me, put me back into bed, and left.

I went downstairs, explained to my Father. Gonzalo came thinking I was in Switzerland, too late for him to go home. He has his key. My Father understood. He got into bed. He said: "Now I understand I am alone in the world."

The next day he left for Switzerland to arrange for the moving of his belongings. Maruca got him a place in Neuilly, a small apartment a block away from the rue du Général Henrion Berthier, where I was born!

And a new law forced all the barges out of Paris, and forced my *péniche* to dock on the boulevard de la Seine, Neuilly, a block away from where I was born.

Bad omen. Return. The Circle. Only I triumphed. My Father could not devour me a second time. He killed my love. I am free. The rest of this nightmare dwindled into errands I had to do for

Maruca and my Father. They used me as ambassador. I had to carry books back and forth, notes, lists, a crystal vase of great delicacy, paper. Lived in a maze of petty details, ugly scenes, disputes, separations. His selfishness predominating.

One day as I was walking to Henry's I met Moricand. "Don't be frightened," he said, "but Henry has had a little accident. He is all right now."

Henry had fallen down the ladder leading to the balcony of his studio, cut himself against the shattered glass door, had wounds on his back and on the soles of his feet. He could not walk.

For ten days I nursed him tenderly, devotedly—stayed all day, fed him, played tricks to stay with him.

And when he was just beginning to walk a little, Thurema arrived.

Thurema. For a month. Thurema, my friend. A Monster. Her visit was a nightmare. I will someday return to it. Thurema a demon. To begin with *she* is a man. Sex-obsessed, a maniac, repressed, teeming with envy, jealousy, fear, hysteria, twisted, unavowed desires. And denying it all. Idealizing herself.

She *clutched* at me, loved me in a death strangle. Violently set herself to take me away from Henry and Gonzalo. Henry still needing me for his errands and food. My Father needing me. Maruca calling out to me because she said, "You feel for me as a woman and your sympathy helps me." Thurema demanding attention, complicating my life, weeping after meeting Gonzalo. An earthquake of possessiveness, selfishness, egotism. Stifling. Always hurt, touchy, on the verge of tears, but brutal and violent with others. Spoiling Hugh's vacation in Trouville because she could not stand a third person. I had to be alone with her. Showering gifts on me; but these gave me no pleasure. She was merely trying to cover me with *her* taste, *her* belongings—to make me hers by indebtedness. I finally could not telephone anyone in front of her without causing a scene. Constant ego, tremendous. A suffocating world of destructive upheavals. Finally she got sick, first after a night when she got drunk and talked wildly about killing Gonzalo and Henry. Then a week of tonsillitis when I stayed in her little hotel room and she gloated over the situation, while Hugh telephoned me begging me to join him at the beach.

She took, appropriated, invaded my *month*—and I hated her for it. Her realization that I could not live with her alone, away from Gonzalo, infuriated her.

To get away from her oppressive, tyrannical atmosphere I used to pretend having to go to the W.C. often. And there I would sit with pleasure, *breathing* a while, free. When I disregarded her scenes to be with Gonzalo late at night, I still felt her presence so strong that I was often frigid. All my nerves were knotted by her own impotent sensuality. She affected me, paralyzed me. I had to fight her. I began to burst out, to attack her, to be severe. I analyzed her mercilessly. I finally cowed her. The creative role in me survived. I analyzed her. It killed me because I rebel against this role. I wanted a friend—not a maniac to watch over.

Well, I was an insane-asylum keeper for a month. Worn out physically, and by my control and struggle to be patient, to be creative when I really just wanted to beat her.

The comedy.

Not to say of my Father: You killed my love, too.

Not to say to Thurema: I hate you.

As soon as she sailed I went to Henry and Gonzalo. I enjoyed them both sensually, wildly. Then Hugh arrived and I got desperately ill, vomiting all that had happened until the blood came.

Meanwhile, the boat is far away, near a sewer infested with mosquitoes. And now moving out, regretting the symbol, defeated by exterior forces: a law, distance, the cost of constant repairs, the rain falling on everything. Problems of all kinds. Expenses. The boat now impossible, too far, lonely. Pains from the dampness. Hugh in London. My only joys: the flesh of Gonzalo, his love, the divine writing in *Capricorn*—all through the month Henry writing like a god. And here I am where I started. What struggles. What infinite circles.

AUGUST 24, 1938

VILLA SEURAT. *HENRY ON MEANING OF Cancer:* For me, *Cancer* means the crab, as it was known to the Chinese sages—the creature which could move in any direction. It is the sign in the zodiac for the poet—the halfway station in the round of realization, which changes when one comes to the constellation Libra. Opposite Cancer in the zodiac (extremes of the equinox—turning points!) is Capricorn, the house in which I am born, which is religious and represents the renaissance in death. Cancer also meant for me the disease of civilization, the extreme point of realization along the wrong path—hence the necessity to change one's course and begin all over again. Nietzsche's doctrine of eternal recurrence, also, in a more profound way, the essence of Buddhism: Cancer then is the apogee of death in life, as Capricorn is of life in death. The two symbols are found in geography as tropics (which is another word for hieroglyphs). Cancer lying above the equator and Capricorn below. I, as I have said frequently in my books, am trying to walk the hairline which separates the two. The line is only imaginary—there is no boundary line to reality.

The anguish of a Neptunian is special. It is not lack of confidence but lack of reality. Entering and then leaving life for the dream, vanishings, and returns. As Henry said about me: A vanishing color that came and went depending on atmosphere. The dream faculty makes everything insubstantial. We need to be incarnated. I am incarnated over and over again in Henry's writing and through Gonzalo's body, which is so powerfully real. Through love I enter the human and awake from my dream.

At certain moments Neptune is like a filter—and I feel disconnected. It's what Moricand calls the *"courant alternatif,"* alternating current.

Henry's writing is a part of me. He *expresses strongly, violently* all that I feel but in a state of nebulae. In me it is clouds. In him it takes form. Concrete and earthy. I love his writing. What it expresses I feel, the extremes of sensuality and the myth, the spirituality and the demon.

I understand every word. He could write it all symbolically and I would feel it. We talked sadly once after he wrote the pages on the black star. Anciently all literature was symbolical—and everyone understood the symbol. Now we can no longer write in terms of symbol or myth.

Henry is a primitive. He loves the sound of words, not their meaning.

The same elements are in Gonzalo—a woman said he has the hands of a savage. It is true. Whenever he is happy, after sensual moments, he always begins to talk about his country. He tells me about the hunting trips he made with his brothers and the Indians, lasting three months in the mountains, sleeping on the ground, never washing. When he returned his mother said: "You smell like an animal."

It took six hours by train to reach the heights, three weeks on foot. It had to be done slowly on account of the heart. Beyond a certain height the horses or mules could not bear it, they would begin to bleed through the mouth and ears. When they reached the snowcaps and the air almost black with intensity, they would look down a sharp, straight cliff thousands of meters high and see way down below, small, intensely green, luxuriant, *the tropics*, the jungle.

Gonzalo was teased by his brothers for dreaming of *"una princesa exsangua"*—the pale *princesse lointaine* he found in me. Gonzalo was so romantic, sensitive, nervous that he says there are many women in the world who are convinced he is impotent. Attracted to a woman for her beauty, once in her presence he could not take her. Timidity, inhibition. Not one of them understood this or found the way to tame this gentle savage.

"How could you ever leave the mountain, Gonzalo?"

"The poison of culture. The full-blooded Indians die of sadness when uprooted."

His laziness in thinking. I see the efforts he makes. And with me he falls back into nature. That is why after our caresses it is the mountain he talks about.

When we first met he too imagined taking me there, living there with me.

I asked Moricand about Lilith in my horoscope—the sexual, demonic Lilith, the woman-not-woman, the unpossessed, the one incarnate in "Djuna" in the novel.

He said: "Your Lilith is at the bottom of a well. She is one of the drowned, imprisoned personages in you, which Henry is exposing to full daylight in *Capricorn*. He calls her June. He often writes about you only he doesn't know it. He thinks it's June."

Never having lived a chaotic, capricious life I began to imitate it to gain freedom. I imitated Henry's erratic behavior, Elena's sudden changes of plans, caprices, Gonzalo's irrational behavior, their unexpectedness, unaccountableness. So they lose track of me. I suddenly decided to go to church at six in the morning to hear the music (to explain my not being at the boat at eight A.M.). I went for a walk in the middle of the night because I couldn't sleep. Elena went once at dawn, walked from five A.M. to ten while the concierge telephoned me she had disappeared. I stayed in the street because I felt like sitting and writing in a café. This permits freedom.

Finally, by imitating this which I had never done out of feeling for the one who expected me, who was counting on my presence (I could never even break an engagement), I began to live this way—breaking promises, lateness, unaccountableness, change, never sticking to what I said.

Anarchism.

I accept and understand this in Henry, Gonzalo—why should I not permit it to myself?

For Jean—who can't read English—I translated a few pages of *Chaotica* and he said: "*Tu marche sur l'eau.* Others will be afraid. They'll see you and they will be afraid to drown."

The day in the boat with my Father was like talking to a madman. One moment the madman is in a lucid mood. He understands he has been a monster. He understands he has lived out his Don Juanism without delicacy or care for Maruca. He knows his faults. But the next morning he has a fit again—a crisis of self-justification. He plunges into lies, he puts the whole blame on the other, he begins to deform, to adore and justify himself. He ends by putting himself back on the pedestal—innocent—and now begins his role, his comedy, his pretenses. A labyrinth. He is so intent on his subjective reality, his fantasy, his pathological lies, that he was doing truly *mad* things which even an idiot could point out to him. He was down south with Maruca. They invited a young violinist to stay with them. She was a virgin. My Father exposed all her defects to Maruca and denied any interest in her. He had not been taking Maruca for a year, pretending it was because of her illness. But Maruca had in her bathroom the pills against pregnancy recommended by my Father. *And these pills began to disappear!* My Father took them. And on top of this a package is delivered to Maruca by mistake, a package intended for the violinist. It is a douche bag for the virgin. And yet my Father persists in *denying* even to me. He says he recommended douches to the virgin to improve her complexion! I said: "Vaginal douches for the complexion—a virgin?" and laughed. But he didn't laugh.

This story, added to the one of the rouge on the handkerchief that I told in my novel, finally opened poor Maruca's eyes. She gave him a lot of money. It was never enough. He invented having to pay a tax on the house. Naturally this was discovered. He said he gave the money to his poor daughter whom he found wearing heavily mended stockings! But it was the thousand francs he spent on a cane which he bought in my presence!

In Caux they had had a Spanish maid he wanted to keep because she was so wonderful. She would take care of him. With that maid, if Maruca would let him have her, all his problems would be solved. At this time he didn't know what a modest life Maruca was planning for him in a service apartment. Yet he knew then that she had promised him merely rent and food money. He dwelt on the need of having this maid (this on the day of his *deepest* sorrow—the day he came from Caux to see Maruca and she would not see him!). After a while of talking about this maid he sighed: "But if I get Maria it will mean I'll have to have *two* maids. Yes, she is not a very good cook."

Regretting *la fête des Narcisses* in Caux, where he was going to preside in his beautiful car. "And if I get sick now, what?"

Gonzalo no longer says, as he used to: "You and Helba." When he talks of going to Russia or China he speaks of taking me. He is willing to separate himself from Helba—not from me.

Helba only holds us with her threats to die! The first time he spoke of me alone I was ecstatically happy. At the beginning it was always: "Helba and you. You and Helba."

What telepathy between us. One afternoon, after my bilious attack, I went to see my Father, after a month of neglecting him. We took a walk through the Bois. I was expecting Gonzalo in the evening. It was a beautiful afternoon. Walking in the shadow of my Father's presence I was dreaming of Gonzalo and yearning for him, thinking we should be together on such a beautiful afternoon. At twenty-to-five my Father said: "Can you return with me or aren't you free?"

"I am not free," I said. "I must be back at the boat about five."

At five o'clock I stood in front of the door getting my key. I looked up at the road and there was Gonzalo coming with the same yearning, the same mood I was in.

Helba, a child in so many ways: Great love of candy and cakes. Infantile with me, as if I were the mother. Complaining to me of Gonzalo's indifference, that he doesn't talk with her, and I have to remind him to take her things she likes or I tell him to stay home and talk to her.

Gonzalo, like Henry, never knows what he feels—neither cold nor hunger, nor loneliness, nor jealousy. Gonzalo doesn't *know* he misses me. But he gets into black moods. Helba *knows*. As soon as I returned from the beach he was full of life again.

But he is tortured.

Pedrito the sculptor asks him: "Does Anaïs live in Montsouris? I have seen her several times. . . ."

I have to explain—Fred lived there, he did typing for me. I went to get the pages.

But it makes my visits to Henry dangerous. I am now full of anxiety. I come to Villa Seurat in a taxi, right to the door. I leave early in the morning. I am anxious now. Each night is a problem.

Gonzalo and I in bed, naked. His sex so large now against my belly. We just lie quiet, feeling each other's body. Gonzalo murmurs: "How can it all go inside of you and not hurt you."

I tell him the lovely story of Marius and Olive. Marius saying that when he gets passionate eleven birds can perch themselves on his sex. Olive protests: "Don't exaggerate, Marius."

"Well," says Marius, "the last one on one leg!"

I think of Thurema at night in her hotel room. No longer the Thurema of New York but a sexual animal who pretends not to be one, a woman who wanted caresses, excitement, sensation without the capacity to yield to it completely. I felt the sexiness and the lack of naturalness. I stopped kissing her on the mouth. If she had been more natural, more yielding, more tender, feminine, it is possible I might have been tempted. She tried so hard but her hardness and aggressivity, her shame, her uneasiness, her mental awareness, sex-consciousness, spoiled whatever adventure we might have had. Surely I do not care for woman sexually—of this I'm sure now.

Thurema stimulated and electrified me at first. She liked to dress me, to come into the bathroom when I was bathing. A friend told her in New York: "When you talk about Anaïs you talk like a man." When I took her out to lunch to meet Gonzalo she began to show uneasiness. When we returned she began to say she couldn't stand seeing us together, absorbed in each other. It was the same with her sister. She couldn't bear seeing her with her husband. They were used to it. Then tears, hysteria, a mixture of envy and jealousy. If I left her room her blue eyes would flash: "You're going to telephone Gonzalo?" If I left her at night, late, after spending the day and evening together it was "abandon." She didn't sleep all night, or she had nightmares and anxieties. The next morning there would be a scene. Finally I rebelled. I told her I couldn't understand her attitude. She always vigorously attacked Lesbianism and said it was disgusting. This ambivalence—hatred of man—spread so much and culminated in a night where she also pushed off Hugh and made it impossible for the three of us to go to the beach. She got drunk, she harassed Hugh because he was quiet, she irritated him, she wouldn't dance with him so as not to leave me alone, she couldn't bear the dancing because it was sensual. I could never tell exactly how she did it but she created an atmosphere of war, hostility, hysteria. At first I tried to tell her what was happening to her. There were reconciliations. Then I ceased feeling for her and began to act like a doctor. My hopes for a *friend* died. She thought I could be absolutely happy for a month away from Gonzalo or Henry. She quarreled with everybody. Even her voice over the telephone grated on Henry and made him bristle. Her voice in my ear was hard and hysterical. No pleasure together. Everything marred by her preoccupation with herself, her shame, self-consciousness, her doubts. "How did I seem? I had a run in my stocking. I felt terrible. I'm too fat for the beach." I. I. I. I. I. I. I. I. I.

I got tired of reassuring her, of bolstering her, of analyzing her. Every meal brought an emotional storm. Once she told me she hated to be thought maternal. A few days later remembering this I said, "You're a *femme fatale*." This brought a storm of protest and explanations. Idealism. She had to appear good, compassionate, selfless. When the last few days came I was on edge. I thought I would break down. I suddenly offered to take her to the beach. She could sail from there. Immediately she became calm and contented. I was able to continue the comedy. Now if I never saw her again I would be glad. But I wanted to let her return without a feeling of failure. So my last words were studied to please her. But after this came indifference—and now? I should have been honest.

She left me nothing to love. No mother, no sister, no friend, no adventure, nothing.

SEPTEMBER 15, 1938

*T*HE PRESENCE OF WAR.

People lived the last two weeks under the threat of war. Everything became ugly, tense, destructive. Individual life was annihilated. Collective panic, collective rebellion, collective fear, or collective fury. People running away. People faced with the problem of a possible invasion or possible catastrophe. Henry ceased correcting *Capricorn*. He had finished the first volume. He got sick at the disruption of his life. Hugo and I went to Bad Rogaz on vacation and then returned after eight days because of our anxiety. Gonzalo at his worst—either jubilating over what the war might mean to the revolution or disintegrated, sick, without energy. All the problems falling on my shoulders. My own health breaking down—attacks of bilious vomiting exhausting me and leaving me weak for days, eye trouble, anemia, fatigue. Black days for the world. The crowds awaiting the news before newspaper buildings. Unrest. Hysteria. Henry's health all year fragile. Last night a hiccup fit which lasted a night and a day and of which one can die. An infected tooth, the consequences of the wounds, dizziness, paleness. So close to Henry: leaving and returning from Switzerland we embrace with the passion of old, but a passion full of tenderness. With Gonzalo greater keenness and less depth. Sharpness, desire, passion, but less depth. I don't want to know. Struggle to save my Father from the pathologic lies which isolate, disconnect him. Wrote him eloquent letters which caused a great storm and roused his sincerity. Wrote Thorvald also a fiery, thundering letter for his *unnecessary* lies to me. Honesty among crooks obtained an honest letter. I can't let them create their own loneliness, alienation, separateness, destroy themselves. I fight, fight, plead, operate drastically like a doctor. Aggressive but constructive. Frenzy of protectiveness again. My world threatened, a world which was a creation, and in its miniature scale beautiful in how it was run. A little universe by itself of pure communism, pure creation, protection, care. This little world, nourished by Hugo economically, by me with all my spiritual power and possessions, whirling into the marvelous— and stopped in its convolutions by the destructive forces of the outer world: Hitler.

This at first caused me so deep a sorrow as you feel when an earthquake destroys a city—Shangri-la and *Nanankepichu*. But now I have stopped sorrowing.

How to protect Henry? What to do? How to get money? Mother. Joaquin. Old Lantelme ill. Father. Order digestive biscuits for him. Get the same for Helba.

Story of the pieces of sugar: Gonzalo never has enough sugar in his coffee. The French look askance when he asks for more, or bluntly refuse it. I started making little packages of pieces of sugar the day I was deathly ill at the Hotel Scribe (all alone in the room, Hugo at the bank), which made Gonzalo laugh. I sent him an envelope full of sugar from Switzerland. I pick up sugar wherever I go and wrap it up in little pieces of paper. I tell this in the middle of the earthquake, because the earthquake is pointless, meaningless, it comes of man's brutality and stupidity, but the sugar wrapped up to sweeten Gonzalo's coffee is human.

What made me ill was moving out of *La Belle Aurore*. Deep regrets. In one day the dream ended—and I have to find another. That day in the summer, the day of the *Fête sur les quais* seems so far, so far away. I should have known it preceded great catastrophes. It came when I have no strength. All I can do is protect, protect, protect.

Bad Rogaz—the womb. But we heard the thunder there through the rock walls while bathing in the soft warm waters.

Photo of Hugh as a child symbolical because he travels constantly by airplane now—back and forth from London. Born under an air sign. So much of the bird in him—and for me he swoops down from the air to gather me up when my battles in the world shatter me.

My spiritual battles: to make my Father sincere, to reintegrate him.

Amazing scene: "You lie, you lie." My letters on isolation created by lies. I showed strength, force, directness. Broke him down. And now he talks the truth. "It is good for me, good for me." Pacing his room sobbing. Beginning of new relationship he never had with woman.

S E P T E M B E R   2 1 ,   1 9 3 8

ALL OF US SHATTERED BY TENSION. WAR DANGER lulled for a moment—dissolved in conferences.

A day: Eight o'clock at the Villa Seurat. Henry and I awakening. Henry worn out, absolutely, by several physical troubles, the last one at the dentist. Worn out by strain of Paris atmosphere. Always desperate at change and insecurity, just when he was writing the most amazing pages of *Capricorn*, the first four hundred pages. We are packing. He has arranged things as if he were leaving for a long time. He leaves instructions about his MS as if he were going to die. I give him all the money I have—a thousand francs—and see him off to the Dordogne region he always wanted to visit. He is pale. We kiss on the platform, with passion and tenderness.

From the Gare d'Orsay I go to Neuilly to see my Father. He is sitting at the piano, fixing a composition. His apartment is meticulously arranged, ordered, polished. We walk through the Bois. He pours out real confidences—absolutely himself. Begins to believe there is a God who has punished him. He always weeps at the end, over the lost mother Maruca—lost for foolish sexual games of no account.

From the Bois I go to see Mother and Joaquin, who are preparing to return to America. Mother is older, sweeter, more easily tired. Joaquin is fixing his quintette, studying his piano. From there to old Lantelme, who has heart trouble at seventy. Then Helba comes, in great need of love and care, and we talk about Gonzalo, who is going through a serious crisis. Conflict in him between the adventurous, restless, danger-loving, sensation-seeking part of him and the Gonzalo who needs and loves and desires me, and who is weighed down by Helba's illness, sentiment, and devotions. He has been ill and depressed for a month. He is tied to me by love, to Helba by pity, and he is restive like a horse, bad humor, violent depressions, sickness. Helba says: "I lifted him up, picked him up until I got sick and lost my strength. You're the only one who can save him."

Part of me responds to his crazy dreams. Didn't I risk all my happiness for hazardous experiences? Didn't I dream and wish to be a spy? I feel such pity for Gonzalo's suffering.

Helba says: "I have the presentiment that I'm going to die."

When we sit at the café together and I have to speak loudly, the people insult me and humiliate us.

Then Gonzalo comes. He is shaking and trembling because he got wet in the rain. He says: "How weak I've gotten physically. If I had gone to Spain in two months I'd be out of the trenches in a hospital." I take him in my arms, warm him. While he lies there I think human life is worth more than anything and men are dying for ideas which betray them, for leaders who betray them, for false ideals. Everywhere a battle against destruction and death. Moricand wrote me: "The angel in you is suffering—will suffer."

War—my antithesis.

SEPTEMBER 23, 1938

A DAY: UP EARLY AND TO THE VILLA SEURAT TO arrange to have it cleaned, to take Henry's typewriter to be oiled, to pick up his mail. He writes desolate letters: "Everything looks dead and dull—I feel like a ghost." I answer: "You created such a marvelous inner world, of such brilliancy that the external decors must look poor and dull." He has no use for nature, beauty, wind, sea, mountains. He is worn and nervous.

From there to a spontaneous visit to the owner of *Isis*, the small white boat Gonzalo and I always dreamed of having, just on a hunch.

Find he is a painter, desperately anxious to leave France—wants to sell his boat and begin a new life far away. Can't stand Paris, as a thousand others, for fear of war, can't work. I can't buy *Isis*, but I dream.

Then to the dentist where I wouldn't go until my last wisdom tooth hurt too much. A nightmare. It won't come out. They even use a little hammer. It is impacted. The woman, the wife of the dentist, says: "It's a *mysterious* tooth," which amuses me. The cocaine effect gives out. More injections. Heart anxiety. And the strain, the violence. When it's all over I break down.

Back to the hotel. Cheerful mood. It's all over. Joaquin comes. Gonzalo, tenderness. Not too bad a night. Letters from Henry. Telephone Hugh. I wear a Spanish handkerchief over the head like a gypsy. Gonzalo's demon appeased by hard work.

Chaotica lies there: "Elizabeth" is lying down in a cell-shaped room of the tallest hotel in the city, in a building shooting upward like a railroad track set for the moon.

I'm drunk on *Seraphita* of Balzac. Moricand says: "*You* are Seraphita." He gives me back my wings by talking all evening of mythólogy.

Writing to Jean I find myself telling him I miss him, that I am less light without him, that he gives me great mystical joys and that when he is gone I feel much more the pressure of the earth, the lead of other people. So much earth in Gonzalo.

The weight of Gonzalo's body symbolical. He lies dead, inert. I must *need* this, lack it in myself. I seek it. It's like the *martial* spirit. I sought it in Henry—earth, war, passion. In Gonzalo—chaos, destruction, war. In June, in Thurema.

What we live through the *other*, what I can't live out myself which lies in me—chaos, disorder, tumult, impulse, obscure instincts, caprices, fears, fevers, bad temper, violence—*they* live out for me. My Karma is to pass through darkness, confusion, violence, destruction—which I dominated in myself, tamed, denied, controlled, transmuted. My loves are like the selves I tried to transcend—the lives I skipped, escaped by swift, mystical ascensions. So the earthy, the demons, the instincts grasped me in the form of Henry, June, Gonzalo, Thurema. I transformed Henry, Gonzalo too. The women could not be transmuted; they didn't have the power to sublimate. They remained all blood, all nearness, all hysteria.

SEPTEMBER 25, 1938

*T*OMORROW I PLACE THIS DIARY IN THE VAULT. I cannot carry dynamite around with me. I have to be lighter for the voyage, for the uprooting that is coming.

War looms again. The women weep in the streets. Crowds stand before the *caissee d'épargne*. There is fear and fever in the air. And Gonzalo, the very soul of destruction, the very symbol of destruction, thrives on the anguish and feels alive. The same day I get him glasses, a great sacrifice of four hundred francs, which was hard and left us without money to go away, he drops and breaks them. In anger he says terrible things.

Just last night I was writing a few pages for *Chaotica*, and we were awakened by news of mobilization. Telephone cut off with London. Henry in Bordeaux. Mother and Joaquin preparing to leave. Disruption everywhere, anguish.

SEPTEMBER 26, 1938

*M*OMENT OF WEAKNESS WHEN EVERYBODY TURNS to me for money and I have not enough, in spite of Hugh's generosity. Anxiety as how to get Mother and Joaquin off. A neurosis of protection. The tooth operation has worn me down terribly. But suddenly I got hold of myself when I got Henry's neurotic letter from Bordeaux. Again I must be strong. A violent reaction. Helba's sickness wearing, weighing down Gonzalo like a stone around his neck. He must live his life his own way. I must remove her to a safe spot. I must get Mother and Joaquin to go. I must see Henry who is absolutely lost and bewildered. OK. Prepare everything. Organize. I wish I could give Gonzalo my gift for organization. Myself and others. I went to the post office. Sent Henry money, Moricand a hundred francs, wrote letters, packed. Talked to Gonzalo, who was immensely relieved; Hugh pleads I should leave Paris.

Mother's spirit is wonderful. At sixty-five she keeps undaunted, active, without panic or anguish. Admirable. It was she who helped me today when I broke down, saying I had been so worried not to have enough. Problems. Moricand begging to take him away with me. Starves when I don't remember him. Fred asking me for work and to get his typewriter out of hock. Gonzalo's mad expenses, like collecting at this moment all the Spanish classics and buying an encyclopedia (reading San Juan de la Cruz and Marx together!).

I lie in bed waiting for Gonzalo to return from a meeting. He passes from demoniac moods, glee over war, to the most human tender moods.

To make Gonzalo drink Carlsbad water when he gets sick, I make a playful speech of it not being a medicine but springing out of the mountain. He believes, as I said, neither in European medicine nor in sorcery.

I cling and clutch at little things to reestablish this only thing I believe: human life. That is why I can't believe in systems. I read Marx carefully.

In Bad Rogaz, in the bath, there was a rubber tube with a tip like a man's sex through which the water came in a hard violent jet. Once I took it between my legs and the water flowing excited me. I had an orgasm in the water. The pulsing of it made my whole body quiver like that of a mermaid flipping her fish tail!

I was born at 7 rue de Général Henrion Bertier in Neuilly-sur-

Seine, but I was conceived on the ocean, on the way from Cuba to France, that is, over the Atlantide.

Moricand says of Gonzalo: "He is tied up—the planets are too close to one another, they suffocate each other." Poor Gonzalo—that is why, one by one, he gave up writing, then drawing, then the piano.

Gonzalo telephones: "I think Hitler will collapse. We will see."

I wrote to Henry: "I am watching over you, I and Seraphita. Do not fear."

When I saw my Father at Caux, in his golf suit, he looked suddenly shrunk. He could not yet believe it was all finished. He wanted to plead with Maruca. She suspected him of having an affair with a singer. He denied this. He said she was homely, fat. The servants told Maruca they had seen him kissing the singer in his car.

He threatened to kill himself but I did not believe it. When we returned to Paris I left him in the barge waiting and I went to see Maruca.

His messages were that he would spend the rest of his life making her happy, that he was heartbroken, that he would atone.

To me he said: "I've been unconscious. I didn't know she minded. You know, at times I don't think I am a man. I am a monster. I feel possessed. I get drunk on this lovemaking. I get reckless. Tell Maruca I had nothing to do with this woman."

"But if you had, wouldn't it be better to be truthful this time? She is angry. She will hate a lie now more than anything. She may have proof."

Immediately he looked alert and cool: "What proof? She can't have proof."

He was still lying.

I found Maruca in bed, having breakfast. Her face, which was always that of a believing child, looked stony.

I pleaded with her. "My Father's unfaithfulness means nothing. He always loved you above the others. He was light, but his deepest love was for you. He was irresponsible. You were too good to him. You never rebelled."

But Maruca defended herself. She was that kind of person. She had great faith, great indulgence, great love. For that reason when she was betrayed she could never forgive. She had wept, endured in silence. She had known for several years that he was lying to her. She had warned him gently, she had been ill over his perpetual infidelities. She had wanted to die. She had waited for him to change. She had been loyal, absolute. But now, once she had cut the ties, it was forever.

This child, this little girl Maruca, who had worshiped her husband as a teacher, god, great musician, was now as firmly aware and unyielding as she had been indulgent. She believed nothing. She even returned to the past, added up all the facets of his behavior and decided he had never loved her. She slowly added and accumulated reckless remarks, selfish exclamations, thoughtless gestures, the expression on his face when she was ill, when he told his impossible stories, his outlandish lies, and determined he had never loved her. Until now her own love had covered all the crevices, her own giving stopped all the fissures, her own faith healed all the wounds. But this small, secret, gentle life that had been nurtured on grievances for fifteen years now erupted like a volcano and nothing could stop its devastation.

I knew that nothing could stop it. I knew the kind of unfaithfulness women could forgive was not the kind of unfaithfulness my Father had been guilty of. I knew that he was not a man one could easily forgive because he was cold-blooded. He was not the natural man, that is, the man who lies, drinks, makes love, cheats, steals, devours others because he is of the jungle where such acts are natural. Those are the men women forgive because they are natural. Because if the lion eats the lamb it is not an act of cruelty, not a premeditated one. Women sense this, and they forgive the cannibal, the man who is not aware of his strength, of his cruelty, of his ferocity. But the man like my Father who is the very essence of artifice, whose pleasure was a deliberate conscious quest, whose conquests were not even born of a natural hunger but vanity, the need to accumulate conquests just to prove his power, this kind of self-indulgent behavior accompanied by hypocrisy, the need to make believe he possessed all the virtues, this was not forgivable. The natural man does not deceive, he is honest and does not pretend to be an ideal being. My Father was always acting the ideal being.

He was constantly saying how faithful he was, he even embroidered on this faithfulness. He was always pretending to be absolutely pure. He covered acts which were completely selfish with a coat of altruism. He pretended to be saving women when he was sleeping with them, to be teaching them when he was seducing them. It was this Maruca could not forgive. It was the fact that even today he was lying, for she had definite proofs of his last escapade. It was that, not content with having his mistress near Caux, he still wanted his wife to invite her to stay in the house, he even taunted Maruca for not liking her, not fraternizing with her.

"Let him cry now. I have cried for many years. Let him think about suicide. I know he won't do it. He loves himself too much. Let him measure now the strength of my love which made life so soft for him and know what it is he destroyed. I feel nothing. Nothing. He has killed my love so completely I do not even suffer. I never knew a man who could kill a love so completely."

She resumed her breakfast. I knew she was honest and would not waver. But still I sought to find some cord to touch. The child and the mother. Just keep saying he is a child and she the mother, for thus are many men's acts covered and transfigured. The woman becomes the mother and then she can forgive everything. The child of course does not know when he is hurting the mother. He does not see when she is tired, he is baffled when she is ill and does nothing for her. The child is passive, yielding, demanding, and giving nothing. If the mother weeps he will throw his arms around her. Then he will go and do again that which makes her weep. The child never thinks of the mother except as the all giver, the all forgiving, the indefatigable love. Thus Maruca might see it. She let my Father be the child. The child devours the mother. But poor Maruca had her answer to this: My Father was not even tender as a child, he did not even have the kind of love a child has for the mother.

As I watched Maruca eating her breakfast in her mother's sumptuous house, I was aware of the whole house, of the servants, of the exceptionally good cook, of the luxury, of the chauffeur and the car waiting at her door, and I knew she was taking refuge in luxury.

My Father wanted to look at his house for the last time. When we stood in front of it he looked first at the window of his room: "I will never see that room again. It's incredible. My books are still there, my music, my piano . . . But I . . . I . . ." Tears fell down his cheeks. "What has happened to Maruca? Such a meek, resigned, patient, angelical woman. A little girl, full of innocence and indulgence. And then this madness. . . ."

At the very moment when we stood there, a slight earthquake was registered in Paris. At the very moment when my Father's life was shaken by the earthquake of a woman's revolt and revenge, when he was losing love, protection, faithfulness, luxury, faith. His whole life disrupted in one instant of earth rage. Earth and the woman and their sudden rages.

On the insensitive instrument of my Father's character no sign had been registered of this coming disruption.

As he stood there looking at his house for the last time, the bowels of the earth trembled. Maruca was quietly eating her breakfast while his life cracked open and all the lovingly collected possessions fell into an abysm. The earth opened under his perpetually dancing feet, his waltzes of courtship, his contrapuntal love scenes. In one instant it swallowed the colorful ballet of his lies, his pointed feet evasions, his vaporous escapes, the stage lights and halos with which he surrounded his conquests and his appetites. Everything was destroyed in the tumult. The earth's anger at his lightness, his audacities, his leaps over reality, his escapes. His house open and through the fissures fell his rare books, his collection of paintings, his press notices, the gifts from his admirers.

Because he was a man without dreams he saw in the barge only dilapidation, the homeliness.

When the night came the shadows frightened him. Each motion of the barge made him uneasy. What nightmares breathed from the creaking floor, the wild garden of designs on the walls. A man had sprung into the room and turned on the light fully on his face, and then off again. A man? Had the Phantom Lover come upon the father asleep, to haunt his soul, to defend the daughter, the barge, the secret, the poem? Who haunted the barge at night protesting against the visit of the father, a nightmare to frighten him away. The Phantom Lover breathing heavily in the night, in the swaying windows, turning on the light to see who was the stranger who had no right to the barge?

The barge sailed on without the father.

When I look backward to the week of the war threat when I stopped writing in the diary, I see a cemetery. That the war in reality did not take place doesn't matter. A great many people died, a great many faiths. The veil of Maya which makes life bearable was violently torn.

I saw Henry terror stricken, trembling and howling although he was the only one who left Paris. The sage in him instantly annihilated. Shangri-la world immediately destroyed by his fear. Henry in agony of egotistic instincts, raging because peace and security were torn away from him by great exterior forces. Henry instantly without faith, or strength. Cabling right and left drunkenly for money to sail to America. Henry a primitive—all fear and rage and impotency. I sending all I could: fiery letters, money, exhortations.

I saw Gonzalo ready to sacrifice all individual happiness to war, to death, gloating because war might have made the revolution possible. Gonzalo physically courageous, but with a courage for death and not for life. Gonzalo whose *Nanankepichu* is only a warrior's resting place—a pause between violent fits of upheaval and utopian faith in a new world.

I would have gone away with Gonzalo—because I do not believe in this war—to seek *Nanankepichu* elsewhere. But he has not the courage to live his own life. He is collective. He would have dragged me into the drama because he *likes* violence and suffering.

When it was all over, everyone felt the death of his illusions. Henry's Chinese sage talk had not stood the test of reality.

We faced each other like ghosts. Suddenly Villa Seurat looked dilapidated. One noticed the stains on the walls, the fissures, the peeling paint.

The Peace was like a cemetery.

Gonzalo was sad because I had not incited him to blood and massacre.

I live in the essence of all things and everyone else in the literal. I live in the eternal and others in the transitory. Gonzalo has the necessary blindness to take sides and die simply for an idea, but I see the falseness of all ideas. I live transcending all laws, prejudices, morals, and communism, in reality, is too narrow for me. I always respected a *man* when I saw one, a character, a human value, and never asked where he was born. But all this applies to me. I see it does not apply to others. And so on October 1, 1938, Saturday night, in the Arabian restaurant, I became a communist *for the others*, because I think it may deliver them, because the poor need it, because it is the right punishment for the egoists and a hope for the slaves.

I believe in it for the others. For myself I only believe in liberation by illusion and poetry, the only world without walls, injustices, monstrosity. I return to the dream and the drug.

It was the night of the peace euphoria. We had escaped a nightmare, a monstrous holocaust, a gigantic tragedy. Gonzalo could not help being happy. When we're happy we go to this Arabian restaurant. We talked so exaltedly and fierily about "liberation" that I was caught in his faith. I said, "I believe, I believe." When I read all the little books on Marx later—synthesis made by the French—I saw the limitation, the error again, for me. But not for the world. The world is earthy. It needs earthy solutions. It cannot liberate itself into space and time. It needs concrete, external change to see, to feel. Communism is right. Gonzalo too is earthy. He cannot escape from reality except with alcohol, morphine, coca, cocaine, ether. Neither he nor Helba dominate disease, drabness, *cannot* transform, cannot metamorphose. Helba is encircled in physical pain. Everything around her is real, monstrous: the medicines, the cotton, the dirty bandages, the ignorance, the weight. No power. Only on the stage. No power in life. Gonzalo only understands outer transformation. He forgets no economic liberation will liberate him from his guilt-service of Helba— nor me from my inability to cause pain. Weakness in us. We never recognizes the weakness in us. Blame society, the doctors, everyone but ourselves.

Society is not to blame for Helba's ignorance—nor for my compassion. When I ascend into illusion Gonzalo calls it a "negative" solution. What irony. What I have created out of the terror and tragedy of life! And he, meanwhile, was on the way to becoming a *clochard*—the great renunciators, the ultimate anarchists who prefer to acquire their liberty by renunciation.

One day, thinking of this, I returned to my hotel room. I had left on my desk a page from my diary written long ago but which still seemed to apply today. Gonzalo had come in, read it, and written his answer to it.

Fragment from a diary: This is my drug and this is my vice. This is the moment when I take up the mysterious pipe and indulge in deviations. Instead of writing a book I lie back and I dream and I talk to myself. A drug. I turn away from reality into the refracted. I turn rock events into mists. The driving, impelling fever which keeps me tense and wide awake during the day is dissolved in abandon, in improvisations, in contemplation.

I must relieve my life each day in the dream.

The dream is my only life.

I see in the echoes and reverberations the transfigurations which alone keeps wonder pure.

Otherwise all magic is lost, and I awake to touch the prison bars.

Otherwise the homeliness, the deformities, the limitations gnaw into every gesture like rust.

This is my diary and my drug. Covering all things with the utter fluidity of smoke, transforming as the night does. All matter must be fused this way through the lens of my vice, or the rust of living will slow down my rhythm to a sob.

*Gonzalo's answer:** I was deeply moved on reading the page you left on the table. You know my attitude regarding this problem, which, after all, is the great problem of the artist today. But in the lines you wrote there is such purity and quality, such an angelic voice, that they touched me deeply. I think about your life and understand completely your attitude "or the rust of living will slow down my rhythm to a sob." Rarely have I read such a delicate phrase. But I know what the "rust of living" is; it is giving yourself to others, sacrificing yourself for others, renouncing what belongs to you so that others may have it, opening your arms so that others may crucify you—that is the true "rust of living."

*In Spanish in the original.

Poetically you want to drop a veil of fantasy, beauty, and forgiveness over all past sacrifices, and to a high degree you succeed; and you call it "dreams" or "magic" or I don't know what. This doesn't interfere with the original Anaïs, who was your own, untransferable, nor with your right to live according to YOURSELF, to love, to breathe the air you choose. You were hindered, oppressed, like a freed slave, and today the artistic being who lives in you is *obliged* to say, "In the echoes and reverberations, I see the transfiguration which *alone* keeps wonder pure." With a gesture of infinite kindness, you don't put the blame where it belongs; you prefer to say that the world is horrible and that it is reality which does you harm. Aesthetically, you take a negative position toward life. Anaïs as a human being, Anaïs in her vital self, is constructive; her spirit is full of energy, her words full of hope and help. TO HELP, HELP, AND ALWAYS HELP—that has been the leitmotif of your life, the device on your shield. Anaïs, literally speaking, wants to flee from life and the world. Anaïs looks for a transfiguration in things, for an artificial fever which will help her bear the terrible weight of reality.

However, I, Gonzalo Moré, who for two years have shared Anaïs's physical and spiritual life, who have seen her in suffering and ecstasy, who have felt her TRANSFIGURED, I affirm that this contradiction between the Anaïses should be laid at the door of the social system in which she has lived. In a word, at the door of the plutocratic, obtuse, exploitative, and vile bourgeoisie.

I affirm that if Anaïs had never had to sacrifice herself SENTIMENTALLY and SEXUALLY (pardon the word), she would never have needed opium nor vice nor black magic. Life in itself is magic. And what magic! I affirm my hope in the future and believe that a day will come, after battling, vacillating, moving forward, and slipping back, when Anaïs will reverse those values entirely and will feel that the prison bars were actually in her dreams. Because today Anaïs lives in a Prison of Dreams. And her jailers will keep her there, feeding her on mysticism, astrology, and magic for as long a time as they can. But one day the bars of her prison will fall as though made of wax and Anaïs will return to see the sun and the light and the mountains with eyes that are NEW AND AWAKE.

During the week of the war threat, Henry sent me a telegram from Bordeaux which Gonzalo intercepted. The message was: "Ask Kahane to forward cables to Hotel Majestic." It was the very day of the worst fears. We were planning to leave together, Gonzalo, Helba, and I. Gonzalo made a scene which I finally calmed by saying: "This only *proves* to you that there is no sentimental link but merely a man turning to me for help at a critical moment. He asked Kahane to get him money to sail for America. Kahane probably didn't answer soon enough and Henry merely asked me to intercede."

The flare of jealousy was stifled by greater anxieties. We would leave Paris, it was agreed, but Gonzalo had to return for his work. I was ready to become a nurse. I could not think of joining Henry in his escape to America, nor of waiting anywhere while Gonzalo was in danger. What black days. The women weeping in the streets. Mobilization. All the trains crowded with people running away. Everybody had left. The trapped ones, Moricand, Fred, who could not move because they had no money, were glad to see me staying on. Moricand was copying out mythology notes at the Bibliothèque Nationale. I was reading *Seraphita* when I was not reading the papers. Gonzalo was like a storm: dark, fiery, full of hatred, anger.

A sunny morning, when we were to meet at Gare St. Lazare, peace came. Several nights after the euphoria—the conversion to communism—I was to meet Gonzalo at my hotel at eight. I spent an hour with Moricand at the Café Flore talking about mythology. Then we walked down the rue des Saint-Peres, leisurely. I had plenty of time. I walked with Moricand to his subway station. When I returned to my hotel Gonzalo was waiting for me. I was gay and full of life. I said: "I've been studying mythology with Moricand."

Gonzalo exploded. He had come out of the post office at the rue des Saint-Peres just as Moricand and I were passing. He had followed us. He saw how intimately we talked.

"Gonzalo, you're crazy," I said. And pleaded with him, *reassured him, reassured him*—cajoled him.

His jealousy subsided. We walked to the Arabian restaurant. I was looking beautiful, and I felt beautiful. When I ate the figs Gonzalo watched my mouth sensually, with admiration. Then I felt his desire. We walked out in the soft evening. And suddenly he began to rave about Henry. He knew I was seeing him all the time. He knew I had never broken with him entirely. The telegram proved it.

I repeated what I said before: I had no link with Henry. Only because of the war crisis did he appeal to me. It was natural at such a moment when everybody lost his head. Appealed only as a friend.

But Gonzalo was like a demon. I will never remember what we said. Violent, ugly, twisted things. Gonzalo was foaming, hurling all his rancor, doubts, furies at me. I was weeping, and denying. Any other woman, faced with such violence, would have confessed, just to bring it to an end. But I never wavered. We went down the streets —people stopping to watch us. I weeping and Gonzalo storming. What violence! Twice I left him, ran away from him. He followed me. When he said ugly things, I struck at him. We reached the hotel but didn't go in. We stood at the corner. I got so desperate I began to hit him with my two fists, striking at his chest. He was black, demented, a demon. Scathing words. Lashing. Bitterness. We went to my room. I never wavered from my story. Gonzalo implored me. I maintained what I had said. I wept hysterically at his cruelty. We got into bed. Finally Gonzalo quieted down: by gentleness he tried to make me admit it. Gently I answered him, denying.

Hugh was arriving the next day. This always unleashes Gonzalo's jealousy. He took me but I felt nothing. I was absolutely shattered. A black day. My face swollen. Hugh arrived.

Now, when I remember this, I love it, like a terrifying storm. We touched the bottom of horror, of hatred born of love, of fear born of blind passion.

This night of storm brought me months of peace. I told Gonzalo that night Henry had left for Mexico. He believed it, I am again running in and out of Villa Seurat, risking every day my happiness, my life.

———

I wanted passion—I got it, and its punishment too. I asked to be loved for my skin, feet, mouth, body, sex. And I got all the violence that accompanies desire.

DECEMBER 13, 1938

WHY IS IT THAT WHEN I GOT A HOME AGAIN I needed the diary? When I left the *péniche* I wrote in it—then I buried it again. Yesterday I began this little book. Why?

Is it because Henry is talking of going to America and I feel the space between us growing too vast, too mystical? I am afraid of complete separation. Gonzalo's great human vitality, his violent fleshy love, his body, almost destroys the mystical link between Henry and me.

I don't know.

I call this walking over water. Walking over the moving ocean of the secrets men will not speak of.

In life I grow more silent. In writing I open all the words because I know nothing can destroy mystery.

I finally amalgamated the three novels—Henry-June, Father, and Confessions-dream book—into one, for which Henry found the title: *The Winter of Artifice*.

Durrell is bringing it out in February.*

In *House of Incest* I wrote about June: "She would tolerate no bars of light on open books." This is true of Gonzalo. When he read the new parts of my MS, the confessions to the analyst, the story of Mischa's crippled leg, he began by reading objectively. He was moved by certain pages. But then it all ended in a scene of jealousy.

---

*This volume, containing the "Henry and June" novella ("Djuna"), the "Father" story ("Lilith"), and the "Confessions-dream book" ("The Voice"), dedicated to Nancy and Larry, appeared as "the third volume in the Villa Seurat Series" under the imprint of the Obelisk Press, Paris, in June 1939.

I took my MS to Henry. We worked on it quietly several evenings. Helba said: "Gonzalo should stay with you and read what you write instead of going so much to the café."

That very evening I sat down and worked with Henry. Gonzalo had stopped halfway to explode with jealousy.

My Father sent for me one day. After seven months of weeping he composed a *"Berceuse pour les orphelins d'Espagne,"* in which he merely wept over his own orphanage, his loss of his mother Maruca. *He* is the orphan.

Jean is in Lapland, working like a farmer, in a little wooden house. One afternoon, it was still summer, we were walking toward *La Belle Aurore.* Knowing his self-doubts I decided to tell him my impression of him as a lover. I told him exactly how good he was, how firmly he held a woman, what I like, etc. He was dumbfounded. "You dare to talk about this, in full daylight! How we suffer, stumble, stutter, grope, because no one dares to say these things. And life, the mystery, remains, greater even in the clarity. The way you illumine leads to greater depths, Anaïs!"

Nothing is destroyed by daring. It is a further advance into mystery. Jean getting inside of a woman—lying still, not moving, and thinking this was all there was to it. This was his first experience. The man with a clubfoot making beautiful shoes of crocodile leather, fur, glass slippers.

DECEMBER 16, 1938

BACK TO THE SCENIC ILLUSION. A NEW HOME made again. I lie in bed and I can see it all. It is one large room with an alcove for the bed. My setting again. Again the black rug, the Arabian bedstead, the oriental lamps, lace patterns of shadows on the ceiling, seashells, atmosphere, voluptuous, and mysterious. With so little material! I don't need very much. I am an *illusionniste.* I can create an atmosphere with valueless objects. I am a prestidigitator. I can give the illusion of luxury, of sumptuosity.

Meanwhile the news is bad again.

Gonzalo came the other night sick with the horror of having had to expose and judge a traitor. He described the scene: a South American who had worked for the Party and then betrayed it. Gonzalo had to question him, break him down, extort his real name, and finally confront him with the proofs of his treachery. When the man broke down and howled and wept, he said: "I thought the revolution was going to take place immediately. I was full of faith. But all this waiting. My exaltation finished. I needed money...."

Gonzalo cannot condemn. He personally always sees the motives, forgives. Forced to *act*, he was ill with pity for the man. He could not sleep thinking of him. Gonzalo says if he is ever shot, it will be for his good heart.

I saw the extent of his idealism. He was revolted, nauseated with the *reality* of politics. He remembered the *Procès de Moscou.** He runs to me now when he is in trouble. When Helba gets sick, when he's sad. I have to act and decide.

Henry says he has some accounts to settle with America, and that the time has come for this. He has been withdrawing from exterior life greatly, condemns all the waste and activities I used to lament in him. He repudiates all that years ago I could not understand him doing: silly friends, empty evenings, futile activities of all kinds, dispersion—the vice of constant motion.

He dreams of Tibet. Says in four years he will retire to Tibet and become a lama.

"And what must I do then?" I asked him playfully.

"You can become Seraphita."

Alas, Henry doesn't know we are still traveling inversely. I am

---

*In 1935 Soviet dictator Joseph Stalin had instituted a series of show trials in which old Bolsheviks were induced to confess political crimes manufactured by the prosecution. These Moscow trials produced deep divisions among the political Left and its sympathizers. By 1938 many of the leaders of the revolution in 1917 had been condemned and executed, and Leon Trotsky, the founder of the Red Army, had been exiled, and many of the generals shot.

doing the route toward June that he left so long ago. I am living out this vivid passion I wanted—only not blindly. I am not given the blessed blindness Henry had. I am *aware*, as the Tibetans are made to be aware of their dying. I am always aware of what I live out in relation to my Karma—I suffer more.

Maybe—now I know—that is why I stopped the diary! I see tonight how it accentuates the awareness and brings pain.

I have been living blindly, like one without vision, always pinned down to earth, suffering. I was cursed. For my *lightness* I was cursed, for it made me need Henry and Gonzalo, who both made me suffer by the *earth* in them.

What a great struggle to keep the balance between: so Henry would no longer destroy himself or me, so Gonzalo would stop destroying himself or me. There are days when I feel the fullness of my inferno on earth.

Human life on earth. There lies all the tragedy. I have all the moods of a mystic. I am most of the time in a drugged, intoxicated state. Most of the time in a dream.

I lie here tonight in a setting of the Sleeping Princess. It is the Sleeping Princess all this is happening to—remember. This makes it all more violent. It is a Sleeping Princess who is traveling in the subway next to an old woman covered with eczema, who is walking up a hill in the mud to a clinic, who is handing Helba the urinating pan, changing the cotton, looking at the tube. It is the Sleeping Princess who is listening to the story of the traitor from a Gonzalo who smells violently of garlic, because he was so nauseated with the scene that he went to the café afterward and ordered a steak covered with garlic to recapture his equilibrium. It is the Sleeping Princess who is cooking because money is more and more scarce. No more taxis, servants. Except that all of us, being Russian, we swing to extremes and spend in one day what we saved for a month. I did buy a piece of stalactite—like a piece of the moon.

I hold this secret drug which does not destroy me and which permits me to hold on to the ecstasies.

Dr. Kaplan on my health: "You are not sick. You have different deficiencies which keep you from being very strong physically—

insuffisance globule rouge, insuffisance endocrine, insuffisance hépatique.
None of them a sickness. I can make you stronger. But nature
has done a queer thing with you. You have such a strength of soul,
spirit, psyche, imagination that if you had a body equal to them
you would burn like a meteor and die. Nature established a weakness which holds you back, which forced you into occasional
pauses."

I would rather have had the animal strength of June or Gonzalo,
burned up and died early.

DECEMBER 30, 1938

When HUGO CAME WE THREW OURSELVES INTO
pleasures: We got a radio, a bedcover from
Madagascar, a couch cover from Marrakech, an electric heater, papaya
jam, sweet potatoes, cranberry, a wine bottle from Mexico, an orange-
painted candle, a holy water holder of old Spanish-Moorish pottery,
seashells.

I gave myself ten days of selfish living, told my Father, Maruca,
people, I was in London. Entrenched myself in the Arabian nights of
my home, lit sandalwood sticks, and contemplated my life.

Such a wave of sadness came up to my throat at this moment that
it frightened me.

But now I know the secret: I can't wake up. I have remained in
the state of wonder of the child. When I cook I do not expect to get
burned. I am surprised when I get burned. When I go out I don't
expect rain. I dress gaily and I am caught unaware by the rain.

Before Hugo came I expected to be happy with him. I get a shock
each time at his appearance—so glum, set, absent, dead. Slowly his
glumness, his mournful predictions, his concern with saving for our
old age, his worries over trifles, his concern with the world's opinion,
his fear of people discovering I wrote the "Birth" piece, his constant

putting the lid on me, his unresponsiveness to joyousness, his sense of realism, limitation, his disbelief in miracles, his underestimation of people's understanding, his expectation of malignity, his fears, doubts, his constant bad health, nervousness, oppress me.

In one day with Hugo, Thurema understood why I exploded so often outside of his orbit.

He—and Helba.

Gonzalo, by a strange instinct which I like, not taking me until Hugo goes, until I am all his again, as if he divined those sad sexual scenes between Hugo and me.

I know the secret.

I do not expect Gonzalo to be enslaved by Helba's sickness. I do not expect him to be late. I do not expect the venality and pettiness of Kahane, the limitations in Durrell's understanding of my work ("You have no form and no objectivity"), I do not expect to run short of money every ten days after giving right and left like a fountain.

Moricand said he identified me with the legend of Arethusa, who, unable to reach for impossible loves, turned into a fountain nourishing others with her tears!

Well, somehow, this made me laugh. I'm a rather ridiculous personage—as ridiculous as Don Quixote.

Il faut rire un peu. (One must laugh a little.)

Moricand said the fountain was the diary.

In London, seeing the movie *You Can't Take It with You*, with Hugo. The theme: A big family all doing exactly as they please. "God" takes care of them, but finally God must take the form of a rich man. I wept abundantly. Hugo didn't know why. In the taxi I explained: "I was weeping over you. You are the one who makes it possible for all of us to do what we please. Because of you, Joaquin can play what he wants, give expensive concerts, compose as he wishes. Because of you Helba can cuddle her diseases, Gonzalo can serve communism and not work for a living. Because of you I can write and live in a dream." (And Henry. I didn't say: Henry is playing with an expensive magazine, *Delta*, printing the "Gold" essay when it had already appeared in a book, and the silly pamphlet on helping Fred.)* "But *you*," I said, "are you happy, are you doing what you want to do, do you feel free? Are you playing as you want to? That's what made me weep."

Hugo was amazed, as he is each time I weep over his life.

"But I'm doing what I want to do. And perhaps if it weren't for all of you, I might never have learned to play too...."

We bring him the pleasures.

It was his turn to weep when we saw *Froufro*. The pretty, delicate Creole girl—whose large dresses made such lovely symphonies—all coquetry, playfulness, lightness, the *toy* wife. Hugo wept because he wants me as a Chinese wife—dressed, perfumed, full of coquetries, sheltered, an ornament, a charm, and instead it is all the beauty of life I have sacrificed. My hands are getting spoiled with cooking. I have only one very feminine, decorative, elegant toilette. I have surrendered things which sound foolish but which I love—coquetries of all kinds—for a tragic and much harder life. I still try to give the *illusion* of riches—and I do. But each time I buy a little incense, how furtively—and only when Hugo is here, never out of my own money. I spend less on myself than I give to Henry, or Helba and Gonzalo, or old Lantelme, or Mother and Joaquin. What I give to Moricand each month forces me to go to the pawnshop, or to borrow and get deeper into trouble. Hugo knows this and it hurts him. He wants to spoil me and I don't let him.

---

*In April 1938 *The Booster* became *Delta* and carried a notice by the editors: "Beginning with this issue *The Booster* becomes *Delta*. It should be remembered that circumstances imposed upon us a title which we did our best to live down to. The change merely marks a voluntary break with an ambiance which never was ours. It neither means a change of heart nor even one of attitude." The April issue was given over to poetry, and among the eighteen contributors were Kay Boyle, Antonia White, Dylan Thomas, David Gascoyne, Michael Fraenkel, and Lawrence Durrell, who apparently had collected the material. Henry Miller's parody of Ezra Pound's theories, dedicated to Ezra Pound, "Money and How It Gets That Way," appeared as a *Booster* pamphlet in September 1938, in an edition of some five hundred copies, at fifteen francs, and was apparently reprinted the same month.

DECEMBER 31, 1938

ALL THIS IS FINE, BUT I HAVE REBELLIONS. AT MID-night last night, 1939, the most terrific sadness. A feeling that I am in a prison. That each time I love and think I will escape, it is I who am sacrificed. Henry did not help me to escape. He made me a prisoner of Hugo by his incapacity to use money in any way but egotistically or childishly. I am a slave of his magazine, of Gonzalo's "altruism" and devotion to the masses, to Helba's "cru-cifixion," which disguises a negative will to die. *I am in prison.* And Gonzalo didn't get me out of it either. He is a prisoner himself. And there is 1939—a prison.

JANUARY 3, 1939

HUGO HAS LEFT FOR LONDON. I'M EXPECTING Gonzalo. Having touched walls so violently again, with my head, broken *élans*, so many of them, so much waiting for Gonzalo while Helba fabricates a new disease, so many shocks, threats from the outside—great mute pain for days. Everybody asking: What's the matter?

A mute, blank pain.

Groping in the dark I find always one little, tiny door open on the infinite. I will write another book, a book like a dance, about the *péniche*, Helba in her rags, sewing, taking buttons out of a box marked "ovarian suppositories," Albertine's abortion in the little cabin. The fetus I had to throw away into the river. Her valise with a child's reader in it. Renatta's masculine footsteps above my head while I was asleep. My Father's shipwreck. Looking at his house for the last time, the day of the *tremblement de terre*. The drunk *clochard* sitting on the quay. Seeing the black sex of old *clocharde*, who sat with her legs drawn up, from the little kitchen window. Debris. Lights on the ceilings. Moricand thinking I took drugs. Jean playing the violin for the first time after many years. Sending penny through hole in the floor for his flute playing. Colored stone window. Dinners. People. Postman afraid of passing over the *passerelle*. The first bath, with minnows in it. Pump breaking down. Noise of ferries. Girl who lost her hat. Man with wooden leg stamping on fallen five-franc piece. Traffic with *chiffonnier* bags. High tide. Little boat. Over the wall and down the ladder. Michel Simon and his monkeys couldn't live there or the monkeys would run on the quays. Floating. Two long voyages pulled by tug. Sitting with umbrella, eating banana, directing. First voyage asleep, loss of time, distance, thinking I was going very far. The suffocated fish. *Chambre de Nuit et de Jour.*

And then, in this *"Casa de las Candelas,"* as Gonzalo calls it (from a Spanish poem), comes Gonzalo—and everything is covered again in the night.

This morning I took Hugo's drawings to be reproduced in a Japanese sketchbook form. Such delicacy and imagination, and primitivism. Moricand called it "the creation of the world."

Hugo on the train to London, Henry on his way back; the Durrells staying with Hugo.

Gonzalo talks about dynamic as against static life: Marxism as dynamic philosophy. He paints a world in constant *revolution* because it matches his tumultuous life. But the adventurer in him is tired. He offers his big arm to my caresses like a giant cat and says he doesn't want any more adventurer life, it is too hard, bitter, terrible.

For most people life is a constant succession of mishaps. They fail to live as they intended. They miss the moment to say what they want to say: at the station, at parting, they are overwhelmed with indifference. The letter that should arrive at the right moment is never written. Always a failed performance. Helba and Gonzalo.

Only in creation is it possible to fashion a world without deserts, eclipses, failures.

Question troublante: My love for Gonzalo seems to give to my love for Henry a mysterious equilibrium it lacked—instead of destroying it. I ask myself whether, because I wept so much over separation, change, and death in life, whether my prayer was not heard.

I have often said I did not believe in *death*, that nothing could die around me. Hugo's love does not die. Eduardo's love does not die. Henry's love does not die. When he returned from London he took me with real hunger, and I responded! We sat down to correct the proofs of *Capricorn*, and his writing moved me profoundly. Gonzalo's desire and passion do not die when he expected them to—because desire and passion rarely last three years in the same exalted form. The night Hugo left and we were together was like a first night. And in myself all the feelings are alive.

Is this a spell? In spite of all the destructive realities, the disillusions, the struggles.

JANUARY 9, 1939

MOONSTORM. PROOFREADING *CAPRICORN*. TRANSported by it, so much that I lay in Henry's bed while he took a walk and wept over him and myself and the terrible truths he utters. Took his book like an earthquake. Felt disrupted. "I must either go home immediately and write a book or begin an absolutely new life!"

Whereas Henry, detached from his past, surprised at my emotion, says: "But I am happy now. I would change nothing in my life today."

But I, I am in prison.

I cannot begin a new life. So it will have to be a book which will begin: I am behind the window of a prison. I am a prisoner. It does not matter whether it is a window of Saint Alley where I first lived.

It was always a window. I was always behind it, looking out and desiring to escape. The window of Saint Alley gave on a small garden. I wanted to be at the sea. The window of the apartment house in New York gave on a backyard. I imagined and desired a park with golden gates. The window of Louveciennes was on a garden and the green gate was closed. I wanted to see Fez. The window of the Barbizon Hotel gave on the park. I was imprisoned by my desire to save others. As a child I was imprisoned in my loves, in my fantasies. But I was not allowed on the street. Whoever gave me a house, costumes, jewels, imprisoned me. The one who kissed my feet and adored me imprisoned me. I surrendered. It was my self I gave. I wanted to dance and roam the world like a gypsy. I did not do it. I wanted to be Joan of Arc. I wanted to be a million-faced actress. Behind the window of my loves and my compassion—and of the worlds I created. And when the doors opened, when I was on the verge of freedom I would take one fatal glance backward and see the one behind me who was not free, and I retraced my steps and enchained myself to this one while the prison door closed again. I never wanted to walk out of my prison alone. I was always preparing the flight for others—and so time passed. I stood behind every window of every city of the world, always looking at something I wanted and I could not have.

But of course, I had the *dream*, this blessed drug which is given to all prisoners of distinction! Only the dreams did not calm my hunger, because my dreams did not lead me away from life but toward it, always guiding me toward dawn and realization, so that I always butted against an impasse: I wanted to live out my dream. It was not enough to be illuminated. And so no matter how marvelous the night, I always awakened to the presence of the barred window. To love was no prison, but to love as I did was, because I wanted my loves free, I wanted them to be fulfilled, I wanted them to live their dream.

It was when I heard music that I awakened. Why? Because music makes my body move. The invisible dance of life, the invisible drama I lived, secretly animated by the music, became incarnated. The foot moved, the hips, the head, the finger. The dance was made visible— and with it, the sense of limited space.

Because I have erected a universe, resting on Hugo's protection,

Henry's creation, Gonzalo's passion—and all that this universe fecundates and protects: Henry sending money to his father; Gonzalo feeding his poorer friends; Helba sending money to her mother, Helba nurturing her illness; Joaquin giving his concerts; Mother having her lost teeth replaced; Gonzalo getting glasses for his failing eyesight; Henry going to London to rest himself; Lantelme's last days relieved from utter misery; Moricand eating. Because of the million webs I threw, of protection, liberation, for this reason I am trapped as no one was trapped. Indebted forever to Hugo's goodness, devoted forever to Henry's creation, crucified to Gonzalo's weakness and Helba's suicide.

How to escape? Where? Henry did not take me away. He needed me, my sustenance, peace. Gonzalo comes when he is tired of being an adventurer.

By a miracle I escaped from my Father's burden. I had the strength to push him away because he killed my love. Yet I can still get sick every time I see him weeping. I cannot escape my vulnerability or compassion. I always look behind me. It is all my fault. I know. Why the rebellions and the restlessness then? I have made a prison out of sentiment, pity, weakness, indebtedness, fraternal loyalties, out of love, devotions. I have done it all. Why do I rebel against my own work? No one frees me in return. Gonzalo awaits the revolution. That is how he wants to free me. Hugo frees me, he believes, but by this generosity binds me more securely with an almost religious gratitude. I have a rich life. Why this feeling of tragedy? I sense the world is big and I am shut in, condemned to live fully only through dreams. When I love it is because this love is part of the dream, as is proved by Henry's writing, or by Gonzalo, who is so clearly a dream image, born of racial memories. Gonzalo belongs to my Spanish blood dream. But why must it all enclose me rather than free me? *Where* is it I want to go? I don't know. I never know except when I feel something, pushing me dangerously outward, like the trips to New York.

What is the prison? Only the difference, the disparity between the enlarged images of the dream and the rhythm of reality, which peels, clips, cuts, interrupts, diminishes, shrinks, shrivels all things. The ugliness of Helba's slow, cowardly suicide. Why not a courageous, clean death since she has not the courage to live? I would never impose my slow suicide on others and destroy them with me. I would never cast the shadow of my desire to die on others around me.

E. Graham Howe, in *Time and the Child*, writes: "Depression is characteristically associated with over-consciousness, and so is particularly liable to befall virtuous people. This is because they feel it is their moral duty to hang on to all good things, fixing them forever against the moving law of time."

It is curious how I have always awaited the one who would *represent* the evil in me—one who would lead me into perverse, dark adventures, who would push me to the end of my curiosities. I needed a leader because this is the weaker part of me, the half constantly submerged by the good in me. June could have done it. June was the one. But then I represented the part of June that was not perverse, not destructive, not dark. The alchemy produced illusion, not adventure.

Then I thought my Father would be the one. I knew his cruelties, his monstrosities, the crimes he was capable of. But he was not honest—he was haunted by the need to idealize himself, especially in my eyes. He lied and kept his adventures secret, deformed, embellished.

Henry—Henry was never the leader in adventure. He was pushed by others.

Somehow the counterpart of the demons in me never crossed my path—or if they did they changed and transformed themselves at my sight. Gonzalo abandoned his nightlife when he met me. He too needs to idealize himself in my eyes.

And so?

It all remains an undercurrent, a desire, something I never fulfill or realize. It is not *strong enough* in me, that is why I need to have it strengthened, asserted, by another. I am pushed by a greater force to save, create, liberate, illumine. This companion never appears. In Jean there was plenty of perversity, but unacknowledged, feared, not audacious.

Alors. Bon.

It is interesting to see that what is not strong enough in us does not realize itself. Nothing could keep Gonzalo away from drugs but while all his friends either died or crippled themselves from abuse, he liberated himself.

Gonzalo had a red-haired friend in Peru who was like an animal. He used to twist his body around so that he could suck his own penis and enjoy himself before everybody. Whenever he felt the need, there he goes, head down, legs in the air, rolled up, and sucks himself off, red hair blazing around this rare bit of self-fecundation.

Gonzalo and another friend stealing the milk bottles of the other tenants and going back to bed saying: now we don't have to go to work today. Gonzalo washing dishes for cafeterias and leaving the hot water tap open once, flooding the place. The Argentine perpetually ironing his trousers and shining his patent-leather shoes. The people from the show in which Helba was dancing.

Why are some people's lives crowded with monsters, madmen, perverts—and not mine?

I write in Villa Seurat, waiting for Henry. I found a note he had made for a dish he wanted to cook sometime, so I made it.

I ask myself—now that Gonzalo will no longer live in Vanves, in the suburb from where, after feeding a helpless Helba, he had rarely the courage to return—my coming here and staying the night will become more dangerous. He has threatened to spy on me.

I wish Henry could realize his desire to go to America—because if I lost Gonzalo now, because of him, I would go mad with pain. It is Gonzalo who is inside my veins and blood now—my love for Henry has transformed itself and become mystical.

JANUARY 13, 1939

MYSTICAL INDEED! I WAS WRITING THE WORD when Henry returned from cocktails with Kahane, a little drunk. He enjoyed his dinner and then collapsed with fatigue and dizziness. I playfully "put him to bed," undressed him slowly, I laughing, and he enjoying the inertia. I almost carried him to bed and he pretended to be half asleep. He was laughing too. Then he ran his hand up my dress—felt me, got excited, and made me lie over him, and we fucked savagely.

The next night Gonzalo and I were caressing each other very late at night when the telephone rang. I answered because I thought it was Hugo. God, it was Henry, saying he had lost his key and would I throw him mine out of the window. All I found to say in a very definite voice was: "Don't do that." (He was saying he was coming.) "Don't do that," and hung up abruptly.

Gonzalo was silent, furious. I said they were two homosexuals, friends of Eduardo, to whom he'd given my phone number. They were a little drunk, they called up to have me join them to go to a party.

This made Gonzalo instantly believe I went out every night to parties. Big scene. Tears. Assurances of my love. Then finally caresses, an orgasm which lasted so long I thought it would never stop. Increased passion, fear of loss, awareness of the love.

Instead of beginning a book I am preparing to safeguard the diaries for war. The last alarm found me unprepared.

JANUARY 14, 1939

LAST NIGHT A SUSPICIOUS GONZALO SNIFFING THE air, restless. Our talk a dissonance. Jealousy. I reproach him for isolating me completely. He finds it natural. He remembers with anguish the first year he met me how surrounded I was with men, all of them in love with me. I sit next to him thinking of my visits to Villa Seurat and feel the danger I am courting, the irresistible fascination of it. Sitting next to Gonzalo discussing whether or not I go to parties while it is Henry I see. He is saying: "At times I imagine the wildest things."

Later I say: "You fight about little things like a telephone call in the night, just when we could be happiest now that Miller is in Mexico. I've been so happy ever since—thinking there was no more danger of your condemning me for some incident not caused by me, some appearance."

The way he answers me I can see he believes Miller is away—story which can crumble any moment if Gonzalo should see Miller in the street, or meet one of his innumerable friends in Montparnasse. Fortunately Gonzalo moves in a different milieu: the communist *"cellule,"* South American newspapermen, not Montparnasse but the little bistro on the rue de Beaune where he talks with workmen and *clochards*. And Henry is rarely in Montparnasse.

Sometimes I get very tired of the tension—I wish for peace, a life without *angoisse* and danger, secrets, lies.

All my diaries and papers are in the cellar. I have to go down the dark stairways and hide in a brick-and-beam room with spiderwebs and coal dust and there hide away copies of *Delta*, Henry's magazine, or the magazines with articles written by him, or the copy of *Tropic of Cancer* translated into Czech, with my preface.* The immense physical fatigue I feel at times is entirely due to the tension.

All this I think of while Gonzalo talks. Suddenly he said: "You're absent. Probably you had an engagement tonight which you had to put off and that makes you uneasy."

"Don't say crazy things, Leóncito."

We went to bed, both hurt. I said: "It's a night of dissonances." He begins to caress me and I get all wet.

Before, he had said: "There are two kinds of men, one kind who likes to be betrayed and who loves the woman more when she betrays him, the other kind who is estranged from the woman if he does not feel she is altogether his."

After our embrace I ask him mischievously: "Am I altogether yours?" He feels I am, yet he also feels I escape, and he can't solve the mystery.

Obratnik Raka, published in Prague, was the first foreign edition of Henry Miller's work, and the only translation to appear before the war. The blue-and-white jacket reproduced a line drawing of a nude by Henri Matisse.

Why I feel *whole* when my loves appear split is because I lead an unreal life. I refuse to accept the limitations of one relationship. I live out all the sides of myself at once. It looks like a split but for me it is wholeness. It looks like betrayal, but it is integrity. It is amazing to note the absolute differences between my relationship to Gonzalo and to Henry. With Henry it is very large, creative, cosmic, almost impersonal. I have transcended the pure woman to be his wife, in the scale in which he lives, to sustain his creation. I accept all the pain. I proofread his love passages about June. I take an objective, creative attitude.

With Gonzalo everything is personal. He is personal, possessive, jealous, emotional. Incapable of objectivity. I live out all my near, personal feelings. He is *near* men and women, personally, not as Henry is. He loves the friend, not friendship. He does not want isolation. He gives himself, willing to die, absolutely. Henry does not. Henry belongs to eternity. Gonzalo to the present.

Even Henry's caresses are impersonal: I become woman—any woman—a cunt. Gonzalo is primarily personal: me. He makes me feel more female, *his* female. He encloses me. Henry's attitude is a result of experience and wisdom, Gonzalo's is romantic.

Real—Unreal. Renatta and Italian hypnotist, who made her play a concert at Baronne de Rothschild's house. Carteret and I sitting in window bay looking on garden at broken mirror.

When I read *Capricorn* I realize how much Henry has suffered. It is enough. Gonzalo never suffered because he never loved as strongly in the flesh.

I want to write about the lost *péniche*—floating—the light—the water changes—the drug. Moricand hanging his beautiful, spotless coat on the *résine* wood walls, rain falling on the velvet collar.

I will make G. an *imaginary* lover—a fantasy! Arriving not by the *passerelle* but by a rowboat, entering *péniche* by the window. Leaving at dawn.

The abortion: Albertine's thin little legs and big breasts. The scanty hair around her sex. The worn-out bedroom slippers. The photo of her fiancé. On a night of *fear*.

Life under the bridge. *Clochards* watching. Rain on glass roof. Life on other *péniches*. Carrying water to and from the fountain. Creaking floors. Revolvers. Mildew. Rocking. At night *péniche* asleep. Dream boat. Stained-glass window.

Larry in a letter to Henry mentioned a mad Hindu poet. Why immediately I pictured him, felt him, I don't know. But in my letter to Larry I asked him: "Will the Indian still be there when I come?" And then this morning I was lying in bed, having my breakfast alone, reading Hugo's letter: "Tambimutu has fallen in love with you. Just from reading your *House of Incest* and going crazy about it. He is going to write a review of it which I will send you. And then from seeing your picture. He is an Indian from Ceylon, but not a calm, philosophical one—a tortured, half-crazy poet. Admits he has been mad for periods. Analysis of handwriting shows 97 percent feeling. Same analyst gives you much the same percentage and says your handwritings are similar. But says he has never seen such an even flow of feelings as yours. Tambimutu says too bad you are married."

Tambimutu. I thought of someone with Gonzalo's body but *altogether* a poet. Not coming to me to tell me how marvelous the fête of the communist *cellule* in Vanves was: All the workmen and families sitting around a table and singing. Such a marvelous atmosphere, real fraternity, the bond of political passion, elbow to elbow. His eyes wet with sentimentalism: "Such a *purity*, such goodness and loyalty."

"How awful," I said.

Tambimutu. Are your arms and shoulders softly rounded like the Indians of Peru, your sex very dark, your eyes full of fire?

Proofreading *Capricorn* with Henry—the amazing pages on June. They are so marvelous that they give me the feeling of a cosmic story. No longer June and Henry but something beyond them both, born of Henry's imagination. I don't suffer humanly because the lover, Henry, even while a puppet on June's knees, had a terrifying vision of her emptiness, and while he writes of her power, he at the same time crucifies her on her own void. It's frightening, the vision of the spiritual man ruthlessly exposing the sex tragedy, woman as nature—soulless, a mirror.

I keep seeing Gonzalo in those pages too because Gonzalo has those instinctive illuminations which appear like a vision but are mere flashes in a kind of animal nature. Henry writes of June: "I thought I had found a female Vesuvius."

At moments I feel like telling Henry about Gonzalo. He would understand. Henry today could read my whole diary and forgive me.

JANUARY 18, 1939

GONZALO WAS QUIET AND GENTLE LAST NIGHT AND after our caresses we talked about political work. When he gets enthusiastic about political activity I have a desire to do it out of love for him, to be nearer to him. For fear this world I cannot enter may separate us. I know I am inadequate for it, not gifted for it, that the words they use sound hollow to me, that I do not belong there. I was honest with Gonzalo. I told him I didn't like the idea of writing letters full of platitudes, heroic bombast, sentimental propaganda, naïf humanitarianism, such as he does; collecting money; entertaining volunteers; attending meetings; listening to news on the radio; reading newspapers. That I wanted to do it to be near him, to understand what it was all about so I could understand his work. He was immensely moved—he understood the tenderness behind this. But he understands, too, that I do not fit in. Even if my love or sympathy draws me toward human beings, even if I desire nearness, sharing collective fears and desires and angers and victories, I can't. Even if it makes me sad to see people agitated, moved by events and happenings which I can only see from afar as *all* dishonest, foolish, erroneous, blind, I must hold on to my own integrity. Out of love I take on atmospheres, costumes, roles, friends, books that I don't really *feel*. But never to the very core. When I met June I wanted to become negligent, stop being "the Princess," have a hole in my sleeve. When I met Henry I wanted to learn to "use" people as he did. Helba and Gonzalo feel uneasy in my surroundings, so I gave up all luxury and found the boat which was right for Gonzalo, and I got more and more careless and poor in my dressing, to get near them, to make them feel good. I took on much of others' colors, out of love, to envelop and help and create and protect. But only superficially. Deep down I cannot change anything. Fundamentally I remain I.

Gonzalo understands. He said: "All I want is your sympathy and your faith. We do not expect political work, service, from an Erik Satie or an Artaud. Erik Satie, when he joined the Communist Party, *wanted* spontaneously to do something for us. He offered to write a symphony on Lenin. Then he tore his hair because he couldn't do it. And when he came to the Party and told them, they understood. I wouldn't have expected Artaud to be useful except by being himself and loyal. You do your work—that's your job."

I was immensely relieved. Because I felt the falseness. I couldn't *act* "La Pasionaria."* If there was a Joan of Arc in me it was to defend and establish a king—but I have done this on another plane. I placed Henry where he belongs, where he reigns over a marvelous world which will live centuries more than the blind convulsions of today's putrid world.

It is because Gonzalo is of the earth that he can swallow Marx wholly. He said last night: "The Indian is not a mystic. The Indian is a pantheist. The earth is his mother. He has only one word for both. When an Indian dies they put real food in his tomb, and they keep feeding him. At night, in the immense solitude of the mountains I used to come upon one of their cemeteries. And there they were, by the light of the torches, eating a banquet right over the tombs, and with diabolical joy, rolling themselves into orgies." It is because he is of the earth that he is jealous, possessive, that he would watch me like

---

*Dolores Ibarruri, the vocal "Passion Flower" of the Spanish Communist Party, once a devout Catholic, rose from poverty to become one of seventeen delegates to the *Cortez*, the Spanish Parliament, which General Francisco Franco set out to overthrow in July 1936, at the start of the Spanish Civil War. By proclaiming the birth of a new world order, and enlisting the sympathy people felt for the Spanish Republic threatened by fascism, while acting at the same time as an *apparatchik* of Moscow, La Pasionaria embodied many of the problems of the "Popular Front" and the confusion of "progressive" attitudes. Anaïs Nin freely used "communist" in reference to the party, ideas, and ideals for a "better" world, and those siding with the "Loyalists" against Franco.

an Arab, spy on me, without faith in an invisible bond, and seeking *proofs* of infidelity. His angers are of the earth. His massive body is of the earth. His feet are made like horse's hooves. His knees of iron to press the flanks of wild horses. His stomach is heavy, not hollow, with drink and meat. He dreams, but like some mythological animal, a centaur.

Seeing the color of my bedspread he said: "The dark red of bull's blood."

In his eyes—I was deceived as Henry was—I thought there were volcanoes and freedom. I thought with the fire in him he could burn through all the chains. But he is bound like an animal, he is helpless. He can set fire to a bed, a room, a house, a whole city, a continent, but he is helpless, wild, blind as an animal. He can scent danger, he can fight, he can sleep on a rock, but he is bound and helpless as all nature is. He yells like a savage, and foams at the mouth, it means nothing. He can kill—and then? He will look around him, innocent, perplexed, tender even. Today communism takes him—hurls him like a human bomb. He will explode. And this bomb is what I love, because it is made of the warmest flesh and the huskiest voice, of a leopard gentleness, of blind fiery eyes which burn me up, of a sex which arouses me to frenzy.

Was writing this while waiting for Henry at Villa Seurat, watching his dinner. Brooding on his description of his passivity toward June—sitting on her knee, ventriloquist. After the proofreading we talked about this. I said he had finally transmuted his negative attitude into wisdom-acceptance. At first it was a weakness. A real female could reproach him for it. I myself, I resented his letting me go to New York—his acceptance. I felt he didn't hold me, never made me feel the bond. But strangely enough, I said: "At times I felt I was held by you by something more subtle than your own personal effort to hold me. I hung on to you by a cosmic hair!"

It is true. At times when I am facing Henry, looking at his blue eyes, at an expression of gravity he seems to have only for me, I feel that he *fascinates* me quietly, by a balance within him, not by tears, clutching, despair, but by a miraculous steadiness of faith, like a Tibetan Master. Something in me beyond myself as woman, something greater than me, answers the established bond unwaveringly, in some greater world. He does not move, he waits, and the cosmic hair holds me—faith. What, I don't know. He is no longer inside me as a child, nor outside, struggling in stormy gestures. We are in some cosmic suspense—here Henry, here Anaïs, as firmly bound across space as planetary distances are fixed, changing but never falling off their course.

Henry always says: "You're not just a woman. You're more than a woman."

I laugh sometimes because I often act like just a woman—the diary shows it. I storm, get lonely, misunderstand, break down, but ultimately, facing Henry, I always end by bowing to this greater thing, by living up to it, this greater world of Henry and I, which no one can understand when they look at the everyday Henry, or at the everyday Anaïs, sometimes acting like a woman, any woman: A little suspicious (he doesn't love me); a little bewildered (how impersonal he is, he never says "You," he goes crazy over *Seraphita* when *I* am Seraphita); a little lost (the distance he leaves between us—he can sleep alone, until now I could never sleep alone); a little lonely (how good the *nearness* of woman, the intimate emotional, personal nearness of woman); *very* jealous (of his interest in so many *people*, so *many* people); all of this being part of the cosmic world! A big world in which woman sometimes swims with a bit of human apprehension— a stellar world of magnitude and mutation by which woman is fascinated and wounded at the same time. Up there I swim in planetary deserts where sometimes I see no trace of Henry at all, but a kind of fevered monster spilling out legends, myths, anthems; or the plain story of a little Brooklyn boy, the stories of Max the Jew, Claude the whore, a strange Henry who fucked impersonally like a goat, all women, and Woman rolled into one universal orgasm; a schizophrenic maniac absent altogether, removed from daily life, whose every tear and cry is being transmuted into diamond words, who emits from the top of his cosmic head white flames of spiritual bonfires, curses from visionary unseeing eyes; a Capricornian goat butting his horns into the same turning windmills of Don Quixote; or a ragpicker sticking his forked cane into all the debris, junk and excrements of the world, philosophically. In all this geological world, peopled with his *creation* of the world, I sometimes walk not as the cosmic counterpart, the great mother, the great whore, the estranged Seraphita, the Sleeping Princess at home in the myth, but like a very simple woman in need of warmth and nearness.

Then I hear Gonzalo's voice so hot: *"Chiquita, mi chiquita, mi chiquita, no quiero que nadie te haga la corte, que nadie se acerque de ti. Cómo te quiero, chiquita. Pégate a mi. Abrázame. Pégate a mi."* I always hear him say: *"Pégate a mi."* (Stick with me.)

Strangely, last night, after the talk with Henry, I raised my arms over my head. I felt my satin pants slipping a little. I felt my stomach so vividly, as if I were a big woman, I felt my stomach and my sex so violently. In the dark we threw ourselves into a prolonged, bestial possession. I felt all the women he had taken, and took all the sex he had ever spilled, every quiver of it, all that his fingers had touched, his tongue, all the sex he had smelled, rubbed against, every desire and lascivious memory, every word he has ever uttered about sex, all his animalism. I took into myself with him the whole Land of Fuck, with Henry inside of me as if I would swallow him into my womb once and for all, as if this were the last of all the fucks, and containing them all, all of them, the ones with me and June and all women, all rolled into one inside of me like a big synthesis of fire, saliva, sperm and honey, tongue and mouths, vulva lips and penis skin—took the whole world of orgasm and spasm in one dark moment of deluge and fever, once and for all, devouring everything in this small dark banquet of flesh teeth.

JANUARY 19, 1939

*T*HERE ARE PEOPLE WHO CAN'T CHANGE FROM THE interior outward, who must be pushed from the exterior. These are the ones who need revolutions. The weak ones. There *are* those who can't rise above life, transform it, free themselves, and for these the revolution is necessary, for the weak ones. It's for the weak and by the weak.

That's why for me personally I have no use for it, but for the *other* I have. No revolution will free me from my sentimentality, pity, weakness.

But it will free those who cannot escape into the infinite, those who cannot create an illusory world. Those who cannot dream, those who cannot transform.

Letter to Lawrence Durrell: Dear Larry: Three cheers for your fine long letter, written, I realize now, I don't know how, in such a turmoil and tumult as you seem to be living. But the last phrase if I remember in a letter written to Gottlieb was: "But happy." Wonderful.*

As to the corrections: When I got your notes I saw the pagination of them no longer corresponded to the page numbers in my MS as I had changed the order around! Well. What to do? I decided not to lose any more time and to give it to Kahané, and then to make whatever changes you wish in the proofreading when I take the proofs over to London. Not that I believe in making any more changes. The changes I made already are all I can do. The rest is you, not me, and therefore you ought really to let me take my chance, let me pay for my weaknesses, defects. You cannot write my book for me. If I am as bad as all that, if I need rewriting, then, you should not publish me, see? Beyond a certain amount of correcting, which I have done, there are the innate defects which no one can fix. It means there is a lot in my writing you, Larry, don't like, can't accept. That makes me sad, especially for the future. But your helping me, or directing me won't do me any good. I can't go around getting fixed up by Hugo, Henry, and you

---

*"Gottlieb" was a name Anaïs Nin and Lawrence Durrell had used for Henry Miller, who had visited the Durrells in London, while they were staying at Hugh Guiler's apartment. Anaïs Nin had sent Lawrence Durrell the manuscript of *The Winter of Artifice*, which Jack Kahane's Obelisk Press in Paris was about to publish, and which initially had been entitled *Chaotica*.

and Fred or I won't get anywhere. I think that you mean to protect me from all attacks, but whatever you do, even rewrite my book, you can't protect me from myself, and I am as much in my good as in my bad pages. I have to be let alone to come to it all by myself. I never could change Henry either, not inherently, not the defects which are part of his character, though I know very well where they lie. I never attempted to transform him, or you. Larry, why don't you let the world attack me? I prefer it to having you revise and examine and disintegrate me. About the world, really, it doesn't matter. But if it's you that wants to overhaul me, remake me, then I get sad, absolutely discouraged, and I say: "Well, he doesn't accept me, that's all."

Gonzalo was born condemned to prison. When his mother was bearing him there was a revolution going on. His father had to hide away from the *guerrilleros*. A warrant was issued against the mother and child.

Letter to Lawrence Durrell: Dear Larry: Funny we used the word *love* at the same moment. I will confess my great weakness, Larry. It's true, criticism breaks me down, because you know I feel handicapped. I feel I am making superhuman efforts to dominate not only a language that is not mine but to say things which I should have said with music and dancing. I am deeply and honestly aware of my faults. I feel like a stutterer at times. Worst of all, I suffer because when I look at the bad phrase I can't see it's bad. Imagine a painter being color-blind. Yes, at certain moments I shake my head like a Chinaman and say: "What's the matter with 'belly-well,' why can't I say 'belly-well' instead of 'very well.' I can't say 'very well.' I know you want to protect me from ridicule. I should not get desperate. But I feel differently now. As soon as I am sure of the faith and love then I feel equal again to this struggle in the dark which is different from the English writer's struggle. Mine is not laziness or carelessness but certain tone-deaf moments. . . .

This after a month of hailstorms from London, Larry questioning all my weak phrases. One little criticism from Hugo, then I overflowed. Storm and lightning and tears. Hugo amazed by my vulnerability. But afterward I calm down. One little magic word of faith and I get my strength back.

Bon.

Living so many lives simultaneously. With Henry a trip to Mexico via moving picture, and a Balzac obsession with research on *Seraphita*. *The Book of the Dead* from Tibet. With Gonzalo gnashing our teeth in despair over the tragic fate of Spain. Barcelona about to fall into the hands of the fascists. Persecution of the communists in France. Gonzalo wondering where he will go. With Hugo, a sick Hugo in bed, tenderness and devotion, sweetness and deceit. All this was possible because Hugo was a somnambulist. As soon as he left the bank he went into a trance. When he came home he noticed nothing. He walked like a somnambulist, unseeing eyes open. But there are moments when he wakes up. So I am having a special version made of *Winter of Artifice* omitting the Henry-June novel, all in part one, for Hugo and for Gonzalo. At the same time I am copying out diary volume nine, written at sixteen, all of it *sur un ton de "Pavane pour une Infante Défunte."* Meanwhile my Father is selling his furniture and his marvelous collection of books on music to go back to Cuba, back to the womb of his cousin's home, swallowed by the birthplace again after seeking to escape for thirty years from his starting point.

Meanwhile *le petit Joaquinito* is playing in Havana before sailing for America to work.

Meanwhile Thorvald is all alone in Bogotá, separated from his wife and children. And at sixteen I wrote: "Thorvald is not as profound as Joaquin." Meanwhile I am metamorphosed into a sponge full of the tears, sperm, honey of the world, all wet with desire and memories, unable to wipe off anything, accumulating an ocean of sensations enough to quench the thirst of several universes.

Hugo passes next to the diary I am writing with his somnambulistic walk, never hearing Gonzalo's telephone calls, Durrell's talk of Miller, fixed on the central point of his obsessional love, waiting only for the moment when he can possess me, with the impatience and frenzy of a new lover. At night, asleep, when he tries to take me I fight him off like a lioness. The next morning he asks me: "What does it mean?"

I answer: "Perhaps when I am asleep I feel virginal."

Hugo says: "I love you more for that."

On the table there are bottles which seem molded by gnomes. Tambimutu waits in London, a Hindu who has lost his Indian basis, that may be why he is mad.

In the *péniche* book there will be a Phantom Lover, dreamed, not seen, who comes every night out of the river with a noise of chains and *clapotis*, splashes of little waves, when the candles are lit and the incense burning, and who is gone when she awakens.

FEBRUARY 1, 1939

*H*UGO CAME WITH THE GRIPPE. I TOOK CARE OF him, but dragged down by his depression, his Saturnian cavernous sorrow, I got ill too. Two weeks of sickness, sadness, imprisonment. Gonzalo's short visits. Hugo cannot accept the separation, that is clear. It is hurting him. What can I do?

Today he left for Brussels. Already yesterday I sought escape into the infinite. Found all I had written in the summer of 1938—metamorphosis and mirror pages beginning: "She was conceived from the seed of the man who was hanged"—is in *The Tibetan Book of the Dead* as *"bardo"* states, leading to rebirth, second birth. I describe the same atmosphere, images, visions, hallucinations, also in the "Paper Womb," beginning: "When I was eleven years old," where I later annihilate sense of time and reappear at the end of the labyrinth the same little girl.

All this, then, exists magically, whereas condemnation which discouraged me at the time was this: I was getting so subjective that what I wrote could not have meaning for anyone. Durrell, Henry, Hugo, a friend in New York, all looked as if I had carried my subjective babble so far I was stuttering some narcissistic foolishness. Hugo was afraid for my sanity. Today he recognizes the mystical authenticity. Writing like *The House of Incest*, and all the fantasies for which I will rarely be loved, contains the purest essence of my feelings and approach to meaning. It comes from the very purest essence of my life which I live continuously on such a high plane that it forbids me all happy relationships, all companionship.

I know it now. I have been humanly the least lonely of women, surrounded by family, parents, brothers, friends, the tenderness of Hugo and his sensibility, the genius of Henry, everything, but there is a world into which I go alone, a Tibetan desert. It is not Henry's Tibet either. Henry takes the wisdom of it, but few of the "states" and alternately, not continuously. I must understand that this is the cause of my sorrow and one that cannot change. I am lonely in the very embrace of Gonzalo, in the very furnace of Henry's concrete image world, because I am lighter, I go further. I disappear. In moments of sensuality I can belong to the earth but that is all. The rest, even my pity, comes from the infinite. I was born disguised.

"After collision with reality comes the departure, the ascension." But I never know where this collision takes place. I may be sitting in a café listening to the music, drinking coffee. The lights are vivid, the music violent. I am keenly aware of everything, from the stain on the table to the face of the man sitting farthest from the table, aware of what the waiters are discussing. I feel my body alive and warm inside of my fur coat. I am wearing a hood with a fur edge. I feel at moments I am an actress. I feel I am a Polish countess, a Hungarian singer, an Eskimo princess, all out of novels. The men always believe in my disguises. They believe. They never step behind the stage to say: "You're lying. You were lying when you sewed the hood. You're not what you seem to be." If I answer: "What am I?," this only precipitates my departure. As soon as someone denies my existence, appearance, and I am exposed as a disguised being, as a spy from another world, this other world opens its luminous jaws and engulfs me. I am here only while someone believes in me, while some human being swears to my presence and loves me.

Someone could spy on me and detect my astral origin. I wash too easily, lightly, I do not wear out my clothes. I cook too lightly and too quickly. I eat invisibly. I do all the earth jobs lightly, invisibly. It is a question of not lamenting. No more sadness and regrets. I must enter very boldly into my world, with all the feelings I have, eyes open, alone. It is not a world where one is humanly married, linked. Marriages happen on earth. It is good enough. Gonzalo, who has momentary visions, a sympathy such as a noble animal might have, the vicuña; Henry, who has his own mysterious but very concrete world, like Swedenborg's comical heaven, or the Negro's "Green Pastures"; Hugh, with his blind love—they all look at me. From the very days in Richmond Hill, when I'm lonely but can't go out with my friends, until today. Only I want to cease lamenting and rebelling, and getting angry when a different Gonzalo returns to me from his drunks, cafés, and newspapermen, an ordinary, very ordinary Gonzalo. Henry did this to me too. They all leave me perched up there and I can't find my way down as easily as they do.

FEBRUARY 8, 1939

STRANGE THINGS ARE HAPPENING. WHEN I DISCOVered the link with the Tibetan world I laughingly said to Henry: "You know, I died a long time ago, and I'm on my way to something else, maybe a rebirth." Henry, meanwhile, is obsessed with Balzac and *Seraphita*. He is writing about them. Once I asked him why I did not feel sad after sex as some people do. He answered: "Because for *you* it is not everything." People for whom it is the only means of connection were sad at this fleeting union. For me it was one kind of union, or an expression of union. Henry is saying now almost what I wrote long ago, about the mystical union getting so strong that it makes the sexual unnecessary. It is this union I have with Henry which Gonzalo cannot break. Gonzalo comes at night and talks to me about the friends who died in Spain, about the treachery of the anarchists in Barcelona, about one of his friends who got his face slashed in a fight in a café. But all the horrors he brings me suffocate me. I dream of Shangri-la while lying at Gonzalo's side. I dream of Shangri-la where Henry sits among his books, papers, notes, a Tibetan guru, more and more luminous, more and more mystical.

The day Gonzalo discovered Miller was in Paris I went to the Porte d'Orleans looking for a place for Henry and myself. I could only find a hotel room. I brought to it all Henry's books, the magazines with his articles, the phonograph, cigarettes, incense, nightgown. I tried to be gay, to make it seem like a second Shangri-la. When Henry came he found two of his watercolors hung on the walls, but we were not happy. You can't transport the spirit, move it at will. It was a strange room, a hotel room. Henry and I went out to dinner, planning to return to the room to do the proofreading of my *Winter of Artifice*. But somehow or other we couldn't. We sat in a café and read proofs there. There was a thick fog outside. At midnight I went home. As soon as I arrived Gonzalo telephoned: "Can I come?" When he came he said: "I'm so happy, so happy to find you in. I was going crazy imagining things. I telephoned you all evening, every half hour."

"What did you imagine, Gonzalo?"

The next morning I said to myself: To hell with precautions. I would go to Villa Seurat. Henry was sitting in the sunny bedroom. I said to him: "I couldn't meet you in the hotel room. It made me sad. I felt as if I had been cast out of paradise."

Seraphita is lying on his desk. Henry is in love with Seraphita. Henry is in love with me.

As we read the Henry-June novel we see new meaning in it. Mystically, it acquires new value, in spite of its bad technique and defects. Just as it made me love Henry to read the despairing pages of *Capricorn*, it makes him love me, to read what I write about him. We are not yet altogether beyond desire. Love can make you desire. So after lunch we get into bed and Henry satisfies his feeling of union by a long, lingering stay inside of me, and Seraphita who is not yet ready to ascend to heaven, she gives to her feelings of union a very passionate human expression.

Gonzalo enters my real being by flashes of intuition. Those are the flashes June had of Henry. But then the blindness comes again. He lives in another world. He has strange moments of perception. We have moments of human nearness. When Helba gets very sick he comes to me like a child, lost and baffled. I decide on a plan of action. We walked together to the doctor. I waited in a café. All along the street Gonzalo was kissing me with deep feeling. In the restaurant he took my hand. It looked so pale lying in his that he got frightened: "My, God, Anaïs, are you all right?" I said yes. It is not true. I feel utterly weak. And today Dr. Kaplan said: "I am not satisfied. I don't like this persistent anemia. I am going to have your lungs examined." In the taxi, on the way back I thought: Maybe I will die like Seraphita. The taxi stopped to let a burial pass. Coincidence. Perhaps I have become Seraphita and I am ready to die.

A few weeks ago I wrote that I was not ready. I still have desire, but this desire is so accompanied by the tune of Helba's death. When she is saved Gonzalo celebrates by taking me.

The other night too, after a quarrel we had, Gonzalo was happy and he said: "I always know when we begin a quarrel how it will end. I like quarrels."

While weeping over the friends who died in Spain his hand seeks my sex, death and sex, disease and sex. "I am sure that when I keep at it so long it hurts you. It can't be a pleasure. I feel I am wounding you." This fantasy persisting I ended by saying: "Hurt me, Gonzalo, wound me." And that is how he thinks of sex. I know he is attracted by my fragility. His mother was "dying" for many years. She is still alive at eighty.

He wrote an article for the newspaper after extraordinary pains. He said: "It's torture. I would rather be running a machine gun."

I was so sad lately, so sad not to have been able to live with Henry alone, to have needed something else, that all my life has seemed tragic, a tragic error. I cannot understand it. It is due to some weakness in me. It is Gonzalo I should not love, Hugo I should not need.

My Father, my poor Father "died" at his concert on the third of February, his thousandth concert in Paris. For the public he had merely a *"syncope,"* a mild stroke. He fainted just before the end. Henry and I were sitting up in the balcony. I was about to say to Henry: "You know I believe in you as much as on the first day. My faith is intact."

My Father was playing, playing perfectly. Then suddenly his arms fell, and he sat back on his chair. People rushed to the stage. It was not the heart. It was anguish, sadness, solitude, death.

I took him to Neuilly. What sadness. The pity I felt was terrifying, but a passive pity, helpless. He "died." I could not weep. For him, yes, for his sadness. Not my Father, all links broken with my Father, but pity for a man—any man. The darling of the gods and of women. White hair. Elegance. Solitude. All the women around him and none near enough. I not wanting to go near, *because you cannot get near him.* He bars the way with his self-love. His self-worship isolates him. One cannot console him. He "died" because he has no other life. With the end of luxury, of protection, of love affairs, of paid-for concerts, his life ends. Something is broken. His ghost is going to Cuba. Father died truly at his one thousandth concert in Paris, at about ten-thirty on February 3, 1939. I did not kill him. I never told him, as Maruca did: My love is dead. I fulfilled my role of illusion giver. I acted compassion, understanding, but I also acted detachment. I did not let him cling to me. Very gently and quietly I made him feel he could not turn to me. I let him see the differences between our lives, between us. I offered to share the simplicity of my life on the boat. I let him know I had a husband, a lover, children to protect whom I would not abandon. He found me firm. I let him die. Because what he demands always, is one's total life, slavery. That night, in his room, pity convulsed me for a moment, but no guilt or regrets. Acceptance. He was fulfilling his destiny. The punishment was great, but so were his sins. He sought only his pleasure. He made not one sacrifice for anyone. He gave nothing. He took his pleasure with a monstrous absence of awareness of what he did to others.

He died alone, on the stage. Today, he weeps over himself. I weep over him. I think even then my weeping is more profound.

Petites Histoires Drôles: The story of the ring. The Indian love ring Henry gave me in New York, like the one I gave him. One night Gonzalo and I sat by the Seine, at the beginning when we had not yet possessed each other, when we wandered the streets kissing ourselves into a frenzy. We sat on some stones by the Seine, a summer night. Gonzalo's shirt was open at the neck. His beautiful neck tantalized me. His mouth trembling. He saw the ring on my hand: "What does this ring mean?"

I answered I would throw it into the Seine. But I didn't. I kept it in my pocket. I carried it in my bag from then on, taking it off to see Gonzalo, and putting it on for Henry. I did this for two years. Then knowing how unobservant Gonzalo is of jewelry and costume, I began to wear it. He never noticed it. In Bad Rogaz I dipped it in the healing waters. *Audace.*

Audace again when Heinz came to see me at the *péniche.* Gonzalo had made such a scene when he found him at quai de Passy one afternoon. I knew he had seemed so unnerved to see a young man there that I felt almost sure he would not recognize him two years later. Anyway, Gonzalo arrived at the *péniche* while Heinz was there. I boldly introduced them as if they had never met. Gonzalo did not remember. I knew too that in Passy Heinz was very groomed and elegant while this time he came with long hair and in a dirty raincoat. My coolness saved everything.

In front of my window here I see heads passing, as if they were cut off, just heads passing.

I got a letter from my school friend Eleanor. Eleanor, her pretty blue eyes and long golden tresses—twenty years ago. "A note in the *Saturday Review* mentions Villa Seurat Series and among them *Chaotica* by Anaïs Nin. You're probably a very important, busy, really famous person, while I'm a housewife...."

FEBRUARY 27, 1939

WHO SAID THAT THE ONLY TRAGEDY IS TIME? I AM extraordinarily happy with Henry now, as I never was before. It took eight years for us to reach a point of absolute happiness. Henry the sage, the mystic, free of desire, fevers, a Henry who lives in a luminous atmosphere continually, delicate, fragile. A Henry who sees few people, who goes rarely to the café, who prefers meditation, reading, who returns to his place filled with ideas, plans, who is writing about Seraphita, who belongs to me as he never did, who writes about his past and June as a great crucifixion. Error. Who gives me full due for what I am—who says in talking about the great liberation he feels: "Of course, for this YOU had to be crucified," and in saying this makes my crucifixion a joy. A Henry who wrote by hand an entire little book for my birthday, who is tender and aware and sympathetic, who imitates my order, who fixes his place, his notes as I do, who was tender when I got sick (Henry hates sickness), who says I am above the artist because I, by the hierarchy of mysticism, live for love not for myself. A Henry who paints beautiful watercolors, melts into music, is contented with his mystical explorations. Before Henry was awkward and slow, blundering in the spiritual world, now he is almost continuously aware. He lives by a new awareness and on a new level. At the same time he remains human and delightful.

Once, laughingly, we talked about his "errors," the only foolish acts he committed which I had opposed: Publications of the joker *Booster*, the letter about Alf, and the "Gold" pamphlet, which was already included in the collection of essays in the "Max" book.* Letters

---

*The self-published pamphlet "Money and How It Gets That Way" appeared in September 1938, prior to the publication in October of *Max and the White Phagocytes*, which included both Henry Miller's "Scenario" and the essay *"Un Être étoilique,"* but not the "Money" pamphlet, which apparently was reprinted separately. Henry Miller also had

from messenger boys, leaflets. All these things cost a lot of money and sacrifices and were wasted. He had to give them away, and even giving them, nobody liked them. I told him how in each case he had been moved by willfulness, by a feeling of autocracy. He wanted to force the world to laugh as they did before the war and printed the childish, prankish *Booster/Delta*, which nobody laughed at. He wanted all the bankers and magnates to laugh at "Money" when their whole life is dependent on this and not one of them saw "the joke." The letter about Alf was what he thought a humorous holdup, but nobody else thought so. In fact, Henry's practical jokes always fall flat, and he overestimates his own humor. It is the child in him. I said all this very tactfully. I said how according to the motive behind our acts, this act failed or succeeded. I said acts out of contrariness just to oppose, affirm, dictate, force, seldom bear fruit. All these were acts of egotism, because I, or Durrell, or someone around him did not back him, then he did it. All these acts lie piled up in his closets. He knows. We were in a highly good humor and I collared him laughing. He admitted I was right, laughing too. Yes, he knew, he confessed, they were acts of egotism, will, contrariness. Then he added: "But I would still do it."

Now he wants to print *"Seraphita,"* involve Durrell in a loss of money, and give the world something which it will reject, vomit, because it is not the time.* Not that I mean one has to wait for the time, no, great sincere works of art are prophetic, advanced, written for the future. Creations are always. But *"Seraphita"* is absolutely out of phase, a disconnected thing, contrary to the epoch and not *opening a new* epoch. It's a work of the past, not of the future. Like Henry's humor. One can't confuse the past and the future. The "Money" pamphlet can't make anyone laugh because those who don't know about money don't see anything funny about the long, heavy, cumbersome

published in 1938, at his own expense, a giveaway broadside, "Henry Miller Wishes to Call," in which he recommended a dozen books, including *The Tibetan Book of the Dead* and Balzac's *Seraphita*.

*Sections of Henry Miller's essay on Balzac's *Seraphita* appeared in the magazines *Volontés* (April and May 1939 issues) and the *Modern Mystic* (May 1939), but not as a separate publication. At the suggestion of his friend, the writer Raymond Queneau, Henry Miller had become an "editor" of the magazine *Volontés*, published by Georges Pelorson, who later became "Georges Belmont."

booklet, and those who do know don't laugh about it. All this talk and Henry ending: "But I would do it all over again!" However, he has dropped *The Booster*, which was bleeding us all; he recognized the futility of it.

Strange, this happiness with Henry, long humorous sessions of proofreading, when we mocked my defects, laughed at my idiosyncrasies, at my dissonances in English, which sound to Henry and Larry's ears like Hindu quarter-tone music, false. How we laughed over the surrealist proof errors: "I want to *much* you," I said to June, instead of "I want to touch you." And proofreading *Capricorn*, when I read the most devastating obscenities in my quiet voice!

Henry sweated over my book, let nothing pass, we combed the book rigorously, regardless of time.

He continually mentions me to his critic friends, pushes me, helps me. He is the one who has most pushed me in my art work, trying always to save me from the other devotion current in which I annihilate myself. We have curious telepathic connections. This morning when I arrived he asked me to look at his latest watercolors. I said about them exactly what he had written about them the night before. Or about dreams. All I wrote in my *Winter of Artifice* touches and excites him. He picked out the last phrase as a beauty: "The poet is the one who calls death an aurora borealis." This was a phrase I dreamed. Or, "Sparked the great birds of divinity, the eternal moments."

We read the same books. We go to see films on Mexico, or on China. The luminous life without jealousy and passion. From this heaven of Shangri-la I descend into Gonzalo's inferno.

One night, waiting for him. I never can sleep. I waited all night. He was drinking. I was angry, feverish. At dawn I went for a walk, in a rage. At dawn he was returning to me, didn't find me, went to his hotel and to bed. At nine o'clock I went to his hotel, entered his room, flung the covers off his face violently and insulted him, said all I could find to rouse and wound him. I left broken by my own violence, thinking I never wanted to see him again. An hour later he was at my place. I wept. He asked forgiveness.

I was waiting for my Father's visit a few days later. I had lit all the little lamps, and perfumed the place. Gonzalo happened to pass on his way back from the hospital. He saw the lights. He came in. I was *"en beauté,"* my hair in one of its good moods. I told Gonzalo I was waiting for my Father but he could come in. I didn't mind their meeting. He refused. He seemed in a hurry. I didn't notice anything amiss. He had agreed he would come at midnight.

In the evening I went to the movies with Henry and I was home at eleven. I disconnected the phone to sleep, I bathed and went to bed. Gonzalo never came. I couldn't sleep. No drugs could put me to sleep. Thinking he had gotten drunk again I was sad and angry, rebellious and disgusted with him. So angry I couldn't sleep. But I decided not to go to his hotel, but to go to London, leave him for a while, hurt him. As all this happened so soon after my sickness (for two weeks I was so weak that Dr. Kaplan gave me a blood transfusion), it shattered me. Henry thought I was ill again. My heart beat in such disorder I couldn't walk. Gonzalo's drunkenness annihilated all my hopes of a changed Gonzalo. He was returning to his old life and I didn't deserve this. He came after lunch, looking very angry himself, which surprised me. I began to say angry things but he stopped me: "Do you know what you've done to me?" I looked at him trembling inwardly but seeking to look innocent. Perhaps he had seen me with Henry. Then he launched into a violent scene of jealousy. He knew I had received my Father like a lover, my house was perfumed and prepared as for a lover and I had made myself beautiful. Returning from a meeting Gonzalo had telephoned me and I had not answered. I was still out with my Father, he thought. So he got terribly desperate and drank all night. Reconciliation. Explanations. Peace.

There was more to that night, I discovered afterward. At the meeting the auto-criticism practiced by the communists had been leveled at him. They had told him all of his virtues and faults, scolded him for drinking, disorder, and weakness, but with kindness. Praising his capacities too, all the gifts he wastes and ruins by chaos. On top of this a maddening jealousy.

At the moment the violent passage from anger, despair, hatred, to passion, peace, seems to bring a deep joy. But it destroys one. The violence destroys me.

Last night he left his drunk friends and came.

With Helba at the hospital, life with Gonzalo is like an inferno. But Gonzalo's own confessions and admissions are disarming. He is overwhelmed by his own weakness, he aspires to order and discipline. He says I should impose it on him. I answered that nothing that is imposed is any good. "It has to come from you." The only real influence is that exerted by what one is.

Again I say to myself: patience. It takes time. In three years Gonzalo has changed, but he can't overnight become different. He says himself: "I'm crazy. I'm a Russian. Crazily jealous, weak. I know it." I don't try to tame him, but to keep him from destroying himself.

I reached a pit of physical weakness, carrying the burden of his terrible moods, Helba's operations, feeling I hold them both alive, that I am giving of myself to the point of death. Such love I give Gonzalo, such love I ask myself, as I did with Henry, how can such a love not make them strong.

This love with which I prop them. I never understood how it did not save them. But now looking at Henry I think: Time, time, time. Time—unless I die in the effort.

Hugo had to come and give me his blood. Gonzalo was jealous of that too, terribly jealous. And after Hugo left Gonzalo and I had a wild night together. He wanted to take possession of me again, to satisfy, assure himself I was his. I gave myself with such fervor he was shouting: *"Ay, chiquita, cómo te entregas. Entrégate más, más, te siento toda mía, toda mía."*

When I see Gonzalo working on his printing press, his shirt open, I look at his neck with desire, at his big hips. He is heavily built from the waist down. I like this, it excites me terribly, his clothes, his pants, his belt, the heavy feet, the tremendous knees. This same brute can sit like a most delicate woman and catch the fallen sea horse of glass in my aquarium to place it right, or talk in the night in the dark saying: "You are too sweet to me, too good to me, too gentle. I'm weak. You should discipline me." "Perhaps I am disciplining you, only you don't know it," I said laughing.

Gonzalo talking about Peru. Gonzalo's house was approached by crossing a river. Then came the front patio which was as large as the Place de Vendôme. Then the church which belonged to the *hacienda*. A priest was sent from town every Sunday to say Mass. The house very large, rambling, with many inner patios of rose stucco. There was a room for firearms alone, all hung on the walls: guns, revolvers. Gonzalo still remembers the cedar-and-tobacco smell of his father's room with more love almost than for his mother's room. A man's love of a noble man's elegance, courage, and manliness. His father was a mayor, a soldier, a leader, head of a big family and vast *haciendas*.

One of Gonzalo's aunts, who was a musician, married a brutal man who made her unhappy. She played the piano all night. She let herself die of hunger. Gonzalo found her music and played it: Bach, Beethoven, Brahms. It was through her he became interested in the piano. But in Peru at that time men did not play the piano. The school of music was only frequented by girls. It was thought to be an effeminate art. Gonzalo had to give up his lessons. He worked alone. Although so rough physically, a hunter, a boxer, a horseman, he liked to play the piano above everything, and to draw, and later to write about animals and sports. He brought into sportswriting a new element unknown in Peru: a knowledge of aesthetics, of sport's link with form, the dance, theater.

I never tire of asking Gonzalo about his childhood. Somehow or other we rarely talk about his later life. Montparnasse and Greenwich Village. He reverts always, after lovemaking, to the beautiful early years. I know he ate a steak for breakfast, a cereal, eggs. I know what he ate for lunch, for dinner. I know the taste of the rich and heavy chocolate served on Sunday mornings. His father possessed many books. Gonzalo's two brothers and nearby cousins were his companions. Sick young priests were sent to them to recuperate in the mountains. The mountain men's obsession was to see the sea. Gonzalo never forgot his first sight of the sea. He was about fifteen. The train arrived at four in the morning. Great change and softening of climate, then he saw the sea. He was profoundly moved, dazzled. Even today he reads the *Odyssey* with the fascination of the dark-souled man for light, of the mountain man for the sea, of the snow man for the tropics.

And it is this he desires in me. He is aroused by my fragility, the luminousness, the sea in me, the tropics, the Mediterranean glow, the Cuban languors, the Creole softnesses. He looks at me at times like a Plutonian from the caverns, with a cannibalistic hunger for my dancing figure, for the light I shed around me, for the Neptunian flowingness. I feel this. I marvel sometimes at the contrast between us, like the contrast between our two bodies. Our two bodies naked, mixed together are so strange, the animal in Gonzalo is so powerful.

What happened to this body made for the mountains and for war? A little blue flame of music, of art from the aunt who was never buried in his mind, from the grandfather who died insane, from the Scotch father who might have been dreamed by the Brontës in *Wuthering Heights*. A little blue flame of restless sulphur escaping from the death of the Indian, and the death of the Spaniards who killed them, from a sixteenth-century Spain of torture and hypocrisy. And the body made for war and hunting sat among the poets of Paris, talked all night with Antonin Artaud, with André Breton, with Tristan Tzara, drank with Léon-Paul Fargue, Picasso, Miró. But only a little blue flame that shines in the long nights of our love. That is all.

It does not blaze into the day. As soon as the day comes this body rises with a strength as if he were going to conquer the world. He begins his day slowly, but the strength he has, what will become of it? He will smash it, crush it, crumble it, fragment it, make dust of it.

Gonzalo wants to write about Artaud, who is insane, unknown, unnoticed, in the madhouse. This will never be. This knowledge of Artaud, intimate and grown out of working with him in his plays, will die with him. He never wrote about his beloved friend César Vallejo, the Peruvian poet. He never wrote what he wanted to write about me, about *House of Incest*. His day is a cemetery of negations, of undone things, of rebellious abortions.

All would be well if he were contented to abort. But no, it gives him despair, melancholia. Gonzalo, when he wakes up, starts a kind of a spool mix-up, tangled threads, in which he chokes himself continuously. Now and then I free him, but his activity using his terrific vitality to entangle himself in nothingness is stronger than my knot cutting. This in Gonzalo at times causes me an intolerable suffocation.

At other times it causes me such a keen pity that it almost looks like the root and heart of my love, this struggle against destruction—and I don't know anymore whether this stumbling, helpless, blind giant child is mine or a curse put upon my desire for supreme lightness, liberation.

At times I think I am Henry describing June. I am writing my own *Capricorn*. And I feel like telling Henry everything, all this that he would understand so well. Henry would understand. Many times I am about to speak—we get so far beyond the personal. But I remember the human Henry in time. It would unburden me. I could almost share this with him. He is writing of it. Only I repeat, I suffer more. Henry was blind while it happened. I am not blind.

MARCH 6, 1939

I DON'T KNOW WHAT IS THE MATTER WITH ME. Such exaltations, such violence of feelings, and such exhaustion. Just before Helba came out of the hospital, when my life with Gonzalo was coming to an end, I had a fit of despair as I so often have when my life becomes, for a moment, an absolute, a unity, only to get shattered into fragments again. For three weeks I lived for Gonzalo, took care of him, cut his hair, cooked for him, our passion became exacerbated, terrifying, an obsession. That night, when I knew Helba was returning home and he would have to nurse her, Hugo was coming from London, I lay awake and wept.

That same night my Father was preparing to sail for Cuba. And though I have fought off all feeling, this departure, this separation forever (I know I will never see him again) hurt me deeply, like a tear, even when I say I no longer love him. Perhaps I was weeping over him too. He did not want to see me; he couldn't bear it. He had come one afternoon and it had hurt him so deeply that he had fainted in front of my house, on the street. I couldn't bear the tear from him and the tear from a moment of absolute love for Gonzalo. I hated the world, my destiny, the inexorable truth by which I live, for it is only when you live by the law of absolute truth that you enter the infinite torture of duality. You live by the law of truth and truth is not one love but LOVE, the total, made out of dual rhythms. Such a paroxysm of love I reached that I understood the law of duality, of life, for I am one who would smash her soul against Oneness in love, die in it, death, death, easily. I could easily die.

The night Hugo was arriving Gonzalo and I got drunk together. He was tortured too. We were saying wild things to each other. Gonzalo wanted me. We were drunk on sadness, regrets, desire. I took this separation tragically because it is so often repeated. Each time I give myself, then the outer rhythm, the fatal rhythm asserts itself, and now comes Hugo's turn, and now Henry, and deep down I am not supple or fluid but I break each time, and finally I will break altogether. Break. That is what I feel.

I feel two ways of action are open to me: Religious exaltation, mysticism, give my life to the refugees, play the organ in church, pass into a religious trance forever. Or debauch, throw myself into pleasure, into the nightlife, drugs.

Meanwhile, the body is failing me. I was given another transfusion. But strangely I don't care. I suddenly lose all sense of life. I cannot write, work. I feel absolute inertia, indifference. Why the order? The *élan*, the struggle, the effort, the creation? Why? The intensity leaves nothing but ashes. Henry has found his realm of joy. I find only suicide and despair. Why? I should be growing toward balance, and I am moving toward violence and extremes, toward contraries and conflicts.

A few days before my Father left, when I was trying not to think of him at all, when I was trying to remember that I had not pitied him at all actively during his fall, not helped, or protected him, nor tried to keep him from going to Cuba, that I had been silent, evasive, and neutral, keeping control of myself not to utter the last murderous words: "My love for you is dead," suddenly I pictured him vividly, first when he fainted at the piano during his concert, then when he was lying down on the bench in the artist room, his collar open, and at this remembrance of his slender, elegant effigy, unconscious, such a burning pity lanced through me that I jumped: My God I love him.

Love what? Someone whose every awake word you hate, whose every act and thought you abhor, whose every desire, aspiration, you despise, whose every tic and mania and idiosyncrasy is distasteful and ridiculous—and this figure lies on a couch, this body empty of its consciousness, lies with eyes closed, the supreme comedian's act, this effigy of my Father. And some inexplicable, remote, puerile detail reawakens a love that died a million times and was buried. The figure, the slenderness of the body, the fineness of its form, its essence that every act and reality denied, this escapes still from the dead tomb of the love, and is alive in you? My God, does love ever die? I ask, and will die asking. For years I buried him. I buried him in the novel which will appear while he is sailing away. I buried him when I let him decide to go to Cuba. I buried him by not acting as the refuge, the third mother. Over and over again I buried him. I buried him under my sensual and vivid love for Henry, under my sensual and vivid love for Gonzalo. I looked at him without illusion, opened my eyes, saw all his faults, his many faults. I saw the truth. Yet when he left, the night before he sailed, I wept over him, and awakened in the morning thinking of him, lying at Gonzalo's side, and parting from my Father even then succeeded in mixing these feelings in myself so well that the parting from my continuous life with Gonzalo seemed the stronger emotion, and the other an echo of something very old. What I tear off and throw away is only a part of my own flesh and is never dead, it keeps on quivering. I do not know death or indifference. Time kills nothing in me. I will die before my lovers and my memories. Each time a little bit of my flesh stirs somewhere, my brother Thorvald in Columbia, I will feel it in my body even though I have tried by art to deliver myself of all possessions.

A possessed being. Succubus and incubus of old loves. No disillusion, hatred, contempt kills love in me. This is my crucifixion.

Les Parents terribles of Cocteau contains this monstrous germ of truth which is beyond good and evil, this fantastic mixture of love and hatred, this *"incroyable"* of foggy motives, base and noble intertwined. Marvelous theme. Nakedness. The aunt, the truthful one, never deceived by her own acts of sacrifice and revenge. Never any falseness. I live by this now, I can't bear self-deception. Helba and Gonzalo can't bear the truth. I know the truth about my feelings toward Helba. Helba hides half of her feelings toward me. Gonzalo does not see that Helba loves me for herself, out of love of herself, because I take care of her, act love and devotion. I am not duped, yet I must act as if I were, because they live in a false Catholic world, a world of untruths, of false nobilities, false sacrifices, false interpretations. I have to act this because as soon as I act otherwise and confront them with a true mirror, they cannot bear it. They prefer the penumbra. I live in a clarity which places me near to Cocteau's play (which revolted everybody), a transparent world.

I know it is remorse and guilt for his joys which sends Gonzalo back to nurse Helba, sense of duty. I know it is not goodness which makes me give life to Helba, mystically I desire her to live, I keep her alive with all possible magic known, because I love Gonzalo and it is for him I do it. And because if she dies I would be afraid of the guilt in Gonzalo and in myself.

When Gonzalo says: "I have loved only twice in my life," I forget how much he suffers from the existence of Henry.

Unmasked by my own honesty, I suffer now from others' self-idealization. Helba accepts me because by this she holds Gonzalo. She believes it is generosity. Our union is our strength, she knows it. She knows we are linked by a certain spiritual resemblance so I do not destroy her but reinforce Gonzalo's spiritual life. Other women, not of her race, unrelated to her, are the enemy. She allies herself with me against women who threaten her possessions. She trusts me.

The truth!

"*Quels monstres!*" said the people as they walked out of Cocteau's *Parents terribles.*

Thurema. I never described her well. She was another liar who could not bear her real face in the mirror. All Thurema's acts were frenzied coverings of an erotic sexual appetite and lesbianism. Her white Negress face proclaimed her sensuality, her avid mouth, her provocative glance. But instead of yielding to it, she was ashamed of it, so she throttled it, and all this desire, lust, got twisted inside her and churned the poison of jealousy and envy. Whenever sensuality showed its flower head, Thurema hated it. She was jealous of everything, of everyone's loves. She bought a black lace nightgown like mine when she came to Paris. She remembered our nights in New York. She said she had bought it for a lover she had after I left New York, but the price tag was still fastened on it.

The night of her arrival, the valises piled into the taxi, the taxi lost in the darkness of the boulevard de Neuilly. I had to get out and walk to find the *péniche*. There was a little hill to descend in the dark. We slipped and fell with the valises. We laughed. In the room where so many times the passion of Gonzalo had blazed in many flames, I now found myself with a woman who had enchanted me in New York, attracted me by the same violence of feeling, the same savagery as Gonzalo. And now? I remember looking at Thurema then with something of the same ravishment. She had grown fatter. I could see the swelling of her breasts at the opening of her white blouse. I liked the vivid primitive eyes, the wild hair, the wide mouth, the round thick nose. A white Negress, with her husky voice, strong teeth, wide jaws, thick lips, vitality. A blue-eyed Negress, with hair in an aureole around her head. Every gesture one of disorder, forest gestures, as if you brought a lioness into the room, and the lioness tried to open a valise and smashed the locks, the lioness pulled out the perfume and jewelry to give me and almost threw them at me. She covered the bed with gifts. She wanted me to put all the jewelry on, smell all the perfumes at once. I was showered with gifts as in the fairy tales, only to each gift was tied a little cord of demand, exactingness, of debt, of domination. Thurema gave as the spider weaves its web. She did not give away objects but threads woven out of her own substance to hold and to fix. The gifts so lavishly displayed on my bed reminded me of Rank's gifts. They were not the fairy-tale gifts I expected all my life.

She brought me dresses, jewels, perfume, slippers. She wanted to dress me. But the dresses were not for me. They were little girls' dresses, Thurema's taste, and I did not like them. Her magnificence did not make me happy, it stifled me. She put too much violence and self into her gifts. I felt this. The night begun in gaiety began to thicken. It was a lovely summer night. The barge was steady. Water was trickling from the little hill, sewer water, but with the sound of a bubbling mountain stream. The island in front of us was dark and murmurous. The candlelight was steady. Thurema was flickering and leaping. We talked all night.

I explained all the discomforts of the barge because I did not want her to stay there without a bath and hot water. I took her to the Acropolis Hotel. We chose a room. I was full of plans to amuse Thurema. I thought she could choose between Gonzalo's world, friends, South Americans, Spaniards (Thurema speaks Spanish), artists, all of Montparnasse, or Henry's American friends, Henry's artists and painters. Or Hugo's more conventional world, American colony, American bank visitors. To meet Thurema the night before I had left a limping Henry getting into a taxi, Henry's first night out after his fall from the ladder. We had agreed that I would bring Thurema to lunch. Henry could not go out for errands yet. I had to get his food for him anyway. While Thurema was hanging up her clothes I told her Henry was expecting her. Her eyes flashed green danger signals, shone with anger. She hated Henry, she said. Hated him. Why? I asked. Her reasons were confused and inadequate. I could only make out that she hated him and did not want to see him. Bang! One door closed. No evenings with Henry and his friends at the Villa Seurat. I explained that he was helpless because of the fall from the ladder. I had to go out and buy him food at least, then I would return and take her out to lunch because she did not know French.

I thought I would have better luck with Gonzalo. She was willing to meet him. We sat at a café. They talked about the guitar, which they both play, they planned a *"concours"* to see which one could eat the most pimentos as Thurema was used to them from her childhood days in Mexico, the hottest pimentos of all. We had lunch together at a little Greek restaurant. I thought that they liked each other. I was even a little jealous because they both loved pimentos and because I remembered they were born under the same sign, and because, strangely, Thurema had a trick of sticking her right leg out of the bed to cool it off, like Gonzalo. But as soon as I was alone with Thurema I saw by her silence that she hated him too. I asked her if she didn't think he was handsome. She answered: *"Es mono!"* He's cute—which is the last word one could apply to Gonzalo. No, she didn't like him.

I was still in an innocent mood and I did not yet detect the true reason for these antagonisms.

When I saw Gonzalo alone he said: "Your friend is a maternal type, not attractive, and so common!"

After this failure Thurema and I were reduced to each other's company, which is what she wanted. We sat at cafés, we shopped, we strolled, we visited the barge in the daytime, we went to the *marché aux puces*. We went gift hunting. Then Hugo came. Thurema could not put him off. She had to endure him. The three of us went boating on the Seine. Thurema wore slacks and was very boyish, comical, delightful. I still found her fascinating. I liked to see her dress up for the evening with her barbaric jewelry. Her face wildly alive. She was not for Paris, for the cafés. She was for the African orgies, dances. But this white Negress was not a free Negress, rippling in natural undulations of pleasure and desire. If her mouth, body, legs, voice were made for sensuality, the true flow of sensuality was paralyzed in her. One felt it in her like a great fear. Between her legs she was impaled on a rigid pole of Puritanism. All the rest of her body was loose, provocative. She always looked as if she had just come from lying in bed with a lover, or as if she were about to lie down. She had circles under her eyes. And energy smoking from her whole body. Impatience. Avidity.

If I had not been so spellbound by Gonzalo, if Thurema had not been so tense and terrified, I might have had an adventure with her. I liked her body, the vigor and violence of it. But she very soon destroyed all my illusions. She had a gift for destruction. She told me stories which revolted me forever against her sexual self, minute descriptions of a disease she caught as a child sitting on a water closet in the *quartier réservé* of New Orleans, where her family stayed in a hotel not knowing it was a whorehouse, of other sicknesses, of hemorrhages, descriptions of her stormy periods. She indulged like Helba in all the exposures of intimate disorders and rottenness. This ended my sexual attraction. At the same time, with an ambivalence which was repelling, she did everything she thought would seduce me, exposing herself, raising her legs in bed when I sat at the foot of the bed so that I could see her sex, dropping her chemise or the bath towel, pretending she had not heard me come in and standing naked in the bathroom.

The nights when I wanted to be with Henry or Gonzalo became dramas. When I could I slept with her—but when I left her at midnight to join Gonzalo I would find her the next morning white and sick with jealousy. I displayed all my gifts for tenderness, consolation, humor, understanding, in vain. I set out to reveal her to herself, reveal her true nature. I spent nights awake to delicately guide her. I was playful, fantastic. Referring to her constant interpretation of everything that was said to her as an injury, I said I would write a Chinese dictionary for her where she could look up each time the real intention behind the phrases. I was patient with her scenes of jealousy, her childishness, her emotionalism. What she liked was that I kiss her on the lips more and more warmly until we both got excited. She thrived on this hysterical undertow without any culmination. I ceased this game soon after she came. I am too sensual for this and it would lead me into full sexual gestures. And my feelings for her were beginning to get mixed with antagonism. One night we went with Hugo to the Bal Tabarin. I admired the women, as I always do, with the appreciative aesthetics of a man. I enjoyed their beauty, their variety. I was enchanted. Thurema got drunk. And jealous. She got furious at my admiration. She leaned over and said: "If I were a man I would murder you." Mixed with everything was her sentimental pity, something more false and sentimental than my compassion. "Oh, poor Hugo, poor Hugo. Poor Hugo, he is so unhappy. Look at him. He is not enjoying himself." "You don't understand Hugo," I said. "He is happy in his own quiet way. I wish you would stop feeling sorry for everybody."

She began to weep. I had to put my arm around her and console her. Hugo was looking on baffled, as passersby look up suddenly at an unexpected, freakish storm. Here it was, chaotically upsetting the universe, coming from right and left, great fury and velocity, and why? She went home and wrote stuttering phrases on the back of a box of writing paper: "Anaïs, don't abandon me, if you abandon me I am lost."

This was the woman I had chosen for a friend. A woman, no, a child, the same egotistical devouring child of always, no better than Helba or Gonzalo. Will and selfishness, caprice and confusion.

I was exhausted. She was so possessive, so harassing, obsessive, oppressive, that when I was out with her for a whole evening I would go to the toilet in the café and sit there for a while just to be alone.

I was physically exhausted. Every word had consequences. If we talked about her children and Thurema reproached me for not having much interest in children and if I answered: "It's true, I am not the maternal type you are," then Thurema threw a fit in the middle of the street because she was "not the maternal type," she was "something else," and if later to soothe and please her I said: "You're a *femme fatale,*" then she made a scene again, because she "never destroyed or hurt anyone." Thurema thought herself good, generous, and with a great capacity for love.

Finally I went to the beach alone with Hugo for a week.

And then Thurema invented a way to get me back. She got sick, serious strep throat. Sick, alone in a hotel, and not knowing French. I had to leave Hugo and return to Paris, call for the doctor, run out for medicines, buy fruit, magazines, then bring chicken soup. Stay in her room all day and all night, while outside the summer nights were passing like gay whores with a tinkle of cheap jewelry. Chained to Thurema's antics, Thurema clapping her hands and confessing: "Now at last I've got you to myself."

Finally Thurema got well. Hugo was angry and alone. I returned to the beach for the weekend.

All I could think of was that the day of Thurema's departure was approaching. By the time she left she had destroyed all my love. I could not bring myself to write her. From then on it has been a lie. I did not want to let her see what she had done. It's a dead love. I dread her coming again. We did not have one moment of pleasure together. Walking the streets her obsession was to see who was looking at us, or following us. In the shops it was anxiety about her plumpness. In the movies it was emotionalism. In the restaurant it was meals turned to poison by scenes and quarrels with the waiter if we were not waited upon instantly, scenes about the bill, a scene with all I said. In the café she sat denigrating all those who passed, dissected those sitting around us. The universe hinged on her injured and defeated self. Every act of hers pushed people away. She could not understand why everywhere we went I could get what I wanted with a soft voice and gentle ways, why I was always waited on first, why the saleswoman would show me what was hidden away, why I was not cheated, why the policeman stopped the traffic for me, why the taxi-driver was gallant and took the shortest route, why the hotel keeper was devoted.

Thurema's commands, attacks, terseness, cockiness, made everyone bristle. Antagonized everyone. As she appeared she brought dissonance. I wanted to make her a gift if possible which would arrest this wounding tension with the whole world. I softened her.

When she wrote me from New York she said: "I should have come to help you with your burdens, and instead I came and became one of your burdens myself—how selfish!" When she left I got sick.

MARCH 10, 1939

WHAT FASCINATES ME ARE THE NUANCES OF EACH day, the change of a character and its relativity. I want to be the writer of the relativity of character, no absolute but duality, no evil or good but *"alternances,"* alternatings and ambivalence, the mixture.

Evil is like a poison, it is not inherent. One can get rid of it, somehow, if one wants to. When I was a girl I didn't like to play the role of the sweet princess. I gave that role to Eleanor Flynn. I liked being the demonic black woman manipulating the strings, ruling the destinies. I was clever, malignant, crafty, artful. I remember the play. I liked power and black magic.

Through love it is I who fall into traps. I who am possessed by others, but when I am possessed, I am like an infinitely subtle animal who seeks a way to trap the ones who caught me. And here I use craft, oriental ruses. My ruses to give Hugo the illusion of love. My veiled subtle darts to make Gonzalo aware of one's own responsibility in the shaping of one's destiny, to take away from him this typical criminal attitude that society is entirely to blame for everything.

What is it that makes us accumulate poisons against a person which their presence dissolves? I always hate Helba from a distance, and feel compassion when I see her. I get angry at Gonzalo's unfecund life, his tangles and messes, but when I see him he looks innocent. And Henry too. Why?

MARCH 11, 1939

WHILE THUREMA WAS HERE, MORICAND SAT IN HIS little room under the roof and meditated on her horoscope. He proclaimed Thurema WAS A MAN. And a monster, like all our friends, he added, alluding to James Cooney, Miller, Elena, Gonzalo, etc. Sitting in his little room, he compared her horoscope with mine and foresaw many perversities and obscure little games going on. He was not far from the truth. Moricand saw what might have happened, the undercurrent of which I became aware at last when I stopped kissing her on the mouth after she described what it did to her.

Decadence all around me. The hard, granite communists escaping from Spain, they live in a new world of strength which Gonzalo is fascinated by and which he tries over and over again to describe to me. A faith—no matter what—has reintegrated them.

Is there a new world somewhere? Some part of me demands this austerity and discipline which I have imposed on my own life. With what active order do I prevent accidents from happening: Order and control among every letter, paper, note around me which Gonzalo or Hugo might find. I live like an adroit spy, taking chances but also always alert. Most accidents are due to neglect.

Now I am finding homes for refugees but they must not know it comes from me, because among the communists I am the daughter of a fascist and a relative of Andrés Nin, who was shot as a Trotskyist in Barcelona. More lies.

Now that Gonzalo is imprisoned by Helba's helplessness, inability to move, to wait on herself, I am running to the Villa Seurat again, back and forth. To rest from the tension I invented that Hugh was still here. I need a rest from the tension of a spy's life. It is this which is exhausting my strength.

MARCH 15, 1939

I BELIEVE IN ORDER, IN THE MATERIAL WORLD, an order among details and trappings which serves the spirit and liberates the dream. If I can find my clothes, my shoes, my face powder and food easily I am free to dream. If the place is in order it is subservient to the dream, self-effacing, obedient. Disorder in the material world hampers motion, magnifies details, is not a liberation but a burden, an obtrusion. To waste time looking for a stocking or a book or a perfume is to be momentarily trammeled, not untrammeled as Bohemians believe. Thus, for the dream, a subservient order. But this order must not become an end in itself, or else it paralyzes the life motion. I arrange my place, but when the life motion begins I accept the disorder which is life. The same suit I brushed and hung in the morning I am quite ready to get into bed with, if Henry is cold and we decide to get into bed. I'm always willing to have my order disrupted. I organize only to be light and free. I like enchantment. The only thing which disorder leads to is drabness. To say that because you are a poet you will not remember to have the towels washed only means that you destroy poetry itself, because you will live with a dirty towel, which kills the poem. Dirt, neglect, destruction only cause death, not liberation. I like abundance, recklessness, profligacy in living. But I believe in rhythm. You oil the airplane which will take you above the clouds. I like lubrication and smoothness. To achieve magic the detail must be mastered. Henry lived in June's disorder. It was not fecund. It was oppressive.

My two great passions have been sensual. Henry's and Gonzalo's sensual magnetism, the moving quality of their voices, their great physical charm, their maleness in sex, their potency. Henry more bestial, Gonzalo more voluptuous. Sensual passions based on a sexual pleasure, prolonged and expanded into mystical worlds—but each time it was the moment in bed which gave me the deepest pleasure. Henry and I at first were not mystically matched, as I am not matched with Gonzalo either.

My rhythm is slower. I have less strength. I sleep as long as I can in the morning. I copy diary fourteen written in 1921. I cook lunch for Gonzalo. I cook dinner for Henry. Henry is taking his Chinese pre-incarnation seriously. He asked me to get him ginger, which he eats with clownish grimaces of dislike. But it's Chinese. He must get to like it. He writes little books by hand, like my diaries, for Emil [Schnellock], Durrell, Edgar, and me. Each one on the theme that links them. For Emil he wrote about painting, how he paints, and all that Moricand told him about the painters he knew well. Henry illustrates these books with small watercolors; they are delightful, personal, enchanting. A delicate Chinese Henry working these *orfèvreries* of friendship with playful spirit. Durrell's is a riotous fancy on words and rare expressions. Mine is about writing. His article on *Seraphita* is appearing in the *Modern Mystic*. He finds similarities between Balzac and himself. Identifies himself to him. Now and then, after very intense days of work, he "goes on strike." Goes to bed and wants to be nursed, fed, cajoled while he replenishes his strength. I mother him, but I do not treat him as a child. I have too many proofs of virility, of maleness. And for this maleness, this fiery sex, I have a respect. I nourish and protect without diminishing, belittling. I know it is a rhythm. If before I carried Henry into the spiritual worlds, today it is Henry who leads me. He is the stronger. He can pass contentedly from reading the *History of Magic*, to writing about *Louis Lambert*, to doing watercolors, to writing by hand in the little books, without other needs, whereas I can only do this for a few hours and then I want an orgy of caresses, or I get restless for a voyage, for adventure, for another life, for escape.

MARCH 17, 1939

*J*UST AS I WRITE THIS I SEE THAT HENRY'S PEACE is not perfect. He has days of rebellion, of desperation at the slowness of the world's response to his work. He rages under the passivity of Kahane, the rejections from the French publishers, the obstacles, the exclusion from the American market. He is not getting his due materially. So now and then he awakens bitter, feeling imprisoned.

Last night he felt murderous, he rejoiced over Hitler's invasions [of Bohemia, Moravia, and Memel in Poland] and brutalities. He wishes France annihilated because the French publishers reject him. At such times Henry the criminal appears, the blind autocrat who would murder whoever crosses him.

I begin to doubt all mystical vocations. None of them seem voluntary. Most of them seem to come by force of external pain and disillusion. The transmutation of art is imposed in the Nietzschean sense: Not to go mad. All around us artists are going mad: Helba, Artaud, Reichel, even Jean. And I myself. When I feel my prison I start again to become transparent. Today I began to work on the "Houseboat" book.

I said to Gonzalo, who makes me read the *Odyssey:* "It lacks shadows." He answered quickly: *"Pero a las sombritas les falta lo que tiene el* Odyssey." (The shadows lack what the *Odyssey* has.)

Eduardo sent me this: Pisces. General Forecast for March 1939 to February 1940. Pisces people are the most imaginative, dreamy, sensitive, subtle, secretive, compassionate, and sympathetic of the zodiacal types. Pisces is the sign ruling sleep and dreams, subconscious mental processes, the unborn, the transcendent. Its sons and daughters are always more concerned than other people with problems of mercy and compassion, of caring for the weak and unfortunate, of isolation and relative obscurity, of sensitivity to those invisible and intangible forces shaping the soul of mankind. On the plane of material circumstances there is in every Piscean life some form of *bondage*. The spirit can never be free of the body, struggle as it may against the weak envelope of mortality. Turning away then, from harsh reality, Pisces lives by faith, "believing things we know can't be so," *or as unity with a higher reality*. All Pisces people tend to experience some sort of frustration, longing for the unearthly ideal, necessity for sacrifice or renunciation, or suffering through the unreliability of partners, or through underhanded competition. Neptune is your own ruler, the power of dream and enchantment which may be either divine dream or nightmare. Some may be married to men out of work, or invalids, and may have to carry the whole burden; others may find they have walked into a life sentence of harder work; others even less fortunate may be severely disillusioned by experience with dishonest, drunken, or parasitic people.

MARCH 19, 1939

I WRITE THE "HOUSEBOAT" STORY TO AMUSE MYself, like a fairy tale, only to enchant and charm myself. I can write endlessly about the river.

For the first time free, I chose to see Henry rather than Gonzalo. And tonight alone, I didn't call Gonzalo. I am tired of dissonance and struggle. I chose solitude, music, and my green-paged "Houseboat" book, *Marche sur l'eau*. Henry is uneasy in my oriental surroundings. When it got dark and I showed him the light effects, he felt like running away, like a Brooklyn urchin. We laughed, because three Americans took him out. One of them was born in the Fourteenth

Ward. When he discovered Henry was, he said: "Now listen, I can talk to you. You're a regular guy. These other two are highbrows." He didn't know he was talking to Henry Miller, a writer, but a regular guy.

Stop thinking about your life, I said to myself the last two days. And wrote *Marche sur l'eau.* The pain and fatigue almost disappeared. The brooding on injustice, ironic injustices. Because of having to help Helba and Gonzalo I had to give up the houseboat, it was too costly. And Gonzalo, forgetting this, urged me to give it up because it was costing too much.

In helping Helba I have to do my own cooking, and Helba forgets this and says mockingly that my cooking is bad. They take everything for granted now. It is my fault. But it hurts.

Gonzalo and Henry both love to give, and they indulge in this without thinking it is not theirs to give, but mine. I am the one who travels in the subway and in buses, who eats leftovers at home, who wears stockings fit for a ragpicker, so that Henry can mail gifts to Emil and Gonzalo can treat all his friends to drinks. At times I get sad. If Hugo only knew all this. He, who is already angry at our sacrifices of luxury, of vacations; who rages because as soon as he buys me a radio I take it to Henry, a radiator I take to Helba. All the dresses Thurema bought me I gave to Helba, my best jewelry. Why? It seems foolish when the faith dies. When I do it I do it wholeheartedly, with love and faith. But my faith seems naive, at least today. Maybe tomorrow I can believe again.

MARCH 28, 1939

MAYBE TOMORROW I CAN BELIEVE AGAIN. COMICAL. It is just what happens. After writing in the "Houseboat" book, solitude, the bigger wings started to flap and up I went out into the cosmic regions again, forgetting all my small

335

grievances, swimming in forgiveness and compassion, indulgence and understanding. I saw again the innocence of Helba and Gonzalo, the childlike egoism. They are real children. I melted. I turned away from them a little. I began to write so intensely that I felt Gonzalo's caresses less. Then my health cracked again. Hugo came. We had three very tender, very sweet days.

APRIL 1, 1939

STRANGE LIFE. ILLNESS. FORCED TO STAY AT HOME a great deal. Pretending Hugo is here when I want to see Henry, a new trick. Henry finished his grand essay on Balzac, a synthesis of his own mystical discoveries. Edgar says to him: "You used to be all for the earth, and now you're all for heaven."

I feel before Henry a gnawing of guilt for my secret. Henry rising above passions. Every moment I want to talk to him, not as if he were my lover, but my friend. We are in his studio so bare and like a cell, strong naked lights, uncurtained windows, talking of Balzac.

If Gonzalo does not speak the language of poetry, mysticism, or thought, or creation, he does speak the language of feeling. He knows quicker than anyone what my mood is. After sensuality he has to hold me closer to reestablish the human feeling, after appetite he takes me in his arms and kisses me with a kind of gratitude. He has to see me, to feel me near, to be happy. He needs the presence, the touch. He speaks the language of sensibilities: *"Tengo mucha pena,"* because Hugo is arriving and we are going on a trip. He is sad.

When I look at Henry I think: It is all underneath. He is really very emotional. But it is all metamorphosed. It is always that love must manifest itself differently by its two expressions. Henry expressed one kind of love with June and another kind with me. I had to live out the two. Eternal sadness—why not all with Henry, all with One. Why isn't Gonzalo Henry too?

———

I live like this now: Indolently, dissolved. But I remember that once I was so awake in the head. Once attained it was impossible to lose the intellectual world. You can live on feeling, in passion, drugged with mysticism and poetry, dissolved in sensation, but always there comes a dawn—the intellect shines like a giant sun, illuminating everything. Eduardo comes and immediately we are having bouts in the air—new ideas, new currents, new synthesis. The colored ball turns. Philosophy, analysis. Pain is deadened.

Henry took me to see the house of Balzac, on the rue Raynouard, Passy. A house where we would like to live, a kind of Louveciennes in the heart of a city, secret, mysterious, and peaceful, a real Shangri-la hidden behind an old apartment house, stairs going down two flights to a lower step of the Passy hill, then the low one-floor house resting behind trees, tower house, protected and secluded. In one of the rooms there is a trapdoor opening on stairs leading to a quiet little back street through which Balzac escaped his creditors and the husbands of his mistresses. Balzac's portrait, the butcher with an illuminated Neptunian brow and eyes. We were permitted to look through a book of engravings of *Les femmes de Balzac*. We looked at the portrait of Seraphita. Henry said she resembled me, and it was true. I expected that.

Henry wants to give the museum a copy of his essay on Balzac. We went there so gently, both of us, in the rain. Henry left me when I got home, after giving me another book on Zen Buddhism.

I am still sick and weak. Devouring my nights with Gonzalo and my moments with Henry as if they were the last. I believe I am going through a kind of second death, to be reborn again. The last time I died was in 1929–1930, I believe, during the John episode, in Mallorca, in New York. And ten years later I am dying again. What will I be reborn to?

Henry is going through the agony of his Ego. He is killing the selfish man in him, the Ego. He wavers between wisdom, understanding, and sudden attacks of dictatorship, aggressivity. He loves to recall all his insolence, his taunting, his moral courage to attack men and boys stronger than himself physically. He could murder whoever opposed him. The war calls out his animal instincts, fear, self-preservation. The spiritual man is struggling to free himself of the animal. I can see the struggle. He simultaneously expresses both. He foams and hurls insults, he starts minor wars, then in the same moment he talks like a Buddha. We go and see the masks and dance costumes of Java and Sumatra, and he looks at all this with great, delicate attention. He goes home to write about the movies. He observes I do not break with people by explosions, or enmities, but by silence, evasion. I glide off. I cut them as firmly, but almost unnoticeably, without clash. My oriental behavior, my outer control, my subtlety, ruse, act on him. He says in talking of war: "I feel like an animal who doesn't want to be caught in a trap." "I have no such fears," I say, "and if I fall into a trap I know I can get out by cleverness." Henry says: "I can't get out once I'm caught."

In a letter to me [February 10, 1935], Otto Rank spoke of the fundamental conflict between maternal and self-love. "This conflict," he wrote, "is your own conflict, always was, and always will be: Henry is but a concretization of the one form, an expression of maternal love, I of the other, the love of the self in the other: Twin.... You cannot make any decision at all—never—as to a choice between the two kinds of love. They are both essential.... The conflict between the two kinds of love corresponds to the conflict between the woman and the creator (artist) in you. Only in you the artist also comes from the woman, not from the self (which is a masculine ideology you adopted) and herein, in your recognition and acceptance of that, lies your only solution...."

JUNE 1939

SAINT RAPHAEL. THE OLD RAGPICKER WOMAN sitting on a bench in the sun at Denfer-Rochereau. She is sewing. She has taken off her overcoat and has thrown it on the bench, exposing the lining to the air. The lining is made of many small pieces sewn together. Sewn on it is a small cross made of two little wooden twigs. On the other side another cross is embroidered in red thread.

Seeing the little girls pass in their First Communion dresses, the white bridal dress, veil, and flowers, and thinking of the mystic marriage it symbolizes. *Le droit du Seigneur.*

All my confusions, contradictions, and treacheries of my real self come from love and identification with the loved one.

English suffer from a disease which petrifies the spinal column.

One morning: Collected Peruvian stamps for collector, stale bread for bum waiting on bench. Sell books and dine *chez Prunier*. To travel one must disguise. One must go unnoticed. Someone said, "I can't change—I'll always be the poor kid from the wrong side of the tracks."

The only murder I ever committed: The rabbit used for pregnancy test died.

Returning from ten days at Nice I said to myself: I won't touch the "Houseboat" book. I must get well first. I won't write. But I was impelled to. I rewrote the whole forty pages anew—added Albertine, the "Mouse" story, and Father episode.

I was getting ready to leave, and now that I am here in St. Raphael I realize it was a need of the body, not of the spirit. Left to myself I would like to burn up until I die, my whole life in a few years of intensity, like Rimbaud, like so many of the mystics. I don't feel attached to life as a continuous thing. I don't want it to last. I want to burn quickly and die early. Hugh fights to keep me alive. And what keeps me alive is my protective instinct toward others. So many people depend on me. When I got ill this winter I realized how many people I failed to sustain. And it was for them I struggled for strength again. *Au fond I have never done exactly what I wanted.*

People say I look like Luise Rainer. She always shows a greater sadness than the role calls for, and swings as I do from gentleness to violence. She is possessed by those she loves, and does harm without knowing it. She can reach the extremes of coquetry and irresponsibility, and in *Toute la ville danse,* the extremes of protectiveness and deep love.* She is tender and passionate. She is all soul and vulnerability. She swings between feminine provocation and tragic devotion and self-sacrifice. She gives herself while remaining true to herself. As an actress I think she is the most moving figure on stage today. Her softness and yieldingness are incommensurable, but her intensity of feeling is still stronger.

Larry—hearing Nancy's description of the Hindu: "Silky and fiery"—saying: "Just what I am not." Yet it's exactly what he is and that is why Nancy likes the Hindu. Larry cannot see himself in the mirror.

---

*Apparently the French version of *The Great Waltz,* a film Luise Rainer had made in America in 1938, the same year she appeared in *The Toy Wife,* which Anaïs Nin and her husband saw together in London.

AUGUST 24, 1939

*D*ESTINY. ALL WENT TRAVELING. LAO-TSE [HENRY Miller] found joy. I found pain. With Helba and Gonzalo one can only share their fears, anxieties, madnesses. One cannot escape the prison of fear, doubt, disease, jealousy. It is an inferno. We had a few days of joy. *Insouciance.* Tahiti beach, bamboo oceans, meat grilled over wood fires, heat, languor, sun, great thirst, pleasure. But Helba and Gonzalo are heavy, earthy beings, sad as the earth is sad, and they only feel alive when in great pain, violent anger, in hatred and rebellion. "Those whom God would destroy he first makes mad." What a great duel of light and darkness, of heaven and hell. For years. This winter they engulfed me. I saved them from death. This summer I was strongest. I gave them days of joy. They give nothing but anguish. What a contrast: the gaiety of St. Tropez, and their cursed life. And my struggle to deliver them.

AUGUST 26, 1939

*H*A, YOU WANTED TO ESCAPE. HA, YOU WANTED TO travel, to be free, to escape the narrower and narrower fatal circle of Paris. Ha, you wore blue shorts and seashells in your hair, you danced around, swam, bicycled, ate fruit, and desired gaiety, eh? And three months later, exactly, you are back in Paris, in the same corner, and with everything unsolved. Still torn, pulled, tormented, shattered. Still imprisoned, still guarded, needed, sacrificed. Still clutched, loved.

Returned in the black anguish of another war menace, returned in a third-class carriage full of soldiers. Returned convinced that Gonzalo's conflicts are driving him insane, and that his neurosis takes the form of aggressivity and cruelty. He is almost the criminal, the one who murders and destroys to feel his strength because that is the only thing he can do. A new Gonzalo appeared this summer, a veritable demon. Returned fully aware of my weakness, of the prison I have made from which only the dream can deliver me. Everything Henry ever said about June is true of Gonzalo.

*Moricand writes:** I have managed to finish not the entire *Winter of Artifice* but only the first section, Djuna, as far as I was able to with my imperfect English. . . . All that concerns Johanna† is splendidly conceived and written—it's a little masterpiece. This book made me nostalgic for all the earthy and fiery lives one misses by one's overwhelming and obviously chimeric desire not to live such lives for the sake of contemplating nothing but the heavens . . . for wisdom, perhaps, but at what price!

SEPTEMBER 2, 1939

*A*RRIVED IN LONDON BY AIR, WITH HUGO. HUGO rescuing me, anxious, possessive: "How good it is to have you. It took a war to make you come home." London. This dismal city of monsters, fair of ugliness and deformities, the man and woman without magic, fleshy like meat in butcher shops, and every wart, every blackhead, dandruff, magnified a hundred times because they make no effort to be beautiful, employ no artifice or

*In French in the original.
†The characters of Henry and June Miller appear in the story as "Hans" and "Johanna." This section, which emerged from what Anaïs Nin often referred to as the "Henry and June novel," was omitted from all subsequent editions of *Winter of Artifice*.

stratagems. A skeletonic thinness that one sees nowhere else, bones and muscles showing as in medical chart, pimples, nonhuman eyes. The proof? Their only connection is with the animal. They are only human with cats, dogs, horses.

Henry safe in Athens, Gonzalo and Helba safe in St. Tropez. I at my post, sending money orders right and left, with my handbag strap slung across my shoulder like Mercury, bearing silver. Monday war was not certain, but anguish was in the air like a poisonous fog. The calm too, the calm before catastrophe. Yesterday in the street I saw the headlines: "Warsaw bombed." When I saw Hugo he said: "Now it means war." Last night London lights were concealed. Not one light showing. Picadilly in darkness. The lights in buses a dim green. One couldn't count the change. Rain and shadowy figures moving as in the Balinese shadow theater. What shadows? Military masks. The gas mask hung over the shoulder. Green lights of hell. Black curtains. Black doorways. The movie house—one detected a slit of light—but one couldn't read the sign outside. Rain. Picadilly Circus black. People stepping on each other's toes. The war. The punishment. The Ego has grown too big. The personal problems, because of the Ego largesse, insoluble. Duality and schizophrenia everywhere. The death instinct stronger than life because of the panic. A million people like Helba and Gonzalo turning into criminals because of their weakness, because of their corruption, capable only of hatred. A million people knowing only hatred, envy, and fear. War was certain. A war of horror and blackness. The drama openly enacted which has been for many years enclosed inside of human beings in the form of nightmares, desires, secret obsessions. So much corruption can only end in bloodshed. I see all this as I walk the streets and I am not a part of it, I am not in the corruption but I share the punishment. When I saw Gonzalo's soul this summer I knew I was not corrupt. I never imagined a soul as black as his. Today, desperately working with my hands to fill the hours of waiting, at six o'clock I felt a strange, crazy relief. I said to Hugo: "There will be no war. I feel something has happened—we are saved." And I became almost cheerful. I wrote to Henry: "Tonight I write in peace." Actually nothing is known. Poland invaded and the world waiting for England and France to declare war. Waiting and piling sandbags against their windows and doors of big buildings. Our destiny is not yet to be taken out of our own hands, which to many will be a relief, so many broken threads will liberate many prisoners even at the cost of their life. Perhaps we will never have a real war, but this poison, fog, and fear, continuously.

For a few days this nightmare dispelled the Heathcliff one. I suffered so much this summer that I do not suffer at the separation from Gonzalo. The break is made. How long our love will agonize, I don't know. In me, something is broken. I try over and over again to understand what happened. Who will understand the horror of discovering one loves a madman? You give your body, you give your faith, your passion to someone, night after night *and he is mad*. In one instant all that was created between you, every word said in the trustingness of caresses, every caress, every link and bond is swept away by madness! It is far worse than death. I had seen mad days in Gonzalo. Looking back I remember the violent scene at the houseboat. I remember crazy jealousies. I remember utterly blind and stupid remarks. But I didn't realize. I thought: He is violent. He is crazy. He is insanely jealous. He is blind.

St. Tropez: The beauty of it, like a tropical island far from France. The bloom and the softness of it. My desperate avidity for health and joy. My hunger for a sun lost for fifteen years, for the sea, for indolence, the pleasure.

After seeing Henry off at Marseilles,* and a few days later Hugo, I had two or three weeks with Gonzalo alone. Then it was a kind of paradise for a while. What I had desired. Gonzalo naked but for his shorts, his body in the sea with me. His body among the bamboo. The animal glow of his eyes, the soft animal glow. Gonzalo among the bamboo like a real tiger, hair wild, the eyes of an animal. Gonzalo climbing trees, cooking over a wood fire on the beach. Gonzalo remembering smells and pleasures of his childhood in nature. Gonzalo,

---

*Before Henry Miller sailed on the *Théophile Gautier* to meet Lawrence Durrell in Athens and stay with the Durrells on the island of Corfu, Anaïs Nin had met him in Marseilles on July 12, before he sailed two days later. Henry Miller had visited various places on the Riviera at that time, including Cagnes and Nice, but apparently did not see Anaïs Nin in St. Tropez.

a gentle animal, hiding his face under my arm to sleep. He seemed to find his youth again, his innocence, his wholeness. He was potent sensually, ardent.

The first storm came with my book *Winter of Artifice*, all in blue, which I received around the sixteenth of July. Eve Adams saw me bicycling by. I showed her the book. We talked about Miller. We arranged I would give her some copies to sell, that we would meet at the café one late afternoon. I told Gonzalo about this. I met Eve Adams. I was dressed in my Spanish cotton dress, with a flower in my hair. As we sat there, her friend came to sit with us, a sad little singer. At a table in front of us sat three people. One of the women looked intently at me. She asked Eve Adams: "Is this Anaïs Nin?" As she asked I recognized her: Mary, the girl of my orgy with Donald Friede.* Mary, beautiful, fatter, married to an editor of an American magazine. Mary talked to me and introduced me to her friends. Just then Gonzalo passed by, never looking at me, mouth compressed. I felt the storm brewing and I left my friends. I went home. Gonzalo had agreed to wait there for me. Instead he had come to the port to watch me. As I came back to the port I met him, dark and furious. I could not see what he was jealous of, so I was gentle. He burst into a wild speech about my sitting at cafés with corrupt Montparnassians. They were drug addicts. And worse, he had met them at a *partouze*. At this I jumped, and said it was ironic that he should get angry at me for meeting in full daylight, in a café, friends he had slept with. How these scenes start it is impossible to say. All reason is swept away. They are really cyclones of blind jealousies and fear.

That was the end of peace. I could never sit at a café again. But that night when he left me at ten o'clock because Helba was afraid to be alone, I went to the port to meet Mary. She was expecting me in her room. She admitted she liked women better than men, that she had married only to be taken care of, that she was unhappy and had run away. I felt that if I had been audacious we could have had a lovely night together as in New York. I wanted to—but I was timid. She was timid. So I only sat at the foot of her bed and we talked

*See entry for March 29, 1936, in *A Journal of Love: Fire. The Unexpurgated Diary of Anaïs Nin, 1934–1937*, pp. 228–231, where Donald Friede apparently introduced her as "Arline."

about her life, her imprisonment. She had been sunburnt and was rubbing cream on her face, which discouraged me from kissing her. As all Americans, she only wanted a drink to release her, but I was stagestruck, and I left her at midnight telling her I was expected. Gonzalo's unjust violence only gave me the perverse desire to escape from his domination. And besides, he is not as sensual as I am, and he leaves me often with a lively source of unsatisfied erotic hunger. How I regretted that night with Mary—walking back in the absolute darkness of the country to my lonely bed. The next day Mary had received a cable from her husband. She felt guilty and sailed for home. But when Hugo arrived a few days later, for only two days, he brought Jean along. Jean had come to see Hugo off, looking very miserable, and Hugo had said: "Why don't you come along?" There was Jean. He was to sleep in the tent we had on the beach. With Jean came stories of his adventures in Lapland, photographs, astrology, and magic again. Gonzalo at first accepted this, but as soon as Hugo left he grew somber and rebellious. I didn't foresee the storm because Jean had come with a skin disease which made him so repulsive physically that I thought Gonzalo would not be jealous. So I went to the beach to see Jean and Gonzalo came, as usual, much later. That very evening came the storm. At first I laughed. Then I saw that Gonzalo was nearly crazy with jealousy and I tried to reassure him. Nothing was effective. He was obliged to stay with Helba at night and meanwhile he imagined I slept with Jean in the tent.

I offered to go with him to another beach. We did. But naturally, the port being so small, we always saw Jean in the afternoon. And as we had to share our money with Jean I had to see him. I told Jean the truth. We agreed to meet secretly early in the morning, inside of Senequier. Gonzalo, who never came to town early, began to come at nine. My talks with Jean were highly mystical and very extraordinary. He made me aware that Gonzalo was stifling me. He observed I was losing my luminousness, my magic. He struggled to free me. Gonzalo, with an uncanny flair, did feel that I shared with Jean a subtle world I do not share with him. Gonzalo, when we sat at the beach, could only read to me a description of the *"Exposition d'agriculture à Moscou."* Gonzalo, faced with the invisibility of Jean, could only rave against astrology, mysticism, and other reactionary anti-Marxist ideas!

Not being able to come to grips with Jean, he attacked the old political ghosts. We quarreled over the most far-fetched theories. He felt his impotence in the mystical world. He had gained my sympathy for communism for the world only, not for myself. I had another world for myself, the poetic. Jean with his skin disease, his beard, his dirty fingernails, his many weaknesses and defects, was a poet. Poor Gonzalo. One morning he came to the port early (and one must know he loved to sleep all morning to realize the extent of his sacrifice) and found Jean had placed his bicycle behind mine. It was an accident, but he said it looked as if we had spent the night together. There was another scene, because I was rebelling at the injustice of it. I was not seeing Jean anymore, having dinner alone sometimes, going to bed at ten o'clock when Gonzalo left to spare Gonzalo suffering. I had to ask Jean to leave St. Tropez. The quarrels became so venomous, so violent, that they broke me down physically. Gonzalo thrives and blooms on quarrels, on base poisonous words, on guerrillas, bitterness, revolt. They destroy me.

Poor Jean left for another village, leaving me as a present a detachment from the scenes with Gonzalo which gave me power over him for a few days. But after Jean left, Hugo began to write me to join him, as war rumors had started again, which made Gonzalo more perverse, destructive, cussed than ever. The last night before my leaving I lost control again. Gonzalo had been drinking as the only escape from feeling guilty at leaving Helba. He wanted, as he had done before, to get so drunk that he could not climb the hill to his home and he had been obliged to sleep with me, forgetting all about Helba in a sexual orgy with me which lasted until dawn. But that night Helba had walked out of her house at dawn to look for Gonzalo (it was during one of his quarrels with me when I had pretended to leave St. Tropez and Gonzalo had said to Helba that if I left him he would commit suicide) so Helba thought maybe he had committed suicide and she was looking for him and for my house (she didn't know where I lived) to warn me. So this night, though our last, I didn't want Gonzalo to torture Helba, as she was still very sick, and as I refused to drink I kept all my lucidity. This angered Gonzalo, who can only forget himself when drunk. He was already drunk. We returned to my house. In his drunkenness he was raving, weeping, uttering the foulest words a man ever uttered, to wound, saying things I can never forget with such an ugly mouth, such a low invention, that I hated him. At this moment I felt he was insane, driven by an insane destructive force. He was like a murderer, murdering all my faith, illusion, our love, the past, in a flood of poison and vindictiveness. I felt his madness, his destructiveness so far beyond my power to alter that I began to beat him frenziedly. I beat him on the chest, I pulled his hair shouting: "Gonzalo, stop that, I'll beat you until you shut up, you're crazy, absolutely crazy." But the horror of facing a madman, the abyss which opened under my feet at that moment, the despair was so great that I broke down and wept. That sobered him a little. He tottered home. I went to bed and wept all night. The Gonzalo who possessed me had died. One pities a madman. One can't give one's self to a madman. Some part of me divorced Gonzalo that night, was severed from him, because of his brutality, his egotism, his obsession and complete unbalance. I wept over this. I had to surrender all hope of union. You cannot unite with someone who has no core. Love is an edifice. Passion can thrive on storms and violence, but not love. I wept all night. In the morning Gonzalo asked forgiveness: He was drunk. Perhaps. But I was not drunk, alas. A drunk Gonzalo is still Gonzalo—the dregs, maybe, but it's Gonzalo. That's no excuse. He loosened the beast—but that beast lives in him, like the vulgar, poisoned demon in June hurling petty, base, stupid remarks or insults. *A million Gonzalos hurling bombs tonight all through the world.*

Thurema too, exposing her jealousies, envies. She was drunk, she said. And that, they think, effaces all. But not in me. I was glad to leave Gonzalo that day. I am still glad. I want to see him because at some fiery point of our natures we meet, touch. I want to burn again, yes, but I will also leave him, because when I beat him, pulled his hair it was at the impotence I felt before his closed, heavy, dense stupidity, his impotence to understand and penetrate my spiritual world.

The war came. And all I could remember was a bitter-mouthed Gonzalo cursing and foaming—as Heathcliff did at Cathy's bedside while she died, after he murdered her with his impotent love, his jealous vindictiveness, his somber cruel love. What love! This image was only diluted by Gonzalo's lonely, anguished, helpless letters* calling for me:

Chiquita: I just received your telegrams. Yesterday I sent a letter to Paris and I suppose that my letters will be forwarded to you. I am very sad because we are apart, and above all because you are in London, which to my way of thinking is much less safe than Paris in time of war.

I am spending bitter days here, as you can imagine. Not only your trip and Helba's health, which is not good at all, but also this incredible whirlwind of international politics. If Helba were in better shape, I would have left immediately to get in touch with my people and with the Legation of my country. They write me that the government of Peru has instructed the Legation to stay in touch with all Peruvian citizens, but I don't dare leave Helba alone.

I am somewhat optimistic, in spite of all the facts announcing a catastrophe. Here I know no one; I haven't a single friend, and this note will tell you how much I miss you. But I have no choice for the moment except to stay here. I have made an arrangement with the old man so that when I go, I will pay only for the days I owe. I bought a tank of gas. Well, *chiquita,* don't forget to write me. With a warm embrace, Gonzalo.

I will soon see him. I have to. New laws made for war would leave them all cut off, without help from me. But I am on my way to Henry. If the fire in my life with Henry had only lasted. Fire cannot last. It is transmuted. Fire draws me. The first air-raid signal, danger, darkness—they compelled me. The next night I was wishing for it, as for a night of love, almost.

A war is going on which some doubt to be a real war. It may be

---

*In Spanish in the original.

a mock war to satisfy the people who clamored for it. It is all a mystery what is happening. We are being deceived.

On Saturday, September 2, I had an intuition of "no war," which was proven wrong by the declaration of war on September 3. But others shared it with me—Graham Howe for one, and other mystics. Why?

After the little death, Sunday, I set about reconstructing an apparently annihilated world for ourselves, for Hugo, Eduardo, and myself. I went to see [Graham] Howe. Together we asserted the eternal against the present, we set up our individual integrity against the decomposition, collapse of our historical world. We severed our connection with the world. Nothing left but to participate humanly in the error, the suffering of the world, but to separate ourselves from the world's death which is not ours. I was never in it, part of it, so I am not to be destroyed with it. I always lived beyond it, and separate (I lamented this separation often enough), therefore I am not in harmony with its explosion and collapse. We have another rhythm, another death, another renewal. That is it. We were never of the world in the present, and therefore we cannot die at its time, but at our own. I am attached to the cosmic rhythm. I am related only to the few human beings I love. I do not belong to my epoch. That is why I can say I believe in communism for others, humanly, and in something else for myself—because I have a separate life. Sometimes I lose sight of this, I get confused, entangled with the world through love, compassion. But anyone who remembers as much as I do, and who can live in the future, and beyond class, race, time, touches the world at certain points but does not belong to it.

SEPTEMBER 23, 1939

I WROTE THE LAST PAGES IN BED, IN LONDON. DAY of loyalty to Hugo. Days of small feminine struggles against defeat. A mystical struggle against death. Desperately I kept my hands busy. I fixed Hugo's apartment, whose pale disorder has an air of inertia, of emptiness, of absence. Whose structure of ideas has collapsed but who finds nothing to fall back on but me. I took his little clay animals and made a stage for them out of the sand given to us to stifle incendiary bombs. I made food provisions for him. I felt death because I felt cut off from Gonzalo, and cut off from Henry because out of his egotism he can so easily make a new life.

Henry's two war letters monuments of egotism: My only concern is whether I will be cut off. Even now if I wanted to cable [James] Laughlin I doubt if I could rely on him. There are others there who might really do something for me, I am sure of it, such as William Carlos Williams, Dorothy Norman, Paul Rosenfeld, Huntington Cairns, Mencken, Dos Passos certainly, Faulkner, Ben Hecht, Ben Abramson, Gotham Book Mart woman. I can think of dozens but how to reach them quickly and effectively I don't know. The best thing would be for me to croak, then they'd all cash in handsomely. I am wondering if you took my things from the safe from the Obelisk Press office. To leave them in Paris seems really risky. The notes and manuscripts I left there are worth thousands of dollars—a fortune to someone, should I die tomorrow. Remember that I carry about with me a will and testament leaving everything to you. . . . If you do go to America, and if it is at all possible, I hope you could take my manuscripts and notebook with you.

Gonzalo's letters full of anxiety for me, of reproaches: "You will forget me." The English life, which I smelled quickly in a few days, impossible. The little houses in the country, Howe's even, bourgeois. Everything bourgeois. Hateful. My God. Would I be imprisoned here. Fortunately my dislike, rebellion, only represents what Hugo, too, feels about England. I persuaded him to go to Paris with me, to breathe. I confess that the fate of my orphans, deprived of money by new money blockades, worries me. Hugo, blindly, works for us to leave London, and we overcome obstacles nobody else could overcome. People waiting in line two or three days for visas which take two or three weeks after that to be given. We pass through. We leave London in utter darkness. Only three passengers in the train and on the boat. A ghostly voyage. I am out of the English prison. But what for? To see Gonzalo again. Slowly the other Gonzalo, the one who sleeps on my breast, reappears, the lost, helpless Gonzalo whose fears make him brutal. To join him I risk Hugo's life and my own in a crazy voyage. Hugo becomes the accomplice of my struggle to remain in the fiery, dangerous infernal life rather than in an English refuge. Out in the open. I calm his fears and open his eyes to the adventure. Yes, he prefers to be bombed in Paris. But now he is stuck and cannot obtain a visa to return to England. Gonzalo is struggling to return to Paris. His letters are human. I spend all my days juggling through laws and difficulties to send money to Henry, Gonzalo, and Lantelme. The police know me. Soon I will have exhausted all my trickeries (such as going each day to a different post office, all over the city). And then Henry will be cut off.

To keep busy I begin packing boxes in the cellar, push too heavy a box, get lumbago, lie paralyzed in bed. When I most need my strength. Every day I thought of writing here: "This ends the personal life." But that is not true yet; I am still trying to save it. At the thought of possible separation from Gonzalo I weep all night. Between the pages of this diary lie his letters, other letters. Moricand comes to say good-bye after engaging himself in the Légion Étrangère. "What else could I do? I was starving." He repeats that I live by a cosmic, not a personal rhythm. But it is all the greatness, vastness, space which I surrender to touch Gonzalo, enclosed in his limited bourgeois pride which hurts him at receiving money, in his limited bourgeois bohemianism, in his Spanish jealousy, his Catholic guilt, his anarchic disorder, his destructive laziness.

Je pleure. I weep because you cannot save people. You can only love them. You can't transform them, you can only console them. Henry's weakness, cowardice. Given food, he entrenches himself anywhere, hides, attains joy by detachment. I cannot attain this, ever. So I have loved Gonzalo, who had no detachment, no philosophy, no power, nothing but his immediate, emotional, personal life.

"Ces choses dont la beauté enveloppe une absence"—Those things whose beauty envelopes an absence—I read in Ramon Fernandez's *Les Violents.* How far a misunderstanding can lead, such as the one between Gonzalo and myself, if both are violent. When letters and money orders were delayed because of the war, Gonzalo thought I had voluntarily abandoned him and wrote me a raging postcard, the kind that makes one bristle and fight back. He arouses all my combativity with his aggressiveness. I have to be indulgent, forgiving.

Paris at night. You step out of a café, a restaurant, into darkness. This causes me a profoundly sensual emotion. You recognize no one. You stumble. Mysterious blue and green *"veilleuses"* here and there. Immediately I desire Gonzalo. When I returned from London after weeks in the prison of a sexless country (the horse-and-dog sensuality of Graham Howe, bah!) to the oriental softness of my place, and heard Arab music from the restaurant where we went—oh, the absence of Gonzalo, the flesh and blood of all this, Gonzalo sailing toward Peru in my imagination.

I cannot ever believe in victims, in martyrs because I believe so strongly in one's own responsibility, ultimately. Helba and Gonzalo posing as victims.

This week, because of the delay in my letters and money order, they went hungry, but it was *vandage* time in St. Tropez and Gonzalo could have made thirty francs a day culling grapes. Why do I love Gonzalo? Certain nights, nights of sensual exaltation, without alcohol, in the fire of my love he seemed lucid. Perhaps my

soul was passing into him then. I clung to these fragments of understanding, as to the inner being of Gonzalo himself. It was the secret
Gonzalo.

In this same way Henry struggled through the forest of June's
beauty for tiny fragments of a soul to touch in the darkness, and the
next morning the vulgar Broadway June began again to speak and
demolish the miracle.

At times I looked at Gonzalo and I knew he was talking like an
ordinary South American, vulgar caricature of a race neither Spanish
nor Inca, made up of worn-out aristocracies, superficial education,
humiliated Indian blood, half animal, half *rasta*, half brute. "But you,"
said Moricand, "you are an enchantress. You are Princess and Guardian Angel. You are much more than a woman."

So I begin each day anew, very simply, as a woman. I powder my
face, I paint my eyelashes, I wear a fuchsia tailored coat and black
skirt, leather moccasin shoes, a leather Arabian bag slung over one
shoulder. I am like a *coccinelle* walking and refusing to use my wings.
I refuse miracles. I do not seek magic. My little purple jacket. A
hundred brush strokes every day to keep the hair beautiful. I am still
walking. I read the newspapers. I wish Hugo were leaving because I
cannot love him for more than a few weeks at a time. He bores me,
bores me, bores me.

I have struggled toward naturalness. I have never adopted or recognized the discipline of *la vie mondaine,* so that today when I am in
the world, I cannot talk according to the ritual, with irony and detachment. I have not the training. I have rejected all who talk and
live by these rules, including my Father.

Reading *Fille de Samourai,* by Etsu Inagaki Sugimoto, I realized the force of form, and my own struggle against it. This
explains my love of Louise because she was a poet, my following
her into her world, and bruising myself against her formal life,
so contrary to her own essence. And the same with Rebecca West.
This form irritated me in Moricand. Strangely it broke down
when he read my *Winter of Artifice.* His letter was a cry of human
sorrow at having missed human life out of squeamishness, over-
delicacy. But as he confessed his unnaturalness, I also became

aware of the nobility of form. So I wrote him this farewell letter:*

It was while reading a book on Japanese customs that I relived once again all the quarter tones of our friendship, a friendship outside of time and space, and certainly outside and far from Europe, and I thought: Conrad is going to leave without knowing what a precious friend he is to me.

I would like to define what you represent for me symbolically. How humiliated I am for you and for myself to have to give you such a small gift, devoid of all spiritual significance. It hurts that I am unable to give you something larger and give it in the Japanese fashion, wrapped in muslin with "This is my gift" inscribed on it.

Europe has forced us so far away from poetry, but you have always appeared to me to embody a noble attitude, like that of ancient races, never sloppy, never lacking manners, grace, or spirit, even in the face of hunger, illness, or misfortune. Poetry as a heroic act. And always a sense of subtlety, delicacy. How often, when I was offended and hurt by grossness and violence, have I rejoiced to find in you again pure spiritual life, a sense of ritual, of ceremony and beauty. I said to myself: Here is an Oriental brutalized by this world. Believe me, not one of your qualities, of your subtle qualities, has escaped me. Sometimes I held it against you that you were so vulnerable, since I knew exactly how you felt. I wanted you to be tougher, for your own sake. As heroic as you are, you suffer, nevertheless.

When one goes away it is good to know that one has been understood, even loved. That your image remains vibrant and alive, an image you can be proud of. I believe I have grasped all the riches of your personality as you have so well understood mine, and I love you a great deal, my dear Conrad.

*In French in the original.

The first money I ever gave to a man was to Gustavo Morales, in Paris, when I lived on rue Schoelcher. He had written a book which I thought good, but nobody wanted to read it because it was hand-written. Gustavo told me that if he could get it typed he could have it read by publishers but that for this he needed five hundred francs. At this time Hugo and I had very little money. Hugo gave me two hundred francs a month for my clothes allowance. I asked him if he could advance me my allowance. I got the five hundred francs. Then I thought out carefully how I could give it to Gustavo without offending him. I wrapped the money in white paper and on it I carefully designed the exterior of a book, with the title of his novel on it, giving the money its symbolism. I didn't know then that Gustavo had been living on women's gifts for years. I remember being shocked because when he came he tore the paper without looking at it and pushed the money into his pocket very negligently, not understanding, annoyed even, not to have received it directly, and that he immediately invited me out for a drink, destroying my illusion about the purpose of the money. My defect is that when such things happen to me I feel that it is I who am ridiculous, overdelicate, and I never try again for fear of being mocked.

I remember another incident. When Gonzalo first slept with me without possessing me, he kept saying that I had the body of an angel, that he could not believe I was made for sex. To tease him, I bought angel hair one night and filled his pockets with it while he slept. When I left him at dawn I imagined he would wake up, find all the silvery white hair, and be amused. But he was simply perplexed. He didn't understand.

Henry never understood that once when he made a row at breakfast because I had not washed his favorite breakfast cup, and had served his coffee in a cup I found clean, I had answered back I thought he was growing into a crotchety old maid. But knowing it was the thinness of the cup he liked I went and got him the finest Chinese cup I could find, finer than the one he liked.

What first attracted me in Gonzalo's nature was the obsessional criticism of the European commercial vulgar life. Against this he set up the civilization of the Inca—his delicacy, his noble behavior, irony, his sense of humor, his sense of form in gesture, his dignity in amusement, orgies even. I became aware of what separated me abysmally from the Americans, what caused me such mysterious suffering because I was ashamed of my "form" which even at parties, even in drunkenness, I could not depart from. I felt it alienated me. Henry mistook this for snobbishness. Such physical bearing, such *maintien,* absence of vulgarity for him was an artificial attitude. He was completely mystified by the behavior of Moricand because Henry was the natural man par excellence. That is why during the week of the first war alarm he behaved like a Rabelaisian personage and gave way to complete panic.

I wanted naturalness. I love it in others, I reached it for myself. But I made the mistake of thinking naturalness excluded poetry and form. I became natural, sincere, but still remained what I am, too. I am no longer artificial, but I still live *en beauté,* with poetry. For a moment these things were confused in me. It is true the poetic sense of the Japanese seems to be based on a rigid form which has become a prison for feelings. Etsu knew it well. That is so. To arrive at sincerity seems difficult if, for example, you have a cult of hospitality. I received in Louveciennes Michael Fraenkel and an American chorus girl who behaved in a way I despised, yet I never let it show while they were in my house. It was enough that inwardly I despised them. That was my sincerity. It seemed to me that this spiritual separation was sufficient. I did not reach the point of condemning or punishing as I felt simply that they belonged to another world and would not have understood my differentiations.

My basis of behavior is feeling. If I feel poetically or symbolically, I manifest it. If I feel desperate and violent, as Gonzalo makes me feel, I manifest it. I beat him because when I see he does not understand my language I try his. Moricand starving but wearing a hard, white collar irritated me until I realized the white collar was a symbol for him. He could not bear decadence in dress or his whole armature was gone. True to yourself.

To make others at ease I renounced luxury—but a certain beauty is necessary to me and I must not betray the princess in me.

To be a natural princess, a natural poet, sincere princess and sincere poet—how different that is from the behavior of the *grand monde,* or of the poseur poets. But difficult, difficult and delicate, and I made some errors.

Hugo awakens in the middle of the night to caress my face, saying: "Poor little cat. I have made you so unhappy. I am always worried and anxious. I have my mother's defect and I can't get rid of it." And by this one phrase of humility he recovers in one second all the ground he loses by his deadening, sententious, intellectual discourses on politics, his utter absence of faith and warmth. With the same humility Henry effaced all traces of his monstrous egotism. But now he is not here to look at me with his very innocent eyes and say with a soft mouth and voice: "It's true I'm an egotist. But all great men were egotists."

Now I get letters in which he describes at length the meals he enjoyed, the flatteries, the visits, not even asking me: How are you? His three letters from Athens are incredible.

I sent him away. To be with Gonzalo. I pushed him to give up Villa Seurat to travel. I knew I risked losing him. I knew too he was ready for a new cycle. Well, I think it is done. This war has hastened the separation. From afar, Henry's self-centeredness looms more immense, without his human presence to blind or enchant me. *Je crois que c'est finis.* I think it is over.

When I returned to Paris I had fits of nostalgia for Henry—when I saw his watercolors, the little box full of odds and ends he left me which he had on his desk. Nostalgia, but not the pain I felt at the fear of losing Gonzalo.

SEPTEMBER 25, 1939

*I*N LONDON I WENT TO VISIT GRAHAM HOWE, TO pass the time. His books *The Open Way* and *War Dance* had affected me. I wanted to enchant him. But it was too easy, and he did not enchant me. He reminded me of John Erskine, and he is a bourgeois. In a one-hour visit I knew I had attracted him, but I was not.

I can attract from afar! We all wrote letters to Dane Rudhyar, astrologer, about his mystical articles in *American Astrology*. He receives tons of mail. We exchange a few letters. Because I let some time lapse, Dane Rudhyar, busy man in Hollywood, writes me a note concerned about my fate in Europe and suggesting I should go to America.

Tout ceci c'est pour m'amuser. Parce que je ne suis pas gai. All this to amuse me because I am not at all jolly.

I was reflecting on the death of houses, how they seem to collapse as soon as we leave them, as soon as we prepare psychically to leave them. I remember the house in Richmond Hill did not show any decrepitude until our life in it came to an end, when my mother's debts and my marriage dispersed us. Then, as if we had sucked the living glow from it, suddenly it appeared decrepit and greasy. So with Louveciennes when I returned from America so changed as a woman, when I became a different woman, when Louveciennes ceased to be the foyer of my life and I spent all my time in Paris with Henry. In one day it grew old, like a deserted lover, old and empty. It withered. I was amazed to see its defects, its moldiness, its death. So with Villa Seurat, which grew suddenly unlivable after Henry left it during the first war alert. Villa Seurat began to lose its life. It began to break down. The rain and the wind came through the window. The hot-water heater was worn out and needed to be changed. The paint, the walls suddenly appeared very dirty. The need of many repairs began to seem almost hopeless because the life glow had been withdrawn. I felt only anguish in Villa Seurat for fear of being discovered by Gonzalo. My anguish forced us all to disperse. It was intolerable, like an enormous menace, a tragedy pending over all of us. The war was only the external reason. And Villa Seurat, once so joyous, began to die right under our eyes simultaneously with the spiritual death. Houses turn to corpses overnight when we move our soul out of them.

Hugo's apartment in London never appears to have been inhabited. Absent. Like Hugo himself. Perhaps because Hugo has no life of his own without me, and I never lived there. This time I tried to instill life into it. I worked very hard, rearranged, changed, shaped it anew, brought it to life. But it remained empty because I was not living in it. I was planning my escape from it even while creating it and giving it all the warmth I could. It remained inert and empty like a desert.

Paris for me has no longer any rich life of its own, it is strewn with memories. When I came back to my home this time it was not to find Gonzalo but to remember the presence of Gonzalo as if he were gone. My God, I am afraid of those words. I speak of the past. Where is my life?

> *Letter to Jean:* You see, Jean, although I am a child of Neptune, I don't believe we should live in the poetic at the expense of others, making others perform Saturnian chores for us. If we do so, we diminish our own strength, because true strength is only in a complete being. You yourself must take care of the material base, the machinery of your life, thereby achieving an independent and complete structure. Otherwise you would be the loser; you would weaken your power, you wouldn't be the master of the material side. That side must be mastered and put at the service of your dream. From that conviction I draw a strength of organization, doing everything myself, including the disagreeable chores. That is the only note of discord between us, because in pushing the weight of details onto someone else you give proof of weakness, not of strength.

SEPTEMBER 30, 1939

IN LONDON I SAW THE CRUMBLING OF HUGO'S world; I have struggled for months now to bring him into the new. Gonzalo did save me. Through his love, I touched the new world, and when this one crumbled I understood.

He opened my eyes to a drama I never would have known. He, as Henry, prevented me from floating back to childish dreams, such as Jean is indulging in, dreams without roots. He forced me into reality which now gives me the strength to witness the triumph of Russia as a dawn. Poor Hugo is the vanquished one, with his attachment to the old system, his economic laws and loyalties. Hugh struggles fiercely against my communism, because it came from Gonzalo. Hugh became passionately bourgeois, which is not his true nature.

I love Hugh now, because he is the one in error. He was identified with the present system. He suffers from its decadence and from its suicide. The war shattered his work, and what he represents. That is why I went to him.

Gonzalo, identified with Russia, triumphs. He returned from St. Tropez full of assurances, of joy even. Events were proving him right. It is his reign. Henry has fallen because he found only a negative refuge in Greece, an escape. He does not fall altogether because he can create. But he can only wrap himself up in egoism. His letters are all escape, escape.

Hugh is dispossessed of his power. He has no role in the world of tomorrow. So all my love has converged to him this month, my tenderness. He has returned to England. I can't enter England. Gonzalo is repatriated free, to New York. Wants to work there. What a conflict. Death in England with Hugo out of pity for Hugo, or a courageous new life with Gonzalo. A new Gonzalo, cohesive, effective, whole. Talking lucidly. His role is to inflame. He is a fire and he is meant to set others on fire. The fire current is strong in him. He has the brilliance, now, the power of Russia itself, an idealistic power against a corrupt Europe. What undercurrents of tragedy.

Pity for Hugh tortures me. Staying with him gives me nothing but human comfort. It is a negative solution. I have wept, been torn. Gave Hugo an illusion of passion, because of the pity, the yearning maternal desire to protect. I stand on the brink, unable to decide. I let myself be pushed. I improvise. Whenever I was true to myself it turned out good for all those I loved. I must remember that. The cruelty is only apparent. If I go to America I can save Hugo perhaps.

Pull him away. Perhaps the quarrels, arguments, talks we had will bear fruit.

What sad days. Human sorrows everywhere. Unlike Henry, who can leave a sinking ship without a backward glance. In one day he turned his back on France—all those he seemed to love so much. I feel a link with France, affection. I hate to leave it to its tragic fate. I awake with horror thinking of Guicciardi and his naive faith, Moricand in the Foreign Legion, of my ex-*concierge*'s suffering, of what I can give or do. Only because of my pity have I touched communism. Without this I would be today one of those set against change, stubborn, closed off, alone, and obliged to die with the past.

Thank you, Gonzalo.

Racked by feelings for Hugo yesterday. During the air-raid alarm weeping because he was on a plane on his way to London, in danger. Then at night, after months of not spending a whole night together, Gonzalo and I found again the oriental corner, the sensual obscurity and softness.

We were shaken by such violent nervous currents of enjoyment that it was like madness, unbearable. I sobbed. The violent pleasure, so acute and tremendous, shaking Gonzalo from head to toes. Gonzalo—when I left St. Tropez, just like an animal with his sorrow. He stopped eating and became thinner and thinner. A new Gonzalo emerged out of that purifying summer. No doubt of his love. He comments himself on "a man who has lived so much knowing what he wants and loves better than other men. When I love, I love."

OCTOBER 2, 1939

I SEE MORICAND SUFFERING THE DISTRESS OF WAIT-ing. I write and tell him what I think of him, by way of nourishment. I see Giselle Couteau, the great love of Joaquin's for ten years, who was to him what I was to Eduardo. Giselle and Thurema—the two women who almost set him on fire, this being of whom Moricand said: "Born to catch fire but does so with difficulty. Smothered by the earth, by conflicts." Both Giselle and Thurema have the same quality: fire and life. Giselle is exactly like me, a Neptunian fire, a mystical fire. Giselle has the better part of Joaquin—his soul. She understands him, permitted him to bloom open before her. Thurema only a moment of fever, because she is only fire. She is confused and chaotic and unable to see clearly into Joaquin.

It's funny, women—the women who reappear in my life, at certain moments, like sisters, when I need them. And then it turns out they need me even more, and soon it is all reversed and I become the mother: June, Thurema, Elena, Giselle. Giselle came with a gift from my mother. Giselle does not look extraordinary but she is. She has green eyes, dark hair, great freshness and vitality, a beautiful voice, freckles. She might be an Irish girl, laughing always, even in sorrow. Giselle came the day I was bleeding from Hugo's departure and the sirens and my fears for his life because he was on an airplane. And naturally I responded to the fire and life in her, and off we went leaving dead Helba sitting in my place, with dead Joaquin, dead Hugo all around us, and she and I talking about them, about her new love.

I came to life again, as I did at Thurema's touch in New York. Gonzalo, in spite of the sensual pleasure, could not give me this because I could not forgive him the love I have for him, I almost hated his great fiery body, hair, voice, hands.

Then Giselle became my pleasure of the day during the bleak, bleak days of sadness. A luminous point. She showed me Joaquin's letters to her which revealed a new brother—a poet, tender, lyrical, emotional, a Joaquin hidden from me always because in my presence he was intent on stifling these things in me of which he was jealous. For Giselle he flowed in cadenced feelings, in sincere appreciation of her, a chant of tenderness with great debacles of renunciation, great desert-making winds of sudden "sacrifices to God" and all the other Catholic disguises for the fear of life. Poor Giselle: caught in the maze of his contradictions, his inexplicable withdrawals; after a move forward, two moves backward. And God, religion, mother, all tangled with fear, timidity. Secretive, like my Father and Thorvald. Even in his diary he disguised the truth.

Je cherche les points lumineux, les points vivants. I search points of light and life. It is no wonder I study Marx—so that this cataclysm, this convulsion may not appear as a death but as a *renversement*. And I want to live in the reversed order. I seek to understand.

Henry's way is not the way. He thinks he has reached Chinese, Tibetan equilibrium. But he has only reached a crystallization of the ego. Being blockaded by pain and sorrow he asserts the Ego's life as supreme. Moricand was equally shocked by his letters. Detachment, objectivity, but with the wrong accent. Descriptions of his delectable meals, of his future pleasure, voyages, of new friends, of the stars. Moricand reaches my own discovery: that Henry exudes an animal warmth, an animal blood generosity which seems like feeling, but in great crises is revealed as the purest egotism. To end pain by indifference is not the mystical solution. No transmutation then, only an inhuman, impersonal anesthesia. Only I, Henry Miller, count. My belly is full. My wallet is full. The world is right.

And I am to blame for this. I nurtured this. I nourished this by my devotion, my constant, continuous care. When I think of the extraordinary long battle I had to wage to be able to live outside of Henry's presence—to live separately. And now I have to do the same with Gonzalo, learn to live outside of his presence, not always through him. My first impulse was to travel with him, to be close, to be near each other. But I remembered St. Tropez. He does not let me live, shine, when he is there.

I shall sail alone, free, adventurous. I am, in reality, timid. I am afraid of solitude. I am not worthy of the adventures I have had. The way I hide within my love and wish to stay there, and I'm afraid of facing the world alone. Oh, the weakness. Out, out, you sentimental unionist. Always close, always together, that's my dream. And Hugo is the only one who practices that. I have all the audaces, when I must save, protect, or join my love. None to live outside of love. And it is the timid, attached me Hugo has kept, he who is always enslaved and like a woman, only able to live when I am there. *Comme c'est triste tout ceci, aussi triste que la guerre.* In war you only lose your blood once, you only die once. In this life we lead, one dies so many times. Is it for this men prefer the bomb, the real fire, the unique death?

OCTOBER 4, 1939

*I*AM ONE OF THE FEW WHO CAN SAY TODAY I HAVE loved each day as if the loved one were to die. I have always loved giving all to every hour, and forgiving all. The war made people love this way: the maximum of love, because death is waiting. I alone didn't change. I always acted as if it were the last moment. I was never careless, thoughtless, inattentive, absent, or asleep. These are the conflicts which have almost driven me insane this month. If I stay with Hugo in London I cannot help Helba, Gonzalo, or Henry or Lantelme because I cannot send money out of England. And I cannot see Gonzalo because he can't enter England, nor can Henry, either.

If I wait with Gonzalo and Helba in some out-of-the-way place, Gonzalo becomes a demon because he has no outlet for his vitality, his need of talk, of domination, of city life, of contact with the dramas of political roles. In St. Tropez he was already regarded with suspicion as the foreigner who did not go to war, and the persecution of Left-wing people had begun in France. I endanger Gonzalo's life. And I can't send money to Henry.

Chess game of horror: Pity for Hugo left alone; desire to follow Gonzalo into the life in New York; to escape the passive suffering the war gives me, a purely destructive experience for me. Pity for Henry, whom I can't leave stranded and penniless. The most alive thing in me today is the life-current of passion I have for Gonzalo, so I must follow this too. I can't kill this without killing myself and making a widower of Hugo.

But the tear—the sudden realization the war gave me of the powerful bond with Hugo, devotion, of the strong, alive bond with Gonzalo. And I can't murder and starve Gonzalo for Hugo. So Hugo has been sacrificed to loneliness, and I leave for America without joy, torn and divided between tenderness and passion. Hating the passion at times.

I must remember it is not final, only temporary. Going to New York I can help them all. I can help Hugo to leave England, Gonzalo, Helba, and Lantelme. But I, I am sacrificed. It is not what I want. It is, after all, what I must do, make a choice which tears me apart. I am not wholly in any love, so I must suffer the consequences. But Hugo—Hugo who at present gets all my pity, why must he be fated to suffer, only because he does not inspire me with passion?

In this hell, I work. At night, at the hour Hugo usually awakens and suffers insomnia and anxiety almost regularly—I awake now. And feel pulled toward his pain—not toward him; toward his goodness, his feeling, his sensitivity. As the day grows, I renew my course, my faith in positive action, in adventure, in risk. The chess game seems solved. At night I suffer again. And, as always, when I suffer, out of this I pour out giving. I take on the burden of Giselle's life; the burden of little Madame Trollet, my ex-*concierge,* whose husband has gone to the front; the burden of Moricand, his testamentary evenings, poor Moricand. I give him his last minutes of pleasure, I give him love, I tell him all his qualities, his importance in the mystical world. We eat in crowded cafés, seeking lights and noise. He says as I arrive: "My God, you look more enchanting and more like a little girl than ever." Enchantress without a magic wand, a useless one, who only traced a luminous route in the darkness and savagery of the world, something only for those I loved. And today, because all my life has been nothing but love, and not art, and not the idea, and not immortality, I carry all my diaries with me so that if I sink into the sea they sink with me and no one I loved will ever suffer.

I leave testamentary letters to destroy all my papers. And that is all writing meant to me. I will leave three small books, nothing. I will be, as fitting for me, thoroughly burnt by love like a mystic.

End of Hugo's letter: "You are all I have in the world—so give me peace of mind and do what I say."

OCTOBER 14, 1939

*H*ELBA ILL AGAIN—ABSCESS IN THE LUNG. THE three of us in hell again. Helba in physical pain, which she dramatizes enormously. Gonzalo caught by the fear of her death. I caught in their suffering. That's all they want, that I should suffer with them. They can't conquer pain. And I can't either, not in Henry's way. All plans of voyage are annihilated. War or no war. Gonzalo keeps saying I am a saint. But I am in a desperate state of revolt, revolt, revolt.

Gonzalo, at first, revolted too: "My God, I am condemned to be a nurse for the rest of my life!"

And I—well. It's useless to revolt.

OCTOBER 15, 1939

*H*ELBA SAVED. IT TURNED OUT TO BE PLEURISY. That night, in their chaotic studio, tending the stove with Gonzalo by candlelight (the electricity had been cut off), eating food I brought from my place, listening to Helba's laments, heating lineament every twenty minutes, I had such a feeling of despair that I went to sleep weeping. And today I passed through a violent crisis of anguish. I suffer from being forced to witness the tenderness of Gonzalo for sick Helba. What a destiny, mine.

First to take care of Henry when he was broken by June and to have to share all his memories, recollections, his writings about her. And now to have to take care of Helba with Gonzalo and console him in his anguish about her. And I so easily crushed with doubt, so unsure of love, so jealous and lonely. Always lonely, a loneliness which is driving me crazy. Loneliness with Hugo, with Henry, with Gonzalo. I have gone to the restaurant carrying my diary, sometimes, because I feel less lonely with this reflection of my loneliness.

Yet I have the courage to study dialectics and materialism thoroughly, profoundly. I want to understand the new world. I do want to evolve and change with it. I do understand it now. Why was I so slow? Always slow—though I am nimble-witted and swift in comprehension. Because I do not take ideas as ideas. I drink, eat them when they form tissue and flesh with life. For me to understand dialectics and materialism with my head meant nothing, but when I began to feel it and live it through and with Gonzalo then it was life, not just an idea. It was an idea which could illuminate the life, not just a concept.

When I loved Gonzalo, who was all caprice, revolution, revolt, it was a continuation of my love for Henry's literary revolts, my acceptance of his changeful nature, relativism against my static fears and absolutism. My Russian life began with Henry. Henry set me flowing. Gonzalo's excesses of emotion liberated my own imprisoned feelings.

I suffered tortures BUT without them I would have been a ghost, absolutely dematerialized, the kind of exalted mystic who can only plunge into death. Today, through Gonzalo, I accept communism as contact with the earth. Because of Gonzalo I feel the drama in which I live, I am in it (at the same time out of it, too). When I first read Marx I said laughingly: "I'm eating earth." And made a face. But it was true.

OCTOBER 17, 1939

*J*EAN AND I. LUMINOUS TALK. HE ELABORATES ON the deep distinction between true mysticism (union with God) and the cosmic ecstasies and exaltations of Neptune. He and I, until last night, lived in a confusion between our exaltations, poetical ecstasies, and our occasional sense of union with the Whole. Jean separated what he described as the joyous *"courbe,"* the arc we make in sensations composed of fixed senses and spiritual meanings, and the direct road to faith. I supplied the word "amorous." Our ecstasies are of the lovers, loving with fever and exalted to tremendous heights. Not always reaching God. When you reach God you reach peace and confidence such as I had after childbirth. When you reach the cosmos you have a sense of rhythm with the universe which gives a tremendous joy. But it is a fevered, tense condition, not the simple joy of faith.

Jean thinks we have the possibility of reaching the highest mystic points, but we don't because being Neptunians we are "caressing" the universe. We seek the mystic as a higher form of joy, but we seek it sensually, for our poetic enjoyment. We are saints at times, in achieving the transmutation of the demon in us into the angel. We have great power for good. But not for renunciation. All this I knew obscurely, and Jean too, and last night we unveiled it. Together we really emit light, a heavenly light. And curiously, when I came home I found Gonzalo and had an equally magnificent talk on Marxism.

I let the contradictions lie. I don't torment myself. They will work out. From both worlds I draw forces. All I admit humbly is that whatever ideology lay behind my life and work before Marxism they led me to an impasse. Poetry and mysticism were separated from vital human drama. *House of Incest* was severed from *Winter of Artifice*. Duality in my life led me to the impasse of anguish when I lived between Henry and Gonzalo last year. Duality between my diary and my creation. Fissures. When Gonzalo talks about the close interrelation, interaction, I understand. I see severed sections flowing together again. I see flow and movement. And wherever I see these I go. What will happen to my life and work I don't know. All I know is that I am in vital contact with vital elements. That I am at once beyond the present and in it. Not cut off, not lost, not speaking like Moricand of death and age and the end; not, like Henry, hiding; but facing openly the cataclysm and the drama. It does not worry me to have to revise all my values again, to be thrown into a world I don't know, to have to note the death of certain parts of my writing. I know I will have to find a way of not saying God. But I know, too, I must not refuse to live any experience and say: My world was made. I won't recognize its errors and weaknesses. I won't admit its passing, its aging, as I am passing and aging.

My beautiful *Winter of Artifice,* dressed in an ardent blue, somber, like the priests of Saturn in ancient Egypt, with the design of the obelisk on an Atlantean sky, stifled by the war, and Kahane's death.*

As Moricand says, we love to rape. Neptune's passion for unveiling, for secret rapes, from the one which enlarges the eyes and makes one breathless, to the one that gives vertigo and leads one to the edge of death.

But the desire to be discovered, raped? I had that. I liked Henry's spiritual and physical rapes. His violent crude way of breaking through secrets and reserves. He saved me. Who will violate the secrecy of the diary and read between the pages of my books? Between the pages of this book there is a lot to read!†

OCTOBER 18, 1939

I HAVE BEEN PARTING FROM MORICAND WITH PAIN. We had several evenings together. Moricand engages himself in the *Legion Étrangère* because he was desperately hungry, because he wants to die in style, elegance, because he loved me and could not have me, because I, being overburdened, could not save him, help him, only intermittently, not completely; because he

---

*Two days after the outbreak of World War II, on September 3, 1939, the publisher of the Obelisk Press had died, unexpectedly, at the age of fifty-two.

†In the typed transcript of volume sixty-one of her diary, Anaïs Nin added after this sentence: "Note made by me while copying this ambiguous statement: The book in which the diary was written was one of uncut pages. Between the spaces created by the uncut pages I slipped letters, horoscopes etc."

died long ago, long before I knew him, because for him it is the end of his world of elegance, grace, noble attitudes, the end of subtlety and delicacy; because he wasted his life on an inert and passive and empty little whore; because he was always terrified of life and never knew it *"au fond"*; because he missed all its deeper vital currents; because in astrology he only found the reflection of his own fatalism and self-destruction; because he could only see demons everywhere; because he really desired young boys and never had them except by caressing them in his drawings; because he had only known two great friendships, with Blaise Cendrars and Max Jacob. Everything else was only an echo for him because he, like the analysts, was condemned to comment on dramas which he could never enter and play a part in; because he was a *mage,* a sage, and a timorous *jeune fille* in life; because he was tired of his own involved and oblique ways, his labyrinthian excuses and apologies, his long perpetual evasions, his hopeless craving for luxury, his struggle to keep until the end his white starched collar; because his possession of the star's secrets was his only possession; because this was the end of the Neptunian age.

We did not know when he would leave. Yet yesterday, moved by a presentiment, he came to see me and brought me his last possessions, two beautiful Venetian crystal bottles with old flowers painted on them, around his initials, which he always kept on his dressing table, and two gold lockets he carried on his watch, in which there is gold and myrrh, the gifts of the sages to Christ. This I put around my wrist. The next day, moved by a presentiment, I looked all through his letters and horoscopes. I wanted to prepare what I needed to re-create his persona in the "Houseboat" story, because I was losing him.

I expected his telephone call at five, telling me he would be on his way. On his way to what life? He may go to Morocco, the birthplace of the Atlanteans, too. This sixth sense by which we all live, which we call Neptunian, and which existed no doubt in Atlantis, is now left only between Jean and myself.

I went to Jean's place yesterday, a true explorer's den. Jean was wearing long, erotic black felt boots from Lapland. He had placed the midnight-blue sled in a corner of the room. The place was carpeted with fur shoes and reindeer fur gloves, bags, leggings, embroidered belts, tree bark, wooden bowls, tools, Lapland matches, dresses, and hats. The colors danced, red, yellow, and green. Red on the bed, red woolen edges on the boots. The two little Greek chairs were placed before the fireplace. An immense pipe, as broad as a young tree. Rolled cords made out of tree roots. And deer horns everywhere. And then Jean talked against Gonzalo, enemy of the spiritual world, and again I saw the duel between light and darkness. I could not deny that with Jean I find space, infinity, and never-ending riches, whereas with Gonzalo, reading me the history of production, I feel limitation and confinement, a world that is powerful physically but limited. And I was sad. I was sad because around Jean, in his place full of fairy-tale objects, there was infinity, and when I returned to Gonzalo all this was snuffed out, yet I was happy to touch Gonzalo, to feel his naked body and his sex inside of mine.

Jean sees in my study of dialectics nothing but a moving act of love; in order to communicate with Gonzalo I seek his language because he cannot ever speak mine.

We speak of schizophrenia, which I saw only as a lack of contact, a kind of withering of feelings. And as I feel contact, I said, I suffered from the opposite of schizophrenia: Identification with, loss into, dispersion, abandon of self. But Jean explained this: We do touch all things by osmosis, we are in contact with a center, and yet a lot escapes us and we often live *en marge,* marginally, instead of beyond. *En marge* we are exiled (hence the feeling of loneliness). Beyond, we are mystics and need nothing, and are not lonely.

When I feel *en marge* I have sought to reenter the human world. Where is Henry?

It's strange and frightening, but I do not suffer from the absence of Henry. I miss him as a world, a mystic world of writing and inventiveness, but humanly I am filled with Gonzalo's presence, and if I oscillate toward Hugo in moments of loneliness and too much suffering, I can live without Henry. I miss him sentimentally, as he reappears to me with the warmth of the past. I miss the passion that existed, but I do not feel him today. I am caught by remembrance, not a present hunger. Whatever pain I feel is before something marvelous that has passed.

One lives according to the nature of the sifter we carry individually. My sifter is terrifically powerful in eliminating the bad, the feeble, and holding only that which can be loved.

Two contrary currents, one of slavery to love, which makes me remember only the alive Henry who brought such riches into my life, the other of destructive criticism, which makes me rebel against the human, the defects of Henry and Gonzalo, and which forced me out of their dependence. I know Gonzalo's refusal to see anything now but a Marxist construction will bore me, already bores me, like Hugo's Saturnian unvarying seriousness. Communism is Saturnian. Helba and Gonzalo are Saturnian. Even her colors are the colors of death and everything she touches turns gray. Gonzalo has a gay, smiling expansive aspect, but only in wine and company, that is when nourished from exterior elements, not within himself. I am beginning to stifle in Gonzalo's presence.

OCTOBER 23, 1939

GONZALO'S PLAN WAS TO STAY IN NEW YORK A short while and then to go to Peru. I realized it was unjust to sacrifice Hugo and Henry to this plan. Gonzalo naturally preferred to take me out of Europe, to feel me nearer in New York. But when Hugo came this time everything changed. Hugo admitted to intolerable suffering at my going. I felt what I was leaving him for was not great enough. I felt I would feel greater anguish over Hugo and Henry left here. Slowly the plans changed. I made this clear to Gonzalo, urged him to go as quickly as possible to Peru and then I would meet him in New York at his return. This gives me time to work out a plan with Hugo for his going to New York, time to await news (I expect a revolution in Germany which would put an end to the war), time perhaps to see Henry. But then what I began to suffer at separating from Gonzalo surpasses all. In two days I am absolutely wrecked, first a violent suffering, a fear of losing him, a revolt against life, anguish, and then death, a collapse, tears. Unbearable.

Jean is wrong to say I entered Marxism out of love. The truth is that the first law of my nature is to understand. Most people don't know what psychoanalysis, astrology, or Marxism are. They take secondhand information, are too lazy to study them, and reject them.

First I believe in an open mind. Then I believe in making a creative use of all material conquered. In all things there is a part of truth, and a great part of nourishment. I have studied Marxism. I have carefully read the *History of the Communist Party,* a marvelously concise exposé of Marxism in action. I have read the synthesis of René Maublanc. I have listened to Gonzalo. I find dialectics inspiring. Materialism uninspiring but necessary. I firmly believe today in the power of justice of Marxism. I firmly believe in its efficacy for the people. I firmly believe it is a solution to many of the evils in the world. I can see clearly today the superiority of Russia over other nations, its superiority in tactics, politics, aims, humanity, and intelligence. Even its severity I accept, because it destroys destructive anarchism, which I hate. It is true that like the Mensheviks I may never be a very fine specimen of a communist—because I am still an individualist. That does not matter. I believe in communism. I know my own Christian remedies have been ineffectual, my individual charity powerless except in a small radius, my individual sacrifices useful only to a few. I know people like me bring nothing to the great suffering of the world, except palliatives, the drugs of poetry, the small individual gifts which change nothing in the great currents of cruelty. I believe communism is the greater solution. I respect it. I can see today that Marxism produces an integrity and a sense of human realities. Up against Russia, England today talks like a puppet, and France is only represented by a mass of putrid politicians. I read the *History* with admiration.

A new expansion, development will grow out of such roots. The exaggeration of the materialism is only a phase, for pioneer creation, the need of concentration and firmness. Since I have an awareness which covers centuries, I cannot be wholly enclosed in communism, just as no one man was ever able to possess me wholly. I am like the air, space, colors around communism, that which is invisible, which it cannot seize upon. But communism is of the earth, is right for the earth, for the poor, the weak, the blind, the humble, the stupid. I overflow its channels because I am not of the earth, as I overflowed psychoanalysis, philosophy, all attempts at controlling all truths in one, so I overflow from my own life and my own self, but in communism there is a truth I bow to and embrace seriously.

I can never be an absolute Marxist. I am like the eternal voyager asked: "Stay in this country. Become a Laplander with us." I answer: "I can't do this. I don't know how long I will be here. I travel onward."

My only religion, philosophy, system, dogma, is love. Everything else I can only betray when passion carries me to a new world. Now I can talk with Gonzalo, feel his desires, fears, hopes, share his reactions, understand his life, his activities. Today he wants to play a role in politics, in Peru. I gave him the strength. I am the cause of this. As a woman I weep desperately, but that in me which is greater than a woman has again fulfilled its task of creation, even if I am to die of human sorrow. I have made another man, out of a *clochard* and a drunken Bohemian. I have made Gonzalo realize his first ambition, his youthful desire to save the Indians from oppression. Like the mother, too, after nourishing and strengthening, I have to accept being abandoned by my sons for the role they wish to play: Henry for his writing and Gonzalo for his revolution. I have to give up after giving all.

ABRAMSON, BEN *(1898–1955):* Lithuanian-born American bookseller and occasional publisher. In 1924 he opened The Argus Book Shop, which, for some twenty years, became a literary Mecca in Chicago, not unlike the Gotham Book Mart in New York. An early admirer and supporter of Henry Miller's work, he carried on an extended correspondence with the author, whose major works published in France in the 1930s remained banned in the U.S. until the 1960s. "I was a little surprised to find that [Miller's] letters were as chaste in word and thought," Abramson recalled in 1941, "as some of his books were unchaste in those ways."

ALLENDY, DR. RENÉ FELIX *(1889–1942):* French psychoanalyst, author, and co-founder of the Paris Psychoanalytic Society in 1926. Anaïs Nin became his patient in 1932 and did some research work for him to pay for her sessions, but their professional relationship ended within a year and she eventually squelched his romantic interest in her. Dr. Allendy also analyzed Hugh Guiler, Anaïs Nin's husband, and her cousin Eduardo Sanchez, who had initially introduced them to the analyst.

ARTAUD, ANTONIN *(1896–1948):* French poet, essayist, actor, and dissident surrealist, who sought to revolutionize the French stage with his concept of a "Theater of Cruelty," which would disturb and totally involve the audience. He was introduced to the Guilers by his longtime analyst and friend, Dr. Allendy, in 1933, and developed a brief and frustrating infatuation with Anaïs Nin, who felt that to be kissed by the drug-addicted, mad genius was "to be poisoned." In 1936, Artaud traveled via Cuba to Mexico to attend a conference on children's theater, to lecture at the University of Mexico, and to explore the world of the Tarahumara Indians. "I shall speak against Marxism and in favor of the Indian revolution," he wrote to a friend at the time, echoing perhaps the fervent advocacy of the Indian cause by Gonzalo Moré, the half-Inca Peruvian revolutionist, who had provided him with much information on Indian myths and mythology during their café discussions in Paris. In the fall of 1937, having been evicted from Ireland after trying to gain forcible entry to a monastery, Artaud began his long ordeal in various mental institutions, which would last for the next nine years. A collection of his essays, *Le Théâtre et son double,* was published by Gallimard in 1938. His letters to Anaïs Nin appeared in English translation in *Anaïs: An International Journal,* Volume 1, 1983, and her letters to him were included in *A Journal of Love:*

Incest. The Unexpurgated Diary of Anais Nin, 1932–1934 (New York: Harcourt Brace Jovanovich, 1992). Artaud also appears as "Pierre" in the story *"Je suis le plus malade des surréalists"* in the collection *Under a Glass Bell.*

BRETON, ANDRÉ *(1896–1966):* French writer, theoretician, and mainstay of the surréalist movement, who set out to destroy "literature" in favor of impulsive living, dreams, automatic writing, chance, and spontaneity but who maintained a doctrinaire and dogmatic hold on its politics. He broke with the Communist Party in 1935 but persisted that only the "Proletarian revolution" could liberate man's mind. His exemplary fiction *Nadja* (1928) was followed in 1938 by *L'Amour fou.*

BUGATTI, RENATTA: Italian pianist, who concertized in Paris in the 1920s and 1930s. Her appearance at a private *soirée* (sponsored by wealthy society patrons, *soirées* sustained much of the musical life in the city) inspired a section in Anaïs Nin's *Ladders to Fire,* which appeared in French in 1962 under the title *Les Miroirs dans le jardin.*

CARTERET, JEAN: French intellectual, explorer, student of the occult, astrologer, who became a friend of Hugh Guiler. Anaïs Nin eventually portrayed him in her story "The All-Seeing," which became part of the collection *Under a Glass Bell.* When she saw him again in Paris, some twenty years later, he was still living in the same apartment—"surrounded by the same objects I had described, but with added layers of dust."

CENDRARS, BLAISE *(1887–1961):* French poet, adventurer, and prolific author, who wrote the first review in France of Henry Miller's *Tropic of Cancer* in 1934 ("a royal book, an atrocious book, exactly the kind of book I love best") and became a lifelong friend of the author. Miller's "Tribute to Blaise Cendrars" appeared in November 1938 in the Shanghai monthly *T'ien Hsia.*

CLAROUIN, DENISE: French literary agent who began, in 1936, without success, an effort to interest British and American publishers in various versions of Anaïs Nin's childhood diary, written in French, and later volumes in which the actual names and places had been only thinly disguised. Anaïs Nin found the Brittany-born young woman a mixture of "innocence and lucidity. There is something mystical, or fanatical, about her."

COONEY, JAMES *(1908–1985):* Irish-American radical who, inspired by D. H. Lawrence, began to publish his literary quarterly, *The Phoenix,* hand-set and hand-printed in a shack in Woodstock, New York, in 1938. He made Henry Miller his "European editor" and introduced Anaïs Nin's work in America. Admiring Cooney's iconoclastic stance against the prevailing culture, Lawrence Durrell wrote to him from Corfu: "It only goes to show that when a man has fire in his guts he cannot be pinned down by the world, however it tries."

DE VILMORIN, LOUISE *(1902–1970):* French aristocrat and author, who met Anaïs Nin in November 1931 and served as the inspiration for "Jeanne" in *House of Incest* and the story "Under a Glass Bell." Her marriage to Henry Hunt broke up in 1935, and her various affairs and other marriages apparently were not successful.

DURRELL, LAWRENCE *(1912–1990):* Anglo-Irish writer, born in Jullundur, India, in the shadow of the Himalayas, where he spent the "happiest years" of his life until, at the age of eleven, he was sent to be educated in England. A student who flunked various schools and, later, his civil service exams, he sowed his wild oats in London, playing in a jazz band, selling real estate, and running a photography studio with his first wife, Nancy Myers. He eventually settled on the Greek island of Corfu to pursue a writing career. There, through a friend of the Guilers, he discovered Henry Miller's *Tropic of Cancer,* which was the catalyst for their lifelong correspondence and friendship and influenced Durrell in the writing of his first serious work, *The Black Book.* When he sent a bound copy of the manuscript to Miller in 1937, Miller found it "the most stimulating thing I have read in years" and "an event in my life." Durrell and his wife also responded enthusiastically to Anaïs Nin's *House of Incest.* "Wow!" he wrote. "Mobile silk." Between 1937 and 1939, the Durrells made several trips to Paris, vacationed in Austria, and occasionally stayed at Hugh Guiler's flat on Campden Hill Road in London. Anaïs Nin's correspondence with Larry and Nancy during those years was published in *Anaïs: An International Journal,* Volume 5, 1987.

DURRELL, NANCY MYERS: English painter and photographer, Lawrence Durrell's first wife, whom Henry Miller described as "tall, willowy, with auburn hair, which fell down her back like a waterfall." Recipient of a modest income, she guaranteed the printing costs for the first three volumes of the "Villa Seurat" series to be distributed by Jack Kahane's Obelisk Press for a twenty-percent commission on sales, which included Miller's *Max and the White Phagocytes,* Durrell's *The Black Book,* and Nin's *Winter of Artifice.* On their first visit, Nancy and Lawrence Durrell stayed at Betty Ryan's studio at 18 Villa Seurat, where Nancy designed the front cover for the inaugural September 1937 issue of *The Booster.* Subsequently, Anaïs Nin helped her to rent an apartment at 21 rue Gazan in Paris. After the birth of their daughter, Penelope Berengaria, the Durrells separated in the early 1940s.

EDGAR, DAVID: American expatriate of independent means who arrived in Paris in 1930 ostensibly to paint, but who remained secretive about his work. Deeply involved in Eastern philosophies, astrology, and mysticism, he introduced Henry Miller to Zen Buddhism, Rudolf Steiner, E. Graham Howe, and triggered his growing enthusiasm for Chinese and Hindu philosophy. Miller called him "a beloved member of the inner circle," and the Hungarian photographer Brassai described Edgar as an "anxious-looking man who almost never laughed."

ELSA: Gonzalo Moré's Peruvian niece, who lived with the Morés in their various Paris lodgings. A gifted painter, she eventually married the painter and photographer Emil Savitry. Recalling a visit to the Morés' dank, cavernous basement in the rue Bulard, Brassai gave this description of Elsa: "Against her pale face her large eyes looked as if they were on fire. Her dark hair fell all the way to the small of her back and was knotted with a piece of red taffeta."

FARGUE, LÉON-PAUL *(1878–1947):* French poet, who began as a symbolist and emerged as the foremost chronicler of Bohemian café life in Paris. He settled in St.-Germain-des-Prés in 1935 and in 1939 published *Le Piéton de Paris,* a volume considered a Baedecker to the literary and political discourse at such landmarks as the Café Flore, the Deux Maggots, and the Brasserie Lipp.

FRAENKEL, MICHAEL *(1896–1957):* American bookseller, publisher, and writer, born in Kopul, Lithuania, who moved to Paris in the 1920s with his Greek wife, Daphne, to live off his investments and pursue his literary interests. He self-published, under his Carrefour imprint, at the St. Catherine Press in Bruges, Belgium, such titles as his autobiographical *Werther's Younger Brother* (1930) and a summary of his ideas, *Bastard Death* (1936), for which Henry Miller provided an introduction. His epistolary exchanges with Miller between 1935 and 1938, which he took very seriously and Miller with tongue in cheek (Fraenkel, he recalled, "would set up the pins and I would knock them down as best I could."), were eventually collected and published in various versions as *Hamlet Letters,* though originally Miller had titled the projected enterprise "The Merry Widow Waltz." Fraenkel, who appears as "Boris" in *Tropic of Cancer,* owned the house at 18 Villa Seurat, but financial problems forced him to leave Paris, first for London and then the U.S., where, in 1938, he stayed with James and Blanche Cooney in Woodstock, New York. He and his wife planned to set up an artist colony in Mexico, to which they also invited Anaïs Nin. "I don't believe in groups," Anaïs Nin responded to the invitation. "Only two people can make a world together, and that only with deep, creative force." Fraenkel, Blanche Cooney later remembered, "was a tiny man, about five feet tall, with paper-white skin, a badger-brush of silver and black hair, a little goatee, his gaze was keen and impersonally benign . . . his intellectual adroitness, his analytic hairsplitting, was fascinating to me."

GASCOYNE, DAVID: Born in Harrow, England, in 1916, he displayed a prodigious talent early on as a poet (*Roman Balcony,* 1932) and novelist (*Opening Day,* 1933). In 1935 he published his pioneering *A Short Survey of Surrealism* and a year later helped to organize the London International Surrealist Exhibition. Between 1937 and 1939 he lived in Paris, where he became friends with many modern artists and a protégé of Pierre Jean Jouve, whose poetry had a profound effect on his own work.

GILBERT, STUART: American essayist, friend and explicator of James Joyce, and translator, who spent most of his life in France, where he became known for introducing the works of many writers, American, English, and French. A champion of modern literature, he also provided an insightful preface (never used) to Anaïs Nin's *House of Incest,* which he called "a clairvoyant's walk on the dangerous tightrope between self-abandon and analysis, the exploration of an unknown world."

GUILER, HUGH ("HUGO") PARKER *(1898–1985):* Born in Boston of Scottish parents, he spent the first few years of his life in what he considered a "tropical paradise" on a sugar farm in Puerto Rico, where his father worked as a design engineer, before being sent, at the age of six, to be educated in the dour, restrictive world of a Scottish aunt and, subsequently, at the Edinburgh Academy. He graduated from Columbia University in 1920, with degrees in literature and economics, and eventually signed up as a trainee with the National City Bank, as literature did not offer a viable livelihood (which became important after he met and married Anaïs Nin in March 1923, a move which estranged him from his family for many years because they disapproved of the foreign, Catholic girl, daughter of a Spanish musician who had deserted his wife and children). In December 1924, he and his young bride moved to Paris, where he had been assigned to the bank's branch office. Over the next fifteen years, he successfully developed the trust department of the bank, which involved a great deal of travel and an eventual transfer to London. In conflict between his artistic impulses, his painting, his graphics, music (he was an accomplished guitarist and Spanish dancer), a growing involvement with astrology, and the perceived need to hide his "poetic" side from his employer and business associates, he became a patient first of Dr. Allendy and later of Dr. Otto Rank, in the early 1930s. His courtship of and marriage to Anaïs Nin is viewed in great detail in the three volumes of *The Early Diary of Anaïs Nin,* spanning the period 1920 to 1931.

HUARA, HELBA: Dancer, born in Peru, who escaped from an arranged marriage at the age of fourteen, with Gonzalo Moré, who became her husband and piano accompanist. After travels in South America, the couple lived in New York, where she appeared as an exotic dancer in a number of Broadway shows, including *A Night in Spain* in 1927. Thereafter, the Morés moved to Paris, where Helba, beset by health problems and occasional deafness, was forced to curtail her dancing, though she appeared at the Théâtre de la Gaieté, where Anaïs Nin saw her perform the "Dance of the Woman without Arms," and undertook an aborted tour of Germany in 1933. In the early 1930s, she danced occasionally at private *soirées,* often before an international grouping of artists. "Helba's dancing may be described as startling," wrote Wambly Bald in the Paris edition of the *Chicago Tribune,* in 1931. "There was something in the manner in which Helba manipulated the castanets and tapped her heels that cannot be explained. The broken rhythms communicated strange meanings . . . they were sinister, revolutionary. She is the only Inca-dance revivalist, and she creates her own legends, costumes, and music. Her inspiration is the fruit of her mother's teaching and research work in museums. Her dancing is quite literary."

HURTADO, ELENA: South American amateur painter, traveler, mother of two children, friend of Henry Miller, who introduced her to Anaïs Nin.

JOUVE, PIERRE JEAN *(1887–1976):* French poet and novelist, who distanced himself from his early, symbolist poetry in 1925 and, during the next ten years, published a series of novels, including *Paulina 1880* (1925), *Le Monde désert* (1927), *Hécate* (1928), *Vagadu* (1931), *Dans les années profondes* (1934), and *La Scène capitale* (1935), which reflected his developing interest in psychology and the unconscious as a source of artistic creation. His second wife was the noted Freudian analyst Blanche Reverchon. From his novels, Anaïs Nin later wrote, she learned "to fuse poetics with prose."

KAHANE, JACK *(1887–1939):* English-born publisher, who left his family's textile business in Manchester in the 1920s to try his hand at writing "naughty" novels under the pseudonym "Cecile Barr." With the financial help of his French wife, he set up the Obelisk Press in Paris to publish his own works and those of other writers who ran afoul of censorship in England and America, among them Frank Harris, D. H. Lawrence, and later Henry Miller and Lawrence Durrell. A cautious businessman, he often sought guarantees for his printing cost or merely distributed books on a commission basis under his imprint, but in his *Memoirs of a Booklegger,* which appeared in London a few months before his sudden death in September 1939, he emerges as a daring pioneer of modern literature.

LOWENFELS, WALTER *(1897–1980):* American poet and writer, son of a well-to-do butter merchant, who, with his wife, Lillian, settled in Paris in the 1920s to pursue a literary career. He served as a rental agent for his friend Michael Fraenkel, his collaborator on *Anonymous: The Need for Anonymity* (1930) and publisher of some of his work under the Carrefour imprint. A devoted Communist, he returned to the United States in the 1930s and became an editor of the *Daily Worker*. He appears as "Jabberwhorl Cronstadt" in Miller's *Tropic of Cancer*.

"Maruca"—Rodriguez, Maria Luisa: Cuban-born music student, daughter of a well-known cigar manufacturer, who had studied with Anaïs Nin's father, Joaquin Nin y Castellanos, in Paris and became his second wife.

Miller, Henry *(1891–1980)*: Brooklyn-born American writer, who arrived penniless in Paris in 1930 and barely survived with the help of such friends as Alfred Perlès and Michael Fraenkel, who at times offered him shelter in their hotel room or at 18 Villa Seurat. Since his second marriage, in 1924, to June Edith Smith (also known as June Mansfield), a former taxi-dancer and professional *femme fatale*, he had tried to produce "literature" but found his voice as a writer only when he exuberantly and extravagantly used his Paris experiences to create *Tropic of Cancer*, eventually published with Anaïs Nin's support in 1934 by a reluctant Jack Kahane. Miller's involvement with Anaïs Nin since 1931 has been extensively chronicled in her diary, especially in the unexpurgated volume *Henry and June* (1986) and in their published correspondence (*Letters to Anaïs Nin*, and *A Literate Passion*). In 1938, at the suggestion of his friend, the writer Raymond Queneau, Miller became an editor of the French magazine *Volontés*, edited by Georges Perlorson (who later became Georges Belmont), which began publishing translations of some of his writings.

Moré, Gonzalo *(1897–1966)*: Born in the provincial capital of Punto in Peru, on the shores of Lake Titicaca, of a Scottish father and a Spanish-Indian mother, he was educated at the local Jesuit-run school and later at the University in Lima. He tried his hand as a boxer, newspaperman, and cultural critic for one of his brother's newspapers, studied art and piano, and eventually escaped to New York with the young dancer Helba Huara, whom he had met at one of her performances in Lima. By 1928, married to Helba, he had become her impresario and accompanist and the couple had moved to Paris, where there seemed more interest in her kind of ethnic dancing and where he could pursue his art studies. Always a champion of the oppressed Indians in his homeland, he had become involved with the newly created Peruvian Communist Party and, with his close friend, the also part-Indian poet César Vallejo, he founded the first Peruvian "Marxist-leninist cell" in Paris, in 1928. With the advent of Hitler in Germany, Mussolini in Italy, and Generalissimo Francisco Franco's attempt, in 1936, to overthrow the left-wing Republican government in Spain, which unleashed a bloody civil war, Gonzalo Moré, like most of the South American exiles in Paris, was drawn more deeply into the political process. With other sympathizers of the Loyalist cause, like the Chilean poet Pablo Neruda and the Cuban poet Nicolas Guillen, he organized various committees for the defense of the Spanish Republic and worked as a propagandist and fund-raiser for *Paix et Démocratie.* A friend of many artists, including Antonin Artaud, he enjoyed great popularity among his café companions, and he was known, according to one of his brothers, Ernesto, for his "uniquely generous spirit."

MORICAND, CONRAD *(1887–1954):* Swiss-born painter, writer, and astrologer, son of wealthy parents, who settled in Paris and became the friend of many modern artists, including Modigliani, Picasso, and especially the poet Max Jacob, who often congregated at his "salon." Deeply involved in the study of astrology, he published a number of books devoted to the interrelation of psychology and the planets: *Les Interprètes* (1918), *Miroir d'astrologie* (1928), *Portraits astrologiques,* which includes planetary profiles of Blaise Cendrars, Paul Morand, Pablo Picasso, Jean Cocteau et al. (1930), and he assembled 365 horoscopes based on the constellations, "Calendrier des mages," which remained unpublished. The death of his parents left him destitute, and when Anaïs Nin met him in 1936 he was, in Henry Miller's words, "living the life of a beggar" but always maintaining the facade of "an incurable dandy." He stimulated Miller's newfound interest in astrology, provided Hugh Guiler with astrological information, and, for 50 francs, or the price of two or three decent meals, provided horoscopes for Anaïs Nin's friends and acquaintances, whom she had urged to help him. He also triggered Miller's interest in Balzac's *Seraphita* and *Louis Lambert* when he handed him a copy of his essay on Balzac and astrology, which had appeared in the *Revue de Paris.*

NIN, ANDRÉS: Catalan revolutionary, who had returned to Spain in 1931, following the establishment of the new Spanish Republic, after spending ten years in exile in the Soviet Union. He had broken with the Stalinist Communist Party over the persecution of Leon Trotzky and established his own splinter organization, the Oposición Comunista. He became a victim of the in-fighting among the various political factions and was murdered in 1938 during one of the many purges of "anarchists" and "deviationists" on orders of the N.K.V.D., the Soviet secret police.

NIN-CULMELL, JOAQUIN: Pianist and composer, younger brother of Anaïs Nin, born in Berlin in 1908, while his father was teaching there at the Academy of Music. In 1914, after the breakup of the family, he went to live with his mother, his older brother, Thorvald, and his sister, Anaïs, in New York. He returned with his mother to France in the 1920s to study at the Schola Cantorum and the Paris Conservatory, with the financial support of Hugh Guiler. He made his debut in New York in 1936 and concertized in Europe before settling permanently in the United States in 1938.

Nin y Castellanos, Joaquin J. *(1879–1949):* Cuban-born Spanish pianist, composer, and musicologist, who married Rosa Culmell (1871–1954), a singer and the daughter of the Danish consul in Havana, in 1902. They moved to Paris, where their daughter, Anaïs, was born in 1903. After a peripatetic life of performing and teaching in France, Belgium, and Germany, he left his wife and three children for one of his young students, in 1913. This separation deeply affected his daughter, as reflected in her diary and her later fiction, and their efforts at reconciliation after some twenty years resulted in a mutual seduction, which is recorded in Anaïs Nin's *Incest: From "A Journal of Love"* (1992). Joaquin Nin returned to Cuba in March 1939 and never saw his daughter again.

Osborn, Richard: Connecticut-born lawyer and sometime writer, he worked in the early 1930s at the Paris office of the National City Bank under the supervision of Hugh Guiler, whom he blamed for his dismissal from the bank for increasingly erratic behavior. He had helped Henry Miller during his early vagabond days in Paris and had introduced Miller to the Guilers by arranging a visit, and the prospect of a free meal, at their rented house in Louveciennes, late in 1931. He appears as "Fillmore" in *Tropic of Cancer.* After his return to the United States, he was treated at various mental hospitals.

Perlès, Alfred *(1897–1991):* Austrian journalist and writer, who worked for the Paris edition of the *Chicago Tribune,* until the paper closed down in 1934. He met Henry Miller in 1928, when Miller and his wife, June, first visited Europe, and helped the writer during his first desperate years in Paris, even sharing an apartment with him in Clichy from March 1932 to late 1933. After losing his job he freelanced, worked for a French politician, and acted as editor of *The Booster,* and its successor, *Delta,* from 1937 to its demise in 1939, when he emigrated to England. In Paris, he published two books, *Le Quatuor en ré majeur,* and *Sentiments limitrophes,* somewhat autobiographical fictions that reflect his tendency to fall "madly" in love, often and hopelessly. Anaïs Nin appears briefly in the latter as "Piéta," and the book is dedicated to Betty Ryan, *"ma bonne fée, jadis du terrain privilégié de Villa Seurat."* Henry Miller remembered some of their adventures in *Quiet Days in Clichy,* and he called Fred, or Alf, or Joey (interchangeably) "a bit of a rogue, perhaps even a scoundrel, *but* a loveable one."

Rank, Dr. Otto *(1884–1939):* Austrian psychoanalyst, author, and protégé of Sigmund Freud, who belonged to the inner circle of the emerging psychoanalytic movement in Vienna until 1924, when the publication of his *The Trauma of Birth* precipitated a break with Freud. He moved to Paris, with his wife and daughter, where, in November 1933, Anaïs Nin became his patient and was involved with him in a brief but intense love affair. She followed him to New York in November 1934, worked in his office, and practiced lay therapy on some of her own patients, until she returned to France in May 1935. Rank's books *Art and Artist* and *Don Juan et le double* greatly influenced Anaïs Nin and Henry Miller, and Lawrence Durrell later suggested they read *The Trauma of Birth*. Rank dreamed of settling in California but died suddenly, a few months after marrying for the second time, in September 1939.

REICHEL, HANS *(1892–1958):* German painter of magical imaginary landscapes, much admired by Paul Klee, who left Germany in 1928, first for Spain and then for Paris, where he lived in great poverty, his promising career having been cut short by his status as a political refugee. He became an alcoholic, which made life difficult at times for his friends, including Alfred Perlès and the photographer Brassai, who introduced him to Henry Miller in 1936. Miller became a great admirer of Reichel's work and celebrated him in his essay "The Cosmological Eye." "Everything he portrays has a symbolic and contagious quality," Miller wrote. "The subject is but the means for conveying a significance which is deeper than form or language." Anaïs Nin also wrote about Reichel and his work in her story "The Eye's Journey."

RYAN, BETTY: American painter, born in New York in 1914 into an old American family, went to Paris in 1932 to study with Amédée Ozenfant. In 1934 she moved into a ground-floor studio at 18 Villa Seurat, where she became involved with the circle of artists and writers revolving around Henry Miller. (It was she who introduced Miller to the world of Greece, where she frequently traveled, and he eventually dedicated his *The Colossus of Maroussi* to her.) She served as a *"secrétaire de rédaction"* on *The Booster,* lent her studio to the Durrells on their first visit to Paris, and organized a show of Reichel's paintings there. Her remembrance of Reichel appeared in *Anaïs: An International Journal,* Volume 10, 1992.

SANCHEZ, EDUARDO *(1904–1990):* Cuban amateur scholar, astrologer, and one-time actor, Anaïs Nin's beloved cousin, who introduced her to psychoanalysis when he came to Paris in 1930, having been analyzed by a pupil of Dr. Otto Rank in New York in 1928. He stayed at times with the Guilers at Louveciennes and introduced some of his homosexual liaisons to them, including "Feri," a young Hungarian who cruised the Paris cafés. He figures prominently in two volumes of *The Early Diary of Anaïs Nin, 1920–1923* and *1921–1931.* (See also *Anaïs: An International Journal,* Volume 9, 1991.)

SOKOL, THUREMA: American musician born in Lima, Ohio, she graduated from the Music Conservatory in Mexico City and lived at various periods in South

America. A harpist, she met Anaïs Nin early in 1936 in New York while Nin was analyzing members of a female orchestra. At the time, she was living with her husband and son on Long Island.

Titus, Edward: Polish-born bookstore owner, editor, and publisher, who moved to Paris in the 1920s, where he established an English-language publishing house, which, between 1926 and 1932, brought out a series of eclectic literary works, among them D. H. Lawrence's *Lady Chatterley's Lover* and *Kiki's Memoirs,* the reminiscences of the famous Paris nightclub personality, for which Ernest Hemingway provided an introduction. He published Anaïs Nin's first book, *D. H. Lawrence: An Unprofessional Study,* in 1932, and edited the literary magazine *This Quarter,* which featured a section from Rank's *Art and Artist* in Titus's own English translation. His magazine and publishing firm collapsed in 1933 when he broke with his wife, the cosmetics entrepreneur Helena Rubinstein, who had underwritten his literary activities.

Vallejo, César *(1892–1938):* Peruvian poet and writer who settled in Paris in the early 1920s where he and his French wife, Georgette, at times lived with Gonzalo Moré and his family. An active socialist and advocate of Indian rights, he visited the Soviet Union several times. Expelled from France, he went to Spain where he joined the Communist Party in 1931. He remained a vocal advocate of the working class and the Republican cause after his return to France in 1936. His ideas, expressed in short notes and brief commentaries, were collected under such titles as *Autopsy on Surrealism* and *The Mayakowsky Case.* "It is not necessary to deceive people by saying that in the work of art all that matters is economics," he wrote in 1934. "Clearly it must be said that the content of a work of art is manifold: economic, moral, emotional. But in these times it is necessary to *insist* above all on the economic—since here lies the whole solution to the problem of humanity."

West, Rebecca (pen name of Cicily Isabel Fairfield) *(1892–1983):* British writer, journalist, and advocate of feminist causes, who carried on a ten-year affair with H. G. Wells and had a son by him in 1914. In 1930, she married Henry Maxwell Andrews, an English banker, who later befriended Hugh Guiler. She met Anaïs Nin in London in 1934, while Nin was trying to interest English publishers in Henry Miller's work, especially his manuscript on D. H. Lawrence. West preferred Nin's own work over Miller's and visited her several times in Paris.

INDEX